The Prentice-Hall Series in Personality

Richard S. Lazarus, editor

NORMAN D. SUNDBERG

University of Oregon

Assessment
of Persons

Prentice-Hall, Inc., Englewood Cliffs, New Jersey 07632

Library of Congress Cataloging in Publication Data

Sundberg, Norman D (date).
  Assessment of persons.

  Includes bibliographies and index.
  1. Personality assessment. I. Title.
BF698.4.S93   155.2′8   76-28501
ISBN 0-13-049585-9

Printed in the United States of America

10   9   8   7   6   5   4   3   2

PRENTICE-HALL INTERNATIONAL, INC., LONDON
PRENTICE-HALL OF AUSTRALIA PTY. LIMITED, SYDNEY
PRENTICE-HALL OF CANADA, LTD., TORONTO
PRENTICE-HALL OF INDIA PRIVATE LIMITED, NEW DELHI
PRENTICE-HALL OF JAPAN, INC., TOKYO
PRENTICE-HALL OF SOUTHEAST ASIA PTE., LTD., SINGAPORE
WHITEHALL BOOKS LIMITED, WELLINGTON, NEW ZEALAND

Contents

Preface

For human beings, the world is, first and last, a world of persons. This book is about psychologists' attempts to measure, describe, and make decisions about personal differences and individuality. It provides an introductory overview of the diverse methods in personality assessment and explores integration through systems theory. Personality is viewed as a system, mediating between biological subsystems and environmental suprasystems, largely social. Many theoretical approaches—the behavioral, psychoanalytic, cognitive, role and organizational—have contributed to this formulation, and one hopes this book moves towards a useful combination of efforts psychologists have made over a century of endeavoring to study personal behavior scientifically.

In writing this book, I have kept in mind a varied readership. At the center of the imaginary conversational group is the undergraduate student beginning to learn about personality. I have also been thinking of students and professional people in neighboring fields, such as psychiatry, social work, nursing, the ministry, and education, who might use the book to survey current personality assessment procedures. Many non-professionals could also find this book helpful in learning more about understanding people and the ways psychologists go about their business. No assumptions were made about previous knowledge of statistics.

In the development of the book, I have benefitted from use of earlier versions with several kinds of classes, including a first year general psychology course, a freshman-sophomore introduction to personality, a junior-senior introduction to psychological assessment, and a graduate course in personality assessment. With the graduate class, several chapters provided a beginning review of basic concepts and procedures. Although the main intent is introductory, the book contains a great deal of information which may be of value for advanced students and professionals. There are many references and suggested readings for those who wish to pursue topics in depth. The undergraduate or graduate should find this a handy reference book for use in developing papers on personality and assessment.

A word about the use of pronouns: I have used "we" extensively—not as a substitute for "I"—but as an indicator of the common exploration of both the writer and the reader. I see a book as a meeting of minds—a consideration of ideas and illustrations that does not communicate unless the reader feels he or she is sharing the experience. I have also tried to balance examples and pronouns between female and male.

The plan of the book moves from general to specific and back to general. The first two chapters have to do with the meaning of persons and systems of assessment and of quantification. Next is a chapter on the basic assessment methods of interviewing and observation. Then there are three chapters on the depth and breadth of the relevant systems involved in assessing persons—the personal system viewed historically, the person in relation to the environment and the person in relation to the functioning physiological system. Next come three core chapters—7, 8 and 9—on the three most developed assessment procedures—behavioral techniques, objective techniques and projective techniques—followed by one chapter on cognitive techniques. The most widely used tests are described in some detail and each chapter has a critique of the techniques. The last two chapters come back to broad perspectives. Chapter 11 looks at ways of integrating information about individuals both in case studies and large assessment programs, and Chapter 12 discusses theory and current unfinished business and speculates on future directions in assessment. Throughout the book I have tried to portray personal assessment as interwoven with the values of society and with ethics and accountability. Each chapter finishes with a summary and suggestions for further reading.

Such a book as this cannot, of course, spring full-blown like Athena out of the head of Zeus. It has taken many months of drafting and re-drafting, and I am very grateful to the staff of Prentice-Hall and Richard Lazarus for their encouragement and editorial assistance. A rather large number of people have read earlier drafts on the manuscript and were helpful in making many improvements but should not be held responsible for the remaining faults. Of particular significance have been the suggestions and editing of Leona Tyler, my neighbor, colleague and co-writer of other books and articles. Other psychologists who have been very helpful in reviewing the manuscript or supplying examples are Gerald Davenport, Susan Gilmore, Peter Lewinsohn, Joseph Matarazzo, Lonnie Snowden, Julian Taplin, Jerry Wiggins and some reviewers arranged for by Prentice-Hall including Donald Brown, William Craig, Margaret Fitch, Benjamin Kleinmuntz and Frank McMahon. I am also grateful to the several students who have critically read parts of the manuscript: Marlena Green, Wanda Lee, Robert Kurlychek, David Moody, Mary Ricci, and especially William Reynolds who read the entire manuscript at two different phases of its development. Morella Bierwag and Andrea Thorsen also contributed special features to the book. As an appreciator of system influences, I am grateful for the empirical climate at the University of Minnesota and especially my mentors, Starke Hathaway, William Schofield and Paul Meehl; for the long support and academic stimulation at the University of Oregon; for two years at the Institute of Personality Assessment and Research at Berkeley, especially the many opportunities to learn from Donald MacKinnon and Harrison Gough; and for other places of learning about the human condition in Spain, India, and Australia.

Finally, my gratitude must go to my family—my wife Donna, who has helped this project in many ways over many days, and our four sons, Charlie, Greg, Scott, and Mark, who have taught me much about young persons growing up in our society. One son, Greg, did the photographs for some of the book's illustrations. To all of these people and to many more unnamed colleagues, students, clients, and people of daily life, my deepest gratitude. I shall be most happy if many of you find this book of assistance in your daily assessments and understandings of persons.

NORMAN D. SUNDBERG

chapter one

Persons,

Personality,

and Assessment

What a piece of work is man! how noble in reason! how infinite in faculties! in form and moving, how express and admirable! in action, how like an angel! in apprehension, how like a god! the beauty of the world! the paragon of animals. And yet, to me, what is this quintessence of dust? —William Shakespeare, *Hamlet,* Act II, Scene II.

Now therefore go to, proclaim in the ears of the people, saying, Whosoever is fearful and afraid, let him return and depart early from Mount Gilead. And there returned of the people twenty and two thousand; and there remained ten thousand. And the Lord said unto Gideon, The people are yet too many; bring them down unto the water, and I will try them for thee there ... And the number of them that lapped, putting their hand to their mounth, were three hundred men; but all the rest of the people bowed down upon their knees to drink water. And the Lord said unto Gideon, By the three hundred men that lapped will I save you, and deliver the Midianites into thine hand; and let all the other people go every man unto his place. —The Bible, Judges 7, verses 2–7.

The aim of this book is to explore the ways by which people understand, measure, and make decisions about the psychological characteristics of other individuals and themselves. Like Hamlet, people wonder at the meaning of being human. Like Gideon, many are concerned with the difficult decisions of selection for collection efforts.

On these pages I shall try to think through with you the most important ideas and procedures for describing persons and making decisions concerning individual characteristics. We are dealing with an intensely human quest which has always preoccupied humankind and remains far from fulfilled. Knowing others and ourselves is still largely an art, though certainly it is aided by an emerging science.

The art and science of the assessment of persons has become a thriving enterprise and an active area of research in the twentieth century. Now millions of people are interviewed or tested every year all over the world. Employers see personality as an important component in the success of people in many kinds of jobs—salespeople, flight attendants, teachers, foreign service officers, corporation executives—any job, in fact. Programs in the U.S.A. and the U.S.S.R. must make careful selections among candidates for their space exploration teams. Mental hospitals and clinics, prisons, and other institutions have many problems classifying inmates and assigning them to proper treatment and management. Selection for graduate school involves decisions about motivation and persistence as well as ability.

The first question in this chapter is elemental: What is the person—the object of our study? The answer is both simple and complex. The obvious fact is that a person s an individual member of the species, *homo sapiens.* A woman or a man is a separate organism, acting, thinking, and feeling in an environment or habitat. The person is the performer of biological, psychological, and social functions—the center of reference in much of the research and theory in the social and behavioral sciences. As we look more closely, however, we will find great complexity in defining and understanding "the nature of human nature" and the manifold differences between individuals.

The second question in the chapter is "What is assessment?" Though the term is fairly new to psychology, its meaning and many of its general processes are more historic. The Chinese as early as the Han Dynasty (206 B.C.-220 A.D.) used written examinations to select people for government offices (DuBois, 1970), and those had developed out of interviews by the emperor dating back to 2200 B.C. In the quotation above, the Lord instructs Gideon how to select men to fight the Midianites. Two assessment techniques were used for this purpose—one was self selection in answer to a verbal question "Are you afraid?" and the other was a behavioral observation. Presumably those who drank with their heads up, looking around, were more alert and ready for enemies.

Selection for hazardous duty has been one of the most important programs in the development of psychological assessment techniques. World War I and World War II required nations to screen large numbers of men quickly. Special missions such as espionage activities behind enemy lines and submarine service needed intensive selection procedures. In peacetime, similar assessment needs arise, such as selection for exploration of the Antarctic and for the missions of the Cosmonauts and Astronauts. These national needs, along with the needs of business, medicine, public service, and education, have led to the development of thousands of assessment devices.

Everyone is engaged in the assessment of personality in some way. Individual differences are what make life exciting and exasperating. People make daily decisions about others on the basis of "assessments" of personality—whether a worker will do a job if requested, whether a storekeeper is pricing fairly, whether we can trust a friend with a secret, or whether to choose a certain person as a close companion. From the beginnings of the human race, individual survival must have depended on quick judgments about who was friend and who was foe and on subtle determinations of how others expressed affection or anger.

ASKING QUESTIONS ABOUT PERSONS

What sorts of questions do people ask in order to "get acquainted" with someone else? In the following three examples we will use ten questions somewhat like those asked on employment or school application forms or in the game of Twenty Questions. The first five are the same for all three cases. Notice how the impression builds up as more information is added.

Person X

1. Is X a man or a woman? Woman.
2. How old is X? Fourteen.
3. What is X's education? She is doing very well in the ninth grade.
4. What work does X do? Besides going to school, she helps with housework.
5. What is X's family situation? She lives with her parents and two brothers, one a year and a half older and another born when she was nine.
6. What is the family income? Moderate, about average for the neighborhood.
7. Does she have close friends? Yes, a girl from her school.
8. Is she in good health? Yes.
9. Is she worried about anything? Yes, her relation with her father and her developing feminine characteristics.
10. What bothers her about her father? His angry outbursts, her need to avoid him, his expecting too much of her.

At the end of the ten questions we have begun to get a small picture of what the girl X is like. In commenting on the autobiography on which this illustration is based, Goethals & Klos (1970, pp. 53–61) elaborate on the importance of the birth of the younger brother in X's early development and her turning toward the older more self-confident brother. An excerpt illustrates some of the poignancy of the young girl's feelings (p. 61): "I'd always expected to grow up and suddenly be beautiful. . . . But I wasn't beautiful at all. . . . And my mother wasn't any help . . . it seemed that she wanted something more from me, that she never taught me how to do." So the picture of X emerges.

Person Y

1. Is Y a man or a woman? Man.
2. How old is Y? Twenty-nine.
3. What is Y's education? Twelfth grade.
4. What work does Y do? He is a housepainter.
5. What is Y's family situation? He is married.
6. Do he and his wife have children? No.
7. What does he like to do on his time off? Go to sports events.
8. Is he in good health? Physically, yes; he is in psychotherapy.
9. What is his problem? Impotence; he cannot make love to his wife.
10. How long has he been impotent? Three months.

These few questions bring out major aspects of the person, such as his sex, age, occupation, and marital status, but to understand the person more fully, we want to go beyond these basic identifying data. Why did Y go to a therapist, and what causes his symptom? These questions are based on an account of "Roy," a case reported by Grier and Cobbs in *Black Rage* (1968), Roy had been married a year and had a very good love life with his wife until he fell off the scaffolding of a building he was painting. Though his injuries were cured, he had developed a fear of the job. The clinicians who wrote the book trace the origin of the symptoms to Roy's early life in the South with a cruel father who was away most of the time and a mother who was demanding and authoritarian. His success as a painter contrasted with his deep inferiority feelings, which Grier and Cobbs attribute partly to the surrounding culture which does not value black skin. "It was as if the proper place in life for him was as an ineffectual, defenseless, castrated man, and that the brief period of competence was but a temporary violation of the natural order of things. . . . For three hundred years his 'place' in America had been shaped by powerful forces, and the small drama of his own life becomes magnified in the shaping of a nation and multiplied by his twenty million brethren." (p. 8).

Person Z

1. Is Z a man or a woman? Man.
2. How old is Z? Forty-nine.
3. What is Z's education? Graduate of a law college.
4. What work does Z do? Unemployed now, a political leader. He also voluntarily does some spinning each day.
5. What is Z's family situation? Living with wife and children.
6. What is his family income? Quite low; lives on donations.
7. Where does Z live? Ahmedabad, India.
8. What is his name? M. K. Gandhi.
9. What is his health? Poor because of a hunger strike.
10. What is his chief worry? Support for his beginning struggle for the freedom of India.

These questions reveal a little about the personality of Mahatma Gandhi. But it took Erik Erikson (1969) an entire book to explore the conditions and personal motivation behind only a small part of Gandhi's life centering around a major event in 1918—the beginning of Gandhi's nonviolent movement in India.

One of the fundamental principles of assessment is asking the same questions of different people to obtain comparative responses. The first five questions here begin to show among the three persons such as differences in sex, age, education, occupation, and family status—basic identifying data. The information is of great importance because we have grown to expect certain things of people with certain background information. The last five questions reveal more individual patterns. Such diversity and individualization of questions is necessary if we are to know specific persons.

Each questioner will have different things on his or her mind. College students were requested to write five questions they would ask in trying to learn about and understand a person "X." Below are five responses:

Beth: What is X's name? Where is X from? What is X's occupation? Is X married? Does X attend church?

Jack: Am I acquainted with him? Why do I want to know this person? Is he interested in the same things I am? Is he champion of a cause? Is he prominent?

Sandy: Is X male or female? How old is X? What is X's job? What is his place in the hierarchy of his work—his status? Where does he live?

Jane: Where was X born? Where did X live most of the time between ages 8 and 17? What is X's educational background? Does he hope to accomplish much and make much progress? Does his salary satisfy his future goals and expectations?

Bob: Where is X's head right now? What turns him on? Who does he hang around with? Where's he going? Can X cook?

As these questions show, each individual has a different viewpoint. Beth starts with typical questions about identity, then adds the rather unusual one about church attendance. Jack wonders about a personal relationship and probably assumes that X is a male. Sandy uses age and status as questions. Jane starts to inquire about the person's history and economic support. Bob emphasizes the "here and now" aspects of the person and the specific ability of cooking. An infinite number of questions can be asked about any individual, and the choice of questions may reveal as much about the questioner as about the object of his questions. Looking at this process as assessors, we see the need to realize the purposes and interests exemplified by the approach to assessing the person.

In these illustrations, we see how the questioners attempted to mark out many of the important common characteristics that identify the target person. Journalists face this problem in writing newspaper reports. They try to communicate the essential elements quickly—name, age, sex, occupation, home town. These elements provide the minimum identification that is normally expected in our western society.

What the questions do is "place" the person or "identify" him or her. How does this particular individual fit into *what* context? The information received locates the person in *time, place,* and *human relationships.* The questions point to ways in which the person is like other people and ways in which he or she is different.

COMPARISONS AND INDIVIDUALITY

The largest part of all scientific study involves comparing things or organisms with each other, or comparing what the same organism does under different conditions. In the study of personality, psychologists have developed many ways of comparing persons with each other and with themselves at different times or under different conditions. These comparisons raise questions about differences and similarities and what they mean.

Problems arise from the fact that the study of personality concerns the *individual.* Few efforts in traditional science study individual events or objects. Physicists do not study individual atoms or molecules, but develop principles that apply to aggregates. Much of science consists of laws that apply to all cells, atoms, and molecules, and ignore the history of a particular unit. Comparison is often assumed to be the basis of science. To what extent can the study of individuals and their particular ways of life be really scientific?

One prominent personality theorist, Gordon Allport (1937 and 1961), strongly encouraged the study of the uniqueness of individuals. Using a broad concept of human knowledge, he made a distinction between *idiographic* and *nomothetic* disciplines—the difference between areas of study seeking the principles of individuality and those seeking universal laws. Some fields, such as biography and art, focus on individual persons or cases. In a similar way, some sciences are primarily concerned with single cases. Geographers and geologists may be interested in a certain country or a particular volcano. Astronomers may study a single star or comet. Biological ecologists may investigate the plants and animals in relation to the environment on one island. Such work is idiographic. Most experimental psychologists, however, are concerned with generalities (that is, nomothetic laws) not with individual behavior. Those who study learning are interested in describing and predicting the learning of all, not the behavior of the particular rats or those special human subjects in their experiments. Individuality is treated as chance variation on a general process. Allport on the other hand, makes a strong case for including both general principles and particular studies in a science of personality. Just as the description of the moon is of interest if you plan to visit it, whether or not you wish to compare it with other astronomical bodies, Allport would argue that an individual person is a worthy object of study simply for himself or herself. He stated (1961, pp. 572–73):

> Each single life is lawful, for it reveals its own orderly and necessary process of growth . . . Most studies of personality are comparative . . . and these tools are valuable. The danger is that they may lead to a dismemberment of personality in such a way that each fragment is related to corresponding fragments in other people, and not to the personal system within which they are embedded . . . Psychology is truly itself only when it can deal with individuality . . . The truth is that psychology is *assigned* the task of being curious about human persons, and persons exist only in concrete and unique patterns.

A quotation from Kluckhohn, Murray and Schneider (1953, p. 53) adds a useful comment: "Every man is in certain respects like all other men, like some other men and like no other men." Each person shares many *universal* characteristics with all human beings—similar functioning of body organs, similar reactions to the weather, similar ways of learning. Each person also shares many *group-related* characteristics with only certain kinds of people—femaleness, ethnic background, cultural values. Finally, each person's pattern of living has *unique* elements. In assessing another person we will find all three components—the universal, the group-related, and the unique. Figure 1-1 shows how these three elements converge into a science of personality and assessment.

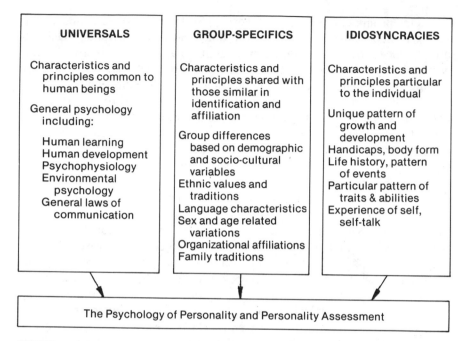

UNIVERSALS	GROUP-SPECIFICS	IDIOSYNCRACIES
Characteristics and principles common to human beings	Characteristics and principles shared with those similar in identification and affiliation	Characteristics and principles particular to the individual
General psychology including:	Group differences based on demographic and socio-cultural variables	Unique pattern of growth and development
Human learning Human development Psychophysiology Environmental psychology General laws of communication	Ethnic values and traditions Language characteristics Sex and age related variations Organizational affiliations Family traditions	Handicaps, body form Life history, pattern of events Particular pattern of traits & abilities Experience of self, self-talk

The Psychology of Personality and Personality Assessment

FIGURE 1-1   Components of the Psychology of Personality and Personality Assessment

CLASSIFYING PERSONALITY INFORMATION

Historically, there have been two major ways of thinking about the characteristics of persons: types and traits. To these we will add a third—transactions.

The oldest of the ways of organizing observations of personality is the use of *types*. The ancient Greek physician, Hippocrates, believed that the four primary elements—air, water, fire, and earth—produced four different kinds of people through corresponding "humors" of the body—blood, phlegm, yellow and black bile. The Roman physician Galen related this theory to diseases. The four temperaments depending on the dominance of the four body elements were the *sanguine* (hearty, optimistic), the *phlegmatic* (calm, listless), the *choleric* (impatient, quick-tempered), and the *melancholic* (pessimistic, sad). A seventeenth century Scottish proverb (Evans, 1968, p. 119) stated folk stereotypes related to complexions:

To a red man read thy rede,
With a brown man break thy bread,
At a pale man draw thy knife,
From a black man keep thy wife.

This popular saying told people to obtain counsel from a florid or sanguine person, and so on. (These admonitions referred to variations in complexions among Scots, not to the racial groups with which we associate the words now.)

Probably the most commonly used typology in the world today is that of astrology. The presumption is that the position of the sun, moon, and planets at the instant of birth determines the nature of the individual's personality. Those who believe in the system speak knowingly about others: "Oh, she's a Sagittarian; she won't get along with him." In some countries it is common to arrange marriages according to astrologers' charts and to make decisions about business, travel, and even political plans only after consultation with the family astrologer. Such attempts to label personality and the concomitant development of rules about personal behavior should be checked for their usefulness and predictability. Research studies show that astrological predictions have produced few or no positive results other than what might be expected by chance and do not give individualized descriptions (Sechrest & Bryan, 1968; Silverman, 1971; Pelligrini, 1973; Snyder, 1974). For instance Gauquelin (1969) found that those born under the sign of the war god Aries were no more likely to be soldiers than others. Silverman found no evidence for astrologers' predictions of attraction or rejection from records of marriage and divorce among people of different signs. He did find, however, that people who were told their signs and the personality descriptions that supposedly go with them chose those descriptions frequently among others—more frequently than people who were not told what their astrological readings should be. This later finding indicates that people are likely to be strongly influenced by a label given them. A person often takes seriously the self-description others give to him or her. The question of classification or labeling of persons then becomes a problem of social influence.

One typology in wide use is based on abnormalities. Beginning with the German psychiatrist, Kraepelin, in the nineteenth century, this system of categorization has been repeatedly refined by the American Psychiatric Association and the World Health Organization. The psychiatrist, psychologist, or other responsible person must first determine if the person is normal, mentally retarded, or mentally ill. If he or she is mentally ill, the next breakdown is into either *psychosis,* which means a severe disturbance and break with reality, *neurosis,* which is a milder condition characterized by anxiety, or several other non-psychotic categories, each of which has subcategories. Psychiatric hospitals and clinics are required by law or administrative custom to classify patients according to one of these labels, such as schizophrenia, paranoia, manic-depressive psychosis, obsessive-compulsive neurosis, personality disorder with drug dependence, or psychophysiologic disorder. Classification of behavioral disorders is still far from satisfactory, however, and even the demarcation line between normality and abnormality is blurred (Sundberg, Tyler, & Taplin, 1973; Ullmann & Krasner, 1975).

Another widely used psychological typology was suggested early in the twentieth century by the Swiss psychiatrist, Carl Jung. He introduced the two widely used terms *introversion,* the tendency to be interested and preoccupied with oneself and one's own thoughts and to be shy and withdrawn; and *extroversion,* an interest in things outside oneself and a tendency toward easy, outgoing relations with others.

The trouble with types is that most people do not fit them exactly. Most people fall between polar oppositions; they are not extroverts nor introverts, but what might be called *ambiverts.* Psychiatric patients are seldom pure schizophrenics or manic-depressives, and people in Freud's typology often have characteristics of different developmental stages (such as both oral and anal personality problems). Furthermore, the same symptoms may be diagnosed differently by different experts, as many court trials exemplify. As for astrological types, they are often so vaguely defined that almost anyone can fit any given description.

Types do have a certain communicative value, however, and "typing" is probably the most popular way to simplify the enormous complexity of human behavior and experience. If the weaknesses can be recognized and the usefulness tested, types can provide a preliminary orienting system for approaching the problem of assessment of persons and a basis for further scientific work.

The other major approach to the "language" of personality is to view persons as having *traits,* that is, characteristics or dimensions in which people differ from one another in degree. Rather than placing people in one discrete category or another, trait theorists assume that each person has some amount of every attribute. A person may be high on one, low on another, and in the middle on the third. Types are like blood classifications: A, B, or O. Traits are like height, that is, people are relatively tall or short. Trait psychologists may even take an obvious dichotomy like male-female and define and measure it as amount of masculinity-femininity, or androgeny, a combination of both interests or qualities (Bem, 1975). Types may be converted into traits by expressing them as adjectives rather than nouns. Thus, instead of saying Sally is an introvert, one says she is relatively introverted.

The trait approach, long dominant in personality assessment, assumes (1) that all human individuals have the same characteristics and differ only in how much of each they manifest, (2) that such manifestations in the individual are relatively permanent; and (3) that the amount of each trait a person manifests can be inferred from behavioral indicators. Research based on the concept of traits has resulted in hundreds of tests for measuring all sorts of things—authoritarianism, neurotic tendencies, attractiveness, political values, and social desirability.

Criticisms can be leveled at trait as well as type concepts. First, neither approach seems to reflect adequately the many ways in which individuals differ from one another. Consequently, some psychologists seek the special character of the person through case histories or descriptive narratives rather than through the simplified approach of traits and types. Second, the trait approach has little to say about personal dynamics—it tends to be descriptive only of surface characteristics. The action of conflicts and tensions is largely omitted in adjectival characterization, although some psychologists (e.g., Cattell, 1950, 1973) use concepts of underlying "source" traits. Third, neither traits nor types are sufficiently concerned with environmental influences—the interplay of the social and physical environment with the person. Fourth, traits are too numerous to be meaningful. (In chapter two we will discuss a technique called factor analysis designed to deal with trait proliferation.) Fifth, trait classification does not pay enough attention to temporary states of the person. Recognizing the last point, trait psychologists have begun to use the term *state* to indicate a condition of limited duration. For instance "trait-anxiety" is a long-term tendency to worry about things and be overly sensitive, whereas "state-anxiety" is a person's feeling of being upset here and now, for instance in a test situation.

An important alternative to the type and trait approaches is to view human behavior as a series of person-environment *transactions*. The units of analysis are then not the personal characteristics of the individual alone but the properties of the person-in-situation. Similarities in behavior result from the concurrence of both personal predispositions and situations. Psychologists have long believed that behavior is a function of person and environment, but the methods of measuring such interactions in real life are hard to apply and are even yet poorly conceived. One very important early study (Hartshorne & May, 1928) found that children did not exhibit a consistent trait of honesty throughout several different situations in school and on the playground. These findings, along with others since then have sparked a continuing debate between those who claim that behavior is a result of personal variables and those who assert the situational variables are most important. The classifications and methods for using the transactional approach are less developed and exact than the type and trait approaches. Some promising procedures will be discussed in the chapter on persons in contexts.

THE MEANING OF PERSONALITY AND SYSTEMS

One of the things that makes personality assessment confusing is the wide variety of definitions of the word personality. Some writers emphasize external qualities, other internal; some list a long set of separate topics of concern, others attempt to integrate; and some highlight social interactions, while others emphasize individual styles. Despite the danger of adding to the confusion, here is another definition—one that expresses the broad purposes of this book:

> Personality is the system whereby the individual characteristically organizes and processes biophysical and environmental inputs to produce behavior in interaction with the larger surrounding systems.

This rather involved statement points toward personality as a *system,* an organized unit of interacting parts embedded in larger systems of inter-action. These interacting parts are to be viewed as largely symbolic, as information processing subsystems. Personality mediates between the internal and external systems. The fundamental concept, *system,* comes from general systems theory discussed by Miller (1971), and others (Berrien, 1968, Emery, 1969) and defined by Allport (in Buckley, 1968, p. 344) as "a complex of elements in mutual interaction." There are many sorts of systems—cells, organs, persons, families, organizations, and even the solar system. Systems have *boundaries* with internal relations that differ from external relations. Living organisms and groups are *open* systems. As Figure 1-2 illustrates, they receive *inputs* from outside, either as *matter/ energy* (food, air) or *information* (spoken or written messages), process those inputs (in operations sometimes called *throughputs*), and produce *outputs* to the environment in interaction with one or more other systems. They regulate themselves to maintain a relatively *steady state* through a process called *homeostasis*: like the temperature control mechanism in a room, the vital functions are regulated within limits so that the organism does not get overburdened or go into uncontrolled fluctuations. However, living systems do not remain completely stable; they are constantly explor-ing in goal-directed ways. Purposive, or goal seeking, behavior is possible because of continuous feedback loops in subsystems and larger systems. *Feedback* involves the return of information based on reactions of the environment to the actions of the system (illustrated by a driver turning a car's steering mechanism when he or she perceives the car veering off the road, or conversational adjustments made by two people in an interview) or internal reactions (such as the body's adjustment to keep blood sugar at proper levels). A particularly important form of feedback is reward or reinforcement from the environment. Thus, the organism (through a control center making comparisons between feedback information and the desired state of affairs) adjusts its activities in approaching a goal. In organizations and large social systems feedback often may be loose, goals unclear, and corrective actions slow and inadequate (such as the sluggish response of a government bureaucracy to the needs of poor individuals).

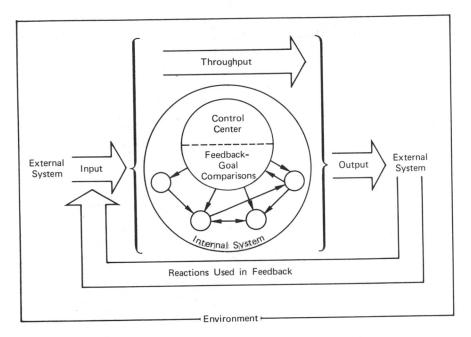

FIGURE 1-2   Schema of personal system interacting with external systems in the environment.

Each system has *subsystems* within it, and is a member of *suprasystems*. Figure 1–3 (taken from Sundberg, Tyler, & Taplin, 1973, p. 101) illustrates seven levels of living systems described by Miller (1971)—cell, organ, person, group, organization, society, and supranational system. These levels are useful in thinking about assessment. One can understand the individual, (or organism) as a subsystem in a group, as a system by herself or himself, or as a suprasystem for an organ or a part of the body.

The processes of physical and cultural evolution have produced in the human being greater independence from the environment and greater self-determination than in other organisms. The information processing, or throughput, capabilities of people are greater and more complicated than those of any other animals.

In applying the systems approach to a person, a useful analogy can be made with a computer in which many different programs are stored for use when requested. Intentions or *plans,* often unspoken, are characteristic of human thought and can be seen as similar to the directing instructions for processing computer data. These internal plans or programs are activated according to the person's perceptions of the environment. We interact and use feedback in one way at the family dining table, another in a lecture, and

Supra National System
e.g., Common Market, United
Nations, satellite communications
network

Societal System
e.g., one nation, a large part
of a nation

Organizational System
e.g., industrial concern, social
agency, professional
association

Group System
e.g., family, work team,
recreational group,
animal group

Personal System
e.g., the individual
organism as a whole

Organ System
e.g., nervous system,
alimentary system

Cell System
e.g., individual cells
within a body

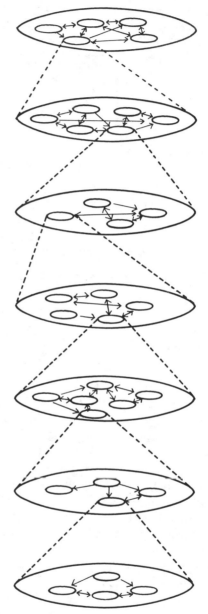

FIGURE 1-3   Levels of living systems (*adapted from Sundberg, Tyler & Taplin, 1973, p. 101*)

still another at a football game. Because of these programming capabilities,
behavior in interaction is *purposive,* allowing the person to approach goals
flexibly and monitor activities by feedback. Internal programming also

relates to the search for new experience and to curiosity, creativity, and self-actualization. The human being is often in a seeking state. The habits, coping mechanisms, knowledge, hierarchy of problem-solving skills, role repertoires, and the like, are carried by each person as potential programs to be used when the situation calls for them. Only a small part of a person's potential is activated at any one time.

What are the implications of systems thinking for assessment of persons? First of all, the systems metaphor leads to an *ecological attitude toward causation* involving considerations of context and evolution. One sees individual persons and individual events as embedded in an interacting environment shifting over time. What the assessor perceives at the present time has evolved from past adjustments between the person's purposes and the environment. One consequence, then, is that the assessor attempts to measure many variables, and often to look for important past conditions (sometimes called moderator variables) related to responses. A second implication is that the assessor sees as a primary task the *identification of systems of importance to the person* over the different possible levels. One recognizes that a person operates in regard to biological, personal, and social systems. In interviews and case histories one particularly notes the symbolic systems and communication networks impinging on the person. A third implication of systems thinking is that it leads to *analysis in terms of systems characteristics* such as boundaries, openness to information flow, inputs and outputs, feedback in systems (especially reinforcements that modify behavior), control center functions (including goals or criteria used in decision-making), and programs or plans available or potentially available.

The internal symbolic subsystems of a person are of particular importance. Assessment often requires that the assessor discern the nature of the perceived internal *self-system,* the person's consciousness of his or her own program, or perceptions of the self and one's possibilities. Assessment also frequently calls for comparisons of the self-system with the environmental system. Depending on its aims, assessment also involves getting to know the person's behavioral repertoire and the potential behavior that might result from learning and situational changes. Perceiving the kinds of situations that evoke potentials is part of the assessment process. Often one is interested in the person as an actor in a larger system, such as a family or business organization. Attempts to change the personal system through counseling, psychotherapy, behavior modification, or education usually require shifts in the inputs from larger systems. Usually these alter external or self-reward patterns or the perception of the interacting systems. Sometimes assessment focuses on limited parts of the system—constructs like anxiety or response sets—especially in research efforts.

We must, however, face the reality that very few current assessment procedures are clearly oriented toward systems theory. Because of the "state of the art" of assessment and the incompleteness of systems theory, it is difficult to maintain the systems viewpoint consistently. However, we will try to keep systems concepts in mind as we look at the major features of the field, and will return to them from time to time.

THE BACKGROUND OF
ASSESSMENT PSYCHOLOGY

Though concern for personal assessment must go back to prehistory, the scientific approach to personality measurement started in the late nineteenth and early twentieth century, a time when a burst of change occurred in many fields of human endeavor. Table 1-1 lists fifty of the major events in the history of assessment. The table provides a rapid overview of important topics of psychological assessment when they first appeared. Some of the topics will be discussed here and others at later points in the book.

The scientific study of individual differences began with a British gentleman, Francis Galton, a relative of Charles Darwin. Over a century ago Galton began systematically measuring human differences such as heights, head size, and speed of calculation. To us it may seem surprising that a simple idea like collecting and describing such obvious character-istics would be revolutionary, but one of the beauties of the way a genius thinks is that his or her ideas seem simple in retrospect. Galton was not only a genius himself, but he was also interested in genius. Much of his work was oriented toward investigating high intelligence and ability, which he believed to be largely inherited. His contributions range from the collection of physical and mental measurements to the development of statistical techniques for determining the relationships between these measures.

TABLE 1-1   Fifty Events in Psychological Assessment*

1869 Galton publishes "Classification of Men According to their Natural Gifts," initiating scientific study of individual differences.

1888 James McKeen Cattell inaugurates testing laboratory at University of Pennsylvania and later (1890) introduces the term "mental tests."

1896 Kraepelin reports comparative testing of mentally ill and normal people.

1898 Ebbinghaus originates the completion test to measure children's mental abilities.

1898 The Torres Straits Expedition (reported by Rivers, McDougall, Myers) is the first study of preliterate people using psychological instruments.

1904 Spearman introduces the two factor theory of intelligence (general and specific) and proposes statistical procedures.

1905 Carl Jung presents the word-association test for uncovering unconscious complexes.

1905 Binet and Simon develop the intelligence test for screening school children in Paris.

1917 Psychologists use the Army Alpha and Beta for mass intelligence testing in the U.S.

1918 Woodworth develops the first major personality inventory, the Personal Data Sheet, for screening American army recruits for maladjustments.

1921 Rorschach publishes *Psychodiagnostics,* initiating usage of the ten ink blots for assessment of mental illness.

1922 J.M. Cattell establishes the Psychological Corporation, first major test publishing and consulting business.

1923 The publication of the Stanford Achievement Test initiates achievement batteries for school subjects.

1926 Florence Goodenough publishes the Draw-a-Man Test.

1927 E.K. Strong publishes the Strong Vocational Interest Blank (men's form).

1928 Hartshorne and May publish *Studies in Deceit,* the first of a research series involving situational tests and showing little consistency of "character traits" across situations.

1934 Moreno publishes "Who Shall Survive?" initiating sociometry, the measurement of the patterning of a group's attitudes and actions.

1935 Thurstone, building on earlier work, develops factor analysis technique and uses it to determine primary mental abilities.

1936 Doll publishes the Vineland Social Maturity Scale for evaluating social functioning of the mentally retarded.

1936 The Soviet Union abolishes psychological tests.

1938 Lauretta Bender introduces the Bender-Visual-Motor Gestalt Test for assessing maturation, brain damage, and personality.

1938 Henry Murray and associates at Harvard publish *Explorations in Personality,* reporting theory and many techniques, including the Thematic Apperception Test (dating from 1935).

1938 O.K. Buros initiates the series of *Mental Measurements Yearbooks* providing critiques and bibliographies on all published tests in English.

1939 L. Frank introduces the term "projective techniques" for ambiguous stimuli on which the subject "projects" inner states and needs.

1942 Hathaway and McKinley publish the Minnesota Multiphasic Personality Inventory.

1947 The Educational Testing Service is formed by merger of the College Entrance Examination Board and other programs.

1947 The American Army Air Force psychology section publishes extensive reports
–48 on pilot selection using many innovative procedures.

1948 The Office of Strategic Services reports on "the assessment method"—a living-in procedure using many tests and situational techniques and many observers.

1949 Allison Davis contends intelligence tests are biased against lower socioeconomic level children.

1950 Adorno and his associates publish the *Authoritarian Personality* in which the California F Scale is a major instrument.

1950 Gulliksen publishes *The Theory of Mental Tests.*

1954 Paul Meehl in *Clinical vs Statistical Prediction* shows that formulae equal or improve on experts' judgments.

1955 Cronbach and Meehl propose the concept of construct validity.

1956 Meehl advocates the development of "cookbooks" for personality test interaction.

1957 Edwards demonstrates the influence of social desirability in the endorsement of personality inventory items, thereby initiating the response set controversy.

1957 Cronbach and Gleser broadened test theory beyond classical concerns to include decision-making and institutional and individual values; book is revised in 1965.

1959 Campbell and Fiske propose convergent and discriminant validation and the multitrait-multimethod procedure for test development.

1959 Guilford proposes a three dimensional "Structure of Intellect" comprising 120 special abilities.

1963 Glaser proposes criterion-referenced testing as opposed to norm-referenced.

1964 The use of group intelligence tests is discontinued in the New York City schools.

1965 Kanfer and Saslow publish one of the first articles applying behavioral techniques to psychological and psychiatric assessment.

1966 The American Psychological Association (APA) publishes *Standards for Educational and Psychological Tests and Manuals.*

1968 McReynolds edits the first in a series of volumes, *Advances in Psychological Assessment.*

1969 An APA task force spells out guidelines for testing the "disadvantaged."

1969 Interpretation of tests is automated as represented by reports in Butcher's book on MMPI developments.

1969 Arthur Jensen publishes an article in *The Harvard Educational Review* questioning the effects of early education on disadvantaged youngsters; a furor follows over the racial inheritance of IQ.

1970 Computers are used in interaction with clients for testing and guidance as represented by Super and others in *Computer Assisted Counseling.*

1971 In the case of Griggs vs Duke Power, a U.S. federal court decides tests used in personnel selection must demonstrate relevance to the job being considered.

1973 Craik publishes first review of environmental assessment in *Annual Review of Psychology.*

1976 First major books on assessment with behavioral techniques are published.

*Readers interested in more details of the history and development of psychological assessment are referred to Dubois (1970), Goldberg (1971), and McReynolds (1975b).

A number of psychologists followed Galton in studying intellectual differences, as Table 1–1 suggests. The most significant was the French psychologist Binet, who with Simon invented a practical scale to be used in identifying which Parisian children could profit from schooling, and thus initiated intelligence testing. To Galton's ideas of collecting quantified data on individuals and applying descriptive statistics, Binet added the idea of asking subjects to respond to complex tasks such as defining words or following directions. Previously psychologists had measured simple psychophysical and sensory performances like reaction times, which had been thought by "mental testers" to be the building blocks of intelligence. In the next two decades the development of intelligence tests became a major enterprise of psychologists. Hundreds of test were spawned, some of which have survived to this day, such as the Stanford-Binet (published in 1916 by Professor Terman of Stanford and subsequently revised several times). Mass intelligence and ability testing became necessary to screen military personnel in World Wars I and II, leading to psychologists' impressive success with the Army Alpha and Army Beta (verbal and non-verbal intelligence tests respectively) in the first war and the Army General Classification Test in the second. Pilot selection on the basis of ability tests was an enormous research effort carried out with considerable success in World War II. A variety of ability and performance test in group and individual forms, were developed during the 20s, 30s, and 40s for industrial selection and classification and for vocational counseling.

It is interesting that while this massive activity was going on in America and Western Europe, the USSR renounced standardized tests, ostensibly because intelligence tests carry a hereditary bias, and probably because they discriminated against children of workers and minorities. Obviously, however, some forms of individual evaluation are still used for admission to higher education and in the selection of cosmonauts. For instance, Soviet high school graduates take high pressure exams, most of which are given orally for admission to prestigious universities such as Moscow, where only one in ten applicants is admitted. Despite attempts to avoid discriminating against children of workers, it is reported that 60 percent of higher education admissions go to children from white-collar families, who comprise only 21 percent of the population (Associated Press, 1974). Psychologists in the USSR have also done impressive work in studying thought processes and psychopathology. Brozek (1972) indicates that tests are in fact used in the USSR, but they are called "tasks," and are not used in routine ways to compare people against standards. The Soviet action is only one of many illustrations that assessment, or any system of evaluating people's characteristics, is closely related to socio-political assumptions and influences. This fact is also demonstrated in America by the controversies over the comparison of intelligence test scores of blacks and whites in the 60s and 70s. These problems were foretold by Davis (1949) in his demonstration that tests were socio-economically biased. Largely because of misinterpretation of IQs as signifying permanent status and the subsequent damage to culturally different children, the use of group intelligence tests was discontinued in New York City public schools in 1964. Selection and classification activities are linked to basic societal issues of equality and hierarchy.

At the same time that the intelligence testing movement was getting started, psychologists were also exploring what is often seen as the other side of individuals—not the ability to do things, but the manner in which things are done—the interests, desires, attitudes, and feeling manifested in life, and the complex unconscious forces which lie beneath the surface adjustments to environment. Jung's word association test related to psychoanalytic theories at the turn of the century. He demonstrated that a person's instantaneous response to a stimulus word reveals something about thought processes. Unusual responses or hesitations reveal idiosyncracies and "complexes." Rorschach, another Swiss psychiatrist, carried this idea further, theorizing that perceptions of unstructured materials like ink blots would reveal the internal organization of the mind and would relate to personality disorders. This whole class of procedures, including word association, the Rorschach technique, the Thematic Apperception Test, the Bender drawing test, and many others, was given the name "projective techniques" by the American psychiatrist Lawrence Frank in 1939. He stated the "projective hypothesis," the idea that individuals, confronted with an unstructured or ambiguous stimulus situation such as ink blots, respond in terms of their own inner needs and perceptions of the world— that is to say they project their nature onto the unclear "environmental screen" around them. This proposition is reminiscent of the adage "Beauty is in the eye of the beholder." In the 40s and 50s projective techniques proliferated in kind and usage. The Rorschach until the 1970s generated more publications than any other test.

Other forms of testing also developed. The personality questionnaire got its start in World War I in response to the need to screen army recruits for psychological disorders. Woodworth's Personal Data Sheet asked questions about personal problems and adjustment difficulties, and the total score was compared with scores obtained from normal and abnormal groups. Some examples of items from the Woodworth inventory are the following (DuBois, 1970, pp. 160–63):

> Are you often frightened in the middle of the night?
> Is your head apt to ache on one side?
> Have you ever lost your memory for a time?
> Do you feel sad and low-spirited most of the time?
> Can you stand the sight of blood?

Items similar to these can be found in modern personality inventories. A few of the Woodworth items show how attitudes have changed with time and appear quaint now:

> Were you considered a bad boy?
> Do you think you have hurt yourself by going too much with women?
> Have you hurt yourself by masturbation (self-abuse)?

Inventories to measure adjustment multiplied along with those used to assess interests. Two of the most widely used inventories are the Strong Vocational Interest Blank, the male form of which was first published in 1927, and the Minnesota Multiphasic Personality Inventory (MMPI), first published in 1943. These instruments were based on the idea that empirical differences in the way significant groups answer questions can be used to construct tests. For example, Strong's Scale for "Lawyer" shows how successful lawyers respond to the items as compared with professional people in general, and the MMPI Schizophrenia Scale was constructed by comparing the responses of schizophrenics and normal respondents. Unlike the Personal Data Sheet, the Strong and MMPI provide scores on many scales rather than a single total score.

This account so far may have given the reader the impression that the history of assessment is a history of testing. While it is true that psychological testing is a very important component of assessment, the process is truly a much larger one. Tests are only some of the tools used to help answer questions that arise in personality theory and in dealing with individual or group problems. A few of the entries on Table 1-1 reflect this larger view of assessment. Moreno's concept of sociometry, the measurement of preferences and attitudes of group members toward each other, led to a variety of methods for showing how an individual is related to the group with which he or she is interacting. Henry Murray and his Harvard colleagues used a large number of methods to study individuals—interviews, ratings, tests, special problem situations—in an attempt to understand the person in depth and develop a comprehensive personality theory. Later the studies of "the authoritarian personality" tried to identify in a variety of ways what went into the development and behavior of people like Nazis, Fascists, and racists. Events in the 60s and 70s reflect the increasing concerns about the relationship of assessment activities to minority groups, the environment, behavioral therapy, and other issues. These are only a few of the events that illustrate how broad and comprehensive the field of assessment is.

DEFINITION OF ASSESSMENT

The word "assessment" first appeared as a psychological term in the book *Assessment of Men* (O.S.S., 1948). This book was a report of the activities of the branch of the U.S. Office of Strategic Services that had been charged with selecting men to serve on special missions in World War II. The pioneers of this approach often refer to it as "*the* assessment method." Some call it "programmatic assessment" or "multiple assessment" (Taft, 1959) because this approach involves many techniques and many judges to collect information on a group of individuals usually living several days in the special testing situation—an "assessment center." Some of these large programs will be described in detail in chapter eleven.

For our purposes personality assessment may be defined as *the set of processes used by a person or persons for developing impressions and images, making decisions and checking hypotheses about another person's pattern of characteristics which determine his or her behavior in interaction with the environment.* The definition expresses three purposes for assessment. One purpose is to develop descriptions and images of the person being assessed. Another is to help make decisions about the relation of that person to his or her environment and potential environments. The third purpose involves the use of assessment devices as research aids in testing hypotheses about personality. The three major purposes then are *image-making, decision-making,* and *theory-building,* including relating theory to practice. The many ways in which these three purposes are carried out will be investigated in subsequent chapters.

ASSESSMENT FOR FORMING IMAGES
OR MODELS OF PERSONS

As part of a social system, assessment is involved in the process of apprehending, organizing, communicating, and creating impressions of persons. "Person perception," "impression-formation," or "attribution," as parts of this area of inquiry are variously called in psychology, entail both the initial impressions formed by the evaluator and the way this person eventually expresses these impressions.

Like the layman, the professional assessor typically develops what might be called a *working image* or *model* of the client or person with whom he is in contact. This image is *a set of hypotheses about the person and his situation, or potential situations.* Trying to obtain as accurate a picture of the person as possible, a psychologist or other professional person considers various plans for further work with the person. Everyone develops informal models of people in daily life, though they are often unverbalized or expressed simply or emotionally (e.g., "What a guy!" or "She's a nice girl."). The professional person is also influenced by feelings and tries to be aware of them and allow for them as he reports to others.

Impressions of a person form very quickly. Meehl (1960) obtained psychotherapists' ratings of clients after each of thirty interviews. He found that, on the average, a therapist's personality description at about the third interview was already almost the same as the final description after the full thirty sessions. Experimental work in social psychology also indicates that early influences are important in the formation of an image of a person which is difficult to change even when later evidence is contradictory.

Assessors must try especially hard to avoid premature categorization —or *stereotypes.* A stereotype is a personality description or label readily attributed to an individual on the basis of a few characteristics thought to be typical. For instance, a person may expect all fat people to be jolly and generous, or she or he may classify any Englishman as stuffy or haughty.

Members of minority groups, mental patients, and ex-convicts especially suffer from such simplistic *labeling*. The tendency to stereotype is understandable; the world would be an unpredictable, haphazard place if people suddenly changed character without notice, and the process of understanding others is simple and short if they can be instantly classified. But the fixed impression in a rigid category system is the basis for racial, nationalistic, and religious bigotry. The humane person and the trained professional try to see other persons as individuals and avoid the incorrect and damaging judgments inherent in most stereotypes.

SAMPLE, CORRELATE, AND SIGN

The assessor, or judge, can look at each bit of information about a person in three ways: "What does it mean as a sample?"; "With what does this information correlate?"; and "Is it a sign of an underlying condition?" In everyday life it is also appropriate to apply these three questions.

Say, for instance, that you tell a joke at a party. A stranger, Mr. Sauer, is sitting in the circle listening. Everyone laughs except this one person. How do you interpret his glum behavior? Perhaps the joke was not very funny and everyone but Mr. S. was being polite, or perhaps most really thought it hilarious; in either case, we may look at Mr. S.'s reaction as being different from others. There are three general ways to interpret this behavior. One, Mr. S.'s silence can be seen as a behavioral *sample,* that is, an observation of a reaction in a certain limited situation, which may or may not apply to other situations and other times. If we make use of traits in describing personality, we would treat this sample as only one of several, which, if consistent, would add up to the conclusion that Mr. S. is a humorless fellow. A more transactional attitude would lead one to emphasize the context of the behavior and seek evidence of other situation-person interactions of a similar or different character. In either case, whether trait or situation is looked at, the notion of seeing observations as limited samples is important. Another way to view Mr. S.'s stony silence would arise from evidence that the response related to some other event or characteristic. The behavior would be seen as a *correlate* of other behavior. For instance, if you had told the joke many times before and had found that everyone laughed except people who disliked dogs, you might conjecture that Mr. S. probably was a dog hater. In treating behavior as a correlate, there is no necessary assumption of causation—simply the probability of a relationship. Finally we might view Mr. S.'s non-laughter as a *sign* of a personality characteristic —perhaps a conflict or repression. Perhaps Mr. S. has such prudish attitudes about sex that the joke is repulsive to him. Perhaps it arouses such strong feelings that he cannot let himself laugh. When used as a sign, an observation is seen as something more than a correlate. It is fundamentally related to a person's nature; it is a pointer to an inner condition, symbolic of a larger personal process. The assessing person is using a "hypothetical construct" about the personality in guessing that the glum silence is a sign of a personality condition such as fear of sex.

The psychoanalyst Theodore Reik (1948, p. 263) gave a remarkable illustration of the use of a behavioral observation as a sign. He reported this intuitive leap—an inference which later proved to be true:

> One session at this time took the following course. After a few sentences about the uneventful day, the patient fell into a long silence. She assured me that nothing was in her thoughts. Silence from me. After many minutes she complained about a toothache. She told me that she had been to the dentist yesterday: he had given her an injection and then had pulled a wisdom tooth. The spot was hurting again. New and longer silence. She pointed to my book-case in the corner and said. "There's a book standing on its head." Without the slightest hesitation and in a reproachful voice I said, "But why did you not tell me that you had an abortion?"

Psychoanalytic theory about symbolism sensitized the practitioner to certain signs—the upside down position of the book, like that of a fetus, the doctor removing something from the body. Such insights, when they prove true, are impressive demonstrations of the skill of the clinician. Skeptical scientists, however, would wonder how often the clinician made such interpretations, that were not confirmed.

In summary, the assessor can always ask three questions about any observation, test score, teacher's report, or applicant's claim:

  a. What kind of sample is this: Is it common or unusual? Will it apply in other situations and at other times?
  b. What is often associated with this behavior? Does it occur in isolation? Does it often follow or precede certain events? With what does it correlate?
  c. Is it a sign of something else? What does it symbolize? Are there personality processes of which it is a symptom?

In asking these various questions the observation will take on meaning and suggest hypotheses for further exploration. The speech therapist hearing one lisp is sensitized to look for more. The psychiatrist listening to a patient tell about being persecuted probes for feelings of special worth or special powers, because such ideas often go together. The personnel interviewer seeking agitation, a flushed face, and changes in the topic of conversation, looks for anxiety stemming from internal conflict. The school psychologist noting a child's poor attention span on a test looks for evidence of hyperactivity and a background of anxiety in home life. Thus working images of persons being assessed build up throughout the process of gathering information; at each stage additional ideas occur to the assessor.

LEVELS OF INTERPRETATION

In the assessment process, between the input (data or observation) and the output (actions), one can distinguish various amounts of cognitive activity on the part of the assessor. At the simplest level, there is very little interpretation. An admissions officer for a college, for example, may look at an applicant's test scores and conclude that the person is not suitable for the college. At a slightly higher inference level, the assessor makes a descriptive generalization from the data he has gathered about an individual, inferring that the person does not exhibit the observed characteristics at times and places in addition to the situation where the observations were made. A clinical psychologist may, for example, report that "This patient, excitable, talkative, somewhat grandiose, is a manic psychotic." It is at the highest inference level that the most complete image of the person being assessed is produced. Based on what he or she has found out about the person's behavior, feelings, and life history, the assessor constructs an integrated system of hypotheses and deductions, a real "theory of the person." This occurs in studies such as Erickson's searching study of Gandhi, *Gandhi's Truth,* and sometimes in connection with intensive psychotherapy. Cognitive processing at an intermediate level occurs more frequently.

If the reader concludes from the discussion of inference levels that the more the assessor uses inference, the more the assessor goes "out on a limb," the reader is correct. The extensive research growing out of Meehl's 1954 book *Clinical vs. Statistical Prediction* certainly confirms this conclusion. The more one uses clinical theory and intuition and the farther one departs from the simple facts of the case, the more complex and questionable the inferences become. Meehl's research showed that statistical formulae based on exact data have repeatedly performed better than clinicians making inferences from the same data. However, such formulae are seldom available, and the assessor must usually rely on his or her good sense and knowledge of the situation. We shall return to this issue in chapter eleven.

ASSESSMENT FOR DECISION-MAKING

In addition to impression-formation, a second important purpose in personality assessment is to aid in the making of decisions about persons. In some cases decisions are made mechanically, as in the initial part of application for an automobile driver's license: the applicant is accepted for further consideration if he or she meets the age requirement and does not have a criminal record; otherwise the applicant is rejected. But in most cases decisions are more involved. The assessor (or a team of assessors) must decide whether to recommend that a person should be hired, or assigned to a certain job, or considered for alternative kinds of treatment, based upon many factors.

Decision-making involves *institutional values* or *individual values* or both (Cronbach and Gleser, 1965). The institution's needs are served in cases when the evidence is used, for instance, to show whether a company would be likely to benefit from hiring a person, or whether society would be protected by incarcerating a criminal. In a typical institutional decision, a single person or department makes a large number of comparable decisions for which standardized and tested ways of making decisions have been worked out. Individual values are involved when a client himself uses the results of the assessment. An example is a college student's decision-making about what career path to embark on, with the help of a counselor and test results.

The growing body of decision theory deals with the problem of rational behavior in the face of unknown states of nature. It takes into account the risks and benefits of different alternatives in a decision situation and the utility of various courses of action. At the present time almost all of decision theory is more appropriate to institutional than to individual decisions, but it is likely that there will be an increasing amount of effort given to individual decision behavior in this complex field where psychologists, economists, and statisticians are working.

Decisions are basically either for *selection* or *classification.* The difference lies in whether or not there is a category for rejection. In the case of selection, such as among applicants for the Navy, the executive position in a bank, or admission to college, the individual is either taken or not. If not taken, he or she is left outside the system; the military organization, bank, or college feels no further responsibility. Classification (including placement or assignment to treatment), however, makes the assumption that everyone in the body of individuals concerned will be placed in some kind of category or given some kind of position or treatment within the system. Illustrations are psychiatric diagnosis, the assignment of workers after they are admitted to a factory for a job, or the guidance situation where the person must make some kind of choice about activity or work. The importance of the distinction between selection and classification lies largely in the responsibility that decision makers assume. In a nation with large numbers of people out of work, with increasing automation, and with prejudices against certain kinds of workers, a pure selection policy leaves many people without means of support. But a nation must consider all of its citizens; it cannot reject masses of people as a private industry can. Therefore it must move toward a policy of classification. One president of the American Psychological Association, Leona Tyler (1973, p. 1023), sees the classification strategy as a hopeful development:

> We are in the process of replacing selection by classification or self-knowledge as a central organizing principle . . . it is possible to begin with an assumption that the purpose of the test is to analyze what each person who takes it has to offer, so that a suitable place can be found for him. Another way of putting it is to say that tests are being designed for the benefit of the test-takers rather than for the benefit of employers or admissions officers.

Tyler's remarks apply not just to testing but to assessment in general.

Another distinction to make is between *single-stage* and *multi-stage* decision making. As the terms suggest, decisions may be made at one time, with the idea in mind of maximizing the decision maker's reward (or subjective utility) and minimizing his costs (or regret). Multi-stage decisions are *sequential.* In planning a career a person must consider finishing first one educational unit and then another. If, as a freshman or sophomore, Joe fails chemistry and biology, his hope for a medical career will probably have to be altered. Multi-stage decision making is usually dynamic, with later information being dependent on earlier decisions, and a complex interplay of decisions and environment influencing future decisions.

In any professional assessment situation there is a sequence of decisions about and with the client or other subject. A typical sequence for many clinical or personnel situations is depicted in Figure 1–4 from the assessor's viewpoint. A person or firm will approach an agency or professional person with a request for assessment. The request will have certain purposes, some of them unstated. In Step 1 the professional assessor must clarify the referring person's interests and decide whether he or she is prepared to help. A referring firm or agency may want something the assessor feels incompetent to give or which would require too much time and money. A self-referred client may be seeking information that is better obtained somewhere else. Step 1 is one kind of selection decision. Once the client is accepted, the decisions may have either selection or classification purposes, depending on the way the institution formulates the assessment situation. In any case, the assessor makes an initial decision in Step 2 to try certain assessment approaches, perhaps an interview or a certain set of tests. As Step 3 indicates, as he or she gets farther along in the task of collecting data and understanding the problem, the assessor may make changes or add extra procedures. After assessment data are collected, the assessor, in Step 4, must choose how to combine, summarize, and organize the information; here again he or she will depend on perceptions of the assessment problem and the agency's needs. Step 5 has to do with the product of the assessment process—usually a conference with a client or a report—and the way this

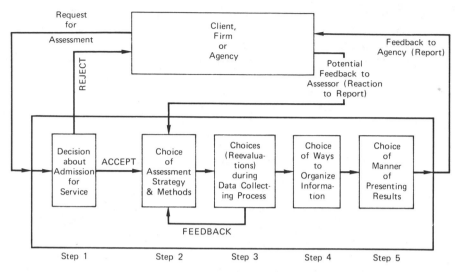

FIGURE 1-4   Chart of typical assessment decisions.

feedback is to be organized and presented must be decided. In return, the reaction of the client or agency may lead to more assessment and feedback. Thus we see that the assessor is a decision maker involved in the larger decision making activities of agencies or individuals. Recognizing the interactions in this larger system should lead the assessor to think about the social and ethical implications of the assessment process.

THE ETHICS OF ASSESSMENT

The measurement of personal characteristics and the interplay between individuals and society—the study of lives—is inevitably intertwined with consequences for the person and his or her environment. Truly professional persons see their responsibility for protecting and enhancing individual functioning, and for being aware of the impact of their actions in society.

Along with other professional groups and psychological organizations in other countries, the American Psychological Association (APA) has been particularly concerned that some human subjects may have been treated badly. After careful study of the problems, the Association published its Ethical Standards for Psychologists in 1953, and has subsequently revised them several times. The APA and most state organizations and licensing boards maintain ethics committees which investigate complaints about psychologists and take action to change unethical practices.

The preamble of a recent proposed revision of the APA ethical code (APA, 1975, p. 18) states the following:

> Psychologists believe in the dignity and worth of the individual. They are committed to increasing knowledge of human behavior and people's understanding of themselves and others. While pursuing this endeavor, they make every reasonable effort to protect the welfare of those who may seek their services or of any subject, human or animal, that may be the object of their study. . . . While demanding for themselves freedom of inquiry and communication, psychologists accept the responsibility this freedom confers: competence and objectivity in the application of skills, and concern for the best interest of clients, colleagues and society in general.

Specific sections spell out rules for the protection of the confidentiality of information from clients or research subjects, the maintenance of a psychologist's competence, the manner by which the public is to be informed about services, the utilization of assessment results, and other professional responsibilities.

In 1973 the APA approved a set of ethical principles specifically for the protection of human subjects in research. One principle they stress is that of *informed consent,* that subjects should receive advance knowledge of procedures to be used in a study insofar as possible, and that they should agree to these procedures. In addition, the APA has developed guidelines for the development of psychological tests (1974) which are influential in setting standards, although they have no force of law or professional sanctions as yet. Most test publishing companies require certain professional credentials for the purchasers of personality tests, since most tests require considerable training for proper administration and interpretation.

Beyond the bare adherence to ethical standards, the responsible professional worker needs to develop a positive sense of respect for both individuality and the community. Anyone who works intensely with people is taking a great deal of responsibility into his or her hands for the psychological state of the person. Individuals often come to the attention of psychological practitioners in times of stress or important decisions. The outcomes of those contacts may influence the future course of life for better or for worse. A deep feeling of concern for others is essential for people who would assess personality.

SUMMARY

The assessment of personality is concerned with patterns of behavior and thought which differentiate one person from another, or different observations of the same person. Locating the person in time, place, and patterns of human relationships is fundamental to assessment. In the field of assessment it is important to carry out idiographic, or individuality oriented studies, as well as nomothetic, or general, comparative studies of persons. A person may be seen as encompassing universal, group-related, and unique components—all worthy of emphasis in the psychology of personality. There are three ways of organizing personality concepts: as types, traits, and transactions.

Personality is the system whereby the individual processes internal and external stimulation and produces behavior in interaction with larger systems. Systems theory deals with inputs and outputs of energy or information and the manner in which these are processed. The system maintains a relatively steady state by feedback but at the same time is purposefully reaching out and growing. Every system is part of higher level systems and also contains lower level systems within it.

The human problems and decisions which psychological assessment addresses are ancient, but systematic study and development of exact measures for assessment date only from the late nineteenth century. Many of the aspects of professional assessment are similar to those of informal, everyday assessment, such as the processes of forming impressions of others. The major advantages of professional assessment are that trained people have special knowledge and skills and feel a distinct responsibility, with ethical concerns about the process. Early development of intelligence tests stems from Binet's work with the Parisian schools, attempting to identify those youngsters who would not profit from regular classroom instruction. The first personality inventory was that of Woodworth in World War I. Rorschach's inkblots appeared in 1921 and eventually were widely used and published. Recent decades have seen an elaboration of concepts about assessment itself and the role it plays in society.

Assessment is the set of processes used to develop images, make decisions, and carry out research on characteristics which determine a person's behavior in interaction with the environment. The formation of an image of another person has two major aspects—one involving the assessor as he or she becomes acquainted with the person and collects assessment information, and the other involving the transmittal of that image to others so that they may develop appropriate impressions of the subject or client. The working image or model of the client is the set of hypotheses about the person and his or her situation. Any information about a person can be viewed as a sample of what might be more extensive behavior of the same kind, as a correlate of something else, or as a sign of an underlying condition in the person. The assessor can use different levels of interpretation in processing informational input and moving to behavioral output.

Assessors are involved in decision making, either about persons or with persons. Decisions are based on institutional or individual values or both. Institutional decisions are primarily for selection (e.g. putting a person in or out of a program) or classification (e.g. choosing among several placements for a person in a factory). Decisions often are sequential and multistaged, with some screening coming first, followed by more exact investigations.

Individual assessment decisions affect the lives of individuals, and institutional policies about assessment may affect large groups of people. Psychologists have developed a code of professional ethics and most American states and some other countries have licensure of certification to protect the public from unscrupulous use of psychological procedures.

SUGGESTED READINGS

ADINOLFI, A. A. Relevance of person perception research to clinical psychology. *Journal of Consulting and Clinical Psychology,* 37, 1971, 167–76. Much of the basic social psychological research on formation of impressions is called person perception. Adinolfi reviews research and ideas on stereotype accuracy, differential accuracy, labeling, and relations between the perceiver and the perceived person. He notes that the highest perceptual accuracy is achieved by those who are most similar to the target person or most familiar with him or her and the situation. Adinolfi notes the problems that middle-class white experts have in perceiving lower-class, non-white people accurately. He suggests becoming familiar with films and art of other groups in order to understand them better. For more extensive coverage of person perception, see Tagiuri (1969); for perception of causes of behavior, or attribution, see R.R. Jones et al. (1972).

BUCKLEY W. (ed.) *Modern systems research for the behavioral scientist: A sourcebook.* Chicago: Aldine-Atherton, 1968. Systems theory attempts to solve the problems of the integration of part processes into active wholes and to interpolate different levels of organization. The theory is for from complete, especially in the field of personality. Buckley's book provides important thinking at several levels. The reprint of an earlier article by Allport (1960) on "The open system in personality theory" is most relevant here. Other helpful sections are the "Foreward" by Anatol Rapoport, "Plans and the Structure of Behavior" by Miller, Galanter & Pribram (who provide a fuller discussion in their book, 1960), and "Society as a Complex Adaptive System" by Buckley, Emery's *Systems Thinking* (1969) also provides a good collection of articles. James Miller (1971) gives and advanced analysis of the theory of living system.

HOGAN, R. *Personality theory: The personological tradition.* Englewood Cliffs, N.J.: Prentice-Hall, 1976. Hogan analyzes eight major approaches to personality theory, according to their treatment of the "root ideas" of motivation, the unconscious, socialization, self-concept, explanation, and psychological health. In his own synthesis, psychological role theory, Hogan is particularly concerned with the relation of the individual to the social context. Hall and Lindzey in their widely used *Theories of personality* describe thirteen major approaches and review relevant research. Some other helpful introductions to theories are *The psychology of personality,* by Wiggins, Renner, Clore and Rose (1971), *Introduction to personality* (1974) by Cartwright, and *Personality theories: A comparative analysis,* by Maddi (1972).

MADISON, P. *Personality development in college.* Reading, Mass.: Addison-Wesley, 1969. Madison presents a series of autobiographical reports by students about their problems and successes in life. He also analyzes the difficulties of the college environment and of the young adult period in life. A basic concept he uses is *reintegration,* the unconscious, automatic tendency for present stimulus situations to recreate feelings and perceptions from similar situations. Readers may wish to look at other first-person accounts such as *Experiencing youth,* by Goethals & Klos (1970), *The inner world of mental illness* by Kaplan (1964), and *Mary Barnes: Two accounts of a journey through madness* by Barnes & Berke (1971). Other good references are White's *Lives in progress* (1975) and King's *Five lives at Harvard* (1973). Coan's *Optimal personality* (1974) discusses different views of the mature or mentally healthy prson and presents a study of college students. Rabkin (1966) has collected literary accounts of mental illness by such authors as Shakespeare, Kafka, Dostoevsky, and Sartre.

WIGGINS, J. S. *Personality and prediction: Principles of personality assessment.* Reading, Mass.: Addison-Wesley, 1973. Wiggins is the best single reference for more advanced discussion of many topics to be covered in this book. He begins with an excellent discussion of correlational analysis and other statistical procedures used in prediction, and then covers clinical judgment methods, problems of quantifying observations, and decision making. His discussion of models and strategies of personality assessment is particularly useful. *Readings in personality assessment,* edited by Goodstein & Lanyon (1970) presents a good collection of original articles and excerpts from books. For more detailed surveys of research, the reader will want to consult the *Annual reviews of psychology.* The series *Advances in psychological assessment* edited by McReynolds (1968, 1971, 1975) includes excellent surveys and discussions of important topics in assessment.

chapter two

Quantifying
Personal Information

Whatever exists at all exists in some amount. To know it thoroughly involves knowing its quantity as well as its quality. —
E. L. Thorndike (1918, p. 194)

One of the marks of a growing science is the increasing ability to specify concepts that can be counted or measured and have mathematics and statistics applied to the findings. If theories are to be tested, and if treatments are to be checked, then there must be a clear specification of variables. Gradually the psychology of personality has been able to clarify some of its concepts and in the last few decades has developed a wide variety of techniques, but personality is elusive, and there are many reasons to criticize existing procedures and to hope for more creative efforts in the future. This chapter will cover the major concepts involved in the quantification of personal characteristics and the use of measurements and tests for personality research and personality assessment. The aim of this chapter is to help the reader develop an understanding of these major principles in order to raise some important questions about tests, and to comprehend journal articles and reports on assessment. Those readers who wish to learn more details about measurement, testing and research methods than is presented here are urged to refer to the suggested readings at the end of this and the previous chapter.

QUALITATIVE AND QUANTITATIVE ASSESSMENT

Both qualitative and quantitative approaches are used in assessment. Psychology has not been able to dispense with the qualitative, impressionistic, subjective, and judgmental descriptions, and probably never will. Qualitative assessment is verbal rather than numerical, and makes use of private knowledge. Society still requires experts in assessment because of the many essentially qualitative decisions to be made about persons. Physicians, social workers, court judges, clinical psychologists, art critics, college administrators, and industrial managers are only a few of the experts on whom organizations rely to make decisions or assist in decision making. Many such decisions about persons do not require quantitative formulations. For example an employer chooses a worker for a job on the basis of an interview, a teacher reports a second grader's strange behavior on the playground, or a psychiatrist writes a case history of the development of schizophrenia in a patient. Even in situations where quantitative procedures are used, some qualitative aspects are present, if only in the judgment about which quantitative procedure to use.

The *quantitative* approach (also called psychometric, objective, exact, numerical, or statistical) relies on public knowledge. These procedures are observable and usable by others. Data may be produced either by *direct measurement* of the subject using an instrument (a scale to measure weight, or the score on a multiple choice test), or through *judgmental measurement* by an observer (a factory supervisor's ratings of a worker's effectiveness, or a psychologist's check sheet describing a patient's improvement in therapy). Many sorts of personal variables can be treated quantitatively, such as the age of menarche, the number of an artist's paintings, the time spent talking with friends each day, and the number of responses to Rorschach inkblots. These variables involve measurement on a physical scale, or counting a defined class of things. An essay examination is not inherently quantitative, but it can be quantified by such procedures as counting the number of words written or having judges assign grades.

Besides using such quantitative *inputs,* assessment may also use numerical procedures in processing the information obtained. These techniques often serve to combine and manipulate data mechanically to produce decisions. Sometimes the decision itself, the *output* of the assessment process, is expressed in quantitative form, as when a student is informed that her predicted GPA is 2.96 or that her pattern of answering a vocational test matches 80 percent of the responses of successful architects.

Quantification has become more and more prominent in all parts of assessment. As mentioned previously, most assessment is a mixture of quantitative "hard data" and qualitative "soft data." By simultaneously considering input, throughput, and output, we can see a variety of combinations, as Figure 2-1 indicates. The pure examples of numerical and subjective activities (A and F) have been discussed already. Examples, B, C, D, and E show other kinds of combinations that can occur. Much of assessment is concerned with D and E, the production of numerical data from subjective reports or impressions. The object of assessment is to make private data describing the characteristics of a person communicable, or public. Often the most feasible way of doing this is to express the result of the assessment in quantitative form.

Some of the simplest operations we can use to quantify descriptive data are to *code* and *count*. We code in everyday life when we classify people into children or adults, male or female, friend or foe. In a research study, a girl's actions toward other children are coded as "aggressive" if she does certain things, and "affectionate" if she does something else. Here

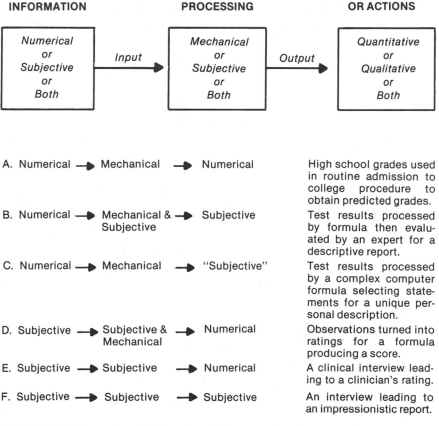

FIGURE 2-1   Mixtures of quantitative and qualitative procedures in assessment

quantitative data are accumulated simply by *counting* the number of occurrences or observations in a defined category. For example, an investigator studying self-centeredness may count the number of times a person uses the pronouns "I," "me," "myself," or "mine" in a sample of recorded speech.

Counting and category assignment produce a kind of measurement called a *nominal* scale, that is, the usage of numbers simply to "name" an object or objects, like a telephone number or a football player's number. Only certain kinds of statistical procedures are admissible with scales of this type, but we can learn a great deal by simply comparing frequencies in different categories and relating the differences to what would be found by chance. For instance, an investigator studying automobile accidents might find that for 100 accidents, sixty-eight were in Volkswagens and thirty-two were in other cars—a difference greater than what would occur by random assignment to those categories.

A scale with more statistical possibilities, the *ordinal* scale, is produced by ranking people or things in an order from highest to lowest with regard to some characteristic. For example, an elementary teacher says "Mary's handwriting is neater than Jerry's but messier than Martha's," or a public opinion pollster reports that of five candidates for office, the first choice of the majority of voters is Mrs. Carr, the second Mr. Williams, and so on. The ordinal scale only places things in orders. It does not have equal amounts or distances between points on the scale. Equal intervals are a property of the next most accurate scale, the *interval scale.* Many psychological tests and ratings can be arranged to have equal intervals between scores.

Besides the three scales mentioned already—nominal, ordinal, and interval—there is a more accurate level of measurement, the *ratio scale,* but generally only physical or physiological data such as height and weight conform to it. What ratio scales possess that even the interval scales lack, are true zero points. A scale must start from zero if one is to make such statements as Cindy's mother is twice as tall as Cindy, and Jerry can lift three times as much weight as Harry. Most psychological variables are *not* ratio scales. Measures of intelligence, anxiety, or defensiveness must not be divided by one another. Mary, with an IQ of 140, is not twice as intelligent as her classmate, Tommy with an IQ of 70.

Rankings and ratings are sometimes confused, but there is a considerable difference between these two common methods for turning subjective impressions into quantitative data. Ranking produces ordinal numbers, but ratings may be set up to produce interval data.

To use *rating,* the investigator must first carefully define the applicable personality characteristic, such as honesty or originality. Then he or she asks a judge to assign a number on a defined scale indicating how much of the characteristic each person has. Person A may be rated 7 (very high) for honesty, Person B rated 5 and Person C rated 1 (very low). One specialized form of rating is the *Q-sort*, in which words or sentences indicative of traits are placed on separate cards, and the judge assigns numbers by placing each card in one of several piles to indicate the extent to which it characterizes the person being rated.

Because all of these procedures—coding, ranking, and rating—involve judgments, it is always important to use more than one judge and to find out how well the judges agree. If the agreement is high, the characteristic being assessed is said to show high *inter-rater reliability*. Figure 2-2 shows how well the rankings given by two observers of a group therapy session agree. The numbers beside the dots refer to persons in the group. The two judges agree quite well about all the participants except Person D, and the *reliability coefficient* turns out to be .76, a high figure. A perfect positive correlation would have been 1.00; no relation at all would have been .00. For a more extended discussion of the calculation and interpretation of correlation, the reader is referred to Tyler (1971) or Cronbach (1970). In general, then, there is good agreement between Observers One and Two about participation in the group they are observing. The advantage of transmuting subjective data into quantitative form is that it gives us an opportunity to check such agreement exactly.

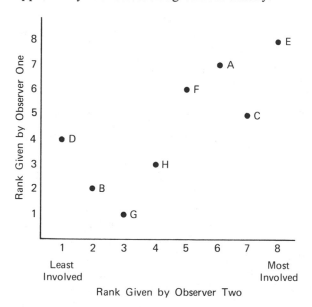

FIGURE 2-2   Ranks on group participation assigned by two observers (Rank difference correlation coefficient, .76)

TESTS AND TESTING

The most highly developed procedures for producing quantitative assessments of personality are psychological tests, and thousands have come into existence since J. M. Cattell coined the term "mental test" in 1890. They vary a great deal in purpose, form, content, and conformity to established standards. It is important for the psychologist to know what these standards are, as well as to know what kinds of tests are available. It should also be kept in mind that concepts and standards set up for tests can be applied to other assessment techniques as well, even interviewing and case histories.

A test is *a method for acquiring a sample of a person's behavior in a standard situation.* In other words, a test is a *specimen* of behavior–in–situation. In interpreting test results, the assessor must always ask whether there was anything about the situation or the person at that time that would be unusual or should be considered in generalizing for other situations.

What is meant by standard situation is that the conditions need to be, as much as possible, the same for all persons taking the test. A completely standardized test would have a particular stimulus presentation using specified equipment and modes of responding. There would also be standard methods for scoring or summarizing the results, and scores could be referred to *norms,* that is, tables showing distributions of scores for similar groups. Tests vary a great deal in the degree and quality of their standardization and how much interpretive information they furnish. Those we call *objective,* like most intelligence tests and personality inventories, are most likely to provide exact norms and information about correlations with other measures. Others such as the Rorschach are classified as *projective,* and have only a loose relation to interpretive material, including suggestions that certain findings relate to categories of diagnoses or personality as stated in a particular theory.

The administration of psychological tests is more complex than "sampling" and "standard situation" may imply at first glance. Figure 2-3 shows the administration of a test. Imagine a different situation in which the subject is a child squirming around in its seat, interested in some parts of the test but not others. Parts of the test are not clear, and the child asks questions that the examiner finds hard to answer. Other problems arise when one tests a resistive delinquent, a paranoid patient, or a handicapped person, or when tests are administered to groups. Good test manuals explain clearly what the regular procedures are, and training helps standardize administration, but each person is different and standardization is never complete or absolute.

In testing situations, the examiner has to be sensitive to the particular nature and mood of each subject. The cooperative and comfortable inter-

FIGURE 2-3   The administration of a test. (Courtesy of Elizabeth Hamlin, Stock, Boston)

action which needs to be established between assessor and assessee is often described as *rapport,* the French word for relationship. In a clinic, counseling center, or personnel office where individual testing takes place, the psychologist usually takes time before testing to "get acquainted" with the person coming in and to informally discuss the purposes of the tests before starting. The psychologist tries to make the person feel at ease and free to reveal thoughts and feelings. It takes skill to create an atmosphere of interest and cooperation while still keeping the test presentation close to standard. If the assessor departs too far from what is intended for the test administration, he or she cannot use the results for the regular comparisons that may be needed. Yet if the client becomes upset, bored, or distrusting during routine testing, the results will also not be useful. Some psychologists (e.g., Craddick, 1975) advocate a very open and sharing testing procedure whereby the client has ample opportunity to ask questions and obtain answers. Even in ordinary college examinations, some students have strong emotional reactions to the stress. In my experience as a college teacher, I have had a few students "freeze" so that they could not continue writing the exam, and a few others have broken down crying. One graduating senior described her feelings about taking examinations:

> I become angry at myself as well as the teacher. Maybe this is because I'm not prepared mentally for the test, and of course nine times out of ten the instructor hasn't been much help either. Many times because of the anxiety

that I go through I get very bad headaches, which causes me to be angry at others who are around me. But when a teacher has reassured the class, tried to put the students at ease, these reactions do not occur.

So part of the whole assessment process is observing and interpreting the subject's *test-taking attitude.* It may be as important for the assessor to know *how* a person took a test as to know *what* test he or she took. Subjects' individual differences in perceiving the testing situation, in interpretation of instructions, in personal purposes in taking the test, and in feelings about the test administrator or the agency for which the assessor works, may enter into the results. A number of studies have identified individual differences in *test anxiety* (e.g., Sarason et al., 1960) and the positive effects of relaxed conditions or special training (French, 1962; Kostka & Galassi, 1974). Some people have consistent tendencies to respond to tests in certain ways that are called *response styles.* For instance, in true–false or yes–no questionnaires, some subjects consistently answer in the positive. In other test formats subjects avoid extremes and stick to middle positions. On open–end tests, some people produce long answers and others are terse. Response styles have been the object of considerable study among assessment researchers and will be briefly covered in the chapter on objective techniques.

In group testing there is less opportunity to attend to individual reactions, but even while applying invariable procedures, the examiner tries to make sure that the instructions are clear and that the examinees are making a maximum effort. Group tests, commonly given in schools, industries, and military organizations, are almost always objective and are usually scored by machine.

In assessment, what comes out of a testing situation is a complex product influenced by the many factors summarized in the following list:

Test stimulus characteristics:

The test content per se.
The test format as it relates to speed, ease, and manner of answering.
Sequential or patterning effects from previous parts of the test.
Culture–bound nature of test characteristics.

Testing situation characteristics:

The method of administration.
The interpersonal context, including examiner influence.
The physical context, such as lighting, noise, and visual distractions.
The social context, whether alone or with others; group attentiveness.
The method of recording responses.

Characteristics of the person:

Personal purposes in taking the test, such as wishing to get a job or to appear
    sick.
Response style, such as acquiescence, defensiveness, or social desirability.
Physiological conditions, such as fatigue, health, visual or hearing defects,
    and motor handicaps.
Fluctuations in attention and memory; internal distractions.
Ability to comprehend test instructions and items; skill in reading.
Emotional state, personal strain.
Previous experience with the test; coaching, training.
Socio–cultural problems in understanding the test and its purposes.
Random "luck" in guessing or willingness to guess.
Intrapersonal variables; the more enduring attributes of personality, such as
    traits, motives and conflicts.

VARIETIES OF TESTS

There are a large number of psychological tests. Recent books edited
by O.K. Buros (1970, 1972), which provide critical reviews and bibliographies
for all tests published in the English language, list a total of 1,270 tests, of
which over a third are personality tests. Unfortunately, many of these are
hardly used and are poorly developed. Buros himself (1972, p. xxvii-viii)
says "At least half of the tests currently on the market should never have
been published. Exaggerated, false, or unsubstantiated claims are the rule
rather than the exception." In addition to the published tests, there are
many unpublished procedures which have appeared in research studies or
reports. Many are described in the handbook of children's tests by Johnson
& Bommarito (1971), and in survey assessment devices (Comrey, Backer, &
Glaser, 1973, and Chun, Cobb, & French, 1975). For almost any personality characteristic one can imagine, someone has tried to construct a test.

Tests can be classified in many ways—individual or group, single trait
or multi–dimensional, verbal or non–verbal, highly structured or unstructured, closed–choice or open–ended, objective or subjective, machine
scored or scored by judgment. They can be classified by content or by
purpose. One of the basic distinctions among tests is the one Cronbach
(1970) makes between *maximum* and *typical* performance tests. A maximum performance test tries to elicit the best possible responses from a
subject. Both the subject and the assessor generally see the situation as one
in which a person will be evaluated according to how well he or she does.
Usually these are ability tests. The typical performance category includes most
of the personality tests, both objective inventories and projective techniques.
Such tests are intended to have no right or wrong answers, and their objec-

tive is to sample the individual's usual ways of behaving rather than skills or achievements. This distinction is not absolute however. Observations about personality can be made on any behavior sample, including ability tests. How a person goes about working a puzzle or the amount of guessing he or she does on a multiple choice exam reveals something about the subject's general personality. Furthermore, it is possible to conceptualize personality in terms of skills as well as typical performances. Proponents of the behavioral or social learning approach to the assessment of persons, such as Wallace (1966, 1967), prefer to see personality as a set of abilities. Wallace advocates a kind of assessment that would determine a person's capability for performance in a situation, rather than traits or typical responses. In other words, he is interested in the behavioral repertoire and the circumstances under which its different components are utilized.

Another interesting system for categorizing tests has been proposed by R. B. Cattell (1950, 1965). Cattell states that there are three major sources of data about personality: the life record, which produces *L-data*; the self-report questionnaire, which produces *Q-data*; and the objective performance test, which produces *T-data*. L-data can be obtained from auto-biographies, school or court records, or behavioral products of the past. In practice, Cattell usually uses ratings by people who know the individual. Q-data are the familiar personality inventories, attitude scales, and self-descriptive statements. T-data are obtained from miniature performance situations, often involving apparatus of various kinds, although some are pencil and paper tasks. Cattell and his colleagues have tried out over 400 of these objective measures (Cattell & Warburton, 1967). Cattell aims to identify traits general enough to appear in all three kinds of data.

The major distinctions in this book are among behavioral, objective, and projective techniques. Chapters seven, eight, and nine will explain these in detail. In addition chapter ten will examine cognitive and ability measurement as it relates to personality, and chapter six will survey physiological methods.

STANDARDS FOR EVALUATING TESTS
AND OTHER PROCEDURES

The person undertaking a particular task of personality assessment has two sorts of decisions to make: (a) Shall I utilize any of the tests available as part of this assessment? and (b) if so, which of several alternative instruments is to be preferred? Many considerations enter into the first decision, such as cost, time available, attitudes of the person to be tested, and the availability of tests that have any bearing on the particular questions to which assessment is directed.

In making both kinds of decisions, the assessor may consult books like Buros' *Mental measurements yearbooks* (1959, 1965, 1972) and *Personality tests and reviews* (1970) and textbooks on testing such as Cronbach (1970) and Anastasi (1976). Test manuals should be read carefully. In evaluating an unfamiliar test, one may wish to take it oneself or give it to a friend to find out whether the instructions are clear and whether there are any particular problems in administration.

In order to make good decisions about particular tests, the assessor must understand the technical standards by which tests or other assessment procedures are judged. These have been set forth in a series of revisions of guidelines prepared under the auspices of the American Psychological Association (1974). Essentially, one must always evaluate the evidence with regard to a test's validity, reliability, and norms. These three concepts can apply to psychological data obtained from coding, counting, ranking, and rating procedures just as much as to tests. They are problems to consider with any psychological measurement, whether it is used for research or practical decisions. Validity is the most important consideration.

VALIDITY

What does the assessment procedure measure? What is it related to? What is it good for? The name of a test or procedure is a poor guide. A test labeled "Creativity" or "Democratic Idealism" may really measure general intelligence. Validity is the property of a test that makes the obtained results useful. A procedure is never valid in general. It is valid *for* something—for measuring blood pressure, problem–solving ability, or aggressiveness. A test is valid if it produces dependable evidence about the characteristic that interests the assessor.

Three kinds of validity (APA, 1974) can be differentiated: content, criterion, and construct. *Content validity* answers the question, "Does the content of this procedure constitute an adequate sample of the subject matter?" It is important for achievement tests, such as those given in educational institutions. An examination in history, for example, must cover the major events of a designated period and area and their interpretation. The author of a personality inventory needs to provide evidence that its items adequately sample certain content areas such as home adjustment, worries and fears, or neurotic symptoms. Some test theorists (Lumsden, 1976) emphasize that test scales should be constructed of items measuring one area of content, that is, the test should be *unidimensional,* not a mixture of all sorts of things. Evidence about content validity is often not as precise and quantitative as one might wish, but an evaluator should consider whatever is available.

Content validity should not be confused with *face validity,* a term used to refer to someone's impression that a test is relevant. While a certain amount of face validity may be necessary to make subjects accept a test, such impressions are no substitute for careful, logical, and empirical analysis of content.

Criterion validity has to do with the relation of the test results to criteria outside the test itself. If the test and criterion measurements are not separated in time, the term *concurrent validity* is used. This is the case, for example, when scores on a heterosexuality scale are correlated with reports of the amount of time spent in activities with the opposite sex. If the criterion measurements are obtained at a later time, *predictive validity* is the term used to indicate the extent to which test scores predict criterion measures. The most common example is the relationship between entrance test scores and later college success. From a practical standpoint, predictive validity is considered to be especially important. For example, psychotherapists wish to know what the implications of measured personality traits are for later progress in therapy and personnel people wish to know what scores on a dexterity test have to do with later success in a factory job.

A related concept is *cross validation.* This process applies when tests are constructed by using items because of their ability to differentiate groups or predict outcomes. Items selected this way may not hold true on another group. Correlating test scores with criterion scores in the original group used in constructing the scales does not produce adequate concurrent or predictive validity coefficients, but inflated ones. Cross validation means validation on a new, independent sample of the population or group with which the test is to be used.

From a theoretical standpoint, the most important kind of validity is *construct validity,* the relation of test results to the theoretical concept which the test is trying to measure. This important concept was first proposed by Cronbach & Meehl (1955). Intelligence, anxiety, ego strength, introversion, and many other terms used in testing are really *constructs* —abstractions growing out of our theories about persons. They are not directly measurable. To decide whether an instrument is measuring one of these traits indirectly, we must understand the theories on which they are based and look for indicators or relationships these theories would lead us to expect if the theories are sound. For example, an inner state like anxiety is presumed to be manifested by behaviors such as restless activity, sweat on the palms of the hands, hyper-reactivity to perceived threats, and self-reports of worry and fear; some kinds of people, such as neurotics, are likely to have more anxiety than others. Studies of construct validity, then, might involve the relation of test scores to measure of palmar sweat, or the amount of reaction to anxiety producing pictures, or the comparison of neurotics with normals. In obtaining positive results, one adds to the confirmation of the theory about the construct as well as to the validity of the instrument. It often takes many studies with different kinds of hypotheses about a construct to establish that a test is a good measure of it.

For construct validity, it is important that the researcher not only show positive relations with similar measures, but also the *absence* of relations with dissimilar behavior and measures. Campbell & Fiske (1959), in an important article, use the terms *convergent validity* and *discriminant validity* for demonstrations of what a test does and does not measure. For instance, Dr. Black is constructing a test of empathy. She would want to check convergent validity by correlating it with other known tests of empathy, role-taking, and the like; she also would want to include in her research some other kinds of traits or abilities with which she hypothesizes the test results should not correlate, such as intelligence or dominance. If she did get a high correlation with intelligence, her test would be of less value because then she would only be getting intelligence test results in a disguised form. Campbell and Fiske proposed getting at convergent and discriminant characteristics of a scale by means of a *multi-trait, multi-method* model. The researcher studies a construct by using several measures of different kinds and includes several traits varying in their similarity to the one being studied so that research exposes variations due to differences in methods and traits.

An important related method in understanding the meaning of tests is *factor analysis.* Although one sometimes sees the term "factorial validity," factor composition of a test is not considered a separate form of validity, though it may contribute to our understanding of the construct we are investigating. Factor analysis studies the meaning of a test or subtest by including it in a set of measures which are intercorrelated. The statistical procedures are involved and laborious, but computers have made them fast and convenient so that it is now common practice to factor analyze any test that has several parts to it to determine its factor structure. Factors are named for the quality in the several tests which seems to account for their high correlation. Several studies of the patterns produced by correlating all ten major MMPI scales with each other suggest that a prominent factor related to elevation of many of the scales is general anxiety. Factor analysis has been heavily used in the development and understanding of ability tests. It is possible to determine if one general ability (e.g., general intelligence) is the basis for the intercorrelation of many tasks or if tasks cluster into groups or if a test is measuring a specific ability and consequently does not correlate with other tests. (For a detailed explanation of factor analysis, see Cronbach, 1970 or Child, 1970.) Psychologists reviewing the literature (Armstrong & Soelberg, 1968) have noted the importance of checking obtained factors for reliability.

RELIABILITY

Another technical consideration in evaluating an assessment procedure is *reliability,* which refers to the consistency, reproducibility, or accuracy of the results. Validity tells about the relationship of a test result to outside matters of relevance while reliability tells about relationships within the test. It indicates to what extent scores are free from the effects of chance determiners and thus answers the question of how trustworthy the obtained score is. No test score is ever a completely accurate indicator of the characteristic it measures. Third grader Barbie Smith taking an intelligence or personality test may be momentarily distracted by a commotion in the classroom; she may be ill or angry at someone; she may suddenly think of an errand she should have done. If we gave her the test again the next day she would probably get a somewhat different score. On any given day her result is one sample of a hypothetical universe of potential scores she might have obtained, given her true ability or personality. In tests and measurements a single observation or score is often considered to be a person's true score plus error, according to classical test theory. If we could give Barbie the test a hundred times without training effects and other distortions, we would expect to get a distribution of scores centering on a mean which would be the best representation of the subject's real performance. Cronbach (1970; Cronbach et al., 1972) has pointed out that scores vary not only with occasions, but also with situations and with observers recording a behavior. When we use a single observation as if it represented all of the person's potential we are generalizing over occasions, situations, and observers. Therefore, some psychologists (e.g., Cronbach, 1970) prefer to use the term *generalizability* instead of reliability.

If it were possible to give the same test to a person many times, the distribution would approximate a normal curve, the mean and standard deviation of which could be computed. (These would be like the distribution and its characteristics shown in Figure 2–4, to be discussed in the next section.) It is possible to estimate this standard deviation from data one obtains when a group of individuals is tested twice, or even on a single occasion. This estimate is what is meant by the *standard error of measurement,* and it is one of the most useful ways of reporting how much chance fluctuation in scores from occasion to occasion must be allowed for. The smaller SE_M is, the more reliable the test is. In thinking about any score from a test or other assessment procedure, we should think of the score as a *zone,* not a definite point and realize that a person's true score lies within that zone.

A more common way of reporting reliability is the *reliability coefficient.* Investigators study reliability in three major ways: by repetition (test-retest), by using two forms or two parts of the test which have the same kind of items (equivalent forms, or split halves of the test) or by studying the consistency of performance across items. The correlation figure for the first kind of reliability is called a *stability* coefficient and the figure for the second kind is called an *equivalence* coefficient. It is often desirable to compute both kinds of reliability coefficients, but their appropriateness will vary with the kind of test. *Inter-item consistency* is established from one test administration through the use of various formulae (such as Cronbach's coefficient alpha and the Kuder-Richardson method, for which explanations are available in books on testing like Cronbach, 1970, and Anastasi, 1976). A fourth kind of correlation figure is *inter-observer reliability,* which has been mentioned earlier. The larger the reliability coefficient, and the smaller the standard error of measurement, the more reliable the test will be. Tests must usually have reliability coefficients in the .80s or .90s to be used with much confidence in individual cases.

Measuring reliability of personality constructs presents some special problems. Many intriguing personal events are of brief duration, e.g., sudden rages, a short love affair, or shifts in attitudes toward presidential leadership. As mentioned in the last chapter, short-term *states* present in one situation and time but not in others can be measured, but only some kinds of reliability determination are appropriate in that limited situation. Because of such measurement difficulties, most research has aimed at long term *traits,* for which reliability is easier to gauge. However, a full study of personality needs both. Reliability, like validity, applies to many kinds of psychological measurement besides tests. It should be noted finally that some test theorists (Lumsden, 1976) are critical of the classical concept of reliability and its recent variant, generalizability. They would place more emphasis on validity and the direct use of prediction tables, rather than estimates based on standard errors of measurement.

NORMS AND DERIVED SCORES

In addition to validity and reliability, a third characteristic to be considered when evaluating a test or other assessment procedure is the information provided about *norms.* In order to understand what an individual's score means, it should be compared with the scores other people have made. For such a comparison to be meaningful, we must be given information about the kinds of people included in the norm groups and the nature of the derived scores which are used to indicate where individuals stand in relation to the group.

Normative data must be *representative* of the population in which a test is designed to be used. The norm group for a children's intelligence test in the United States should include children from all socioeconomic levels and various areas of the country in proportions similar to those occurring in the population. A personality test for hospital patients should use a sample of the population from which these patients come. An achievement test for high school students should use students from several kinds of high schools to construct norms.

The second technical matter that arises in interpreting individual scores in terms of norm groups is the meaning of various kinds of transformations that raw scores undergo in the process of interpretation. Two varieties of derived scores predominate, the percentile and the standard score. A *percentile* score indicates the proportion of the scores in the norm group that are lower than that of the individual. If one obtains a percentile rank of 46, it means that 46 out of a hundred of the scores in the normative sample were lower than this. It is simple to compute and to explain, but has one serious disadvantage—percentile scores near the middle of the distribution are very close together and the practical significance of differences can easily be overestimated. A person who obtains a percentile score of 55 on a test is probably not sufficiently higher than another person with a percentile score of 48 so that any distinction between them should be made. It would be misleading to classify the first as definitely above average and the second as definitely below.

Test publishers are likely to transform all of their raw scores into some variety of *standard score.* The name comes from standard deviation, which is the basis for such transformations. Because the scores of a large sample of persons produce a normal distribution (or can be made to do so by careful selection of items), the mean and standard deviation can be used as a basis of relating individual scores to group norms. A simple illustration of how this is done is shown in Figure 2–4. A student who obtained a score of forty-nine on exactly the same standard score (z-score) on both, because in each case the score is one standard deviation above the mean. Sandra received a score of fifty-two on the first test, thus a z-score of 1.5, and a score of twenty-four on the second, thus a z-score of – .5.

We can transform the z-score scale, which can be obtained for a normal distribution in many different ways, by adding constants and multiplying by constants. Multiplying by ten and adding fifty gives us a widely used standard scale, used by the T–score, in which the mean is fifty, the standard deviation ten, and the total range usually lies between twenty and eighty. Multiplying by fifteen and adding 100 produces the scale on which Wechsler IQ scores are distributed. (The original ratio IQ obtained by dividing mental age by chronological age and multiplying by 100 is now seldom used.) Another variation is the *stanine* score (for standard nines) used in the Air Force and in some college entrance tests. It divides the whole range of the normal

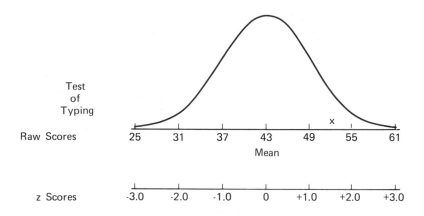

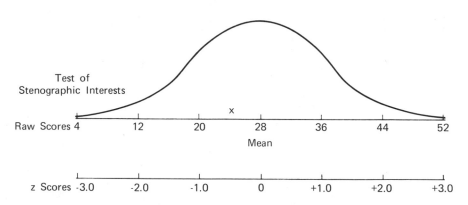

FIGURE 2-4 Two distributions with standard scores

curve into half standard deviations, the middle one straddling the mean. Figure 2–5 shows how these and other scales are related.

Derived scores make possible another useful test device—the *profile* or psychograph. This profile is a method of putting scores on several aspects of a test side by side, to show an individual's pattern of highs and lows. What makes it possible to compare them is the fact that all scores have been converted to standard scores.

Figure 2–6 illustrates the results of a college student on the California Psychological Inventory, a widely used objective personality technique. The T–score for each of the eighteen scales is plotted on the standard profile and all points are connected with lines. Mr. Heinrich (a fictitious name) scores

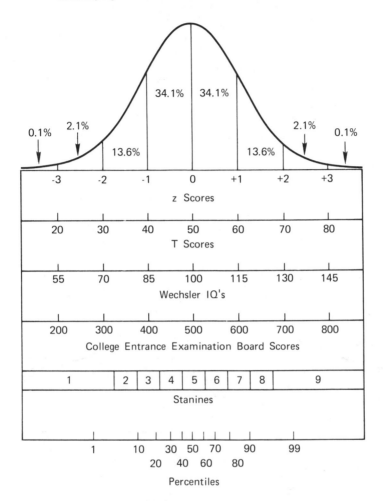

FIGURE 2-5   The normal curve and derived scores

very high on scales called Flexibility and Social Presence and quite low on Commonality. An assessor who uses the CPI, or other tests, develops an understanding of the meaning of the different patterns for interpreting the results.

Non-norm-based Comparative Methods.   The most traditional and commonly used form of comparison is the one we have been discussing—relating an individual's score to norms of a relevant group. Like "grading on the curve," the basis of reference is whatever other people do in the sample used for the norms. There are other ways for comparing a person's results to give them meaning. Glaser (1963) has called one of those ways *criterion-referencing* (as opposed to *norm-referencing*). What he means is that the person is to be compared with a set performance standard rather than with the relative standard provided by norms on other people. A test is criterion-referenced if it provides information about the behavioral level of the person being assessed. Criterion-referencing can be broken down into three forms called content referencing, expectancy referencing, and self referencing.

Content referencing, perhaps more properly called *performance referencing* provides a statement of what the person has done on the test. For instance, on a typing test one might say, "Sandra achieved at a 95

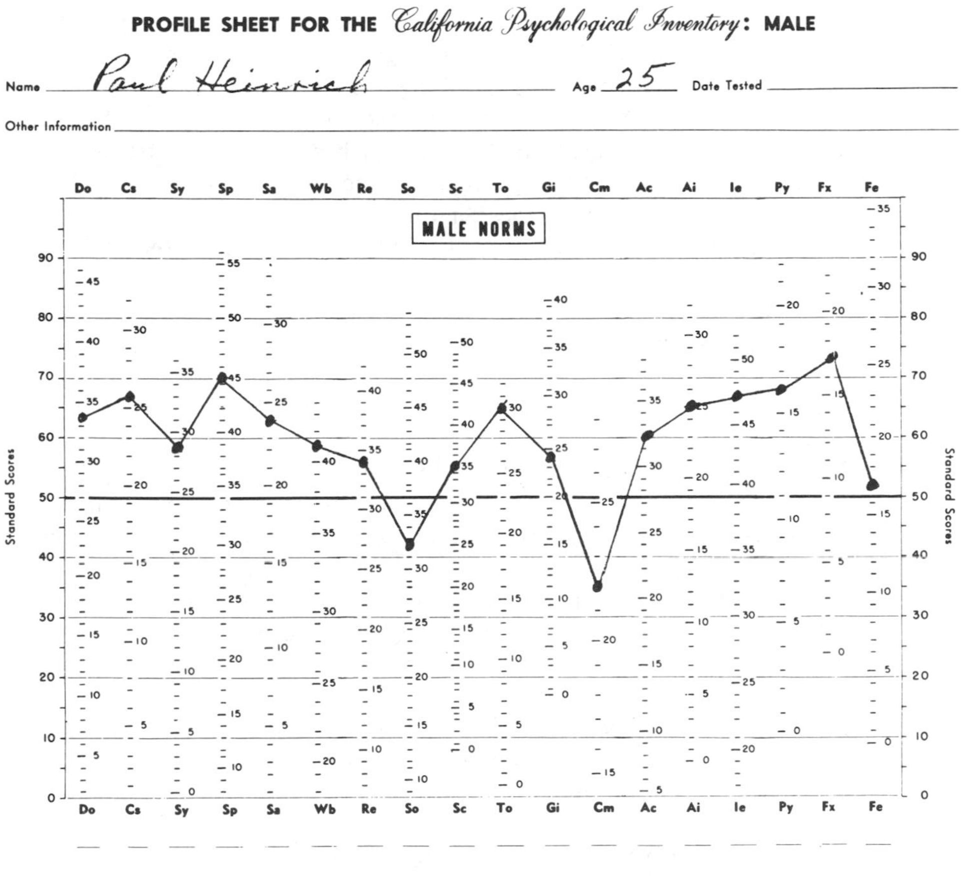

PROFILE SHEET FOR THE *California Psychological Inventory*: **MALE**

Name _Paul Heinrich_   Age _25_   Date Tested _____

Other Information _____

Male Norms

FIGURE 2-6 CPI profile of a twenty-five year old man (Reproduced from *Manual for the California Psychological Inventory,* by Harrison G. Gough, Ph.D. © Consulting Psychologists Press, Inc., Palo Alto, California, 1957. All rights reserved.)

percent level of accuracy.'' This statement does not compare her with other people, but it does compare her with an absolute standard—the possibility of getting 100 percent correct. Similarly on a personality test, a psychologist might say ''Mr. Thompson completed fifteen of twenty sentences with expressions of hopelessness and despair.'' Knowledge of performance level may be sufficient for hiring a person for a job or for making a decision to investigate a problem further.

Expectancy-referencing (Cronbach, 1970) relates a person's test results to expectancy information based on past experience with test results. For instance, we might want to know how Sandra's typing score relates to success in clerical jobs. Her score might be compared with records (expectancy tables) kept on others who have already been working, and the assessor could make a statement like this, ''Women with Sandra's score typically have received a rating of 'excellent' in beginning clerical positions,'' or ''Sandra has a 3–to–1 chance of finishing the secretarial course she has begun.'' Similarly for Mr. Thompson, it might be said, ''His number of negative emotional responses on this test has been associated frequently (80 percent of the time) with a psychiatric diagnosis of depression.'' Expectancy statements compare the person with relevant information on future performance or on some present performance that is different from the test itself. This approach amounts to interpreting test results in terms of data on predictive or concurrent validity.

Finally, through *self-referencing,* a person's score can be compared with his or her performance at a different time or situation. If a person is tested repeatedly, one can make statements like these, ''Sandra types twice as fast as she did a year ago,'' or ''When Jimmy reads with others, he scores much lower than when he is in a room by himself,'' or ''Mr. Thompson's scores on depression have become progressively lower as he moves along in psychotherapy.'' Many behavioral techniques described in chapter eight are self-referencing.

At least three social trends are pressing assessors to use more non-normative comparisons. One trend is the need to find jobs for people who have cultural or social–economic differences from the dominant society that may handicap them in the traditional comparisons with relative standards. Such people may nevertheless possess the abilities to perform if compared with absolute standards. That is, a minority person may be able to perform a skilled job very well, though he or she may not achieve one of the highest scores on a test. A second trend is the increasing emphasis in education on competency based learning, i.e. grading by achievement of a given level of mastery rather than by a curve based on a general distribution. The third trend comes from the behavior modification movement. These psychologists and other specialists emphasize improvement in comparison with measured *individual* performance.

In review, we can apply all of these ideas to Sandra's typing performance:

"Sandra achieved a T-score of sixty-five (the 93rd percentile) in comparison with high school students graduating in commercial courses." (Norm referenced)

"Sandra typed fifty-two words a minute with 95 percent accuracy, which meets the minimum level of civil service requirements (fifty words a minute) but not the higher levels required for certain jobs." (Performance referenced)

"Sandra's score is associated with an 85 percent likelihood of finishing her training course." (Expectancy referenced)

"Sandra's typing speed this week is five words per minute faster than last week." (Self referenced)

QUANTITATIVE CONCEPTS OF ASSESSMENT
IN THE LARGER SYSTEM

So far, we have concentrated on the characteristics of individual tests or other assessment measures. But in real life situations, the whole assessment process is likely to involve several procedures—a battery of tests or application forms, interviews, and observations on a work simulation. Now we will look at some of the concepts and procedures for handling assessment data for decisions beyond the test situation.

The findings from a single test or a group of tests or other procedures need to be compared with the results ultimately achieved. The quantitative results of several procedures can be combined in a formula or equation to give a prediction. This prediction can then be compared with the criterion of success or failure. For instance, let us say that we wish to predict the outcome of a new kind of drug therapy with depressed patients, from a battery of psychological tests and a rating from interviews. From previous research we have derived a formula for combining these measures to make a prediction of those patients who will improve and those who will not during a month of taking the antidepressant drug. Treatment is started with a new set of 100 patients on whom we have the required psychological data. At the end of a month a social worker visits the homes and determines if the patients are improved or not. The criterion is the social worker's rating. Figure 2-7 shows the kinds of representations that can be made of data in studies like this. At the top the 100 scores on the prediction equation are divided in the middle—fifty predicted not to improve and fifty to improve. The two distributions of actual results with the study based on the social workers' dichotomous rating are spread over the range of equation scores; the two distributions overlap. Thus four different outcomes are produced—

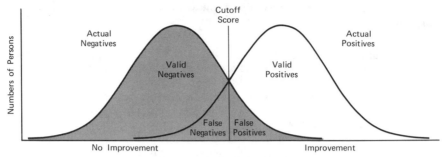

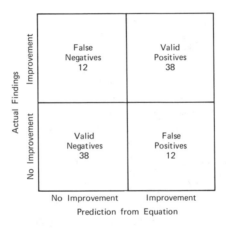

FIGURE 2-7   Two different ways of representing hit rate categories from predictions from psychological measures (From Wiggins, 1973, pp. 241 and 243.)

the two which are desired, the valid negatives and positives, and the two which are not desired, the false negatives and positives. These results are reproduced in the lower figure. In this imaginary study the results are highly significant as compared with chance, and the investigators could conclude that the psychological procedures can predict how a patient will respond to the new drug treatment. When such information about a test or equation based on a set of tests is put in table form, it is called an *expectancy table,* which can be used to make predictons.

Another important and related consideration in the application of testing is the *baserate*—the incidence of a characteristic in the relevant population. If one is making decisions about a characteristic or theory, the question is how common is it already? There are some practical questions:

Will a new driver's examination affect the existing statistics on automobile accidents? In hospital X what percentage of new admissions are diagnosed schizophrenic by present procedures? In setting up a crisis service, can we reduce the present suicide rate among college students? Insurance companies develop actuarial tables based on age, occupation, sex, and other variables which are related to death or disablement. In the same way it would be possible to develop baserate tables, or expectancy tables, for any kind of outcome related to personality assessment, such as diagnosis or reaction to certain kinds of treatment. As Meehl and Rosen (1955) in an important article pointed out, general validity figures for a test are not enough. The value of a test has to be demonstrated by how much it improves prediction over the baserate. If 90 percent of the patients coming to a certain mental hospital are diagnosed schizophrenic, anyone calling all newcomers schizophrenics would be right nine times out of ten. Cronbach (1970, p. 540) presents an illustration of the effects of different baserates on the probability of identifying a depressed patient. As Figure 2–8 shows, the probability that the patient is seriously depressed increases as the T-score on the MMPI scale for depression increases and as the baserate increases. The value of the test is closely related to the baserate. Taking a T-score of eighty, the psychologist calling the patient depressed is right only 15 percent of the time when only 2 percent of the patients coming to the clinic are depressed, but she or he is right about 95 percent of the time if the baserate is fifty-fifty. Of course if the baserate is much higher, the probabilities of

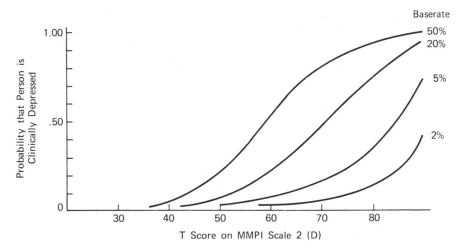

FIGURE 2-8 Probability of correct identification of depressed patients. (From Cronbach, 1970, p. 540). Copyright © 1970 by Lee J. Cronbach. Reprinted by permission of the author and Harper, & Row, Publishers, Inc.)

being correct are higher, but the test is of less value because almost all patients are depressed. A valid test is most likely to be practically useful when the baserate is about 50 percent.

At a low baserate, special problems arise if the decision is of great importance. Only a small percentage of depressed people commit suicide. An out-patient clinic may have less than 5 percent of its patients threatening or attempting suicide, but decisions about taking the patient into the hospital are literally life and death matters. If a test increases the probability of detecting suicide and can be appropriately administered, then the clinic may want to use it even if the baserate is low. Using a cutoff score in Figure 2-8 of eighty on the MMPI D scale, one would catch about 35 percent of those actually depressed. If among those actually depressed, one quarter are potentially suicidal, then it may be worthwhile to use the test and check those people caught by this screening procedure more carefully.

Among the many concepts Cronbach (1970) has contributed to assessment, there are two more that should be mentioned when discussing the larger system of assessment. Borrowing from communications theory, Cronbach notes that some tests have a wide *bandwidth,* others have high *fidelity.* The two are inversely related. A screening device allowing the patient to talk or write about almost anything, such as an unstructured interview or projective technique, has wide bandwidth. Other assessment procedures are capable of being finely tuned and exact in the sampling of a limited range of behavior relevant to specific decisions, such as some tests of clerical ability, memory, or certain kinds of behavioral testing techniques. Highly selected content with careful psychometric development leads to high reliability and sometimes to high validity, but it also makes for narrowness. The same instrument cannot have both breadth and depth. In developing assessment strategies, the assessor must decide whether and when he or she seeks fidelity or bandwidth in the sequence of information gathering. The most common solution in clinical and counseling work is to start with *scanning* and *hypothesis forming* procedures using broad bandwidth devices, such as the interview. Then later one proceeds to *focusing* and *hypothesis checking* as the client's needs become clearer and alternative possibilities emerge.

A final consideration useful in assessment is the concept of *incremental utility* or incremental validity (Meehl, 1959; Sechrest, 1963). A test or other assessment instrument ought to add something not uncovered by simpler or required procedures. The necessary routine administrative procedures in an agency already assist in certain decisions. If a new procedure is to be of value, it must improve upon their usefulness. One must also compare any given procedure with other potential procedures. For example, does the Rorschach provide increased diagnostic accuracy over case history data which must be obtained anyway? A few studies of incremental utility have shown the importance of certain kinds of information, especially case history data (Kostlan, 1954; Winch & More, 1956). In choosing tests and other devices the assessor must study their effectiveness in the particular situation. A device can have impressive reliability and validity with samples on which it was developed, but have no relation to the practical problems facing the assessor.

SUMMARY

This chapter has rapidly covered many concepts in quantitative assessment. Most assessment is a combination of qualitative work, involving subjective judgment, and quantitative work, involving numerical or categorical data and statistical procedures. Qualitative information can be made quantitative by such procedures as coding, counting, ranking, and rating, or by the use of psychological tests. We noted that there are four ways in which numbers are used that progressively offer more opportunity to employ mathematical procedures—the nominal, ordinal, interval, and ratio scales. Most tests provide interval scales, for which raw scores are converted to standard score units.

A test is a method for acquiring a sample of a person's behavior in a standard situation so that the sample can be systematically compared with other information. The test results originate from an interpersonal situation, and many variables affect results. The large number of tests can be divided into two major categories according to whether they measure maximum performance (ability, achievement, and aptitude tests) or typical performance (personality inventories, attitude scales, and projective techniques). In evaluating a test one should become acquainted with the test manual, the situation for which the test is to be used, and practical matters like cost, acceptability to clients, and training required to administer the test, as well as technical details.

Technical characteristics that are important in a test are validity, reliability, norms, and other special aids to interpretation. Validity is the property of the test that tells what the test means; it has to do with relating test information to external information. The different kinds of validity are content, criterion (including both concurrent and predictive), and construct. Predictive validity is most important for practical purposes in the use of tests, and construct validity is most important for theoretical purposes in personality research and measurement of personality concepts. Reliability has to do with the consistency and trustworthiness of obtained scores, and is a matter of internal relationships. The standard error of measurement, which is dependent on how high the reliability coefficient is, estimates the dispersion of scores obtained for an individual, and can be interpreted as the degree of trust one can place in the accuracy of the score. Norms make use of derived scores such as percentiles or standard scores to indicate how a given individual compares with large samples of relevant populations. Several scales plotted on derived score forms portray a profile, which makes it possible to identify many individual patterns. Individual results can be compared not only by the traditional norm-referencing, but also by performance referencing, expectancy referencing, and self-referencing.

Assessment takes place in the larger system of an agency or organization. It usually involves a combination of several procedures which need to be compared with the rates of success and failure in prediction. Baserates, or the incidence of the particular behavior, influence interpretation. At times the assessor starts out with wide bandwidth procedures, such as interviews or projective measures, and narrows down the questions to be investigated by high fidelity instruments. Another final consideration in testing is incremental utility—how much does a specific test or procedure add to other procedures that may be more easily and economically obtained?

SUGGESTED READINGS

CAMPBELL, D.T. & D.W. FISKE, Convergent and discriminant validation by the multitrait–multimethod matrix. *Psychological Bulletin,* 56, 1959, 81–105. This article was an important part in a shift in the orientation of validation work toward the context in which tests operate. It advocates using a matrix of intercorrelations among tests representing at least two traits, each measured by at least two methods. Convergent validity means that independent measures of the same trait should correlate higher than measures of different traits. Discriminant validity means that measures of different traits should not correlate highly. To establish the meaning of a trait or construct, correlations between different methods for measuring it should be higher than correlations with other traits. Another article that advocates the importance of relating validity to the context of operation is Sechrest's "Incremental validity: a recommendation" (1963). Also see Wiggins (1973) for an excellent discussion of classical and newer conceptions of validity, and Messick (1975) for a searching consideration of meaning and values in relation to validity.

MEEHL, P. E. & A. ROSEN, Antecedent probability and the efficiency of psychometric signs, patterns, or cutting scores. *Psychological Bulletin,* 52, 1955, 194–216. This paper has been another important influence in the development of assessment, although its recommendations are not carried out with nearly the frequency that they should be. It describes the importance of evaluating any assessment technique's results against the baserates, that is, the distribution of the particular variable in the population. The authors show how test development should ordinarily be concentrated on characteristics having baserates near a fifty-fifty split, that is, where a person is about as likely to be classified one way as the other. They illustrate some of the practical clinical problems having to do with baserates. This article has been reprinted in a number of books of readings on assessment. Perhaps the best place to see it is in Meehl's book, *Psychodiagnosis* (1973), which has a number of other important papers by Meehl on assessment such as "Wanted—a good cookbook" and "When shall we use our heads instead of the formula?"

MOURSUND, J.P., *Evaluation: An introduction to research design*. Monterey, California: Brooks/Cole, 1973. Although research design is not specifically covered in this chapter, assessment psychology must progress by use of general research principles. Moursund's book is a helpful, clearly written introduction to the ideas and problems involved in planning and carrying out evaluative research. Without complex statistical details and proofs, it presents concepts and principles so that a student can understand how statistics can be helpful in research and can read a statistician's discussion of research problems. Other more advanced books for use in applied social science are *Research on human behavior* by Runkel and McGrath (1972), Chassan's *Research design in clinical psychology and psychiatry* (1967), Shontz's *Research methods in personality* (1965) and the *Handbook of evaluation research* by Gutentag & Struening (1975). Those interested in the possibilities of rigorous methods for studying a single case, which is an important problem in personality research, should see $N = 1$ by Davidson & Costello (1969), or parts of Chassan. Students entering the assessment field will need to be acquainted with certain statistics in order to read the professional journals in psychology. Edgington's survey (1974) of seven leading research journals showed that 71 percent of the articles reporting research made use of analysis of variance, 25 percent used correlation, and 12 to 15 percent used chi-square, t-tests, and nonparametric statistics. Child's *Essentials of factor analysis* (1970) provides a good introduction to that important research and development technique.

TYLER, L.E., *Tests and measurements* (2nd ed.). Englewood Cliffs, N.J.: Prentice-Hall, 1971. In clear simple language, Leona Tyler explains basic statistics and the major concepts underlying psychological tests. She briefly describes leading tests of intelligence, special ability, and personality. This short book is an excellent introduction for students completely unfamiliar with the field. For a much more intensive introduction see Cronbach's *Essentials of psychological testing* (1970, Palmer's *Psychological assessment of children* (1970), Kline's *New approaches to psychological measurement* (1974), or Anastasi's *Psychological testing* (1976). Anastasi's book is particularly useful; along with an excellent introduction to testing, the reader will find appendixes giving handy references to U.S. federal guidelines for insuring equal opportunity in testing, a list of test publishers and a classified list of over 250 tests. Readers interested in applications to business and industry should consult books such as Dunnette's *Personnel selection and placement* (1966). As mentioned in this chapter, see the several Buros books (1959, 1965, 1970, 1972) for extensive descriptions and critiques of specific published tests. Buros is a "must" as a reference book for those interested in psychological testing. Another important reference is the APA's *Standards for educational and psychological tests* (1974).

chapter three

Interviewing
and
Observing

"He that has eyes to see and ears to hear may convince himself
that no mortal can keep a secret. If his lips are silent, he chatters
with his finger-tips; betrayal oozes out of him at every pore."
—Sigmund Freud (1905, p. 77–78)

I can tell that you're a logger
And not just a common bum,
'Cause nobody but a logger
Stirs his coffee with his thumb.
A waitress's song, "My Lover Was a Logger," in Webb et al.,
Unobtrusive Measures (1966, p. 141)

The two main ways to learn about people in daily life are questioning and
observing—we either "ask 'em" or "watch 'em." In systematic assessment,
these are also the most commonly used procedures. Tests, too, are usually
interpersonal events in which the assessor sees and interacts. The major
exception to the use of these direct assessment techniques is the assessment
of personal documents or products, which we shall briefly mention at the
end of the chapter.

THE INTERVIEW—ITS MEANING AND ILLUSTRATIONS

It is likely that the reader of this book has participated in many interviews and will conduct many in the future. Interviews are common, and they bear some resemblance to ordinary conversations. One of the first and clearest definitions of an interview is "a conversation with a purpose" (Bingham and Moore, 1924). An interview is an "inter-view"—a sharing of perspectives and information between two people meeting together. Unlike most conversations, however, the sharing is not equal; the roles in this dyadic (two person) system require more information-giving from the interviewee and more questioning from the interviewer. An interview also often provides an "inner-view" of the interviewee—personal memories, self-concepts, plans and intentions, and ways of thinking through a problem. The interview's potential for flexibility, adaptability to any setting, and similarity to normal conversation make it the most commonly used assessment procedure. But its strength is also its weakness. An interview is deceptively easy to conduct, and research has shown that loosely organized interviews are of questionable validity and reliability. A good interview has more unity, progression, and serious purpose than ordinary conversation. The interviewer is responsible for directing the interaction toward a goal, and the interviewee usually shares that goal and facilitates its achievement.

One of the obvious characteristics of an interview is that it has a beginning, a middle, and an end. The reason for noting these obvious aspects is that, in learning to interview, a person needs to become aware of the movement of the meeting, the significance of starting a relation so that there is openness and acceptance of a common purpose, the proper use of timing so that important topics are covered, and the conclusion of the interview with some feeling of mutual accomplishment and an adequate knowledge of what happens next. There are many varieties of interviews but each needs to relate its purposes to the way the process is timed.

Let us look at these points in two illustrations of ways an interview might be handled in different settings. Each agency has a "gate-keeping" function, for letting people in and out of the system or redirecting them. Interviews are often used as the initial information exchange involved in gate-keeping. The first illustration is a short interview which occurred when a college student, named Charles, stopped to see a university student loan officer.

(After a long wait in a hard chair on the other side of the room, Charles goes to the loan officer's desk in response to his beckoning for the next person waiting.)

L-1 (standing and shaking hands): "Hello. My name is Mr. Lowell. You're Charles Carson, I see from the form you filled out. Please have a seat. Tell me why you need a loan."

C-1: "Well, Mr. Loan—er, I mean Mr. Lowell—I can't pay the rent on the apartment, and I can't buy some books I need."

L-2: "Really? But our records show your father has an income of $30,000 and you're the only child in the family."

C-2 (rather irritated): "Yeh, I know, but he doesn't give me enough."

L-3: "How much does he give you? Perhaps you could budget your money more carefully."

(After discussion of the amount and the needs of the student, possibilities for work and other alternatives are covered and the interview comes to an end.)

L-4: "I'm sorry our rules do not permit giving loans to students from homes as well-off as yours, except in very unusual circumstances. Try looking into other possibilities. If nothing works out, come back to see me, but I can't be optimistic."

C-3: "Well, okay, I'll see."

There are many items to consider in such a short account—the implications of a waiting period and the provisions for people who wait; the early attempt by Mr. Lowell to establish a mildly friendly relationship through the handshake and knowing the interviewee's name ahead of time; Charles' early nervousness; the manner in which the relation altered during the remarks L-2, C-2, and L-3, leading to some defensiveness; and the way Lowell terminated the interview by making his position clear but still leaving the door open in a rather friendly manner. Perhaps of most interest is L-2, which seemed to change the tone of the interview. Lowell's "Really?" said in a sharp and confrontatory manner led to Charles' defensive response. Then in L-3 the Loan Officer implies possible mismanagement. Whether Charles does handle his money wisely or not, the loan officer is close to taking the role of adversary (or father figure?) and is likely to lose a sense of common purpose with Charles. He was *judgmental.* His concern for helping would have been better expressed not by making a hasty judgment, but by first gathering information about how the student uses money and then going over alternatives in such a way that the student would make the decision himself.

Even in brief and rule governed contacts like those in a college loan office, there are influences from the different personalities involved, and personality judgments enter on both sides. Parenthetically it should be noted that in a community there are thousands of similar daily contacts. The manner in which such interviews are conducted generates a climate that probably has important implications for community mental health.

For comparison, let us look at another interview that might have happened if Charles had gone first to a college counseling center or mental health clinic. Coming in without an appointment, Charles was asked by the receptionist to return in a half hour, at which time he could see the psychologist for an initial, brief discussion. He is sitting in a comfortable chair in the reception area.

> I-1 (Coming out to the reception area and holding out her hand): "Hello. You are Charles Carson? I'm Mrs. Infield. Come into my office where we can chat for a few minutes." (Later, with both seated in I's office) "Tell me what brings you here."
>
> C-1: "Well, er, Mrs. Infield, I can't pay the rent on the apartment, and I can't buy some books I need."
>
> I-2: "That's a difficult situation to be in. How did this come about?"
>
> C-2: "My dad makes enough money, and I don't have any brothers and sisters, but we haven't been getting along very well."
>
> I-3: "You believe that your financial situation would be better if you and your father were getting along better?"
>
> (After a discussion of Charles' feelings about his father and about his desire for independence and the immediate financial problem, the interview moves to a close.)
>
> I-4: "The half hour I have available is just about over. We've talked about your looking into a loan from the university, but the rules make that seem unlikely. There may be other possibilities for making some money. You could go to the Student Employment Office. We've also talked about your relationship with your father. Would you like to discuss that further in an appointment with another counselor?"
>
> C-3: "I guess I'll see if I can get a loan. I would like to talk some more; so please give me an appointment."

In this example the interviewer must also make a judgment about how relevant her service is to the client. She defines her role as being interested in personal and family relationships, not just the financial side of the person's life. Recognizing that feelings may take a long time to come out and the client may not wish to explore them at this time, the interviewer allows for different directions that the conversation might take. She deals with the financial problem, passes on information, but does not assume responsibility for it. She ends the interview within the time limits of a busy counseling center. Both examples of interviews are examples of organizational response to individual needs, but they take different forms.

FORMING THE INTERVIEW
AND FACILITATING COMMUNICATION

Because the interview is a conversation *with a purpose,* the interviewer needs to be conscious of several ways in which he or she might let the interview vary. For one thing, there is the *timing* mentioned earlier—when to begin, when to introduce new topics, and when to move to a close. The interviewer must also decide on the *content of the interview,* including both the kind of information and the degree of focus on content. As mentioned in the last chapter, the interview is a broad bandwidth assessment procedure. It is usually used to scan content in many areas, then to focus on certain problem areas. Interviews vary in degree of planned structure for content. Some interviews include a set of specific questions about such topics as health, family relations, or financial matters. Many individual tests are really interviews that are highly structured as to content and use of standardized stimuli. The usual loosely structured interview starts with general questions that allow the interviewee to participate in the direction that it takes and to reveal his or her interests and interpretations. For instance, the interviewer may say, "What brings you here to the clinic?" or "Tell me about your childhood." Unless the interviewer's purpose is narrowly defined, he or she will want to avoid leading questions that limit the interviewee's area of expression. After scanning the major facets of a person's situation through general questions, the interviewer will probably concentrate on details that help clarify the decisions to be made.

In addition to the structuring of informational aspects, the interviewer needs to keep in mind *the degree of distance in the relationship* with the interviewee. One can vary this closeness by the amount of sympathy or feeling expressed, the degree to which one talks about oneself and the similarities of one's experiences to those of the interviewee, the degree to which one is interested and friendly, the acceptance or rejection of proffered help, the amount of digression permitted, and the degree to which one shows a cold, businesslike manner. For most professional interviews it is not desirable to be either overly friendly or overly distant. The interviewee should feel well-received and relaxed, but still be in a "working" frame of mind. Unlike the conversations of daily life, assessment interviews should not ramble and respond to whatever is entertaining. The interviewer needs to control the situation, remembering the purposes of the meeting, but also be sufficiently involved and interested to enter "the world of the person" in order to understand what he or she says.

A third way of shaping the interview is through attention to *the manner of response.* The degree to which questions are *closed or open* is important. Public opinion interviews often ask people being polled to answer "yes" or "no" to a question or to choose a name or a numbered response from alternatives on an answer card. Psychological tests given as interviews often limit response possibilities quite closely, e.g., "Repeat these numbers after me," or "Who is the president of the United States?" Open questions require more than a short answer or a choice; for instance, "What happened to bring on this situation?" or "Tell me about your family." On the extreme end of openness is the interviewing technique Freud developed called *free association.* He asked the patient on the psychoanalyst's couch to say anything which comes to mind, no matter how seemingly irrelevant, objectionable, or trivial—a kind of "rule to be unruly" in thought.

The interviewer may unintentionally structure a response by negatively phrased or loaded questions, or by the responses given to the interviewee's answer. In training, the interviewer needs to learn to see how he or she acts as a stimulus and controlling agent. Studying phonographic or televised recordings of one's own interviews and obtaining supervision by an experienced person is helpful. One can also learn from watching expert interviewing on television "talk shows."

Perhaps the best way to look at interviewing is to examine it as *communication*—a process of sending and receiving messages. Each message has a source and a destination, and it uses a medium of communication, both verbal and nonverbal, in which varying amounts of "noise" accompany the message. The person who is the source must *encode* the message has a source and a destination, and it uses a medium of communication, both verbal and nonverbal, in which varying amounts of "noise" way. Poor knowledge of Spanish may lead an English speaking visitor in Mexico into some peculiar situations as he or she tries to ask questions or understand what the answers are. In India a slight twist of the head meaning "yes" to an Indian may look like "no" to a European. Speech differences among groups in the United States make it difficult for some interviewers to understand their clients. It may be important to know the special argot of the streets or the ghetto to be effective with certain people. If in doubt about the meaning of a term, the interviewer will usually find clients willing to explain and demonstrate their special knowledge.

A useful term from systems and communication theory is *feedback.* In an interview, the participants are constantly reacting to each other verbally and nonverbally. The response to a person's message tells that person how well he or she has communicated. Interviewers often use specific feedback techniques to give the interviewee a chance to clarify meanings.

One technique is called *paraphrasing,* which is a restatement which captures what the person has just said. It is intended to move the interview forward, implying "I'm with you; I understand; please go on" (Gilmore, 1973, p. 241). Paraphrasing is not merely an echo. The response captures the sense of a statement and the person's frame of reference. It is non-evaluative and attempts to be as accurate a reflection of content and feeling as possible. Gilmore (1973, p. 241) gives the illustration of a sullen high school boy plunking himself down in the counselor's office and saying "Mr. Steele said I was supposed to report to you." The counselor's paraphrase might be "The reason you're here isn't exactly 'cause you're dying to see me today." This response captures what the boy has said as well as the tone of resentment. Another example of paraphrasing, more content-oriented, is "You have been mentioning several directions to go; you are exploring your interests in both law and engineering."

Another important and closely related feedback technique in interviewing is *perception checking.* The perceptions we have of the other person's communications and feelings are subjective. The interviewer will often wish to see if these impressions are correct or if she or he and the interviewee share the same understanding of what they are discussing. Perception checking is, as the term implies, a way of reducing the discrepancies. The interviewer describes his or her own perceptions of the interviewee's feelings and asks the interviewee if this perception is correct. Perception checking emphasizes feelings more than paraphrasing and often goes a little beyond what the person has said. Gilmore (1973) cautions interviewers against imposing one's own perceptions on another person. She demonstrates both paraphrasing and perception checking in the following illustration (pp. 248–49):

Suppose you are a junior high school counselor who, at the request of a seventh grade physical education teacher, is attending her conference with the irate parents of a girl who became upset during a discussion of sexual reproduction in a health class. The mother immediately declares that her daughter did not have a problem until the teacher began talking about intimate topics that belong in the home. You respond with a paraphrase: "Things were just fine with your daughter 'til the school began taking over what is rightfully a parent's responsibility." The parents go on to say that the breakdown of morals in the modern world is due to sex becoming a common topic. The father says "We believe sex is a sacred thing that is between a man and his wife . . . of course Sally would be upset, hearing all about it for the first time as if it was just some physical thing." At this point you decide you need to check your perceptions, and so you may say, "I need to see if I'm understanding you completely . . . it's not that you think Sally or someone her age ought to be kept ignorant of how babies are conceived and born, but rather that sex and reproduction are such important, personal, and sacred experiences, that they should be dealt with very carefully, so that the proper values are taught along with the facts . . . is that what . . . am I following you?" They nod "Yes" and you go on to say, "The feeling I'm getting is that it's pretty difficult to see how in a health class you could talk about sex with the care you feel must be given to it and that in a sense the school has sort of taken advantage of your trust or tried to put one over on you . . . does that come anywhere near fitting with how you see it?" Until you and the parents and the teacher share a clear perception of how the parents see the situation and how they feel about it, there is no point in raising the question "What shall we do about Sally and the whole situation now?" The parents are not likely to ask why the school teaches sex education honestly, with a desire to hear the answer, unless you spend a sufficient amount of time and energy understanding their perceptions and letting them know you truly understand how they feel.

KINDS OF INTERVIEWS

Interviewing is regularly used by news reporters, lawyers, police inter-
rogators, physicians, poll-takers, and many others. Its purposes are not
always benign. Lawyers' cross-examinations, some television interviews,
and espionage contacts are designed to produce stress or to put the person at
a disadvantage. Here, however, we will concentrate on some of the common
kinds of interviewing done by psychologists, psychiatrists, social workers,
and researchers in the social sciences who try to understand personality or
make decisions that must take the personality into account.

The *personnel interview* is the most widely used assessment procedure
for hiring purposes. With small companies it is likely to be the only procedure. The interview usually emphasizes the applicant's work history,
interests, and abilities. The employment interview also provides opportunities
to inform the applicant about the organization and the advantages of
working there.

Interviews are also used in personnel work for purposes other than
hiring. Most large organizations require periodic *personnel evaluation
interviews.* Supervisors interview the employee about the work she or he is
doing, and after the personnel ratings are made, good personnel practice
requires that the ratings be discussed with the employee. Through *exit
interviews* with employees, a business or industry attempts to assist with
retirement plans or to learn the causes for job turnover. Occasionally in
industrial or business situations or in research, a *depth interview* is used,
though this type of interview is more common in clinical work. Depth
interviewing aims to collect information for an analysis and report on
motives, conflicts, and relationships that go beyond the *manifest content* of
the interview (Banaka, 1971).

There are a wide variety of *clinical interviews* used in medical, educational, or social agency settings. A specially trained *intake* interviewer,
often a social worker, sees all new patients or clients. From the patient or a
family member, he or she collects information such as the problem or
complaint, the duration of the problem, previous contacts with similar
services, and personal data like age, income, and residence. In many cases
the intake worker will proceed immediately to the *case history interview,*
which we will take up in the next chapter.

Clinical services also have several specialized kinds of interviews.
Psychiatrists and psychologists often conduct a mental status examination,
which traditionally covers six topics: *mental content* (including questions
like, What are the patient's main preoccupations and fears?), *sensorium
and intellect* (How well is the patient oriented to time, place, and person?
How well can he or she reason?), *emotional tone* (What signs of emotion-

ality are observed, and what does the patient report?), *insight* (Does the person realize his or her behavior is unusual? What does he or she think the causes are?), *stream of speech,* and *attitude, appearance, and manner.* Other kinds of clinical interviews include test related interviews initiating or terminating a psychological testing sequence, psychotherapeutic or counseling interviews for assisting a patient or client, and crisis interviews, which are often telephone conversations on a "hot line" to help deal with people under severe and sudden strain who might be considering suicide or some other drastic action. Interviewing for assessment purposes blends into interviewing for assistance purposes. Asking questions about family, schooling, or attitudes toward society often starts people thinking about matters that are important to them.

In the *research interview,* the interviewer initiates the process. Such interviews require considerable preparation so that information can be either quantified immediately or coded later. The *survey interview* is one widely used example. A prototype for this kind of interview is the periodic census conducted by most nations of the world. More closely related to personality are attitude surveys, such as one leading to the book *Americans view their mental health* (Gurin, Veroff, & Feld, 1960). The authors carried out two hour interviews with 2460 adults, selected to be representative of the population in their area. They found, for instance, that feelings of happiness revolved around the home and were conditioned strongly by feelings of economic security. Amount of education correlated with symptoms, where people with less education had more physical symptoms and those with more education had more psychological complaints. Forty-two percent of those interviewed reported problems related to marriage, and the professionals most frequently consulted were clergymen and physicians.

Finally, we should note that research is being conducted on *interview simulation* by means of a computer and the necessary mechanisms to send and receive messages with the person being interviewed. The "Mad Doctor" program of Colby, Watt & Gilbert (1966) can perform such sequences as the following (quoted in Abelson, 1968, p. 313):

> Doctor: Tell me what is troubling you.
> Patient: I feel alone in the world.
> Doctor: Why do you feel very alone in the world?
> Patient: I can't find any friends.
> Doctor: Have you tried?
> Patient: Of course I've tried. Otherwise why would I come to you?
> Doctor: Why do you ask?

As the reader will note from the "Doctor's" last response, the computer program may not react with appropriate social skill. It is built on simple principles, such as always saying "Have you tried?" when the person emits the phrase "I can't." Other simulations of interviews are promising (Hummel et al., 1975). Since programs have also been developed to simulate the thought processes of patients (Colby et al., 1972; Colby, 1974), machines could interview other machines!

VALIDITY AND RELIABILITY OF INTERVIEWS

The same questions can be asked about the interview that are asked about other assessment devices: How adequate is the interview in getting at the constructs we wish to explore or at predicting future success? How well does one measurement correspond with another? How precise a tool is the interview? Does it add anything beyond other, less costly assessment procedures? The trouble with answering these questions is that there is such a great variety of interviews that answers cannot generalize from one form of the interview or from one interviewer to another.

There are many potential sources of inaccuracy and error in interviews. The interviewer is a limited observer and recorder. The interviewee may have limited memory or may try to conceal or distort information. Bias may be built into the questions. The feelings between the two participants may be unfriendly and nonfacilitative. Some studies have shown that ethnic differences, such as a white interviewer with a black interviewee, pose problems of rapport and openness (Canady, 1936; Pasamanick & Knobloch, 1955; Ledvinka, 1971, Grantham, 1973). Interviewer bias is demonstrated in the classical study by Rice (1929) with social workers interviewing destitute men in New York. When asked for their judgments as to the cause of the interviewee's condition, the ardent prohibitionist reported that 62 percent of the men were poverty stricken because of alcoholism and only 7 percent because of adverse economic conditions. The socialist interviewer judged that only 22 percent were destitute because of drinking, but 39 percent were in their plight because of economic conditions.

The question of *inter-interviewer reliability* also arises. For instance psychiatrists have been found to vary a great deal in independent diagnoses of the same mental patients, especially if fine differentiation is required (Ash, 1949; Schmidt & Fonda, 1956). However, in cases where training is good and classifications are rather broad, reliability coefficients greater than .80 have been obtained (Newman et al., 1946; Beck et al., 1962; Sandifer et al., 1964).

The validity of interviews varies greatly with the purposes for which they are conducted, the care with which they are structured, and the way the data and judgments of the interviewers are recorded. Questions can be raised about the accuracy of respondents, or the validity of self report. For instance, as many as 40 percent in a survey may inaccurately report contributions to community fund-raising appeals and even 10 percent inaccurately report possession of a driver's license (Cannell & Kahn, 1968). Some brief psychiatric screening interviews have been effective in predicting gross maladjustments (Wittson & Hunt, 1951), but in general, interview methods are susceptible to considerable distortion and bias. Research on more specific ways to get at certain problems is needed in this unwieldy field. One direction is that taken by Burdock & Hardesty (1963); they have developed an inventory form, the Structured Clinical Interview, to be checked by the clinician while he interviews a patient. The inventory produces scores on ten "subtests," covering such topics as anger-hostility, lethargy dejection, physical complaints, and sexual problems.

There has been considerable research done on interview speech itself as to content (what speakers say) and manner (how they say it). Matarazzo & Wiens (1972) have reviewed the research, much of which has used an instrument for recording and timing interviewer and interviewee utterances called the Chapple Interaction Chronograph, or Interaction Recorder. The authors and their colleagues have produced an impressive series of studies on the effects of variations in such characteristics as duration of utterances and silences on the speech of different psychiatric groups. In general it is clear that an interview is a mutual achievement in which there is a reciprocal effect between the partners.

Despite questions about its reliability and validity, the interview is here to stay. In many instances there are no alternatives to the flexible way that the interview gets at thought patterns and pursues topics in depth. People also *feel* more comfortable about hiring a person or making other decisions if there is a face to face meeting. They know they can picture the person, relate to him or her, and recognize the person if they should meet him or her again. Most psychologists avoid doing "blind" interpretations of tests, though some recommend this procedure as an independent check on the extent to which conclusions are based on nontest information. The interview provides the assessor with the kind of difficult to qualify impressions that may be valuable in supplementing and interpreting results from testing procedures. "Knowing" the person we are assessing seems a sensible state of affairs, but satisfied feelings we derive from an interview should not permit us to make poor or random decisions which affect the course of others' lives. There has probably been an increase in the reliance on interviewing as a result of the attacks on psychological tests in the 60s and 70s and some professional wariness about formal assessment devices. But the wise assessor will question the interview just as any other form of assessment. She or he knows that the interview includes personal prejudices and preferences more than a written document might.

OBSERVING

Like interviewing, observing is a common means for assessing persons and situations. By its nature observation directly concerns the present, while interviews reflect the past (or more properly, the past as seen from the present) or surmise the future (as seen from the present). We do, of course, use observations to make inferences about the past or the future; the clinician seeing slash marks on a patient's wrist guesses that there has been a suicide attempt and may predict another attempt in the future. Observation and interviewing supplement each other. For example, a physician notes the shaky hand movements of a patient and interviews to check for signs in the patient's recent history suggesting a brain lesion. The psychiatrist notices the way a schizophrenic seeks to be alone and the depressed person moves slowly and modifies the mental status examination accordingly.

In everyday life, we constantly use observation in our attempts to understand other people. We observe a tennis player's skill and speed and guess whether he or she is a match for us. We judge by voice and manner how interesting a speaker is and whether we want to hear that speaker again. Haggling in an Asian bazaar, a person judges from the merchant's eager movements whether he will sell at a lower price. A teacher "feels" the restlessness of the class when the bell is about to ring. One social scientist interested in body movements describes how a smile may mean the opposite of approval and friendliness (Birdwhistell, 1970, p. 52):

> My mother took great pride in her role of gracious hostess. She would say firmly, "No matter how much I disagree with a guest I never allow an unchristian word to cross my lips. I just smile." Well, my mother's thin-lipped smile, which could be confined to her mouth, when accompanied by an audible input of air through her tightened nostrils required no words—Christian or otherwise—to reveal her attitude.

An experienced observer of interviews (Wiens, 1976) notes that eye contact plays an important role in signaling verbal interaction. A listener indicates attention by looking at the speaker's eyes or mouth. When the time comes to change speakers, the talker will look toward the listener, who will usually glance away momentarily.

Psychologists and other social scientists have developed systematic ways of observing persons and situations. However, much of this assessment work has been for research, rather than for practical assessment purposes. The bulk of clinical, educational, and industrial assessment using observation is still informal.

CONDITIONS FOR SYSTEMATIC OBSERVATION

The systematic approaches to observational assessment can be grouped around answers to the questions where, what, how, and when. The "where" question indicates the importance of the situation in which observation is done. The major dimension of observational settings is the amount of control exercised by the observers—whether the setting is natural, contrived, or controlled.

At the lowest level of external control, observations take place in natural settings. There are field observations of the ongoing life of the persons being observed. The psychologist who has done the most to establish field observation as a valid scientific technique is Roger Barker (1968). His contribution has been in theory and analysis based on observers' running accounts of observations, primarily with children. Barker argues powerfully for the study of the *ecology of behavior.* He points out that most psychologists are interested in real life phenomena, but the ones they study are mostly artificial, because they use settings such as laboratories and clinics, and data gathering devices such as tests, that distort the behavior of the individual. Psychologists act mostly as *operators,* producing data whose conditions they have dominated, instead of *transducers,* simply translating and coding what happens naturally. It has been demonstrated that the behavior of animals in zoos and the behavior of people in prisons are very different from behavior "in the wild." The "natural" situations for human beings, however, are not immediately obvious. For children, observations in classrooms are natural and for patients, observations in the hospital setting are similarly "natural." In clinical work, home visits may be used for assessing family interaction. A growing technology of observation is making meaningful field assessment possible due mainly to behaviorally oriented clinical psychologists.

Despite psychologists' concern for real life behavior, the great majority of their research and assessment work takes place in laboratories, clinics, or classrooms. The major reason is that field observations are inconvenient and expensive, and the results are often complex and confusing. One may also be interested in specific behaviors such as reactions to frustration that occur rarely in real life, so that experimental situations are required to produce them. There are, however, degrees of control in non-field situations. At an intermediate level of control, observations take place in a *contrived or simulated setting.* The most realistic settings are *work samples* duplicating the conditions one is interested in, perhaps using the actual site in which the person will ultimately be performing. Another technique is the so called *situational test*—a contrived situation in which the subject is given a task to accomplish. One set of investigators (Mills, McDevitt, & Tonkin, 1966) used some clever situational tests to select police recruits, including measures of observations made on a simulated patrol and in the search of a room from which a person had mysteriously vanished. Another kind of work sample on situational test is the In-Basket Test, a method developed for British civil service examinations (Vernon & Parry, 1949) and adapted to many American situations in the training or selection of managers and executives (Lopez, 1966; Bray et al., 1974). The subject receives basic information about a company and is told to play the role of an administrator whose job is to handle a series of memos, letters, forms, and other requests like those typically coming to a manager's in-basket. Assessors may use visual impressions and analyze the quantity and quality of the subject's products and decisions. There are many other kinds of role playing situations in this category, some to be mentioned in later chapters. Simulations of complex situations using audio-visual equipment and computer processing of data are possible and are occasionally used for research and training (e.g., flight simulation, Huff & Nagel, 1975).

Finally on the continuum is the *controlled or laboratory setting.* At the extreme, psychologists use enclosed soundproofed, electrically shielded rooms to eliminate all external stimuli. The laboratory psychologist attempts to control all stimuli except the ones he or she wants to vary systematically; the laboratory setting is also set up so that only the particular behavior of interest will be measured. For example, if the personality experimenter is studying dominance behavior by presenting pictures of people interacting, he or she will avoid contaminating the results with stimuli that might elicit other motives, such as orderliness or sexuality. In giving standardized tests the clinician may approximate the controls of the laboratory, trying to minimize distractions and vary the appropriate stimuli intentionally.

Each of the three kinds of settings—field, simulated, or laboratory—has its advantages and disadvantages. A fully articulated assessment science would include all three. Because the ultimate purpose of assessment is to relate to real life, assessment instruments need some kind of validations in the field, now the weakest link in the chain of assessment.

The "what" question about observation involves several decisions: Should the assessor observe one person or several, the whole situation or a small part? How selective should observation be? The stream of behavior in interaction must be cut up in some way. One procedure is to look for only certain content or happenings; another to sample extensively, but for only a limited time. These procedures are called *event-sampling* and *time-sampling*. In the first method, instructions call for observers to record only a certain class of behavior, such as instances of aggressive actions. Watching Jimmy on the playground, the observer would tally or describe each instance when he hit, teased, or verbally abused other children. In the second method, observers would record what they see happening at certain time intervals. For instance, on the school playground, an observer would jot down what Jimmy was doing every five minutes, whether he was hitting someone, playing cooperatively, or sitting alone. The observer's clipboard might have a timer which activated a light or a buzzer in a "hearing aid" to remind the observer when to record.

A procedure related to event-sampling is the *critical incident technique* (Flanagan, 1954). This technique requires an observer to record instances of behavior which illustrate good or poor performance. Recording is done on a daily basis as soon after the event as possible. A psychologist may ask a mother to write down examples of a child's helpfulness or negativism over a two or three week period. A plant supervisor may be asked to report the specific actions and surrounding situations characteristic of effective and ineffective production. From these examples, tests or other procedures can be developed to chart performance and plan a training situation.

The "how" question about observation is also a large one. It may involve recording by mechanical means, such as with audio-tape or by television, so that assessors can listen or view the records at leisure. If human recording is done, procedures must be developed for checking, writing, or dictating the observations. One important related question is the decision about the relation of the observer to the observed person—whether to interact directly or be out of sight. *Participant observation* occurs when the observer is visible to the people being observed and taking part in the action. An anthropologist may live for many months with a tribe he or she is studying. The psychological observer may play with the children he or she is observing or even take the role of a patient in a mental hospital along with other patients (Rosenhan, 1973). When the participation is active and heavy, the observer must, of course, postpone note taking, dictating, or writing up observations until a time as soon as possible after the observation period ends. The observer may be visible, but noninteractive, as were the trained recorders who followed a child for a full day in a Barker & Wright study (1951). As space exploration has shown, technology also makes non-participant observation at great distances feasible. One study (Matarazzo et al., 1964) investigated the durations of the conversations between astronauts and the ground station. Telemetering of heart rhythms of patients at home or work can be accomplished through radio transmitters, or portable tape recorders (Sandler et al., 1975). There are a few examples of the use of portable transmitters to record psychological data. One research team (Soskin and John, 1963) obtained the cooperation of a young newly married couple to record their conversations during a vacation at a lake resort. Another investigation (Moos, 1968) found it was feasible to use a wireless radio transmitter in a psychiatric ward, but patients showed sizable individual differences in their acceptance and self-consciousness. Miklich (1975) reviews several successful studies with children using radio telemetry. The most common procedure for reducing the visual and auditory intrusion into the subject's activity is a room with a one-way mirror through which cameras can record or observers can watch children's play, an interview, or group therapy. Ethical considerations must always be kept in mind. The assessor should inform and receive the consent of the subjects (or the parents in the case of young children) for such observations or recordings.

Finally, the "when" question about observation arises. This refers not only to the period and timing of the observation that will constrain the sampling of behavior, but also to the time that observations are recorded. *Immediate recording* avoids much of the problem of memory distortion, though perception is still selective. *Retrospective recording* occurs when the assessor jots down observations after the conclusion of an interview or testing session, or uses a checksheet or rating scale to record impressions. Such recording suffers from problems of condensation and forgetting, but may be the only feasible way to obtain some observations.

ILLUSTRATIONS OF THE RECORDING
AND CODING OF OBSERVATIONS

Weick (1968, p. 360) defines the observational method in research as "The selection, provocation, recording and encoding of that set of behaviors concerning organisms 'in situ' which is consistent with empirical aims." Such a definition places emphasis on the aims of the process and also on the plan for systematizing the data. The arrangements for gathering information and transferring it into quantifiable form must be consistent with the purposes of the experimenter or assessor. One must decide where, what, how, and when to observe. Observational methods show considerable diversity in the important basic processes of recording and coding.

Barker and his colleagues are near one extreme in the amount of their unselected material which is kept for the record. Consistent with Barker's view that the natural ecology of human behavior is the important thing to understand, he tries to record the entire behavior stream of the person being observed and avoids disturbing the environment as much as possible.

Observers make a *specimen record* by writing a running account of observed behavior. Later they code the behavior by content or by units based on goals, that is, episodes with a beginning and an end. Figure 3–1, from Barker (1963, p. 8–9) is a record of Brett Butley, age 7 years and 2 months, as he wanders on the school yard in a County School in Yorkshire, England, eating an orange.

Unlike clinical or applied psychlogists with a practical purpose underlying the observations, Barker is simply recording behavior and "trying to make sense" of it. He and his colleagues identify units within the "stream of behavior" as *behavior episodes*. Episodes may have subunits and they may overlap with other episodes. Brett's major units in Figure 3–1 were;

> Eating an orange (containing the subunits noting hurt child and watching cricket)
> Noting hurt child
> Playing cricket (containing the subunit waiting for boys to move away)

Unlike Barker, many psychologists try to select and condense at the time of observation. Patterson and his colleagues are also interested in naturalistic records of children in their homes and schools. Their concern for behavioral improvement of disturbed and aggressive children (Patterson, 1971) has led to the development of procedures for reporting these kinds of behavior and to training programs for observers to apply these procedures rapidly and precisely. The Behavioral Coding System (Jones, Reid, & Patterson, 1975) contains twenty-eight categories, each of which has a two letter abbreviation, like CM (Command), LA (Laugh), or DS (Destructiveness). The trained observer codes the behaviors as he or she watches them occur. The record sheet shows the person and the time of the behaviors in a running sequence. Patterson and others have studied reliability, generalizability, validity, and observer effects with the Behavioral Coding System over many years. We will return to observation and coding procedures in chapters five and seven.

Another kind of approach to obtaining a quantified record of observations is to use a checklist or rating scale retrospectively. For instance, the Inpatient Multidimensional Psychiatric Scale (Lorr, et al., 1962) is used by clinicians to rate symptoms observed during interviews with psychotic patients. The clinician checks whether speech was slowed and labored and whether postures were peculiar, rigid, or bizarre. Another behavioral checklist might ask nurses to indicate whether a patient refused to eat, ate indifferently, or ate an adequate serving enthusiastically. Another might ask a teacher to rate the degree of attentiveness of a child in class. Figure 3–2 illustrates the principal kinds of ratings and check sheets.

The numerical rating scale quantifies the amount or intensity of a specified characteristic. The graphic rating scale is another way of doing this. The cumulated-points scale used with a checklist provides a score by a count of

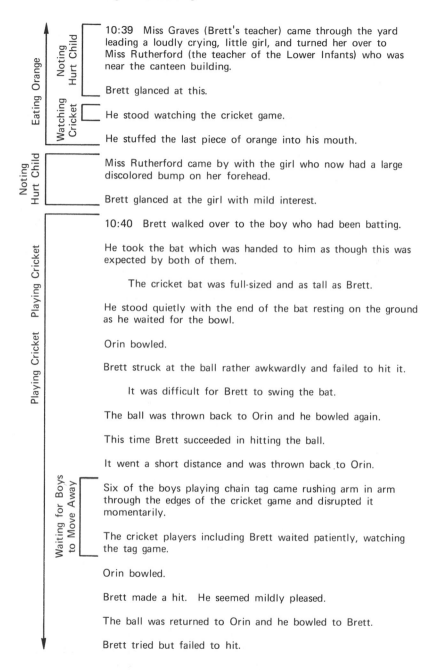

10:39 Miss Graves (Brett's teacher) came through the yard leading a loudly crying, little girl, and turned her over to Miss Rutherford (the teacher of the Lower Infants) who was near the canteen building.

Brett glanced at this.

He stood watching the cricket game.

He stuffed the last piece of orange into his mouth.

Miss Rutherford came by with the girl who now had a large discolored bump on her forehead.

Brett glanced at the girl with mild interest.

10:40 Brett walked over to the boy who had been batting.

He took the bat which was handed to him as though this was expected by both of them.

The cricket bat was full-sized and as tall as Brett.

He stood quietly with the end of the bat resting on the ground as he waited for the bowl.

Orin bowled.

Brett struck at the ball rather awkwardly and failed to hit it.

It was difficult for Brett to swing the bat.

The ball was thrown back to Orin and he bowled again.

This time Brett succeeded in hitting the ball.

It went a short distance and was thrown back to Orin.

Six of the boys playing chain tag came rushing arm in arm through the edges of the cricket game and disrupted it momentarily.

The cricket players including Brett waited patiently, watching the tag game.

Orin bowled.

Brett made a hit. He seemed mildly pleased.

The ball was returned to Orin and he bowled to Brett.

Brett tried but failed to hit.

FIGURE 3-1   Section of specimen record of Brett Butley's stream of behavior on the school playground. (Barker, R.G., ed., *The stream of behavior.* New York: Appleton-Century-Crofts, 1963, 8–9. Reprinted by permission of the author.)

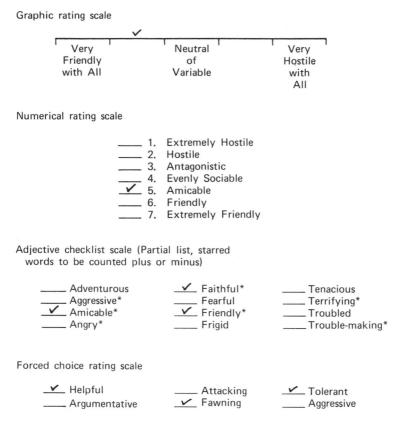

Graphic rating scale

| Very Friendly with All | Neutral of Variable | Very Hostile with All |

Numerical rating scale

_____ 1. Extremely Hostile
_____ 2. Hostile
_____ 3. Antagonistic
_____ 4. Evenly Sociable
__✔__ 5. Amicable
_____ 6. Friendly
_____ 7. Extremely Friendly

Adjective checklist scale (Partial list, starred words to be counted plus or minus)

_____ Adventurous	__✔__ Faithful*	_____ Tenacious
_____ Aggressive*	_____ Fearful	_____ Terrifying*
__✔__ Amicable*	__✔__ Friendly*	_____ Troubled
_____ Angry*	_____ Frigid	_____ Trouble-making*

Forced choice rating scale

| __✔__ Helpful | _____ Attacking | __✔__ Tolerant |
| _____ Argumentative | __✔__ Fawning | _____ Aggressive |

FIGURE 3-2 Four kinds of scales for rating friendliness-hostility (From Wiggins, 1973, p. 311)

the number of checks relative to the trait being measured; other traits can be measured on the same list. The forced-choice scale is so named because it requires the observer to choose between a pair of adjectives, equated by prior research for desirability or negative implications. The last technique was developed to avoid the common tendency of people to be overly lenient or generous in their ratings.

CRITIQUE OF OBSERVATION

What has already been said about reliability, validity, norms, and problems of interpretation can be said about observational techniques. Most observational systems depend heavily on human perception and judgment which provides many opportunities for bias and inaccuracy. It is impossible to notice and remember all details; memory tends to be selective and to abbreviate the many events in the stream of observed behavior. The more time elapsing between the event and its recording, the greater the likelihood of distortion. Observations are also influenced by the observer's previous experience in similar situations. He or she may expect that certain things will occur or that people occupying roles such as teachers will invariably manifest certain behaviors, such as authoritarian demands. The reputation of the subject of the observation will also create what is called a *halo effect*—a spread of positive or negative evaluations to observations other than those directly related to the reputation. A number of studies have shown that, if raters are told an important positive trait, such as intelligence, is characteristic of a person, they will tend to attribute other traits, like honesty or effectiveness, to the person. Although direct and immediate reporting of behavior may avoid some of these biases, there are still factors which can distort observations (Weick, 1968).

Having several observers helps to overcome biases and check inter-observer reliability. Watching the same situation, different observers notice different things. Large personality assessment programs often use several observers or judges. Training the observers and carefully defining what is to be observed and the categories to be coded or rated can also help reduce chance errors.

A special problem related to the validity of observational data is that few observations are without an effect on the behavior of the persons observed. The classic example of observer influence is the study of the workers at the Western Electric Hawthorne plant (Roethlisberger & Dickson, 1939). Interested in the effects on productivity of various changes in the environment, the experimenters observed relay assemblers in a small room of the plant. Almost any experimental changes increased production, even after privileges were taken away. The explanation given was that the attention given to the workers was very rewarding in itself; this positive result of experimenter interest has been called the *Hawthorne effect.* There are many other illustrations from ordinary life of people behaving differently when "under the spotlight." For example, amateur photographers bewail the stiffness and unnatural quality they get from posed portraits and drivers behave differently when they see a police car on the road.

Mischel (1968) presents another vexing question—the degree to which an observer's report is a representation of "what's out there" or is simply a representation of the observer's mental organization about persons. The observer may simply be indirectly reporting his or her own way of classifying people—his or her implicit personality dimensions. Mischel's criticisms particularly apply to retrospective ratings. He points to the work of Passini & Norman (1966) who found that a factor analysis of students' ratings of strangers resulted in the same factors as those of expert observers. Mischel agrees with Vernon's earlier conclusion (1964, p. 59), that "It seems best to regard ratings not so much as summaries of objectively observed behavior as rationalizations abstracted from the rater's overall picture (his homunculus) of the subject.'' This conclusion refers to personality ratings, rather than specific behavior records, of course. It seems likely that all observational data to some extent reflect the personality structures in the observers' minds, but the problem is less acute when clearly defined *behaviors* are recorded.

Despite its problems, observation is an indispensable part of assessment. As the technology of observation and data organization develops, and as research design becomes more sophisticated, all assessment is likely to become more effective. Wiggins (1973, p. 292ff), referring to Cronbach and his colleagues, discusses generalizability theory—the measurement theory combining reliability and validity considerations. He proposes the simultaneous treatment of variations arising from these five facets of observation: settings, observers, instruments, occasions, and attributes, when applied to differences among persons. With this complex design, investigators would be able to tease out variations due to all of the separate complicating factors.

One of the most intriguing questions for future development in assessment is the meaning of incongruence between messages sent by the verbal channel and those sent by the nonverbal channel. Some students of schizophrenia (Bateson et al., 1956) see the confusion caused by saying one thing and acting another as a causative factor in making the schizophrenic "reality" different from that of most people. It may be that in order to function reasonably well, we must have considerable congruence between what we gather from conversation and what we observe. Other students of psychotherapy (Ekman & Friesen, 1968, p. 215) have noted the importance of understanding messages from both the verbal and nonverbal channels: "When there is conflict within the individual either about communicating or about the topic of communication, it is likely that the two channels will be discrepant." Whether actions speak louder than words is a topic for much potential investigation.

PERSONAL DOCUMENTS
AND UNOBTRUSIVE MEASURES

In addition to gathering personal information by interviewing, observation, and testing, there are a few less commonly used sources of data. One of these is *personal products and documents.* The painting of an artist, the performances of an actress or musician, and the writings of a person are opportunities for personality analysis. Allport (1942, 1961) has been a particularly strong advocate of the use of personal documents. In the next chapter on life history we will see illustrations of some of these sources.

Another direction of investigation has been *unobtrusive measures*. Much of personality study and all of social science is open to the charge of bias and distortion as a result of subjects knowing they are being observed or investigated and reacting accordingly, showing what might be called the "guinea pig effect." Unobtrusive measures are "nonreactive" ways of providing data about people. Several psychologists (Webb, Campbell, Schwartz, & Sechrest, 1966) have collected a set of assessment possibilities which do not depend on interviews, questionnaires, participant observation, or other obvious techniques. They suggest using such items as physical traces of behavior (garbage collected from a home), archival materials (diaries, public records), and hidden hardware (such as taperecorders) for observation. Some countries, such as Denmark, have such good archival records on their citizens that researchers have been able to find out a great deal about the inheritance of schizophrenia over several generations. The celebrated tape recordings of former President Nixon are gold mines of personal information for researchers, and a study of the television series "Candid Camera" would show how people adapted to unfamiliar, stressful, and ridiculous situations filmed without their knowledge. All such techniques that involve collecting information about persons without their knowledge pose threats to privacy and raise the possibility of misuse of the information. Scientists need to be very sensitive to the ethical problems involved in such research.

SUMMARY

Two nearly indispensable methods of assessment are interviews and observation. The interview is a conversation with a purpose. The interviewer in training needs to learn how to differentiate the rambling self-expressiveness of conversation from the structured and purpose-oriented nature of the interview. Interviews may be structured for timing, content, closeness of relationship, and manner of response. Two forms of interview technique involving feedback are paraphrasing (the interviewer's restatement of what the interviewee has said) and perception checking (the interviewer's description of impressions received, asking the interviewee if they are correct).

There are many kinds of interviews in personnel work, clinical work, and research, such as hiring and exit interviews, personnel evaluation, intake interviews, case histories, mental status examinations, and survey interviews. Some experimentation has begun on the simulation of interviews by computers. The evidence on validity and reliability is patchy and unclear because of the lack of standardization of interviews. In general, the better structured the interview and the clearer the judgments to be made, the higher the reliability and validity. It can be concluded that the typical unstandardized interview is open to a great deal of bias and inconsistency.

Most observation is done in a casual, unsystematic manner. We are seldom aware of the aspects of our environment and of people on which we base our impressions and feelings. As with interviewing, training in observing can increase one's sensitivity to nuances of behavior. In planning observations, the investigator must consider where, what, how, and when. The conditions for systematic observation vary from natural settings to contrived situations to highly controlled laboratory settings. Observation may involve event-sampling or time-sampling. The critical incident technique is a procedure for collecting observations of effective and ineffective behavior. The observer must plan the degree to which he or she is a participant in the scene and choose the means of recording the observations. Recording can be based on a complete specimen record or on immediate use of symbols for behavior. Different kinds of rating scales are used to record judgments of observations.

Questions of reliability and validity should be asked of observational methods. The halo effect refers to judges' tendencies to rate a person high on everything if they value one variable, like intelligence, highly. The Hawthorne effect refers to the influence of attention on observed people. Questions are being raised about the degree to which observers' ratings are primarily influenced by the mental make-up of the observer rather than by the behavior of the observed person. It is important to develop ways of comparing what people say and what they do.

Other sources of data are to be found in personal documents and products such as diaries and drawings. Some of these are so called unobtrusive measures, that is, data collected without disturbing the person's activities or letting him or her know of the data collection. Looking for wear or markings on books in a personal library or using hidden tape recorders or cameras are examples. Ethical questions are raised by the use of some unobtrusive measures.

SUGGESTED READINGS

ENDICOTT, J. and SPITZER, R. L. The value of the standardized interview for the evaluation of psychopathology. *Journal of Personality Assessment,* 36, 1972, 410–417. The authors, members of a biometrics research team in New York, discuss the value of a guided interview about psychiatric status and show the profiles produced by different groups of disturbed patients.

WIECK, K. E. Systematic observational methods. In *The handbook of social psychology,* Vol. 2 (2nd ed.) G. Lindzey and E. Aronson, (eds.), Reading, Mass.: Addison-Wesley, 1968, 357–451. This overview provides an extensive coverage of the methods and problems of observation in research. Topics include the definition of observation, the occasions and settings for observation, the observer as an artifact, nonverbal behavior, spatial behavior, linguistic and extra-linguistic behavior, issues in recording, category systems, and methods of overcoming observer bias.

WIENS, A. N. The assessment interview. In *Clinical methods in psychology,* I. B. Weiner (ed.), New York: Wiley, 1976, pp. 3–60. Wiens' chapter is an excellent introduction to the interview method, particularly as it is used in clinical assessment. He compares interviews with conversation, reviews studies of validity and reliability, discusses the characteristics of a good interviewer, and provides an overview of major research on the structure and process of interviewing. Some specialized introductions including good examples of interviews are Benjamin's *The Helping Interview* (1969), Gilmore's *Counselor-in-Training* (1973), Kadushin's *The Social Work Interview* (1972), Rich's *Interviewing Children and Adolescents* (1968), and Morganstern's chapter entitled "Behavioral interviewing: The initial stages of assessment" (1976).

chapter four

Assessment of Life History

All the world's a stage,
And all the men and women merely players;
They have their exits and their entrances;
And one man in his time plays many parts,
His acts being seven ages. At first the infant,
Mewling and puking in the nurse's arms;
Then the whining school-boy . . . —William Shakespeare,
As You Like It, Act II, Scene VII.

In this familiar quotation from a sixteenth century student of people, we find portrayals of two important ideas psychologists and others are trying to conceptualize and assess today—the view of the person in context (playing a role in a setting) and the view of the changes in life from birth to death. These two views will be covered in this chapter and the next. The task of the assessor is to understand the person of this minute's observation and the relation of these observations to the days and years of the person's developing life. Each individual may be viewed as a long story, of which we are reading only one page. Shakespeare conceived the story as having seven ages—infancy, school age, young adulthood (lover), early occupation (soldier), mature occupation (judge), old age, and second childhood. Others would mark different periods.

Each assessor is to some extent a historian, analyzing the meaning of the person's background for the purposes of today's decisions. One of the major debates in the field of history is between those who attribute the great movements of change to the nature of outstanding persons and those who attribute them to the spirit of the times—the "Great Person" versus the *Zeitgeist*. Personality theory and personality assessment present a similar question: are the major forces involved in an individual's behavior those of inner development or outer environment? Some personality theorists and psychotherapists, especially those in the psychoanalytic tradition, emphasize childhood experience and unconscious conflicts derived from that early period. Others, especially behaviorists and field theorists, concentrate on the current situation and the forces and reinforcements which are affecting the individual right now. Probably, as in many things, "the truth lies somewhere in between." A person's behavior grows out of both internal predispositions and external interactive influences, and no doubt there are great individual differences in response to the environment and to one's inner tendencies.

In this chapter we will be concerned with the systematic ways psychologists have used to conceptualize and quantify life history and time variables in personality. Such assessment is important in several ways. Every clinical and personnel assessment must pay some attention to history. Life history is crucial when the purpose of the assessment is an extensive analysis of an individual personality. Questions of life history also enter into predictive studies, where, as we shall see at the end of the chapter, they often lead to the most useful data available.

THE STUDY OF LIVES—INBURN

To illustrate one way to analyze life history, let us look at Inburn, a college sophomore whom Kenneth Keniston described (1963, pp. 41-2, 45-46):

> Like many of his classmates, he came from a middle-class family outside of New England, and he had gone to a good high school where he had graduated near the top of his class and been editor of the school paper. . . . His father was an executive in a large Detroit corporation, and his mother, for a time a school teacher, had early abandoned her career for domesticity. Inburn himself had been undecided for a time as to his major, but had finally settled on English literature as a field in which he could combine his interest in writing and his superior high school training in literature. Like other students with artistic interests, he had tried his hand at student dramatics and at writing . . . He was a student who was in good standing with the college authorities, who had caused no one any trouble, and who would not easily be picked out in a crowd.

In the most public sides of Inburn's personality, then, there was little to suggest what was the case: that he was deeply dissatisfied with society, the world, and himself; that he almost completely rejected the institutional forms within which he was living; that he would spend his first reading period for exams in a platonic partnership with a call girl whose memoirs he was ostensibly recording for future use; and that, though he passed his exams, he would withdraw from the college at mid-year, never to return, heading instead on a motorcycle across the country to live with an "irredeemably dissolute" high-school friend in San Francisco. . . .

Inburn's autobiography . . . begins to provide some clues as to the development of his alienation . . . He began his autobiography in the third person:

> He came screaming and red-faced into the world on a December night in 1938, loath to leave his insensible sanctuary . . . It was in a hospital in St. Louis. His mother was a small young woman and she never had a child again. His parents were both schoolteachers and poor, after the ravages of the depression. His mother was particularly good-looking when she was young—black hair, a good nose, striking dark eyes, a sensuous lip, and a delicate yet hard, vibrant, vivacious body.

Inburn goes on to describe his mother's Greek immigrant parents, her mother "a simple, exuberant, and cruel woman," and her father, who ran a small restaurant, "strong man, and strong-willed, tireless, too tireless." . . . Inburn describes his father as a "phlegmatic, deliberate, steady-minded Welshman," noting the extreme contrast with his mother. "Father is pretty much of a failure in his own eyes," he comments, adding: "He's done pretty well as far as the world is concerned, though." Elsewhere he calls his father "a pillar in the community," adding parenthetically, "Small pillar, small community." He describes "a great distance" between himself and his father, noting rather unenthusiastically, "We are friendly, though, except when my Greek side is up and I become disgusted with him and he annoyed at me." . . . But as with most children his age, the Second World War profoundly affected Inburn:

> When he was five years old, his father went into the war, he was gone for four years. In these four years he and his mother had the most intimate of relationships. They were one. Every thought, every action of one could be anticipated by the other. Somehow it seemed more than a mere mother-and-only-child relationship. We were in complete spiritual and mental and physical harmony with each other. Sometimes she was even shy with me. It was a strange relationship.

Keniston uses Inburn's autobiography and the stories elicited by the Thematic Apperception Test cards to identify the major themes of his life. In a narrative and qualitative way, Keniston brings together repeated examples of Inburn's longing to return to the shelter of his mother's affection and physical care in early life, of which he was sole object before his father returned from military service. Keniston interprets Inburn's Oedipal desires for his mother as the basis for his later alienation. Really having his mother was impossible, and as Inburn grew into late childhood and adolescence, he could not view his father as providing an attractive model for the future; so there was no solution to his internal conflict. Inburn found an intellectual outlet for his desire to reenter the "insensible sanctuary" in one close friend in high school, a profoundly cynical and sarcastic young man, and he turned his anger against established society.

Keniston (1963, p. 60) summarizes his approach to the analysis of lives, saying "only when we have begun to understand the subtle inter-weaving of themes, the 'overdetermination' of any single act, belief, or fantasy, and the multiple functions that every dream, wish, behavior, and philosophy serves, do we begin to understand something of an individual." Keniston also points out the importance of recognizing the press of history on individual lives, for example the contrasting cultures of Inburn's parents, the social mobility which makes for unsettling change, the contrast between the intimacy of childhood and the impersonal bureaucracies toward which young people feel they are headed, and the corruption and sordid behavior of some public figures—difficult models with which to link one's enthusiasms. Thus, Keniston found in Inburn a symbol of the restless, disenchanted youth of the 1960s—a prototype of alienation.

Keniston's Inburn study represents a major approach to the assess-ment of the life of an individual in its *search for themes* that run through the account and help explain many events. The personality theorist Henry Murray used the word *thema* to indicate a description of an event in terms of the way a perceived environmental pressure interacts with a particular personal need to provide satisfaction or nonsatisfaction. The assessor looks for the underlying plot of the life story and analyzes the person's major concerns and conflicts. Another analytic approach, derived from medical techniques, is the *search for etiology*, or the causes or origins of a disorder. The assessor looks at a case history for sources of stress, impaired relations, and perhaps physiological conditions, and tries to determine the antecedents of a present disorder. A third general approach to the assessment of life history is to *search for predictors*. The assessor analyzes the material to locate specific events or characteristics that correlate with later criteria. The last approach is generally the one used by personnel psychologists. All of these approaches can be used either for research or clinical purposes. The intensive study of a person such as that of Inburn is usually done for research. Such studies can lead to insights into the nature of personality which superficial exposure cannot provide. These studies help to form the basis for much of the present theory of personality but most assessment does not have the time or the purposes of intensive study. The usual assess-ment of life history runs from three or four questions on an application form to three or four pages of case history in a clinical report.

Information for developing the biographical account is usually obtained through interviews or documents. The respondent may be the person himself or a close relative or friend, or both. It is advisable to inter-view someone besides the person in order to obtain different viewpoints on

important events. Corroboration or disagreements are valuable in understanding the person's perceptions and approximating the reality of events.
With children or very disturbed patients, it may be necessary to rely heavily
on family members.

Usually the history is retrospective. The assessor has to rely on the
recall of the client or informants, and of course memories are often vague
or faulty. An alternative to such "follow-back" is to plan to obtain life
histories by "follow-up." Some research is *longitudinal,* that is, the study
of the same persons over a period of time, in contrast to *cross-sectional*
research, which samples persons of different ages at one particular time.
The aim of such developmental research is to observe personal changes and
situational shifts over time. Follow-up studies of clinics and hospitals can
also be sources of checking on life history.

The life history cannot be confined to the person alone. As suggested
in the case of Inburn, the careful assessor will also investigate the historical
and cultural context within which the person lived that may help account
for the person's problems and changes. It is important to emphasize the
image of the person as a subsystem within other systems. An American
growing up during the Vietnam War is likely to have strong emotions and
attitudes toward the military. Generational and historical changes have
been shown to be significant in longitudinal studies of adolescents and
adults (Schaie and Labauvie–Vief, 1974; Nesselroade and Baltes, 1974).
Cultural context must also be considered because, for example, being forty
years old in some countries is much different from being forty years old in
others; the average life expectancy in some parts of Africa and Asia is only
forty-five, while it is seventy in the United States, Japan, and Europe.

DEVELOPMENT AND ASSESSMENT

In preparing for interviews and analyzing life history information, it is
useful to keep in mind the long term developmental *processes* over the life
span. As with any living creature, the human being develops through a
period of growth, a period of stability, and a period of decline. This developmental approach has generated several approaches to the assessment
of personality.

One approach is the *analysis of life histories by developmental stages.*
This concept requires collecting a biography or autobiography of a person
and breaking down the span of activities into periods with predominant
themes or purposes. This approach will be illustrated by the work of Buhler.
Another approach is the *use of testing procedures to identify level of
development.* This method assumes that persons do not mature at the same
rate and that the stage of maturity attained will be manifested by certain test

responses. Loevinger's work is one of the few specific applications of this method to personality study. A third approach is the *longitudinal measurement of personality change,* and we shall look briefly at the use of assessment procedures for this purpose.

Charlotte Buhler and her colleagues have conducted a number of studies over many years (Buhler and Massarik, 1968). She posits five periods in a person's life:

1. Progressive growth without reproductive ability (roughly 0–15 years).
2. Progressive growth with the onset of reproductive ability (roughly 15–25 years).
3. Reproductive ability and stationary growth (25 to 45 or 50).
4. Beginning decline and loss of reproductive ability in the female (45 or 50 to 65 or 70).
5. Further decline and loss of reproductive ability in one or both sexes (65 to 70 and beyond).

Buhler relates each period to the development and reassessment of life goals and points out that society assigns roles according to age. She and her colleagues have conducted several studies of creativity and productivity in the life spans of eminent people and found two factors related to the highest periods of productivity. Those activities requiring *vitality* tend to reach their highest point early (in the 20s and early 30s), especially those requiring physical ability and acuity, but also some creative activities in science and literature (Lehman, 1960). Those activities requiring *mentality* and social knowledge and experience, like philosophy and statesmanship, reach their heights later in life.

The series of products or public records in a person's life can be used for assessment in Buhler's system. For instance, Figure 4-1 shows the results of Althea Horner's study (1968) of the autobiography of Clarence Darrow. The American lawyer, who lived from 1857 to 1938, is famous for many court cases including his defense of John Scopes, the high school evolution teacher, in the "monkey trial" in Tennessee in 1925. A glimpse of Darrow's sense of purpose, as he assessed it himself when later writing his autobiography, is apparent in a quotation (Horner, 1968, p. 70) after he had been asked to defend Leopold and Loeb in their trial for the murder of Bobby Franks. He wrote,

> I knew of no good reason for refusing, but I was sixty-eight years old, and very weary. I had grown tired of standing in the lean and lonely front line facing the greatest enemy that ever confronted man—public opinion. But I went in, to do what I could for sanity and humanity against the wave of hatred and malice that, as ever, was masquerading under its usual nom de plume: "Justice."

Darrow's highest productivity in law and writing came later than the usual Buhler periods, after a number of years of work as a small town lawyer

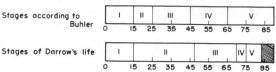

COMPARISON OF LIFE STAGES AS SEEN BY BUHLER
AND LIVED BY DARROW

Stages according to Buhler

| I | II | III | IV | V |

0 15 25 35 45 55 65 75 85

Stages of Darrow's life

| I | II | III | IV | V |

0 15 25 35 45 55 65 75 85

Figure 1. Comparison of Life Stages.

I. Prior to self-determination.

II. Experimental or preparatory self-determination.

III. Definite and specific self-determination toward goals and fulfillments.

IV. Self-assessment of obtained results.

V. Return to need-satisfaction orientation of childhood and/or a continuance of previous activities.

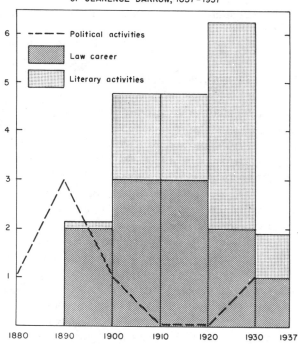

ACCOMPLISHMENTS AND PRODUCTIONS
OF CLARENCE DARROW, 1857-1937

- - - - Political activities

Law career

Literary activities

Figure 2. Accomplishments and Productions.

Political activities were determined by the number of offices held during a ten-year period.

Law career was determined by the number of cases of nationwide interest which Darrow defended during each ten-year period.

Literary activities were determined by the number of publications written by Darrow during each ten-year period.

(Adapted from McNally, 1941.)

FIGURE 4-1 Life stages and productivity of Clarence Darrow (b. 1857, d. 1938). (From Horner, 1968, p. 74)

and a try at politics. In the final phase, Buhler maintains that the individual often returns to the need-satisfaction orientation of childhood. This hypothesis seems to coincide with Darrow's words: ["An automobile ride in the evening or a game of cards or just a visit with my son and his family at the end of the day has grown all-sufficient for my social needs, and it is an effort to do more than that." (Horner, p. 72)]

In assessing any given individual, the psychologist or other assessor must be careful not to assume that the average will apply. Darrow's "late blooming" is one illustration. The curves of measurements of intellectual growth and decline also show wide individual differences. Figure 4–2 from Matarazzo (1972) gives Wechsler–Bellevue means and their standard deviations for different ages based on norms of the twenty to thirty-four year old group (the age group achieving the highest scores). As the reader will note from the large standard deviations, many persons on a distribution of scores for those over sixty-five would excede the achievement of the average twenty year old, even though the average sixty-five year old scores lower than the average twenty year old. It should also be noted that the results in Figure 4–2 are based on cross-sectional testing, that is testing people of different ages at the same time. Longitudinal studies, in which the same people are retested repeatedly over several years, do not show much decline, especially in information and vocabulary, the so-called crystallized abilities. (For a discussion demolishing the "myth of serious intellectual decrement" in the aged, see Schaie, 1974).

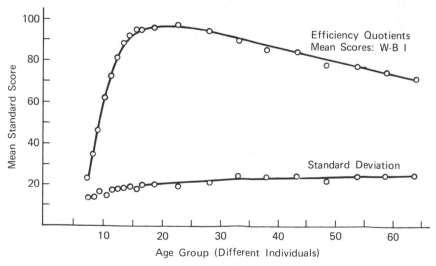

FIGURE 4–2 Full scale scores of the Wechsler-Bellevue I Scale-ages sixteen to sixty-four (using norms for the twenty to twenty-four period). (From Matarazzo, 1972, p. 233)

A well developed methodology has not yet been produced for that important relationship between developmental theory and assessment. However, there have been some attempts to create assessment devices specifically for maturity levels of personality.

Jane Loevinger is one of the few psychologists who have done notable work relating developmental states to assessment (Loevinger, 1966, 1969, 1976; Loevinger & Wessler, 1970, Loevinger, Wessler, & Redmore, 1970). While Buhler concentrated her life history work on maturity and old age, Loevinger has worked primarily on the ego stages of childhood and young adulthood. Drawing on a wide theoretical base, she views the self as an integrator of experience as the individual meets the successive problems of life, growing from infancy to adulthood. She uses the sentence completion method to assess the stages that a child or adult may have reached. Sentence completions (to be discussed again in the chapter on projective techniques) are simply a few words which the subject is instructed to use as the beginning of a sentence, for example, "A good father . . ." or "When people get angry with me, I . . ." Loevinger and Wessler (1970) have developed a way of scoring the subjects' completions that indicates the degree to which the person has reached a developmental level. Loevinger has defined eight stages of development. In the first two, *presocial* and *symbiotic,* the infant has not yet differentiated itself from the world around it; a self has not emerged. In the first differentiated ego level, the *impulsive* stage, the person presents thoughts on the completions that indicate that she or he views the world as one of immediate rewards and punishments, a kind of illogical jungle where "good guys give to me, mean ones don't." Answers to the test are simple and evaluative; for example, "Father is nice" and "When people are mean I run to mommy." Loevinger's other stages are *Self-Protective, Conformist, Conscientious, Autonomous* and *Integrated;* each of them being described and linked to certain kinds of answers on the sentence completion test. For instance, a person high in integration might say that a good mother "helps guide children, if possible" or "loves without being demanding to her own standard." These short illustrations give only a little of the flavor of the Loevinger system of relating development to assessment. The point is that the assessment of development can be accomplished through careful specification of the meanings of different levels of maturity based on a systematic theory.

Erikson's well-known theory (1950, 1968) of developmental crises and identity has been tested through interview and rating techniques with college students (Waterman, Geary, & Waterman, 1974). Many seniors had significantly consolidated their occupational and ideological identities, but a substantial proportion were still leaving college in a state of identity diffusion. Other research with an inventory (Constantinople, 1969; Reimanis, 1974) has also found Erikson's stages useful.

The third approach relating development to assessment is that of the longitudinal studies. In this approach an assessment technique starts with a sample of people of the same age, called a *cohort*. This group is followed up by tests and interviews in later years. Because of the expense and difficulty of keeping in touch with such cohorts over long periods of time there have been rather few long term longitudinal studies. Most of them present examples of assessment methodologies that we are describing in other parts of the book so there is not much point in repeating them here. (Those readers interested in such studies are referred to the readings mentioned at the end of this chapter.)

Here we will consider one example of a method for grouping and understanding the results of a longitudinal study—the work of Jack Block entitled *Lives through time* (1971). Block's idea was to use a Q-sort to develop types of people who have *similar directions of development,* those whose Q-sorts co-vary across time. Block's subjects were cohorts in longitudinal studies conducted by the Institute of Human Development at Berkeley, California, starting either from infancy or grade school days. Block asked psychologist judges to read the case material in the files on eighty-four men and eighty-seven women obtained in adolescence and adulthood. The judges recorded their impressions separately for each of these persons at each of these periods by means of a Q-sort of terms descriptive of personality. Each judge placed the statements of the Q-sort in one of nine piles according to how well he or she thought the statement described the person at that time. The wide ranging statements included the following: "Is critical, skeptical, not easily impressed," "Is a genuinely dependable and responsible person;" and "Has a wide range of interests." The completed sort is a description of the person that can be quantitatively compared with other such descriptions. This technique permits the correlation of persons rather than tests. If the correlation is high between two people, they are said to be similar. When the whole sample of individuals was intercorrelated, Block applied the technique of factor analysis to find clusters of persons who are more like each other than they are like others not in the cluster. Thus, using this method, Block identified several groups of persons whose Q-sorts changed in a similar manner between adolescence and adulthood. The clusters or factors that emerged were called types. Not all the subjects fit easily into types, but about four-fifths did. The types resulting from the study are depicted in Figure 4–3 (adapted from Tyler, 1974, pp. 202 and 204).

The radiating lines in Figure 4–3 are meant to indicate only low correlations between the different directions. In the findings with males, Block's Type A, called *Ego Resilients* started out with many advantages and did well in school; judges described them in junior high school as being dependable, bright, sympathetic, poised, and perceptive and they continued to function this way in adulthood. Type B men called *Related Adjusters* are chiefly

marked by distinct and desirable changes between adolescence and adulthood. Type C persons, *Vulnerable Over-Controllers,* were a cluster of men
who had grown up with neurotic parents and were introverted and tense in
high school; although they were better adjusted in adulthood they were still
hostile, anxious, and unsuccessful. Type D men, *Anomic Extroverts,* came
from large families who gave them little attention; in high school they were
sociable, cheerful, and conventional but as time passed they became more
rebellious, unhappy, and defensive. Finally, Type E persons, *Unsettled
Under-Controllers,* started out with intelligence and many advantages but
were handicapped by their involvement in conflict between their parents,
and became rebellious, impulsive, and inconsiderate in high school and
retained some of these qualities in adulthood which prevented their progress
in responsible positions or in relationships with others. Six somewhat
similar types were found for female cohorts. The *Female Prototypes* grew

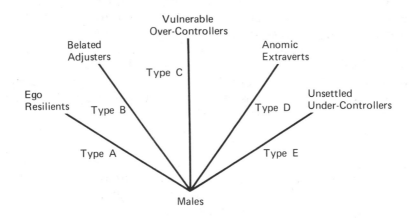

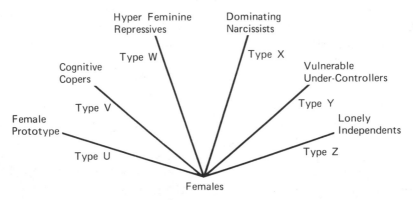

FIGURE 4-3 Types of developmental direction from adolescence to adulthood in Block's study.
(From Tyler, 1974, pp. 202 and 204)

from being bright, pretty, poised teenagers to good wives, mothers, and contributors to the community—stereotypical women's roles. The others are well described by their titles, and Block provides a similar analysis of their development. Block's study shows that there are identifiable individual differences in the way people develop over time. The derived types may not stand up in another study, but they are a step toward building a conceptual framework for personality development, and they illustrate a useful method of investigation.

LIFE CHANGES

In addition to the broad trends associated with developing, maturing, and aging, there are special times of shift and choice within individual lives. The general label, *life changes,* includes both episodes of sudden distress and crisis and of high achievement and pleasure. Important experiences are likely to be associated with change in the direction and commitment of one's life and the kind of efforts one makes. The individual may enter a new social system or reorganize an old one. A person looking back over the course of life is usually able to identify a number of important shifts or choice points. For example, Figure 4-4 illustrates what one woman drew when asked to trace her "life line" from birth to the present, marking each life change with a shift in direction. Her remarks about the drawing are summarized.

The psychiatrist Thomas Holmes and his colleagues have developed systematic ways of studying life changes and relating them to personal characteristics such as physical or mental disorder (Holmes and Rahe, 1967; Holmes and Masuda, 1973). Their procedure, called the Social Readjustment Rating Scale, is based on a patient's self-report on the Schedule of Recent Experience. This Schedule contains a personal history section and a list of forty-three life changes to be checked if they happened in the previous three years. Each of the life events receives a life change score based on judges' ratings of zero to 100 according to the seriousness of readjustment required. There is considerable agreement on ratings from several different groups (Holmes and Masuda, 1973; Klassen et al., 1974). Examples from low to high stress and their scores are: going on a vacation (thirteen), taking out a loan (seventeen), substantial change in work (twenty), birth of a child (thirty-nine), being put in jail (sixty-five), divorce (seventy-three), and death of a spouse (100). The patient's total score has been found to relate to physical illness; that is, the more life changes, whether positive or negative within a given period, the more likely that the person will become physically ill. Holmes and Masuda (1973) found a correlation of .65 between life change magnitudes preceding onset of a disease and the actual onset of

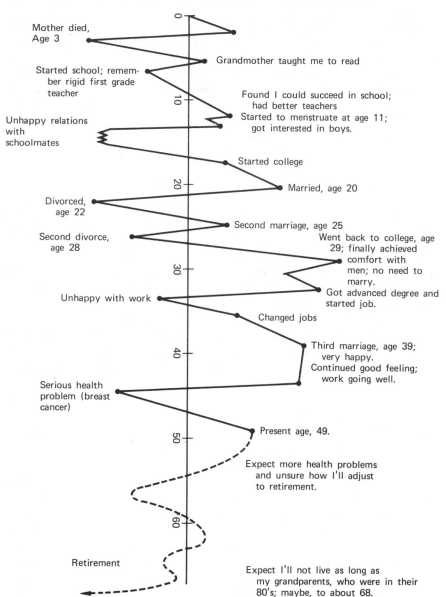

Low Sense of Competence-Happiness   High Sense of Competence-Happiness

Mother died, Age 3

Grandmother taught me to read

Started school; remember rigid first grade teacher

Found I could succeed in school; had better teachers

Unhappy relations with schoolmates

Started to menstruate at age 11; got interested in boys.

Started college

Married, age 20

Divorced, age 22

Second marriage, age 25

Second divorce, age 28

Went back to college, age 29; finally achieved comfort with men; no need to marry.

Unhappy with work

Got advanced degree and started job.

Changed jobs

Third marriage, age 39; very happy.

Continued good feeling; work going well.

Serious health problem (breast cancer)

Present age, 49.

Expect more health problems and unsure how I'll adjust to retirement.

Retirement

Expect I'll not live as long as my grandparents, who were in their 80's; maybe, to about 68.

FIGURE 4-4 Personal life-line as perceived by a forty-nine year old woman.

chronic diseases in a sample of over 200 patients. Working with this procedure, researchers were even able to find a correlation between the performance of football players and the number of life changes they had recently experienced. Felner et al. (1975) confirmed the impact on children of crisis events such as death of a parent. Dohrenwend (1973 b), using a technique similar to that of Holmes, found that the rate of life change was greater for persons of low social status than high status and greater for women than men. Life change scores were also positively correlated with symptoms of psychological distress. One of the interesting results of these studies is that problems are related to positive as well as negative changes (Dohrenwend, 1973 a). Any demand for adaptation seems to call for increased energy output, creates stress, and lowers resistance to disease.

HISTORY-FINDING INTERVIEWS

Interviews are the most common way of obtaining life histories, and every year clinics, hospitals, and research workers record thousands of case histories. One semistructured outline for clinical work with adults includes these major topics:

1. *Identifying data,* including name, sex, occupation, address, date and place of birth, religion, and education.
2. *Reason for coming* to the agency and expectations for service.
3. *Present situation,* such as description of daily behavior and any recent or impending changes.
4. *Family constellation* (family of orientation), including descriptions of mother, father, and other family members and the respondent's role in the family in which he or she grew up.
5. *Early recollections,* descriptions of earliest clear events and their surroundings.
6. *Birth and development,* including ages of walking and talking, problems compared with other children, and the person's view of his or her early experiences.
7. *Health,* including childhood and later diseases and injuries, problems with drugs and alcohol, and comparison of one's body with others.
8. *Education and training,* including subjects of special interest and achievement.
9. *Work record,* including reasons for changing jobs and attitudes toward work.
10. *Recreation and interests,* including volunteer work, reading, and the respondents report of adequacy of self-expression and pleasures.
11. *Sexual development,* covering first awareness, kinds of sexual activities, and view of the adequacy of sexual expressions.
12. *Marital and family data,* covering major events and what led to them, and comparison of present family with family of birth and orientation.
13. *Self-description,* including strengths, weaknesses, and ideals.
14. *Choices and turning points in life,* a review of the respondent's most important decisions and changes, including the single most important happening.

15. *View of the future,* including what the subject would like to see happen next year and in five or ten years, and what is necessary for these events to happen.

16. *Any further material* the respondent may see as omitted from the history.

This sixteen point history (elaborated further in Sundberg, Tyler, & Taplin, 1973) with a talkative adult could easily take two or three hours. In the interview, topics are not likely to follow as neatly as in the outline, but an outline can help remind the interviewer to cover all important points. In making a thorough history, it is useful to diagram the chronology of the subject's life year by year, as in Figure 4–5. Studying this chart, the assessor can see relationships between psychological events and environmental occurrences, and find gaps in the chronicle which might be checked in later contacts with the subject. Note that the subject is asked to divide the life span into major periods. He or she should be asked to describe each period and the "marker events" between periods. This division is usually easy for a subject to do.

An interview must be adjusted to fit the needs of the individual client and the assessment purposes. The language should be relevant to the client. Dailey (1971, pp. 67–68), using a "humanistic" approach, would recommend a less structured beginning than the one detailed above, such as "Tell me about your life. Where are you heading? What do you want to do?" and later ask such questions as "This year, has anything happened that 'turned you on,' deeply and fully expressed the kind of person you think you are?" Dailey strongly recommends exploring the person's *scenario* for the future, what directions he or she might go, and what kind of career alternatives he or she might choose. Peterson (1968, pp. 121–122) in contrast, takes a behaviorist point of view. He focuses quite sharply on the problem that brought the client to the agency and explores the situations surrounding the behavior in the past. He recommends questions like these: "As I understand it, you came here because of such-and-such a problem. I would like you to tell me more about this. What is the problem as you see it? . . . How often does this occur? . . . How long has it been going on? . . . Now I want you to think about the times when the problem gets better. What sorts of things are going on then?" Other personality assessors with different theories and treatment approaches would produce different kinds of interviews.

Gilmore (1976) has developed an important aid to history-taking which she calls a *photo-history.* This special interview procedure is valuable both for personal assessment and for therapeutic intervention designed to assist a person develop a clearer sense of self and accomplish what Gilmore (1973) calls confusion-reduction. Early in a series of counseling sessions the client is asked to bring photographs—loose rather than in albums, if

LIFE-HISTORY CHART

Subject's Name: _____ Age:_____ Sex: _____ Occupation:_____ Education:_____
Date of Interview:_____ Interviewer's Name:_____ Place:_____
Information about Subject:
    Date and Place of Birth: _____

    Family Constellation (names of brothers and sisters and number of years older
       or younger than subject) _____

    Father (occupation, education, and age at time of subject's birth)

    _____

    Mother (occupation, education, and age at time of subject's birth)

    _____

    Major childhood community (kind of neighborhood, friends, activities)

    _____

Subject's earliest recollections:
Marital Family (names and dates relative to spouse and children) or other family-type
    living group:
Subject's Major Periods of Life:

*   *   *   *   *   *   *   *   *   *   *   *

Major Life periods Year Age	Major Events in life situation	Physical and medical events	Behavioral functioning	Subject's impressions
19-- Birth to to 19-- age _____	(for each describe major life sit- uations with particular attention to changes	(Describe on- set, ces- sation and changes in illnesses, injuries, symptoms;	(Describe behavior and effective- ness in adjustment, changes in	(Locate subject's periods of greatest satisfaction, inner
2nd period 19-- _____ to 19-- _____	e.g., who cared for subject at birth, births of siblings,	locate time of adolescent growth spurt.)	psychological problems and productivity)	peace and disturbance, and feelings of expansion
3rd period	deaths, divorce, school problems)			and contraction.)

FIGURE 4-5   A form for recording and comparing the periods of life and person-situation
relationships

possible. Anywhere from fifteen to fifty snapshots and/or portraits,
covering the period from birth to the present will provide a rich developmental history.

    Gilmore begins by taking the pictures from the client and ordering
them chronologically; from this chronological ''deck'' she rather slowly
and gently begins moving through the client's life—infancy to the present—

one picture at a time. Questions such as: "Let's see, how old were you here?," "Where are we now?," "This person is . . . ?," and "Where was the rest of the family at this point?" are used to elicit information. Time and space are transcended; the client is plunged back into the thoughts, feelings, and happenings captured in the pictures. An intense, intimate experience is shared by client and counselor as the history unfolds before them.

Figure 4–6 is the photo-history of one person's life. Early she is a happy, active, racing-to-meet-life child; slowly the awkwardness, turned to agony, of adolescence becomes more vivid. Then, with the transition accomplished, we see her as a graceful bride and joyful mother.

The photo-history results in an integrated experience of the client's development that is rich, personal, and powerful. One interesting related study has shown that delinquents will improve their self-concepts by taking photographs of themselves and making personal picture albums; these findings attest to the power of photo induced self-consideration. (Fryrear et al., 1974)

USE OF PERSONAL DOCUMENTS AND ARCHIVES

The last illustration moves to other important possibilities for data. In addition to the interview, an important resource for personality assessors, especially for research purposes, is *personal documents*. (R. B. Cattell would use a broader term, L; or Life Record, Data.) Psychologists and psychiatrists have analyzed records and biographies of eminent people in an attempt to understand their lives. For example, Freud studied notebooks of Leonardo da Vinci, and Erikson used an autobiography and interviews to write *Gandhi's Truth* (1969). Gordon Allport (1942, 1961) has particularly urged the use of personal document analysis for psychological studies. He includes in his definition of personal document any freely written or spoken record providing information on personality structure and dynamics, such as autobiographies, biographies, diaries, letters, verbatim recordings or certain literary compositions, and art products. He notes that the first step in analysis is to comprehend the author's motives for producing the document—to prove his innocence, confess his sins, show off his accomplishments, gain relief from strong feelings, carry out an assignment, make money, accomplish social reform, or study himself scientifically. The possibilities for the distortion of such documents through poor memory and bias need to be evaluated. Documents vary in the degree to which they reveal subjective and highly personal experiences and also in the degree to which they are topical and selective, or comprehensive. A *journal intime,* a diary meant for no one else to read, is of particular value for studying the person's experiential world; however, Allport cautions that such diaries deal mainly with personal conflicts and problems, noting for example that a

FIGURE 4-6   (Used by permission).

person in good health seldom mentions the body. To gain true perspective on the person, one has to place him or her in the context of routine living, a context which the diarist merely assumes and seldom bothers to explain.

Allport's *Letters From Jenny* (1965) is a fascinating report and analysis of 301 letters written to friends by Jenny Masterson between the ages of fifty-eight and seventy, revealing her pleasures, hopes, jealousies, and frustrations. These often center around her son, Ross, and the women in his life. In the last part of the book, Allport analyzes the background of Jenny and her letters from several theoretical vantage points—existential, psychoanalytic, and structural-dynamic. He also presents a *content analysis* of the letters; that is, a systematic and quantified description of the terms and sentences used in the letters (which contained 46,652 words). The investigator tallied the different topics Jenny discussed and counted her expressions in favor of or opposed to a person or a condition. One study, using data from Jenny's letters coded on punch cards and analyzed by a computer, revealed such factorial traits as aggression, possessiveness, and martyrdom. Computers have also been used for a content analysis which show that Freud's interpretation of a certain case was better than an alternative one, by comparing the incidence of associations between various symbolic words (Klein and Iker, 1974). One study (Welsh, 1975a) obtained adjective check list descriptions of Freud and Jung based on biographical and auto-biographical material. The styles of logic of John Kennedy, Richard Nixon, and Nikita Khrushchev have been the subject of content analysis (Shneidman, 1963). Political documents, such as the Nixon White House tapes, offer rich resources for research in both personality psychology and political science. (For a thorough discussion of the use of content analysis in social science research, see Holsti, 1969.)

As mentioned at the end of the last chapter, Webb and his associates (1969) have emphasized the importance of using unobtrusive measures in studying persons. Among such data resources are personal documents, including archives. School records, for instance, preserve a great deal of material that would be valuable. As one example, Barthell and Holmes (1968) looked into the activities listed in high school yearbooks for normal people and for individuals who had later become schizophrenic. They were able to confirm the hypothesis that schizophrenics show withdrawal tendencies in adolescence; they participated significantly less than normal people in high school social activities. The ingenious investigator may find other records that could provide "follow-back" for testing historical aspects of personality theories.

The objective of the psychologist who studies personal documents and archives is to supplement common sense impressions with more exact techniques that can be communicated to others. She or he is not interested in chronology, but also in discerning the meaningful and important aspects of the person's individuality. The analyst will go to considerable effort to find central themes and shifts in personality. The problem of analysis is conceptualizing and making inferences about causal relations. Personality theories are helpful in guiding one's attention and making sense out of the massive amounts of data obtained in interviews and personal documents, but an inductive interpretation growing out of the case itself rather than the assessor's theoretical predispositions is also desirable.

Dailey (1971) describes his process for developing a model of a person using life history information. It involves listing episodes and related environments by stages in life such as those used by Erikson (1950), or around certain significant people. By comparing episodes, the analyst intuitively groups them into themes and sequences. He or she keeps asking the question, "What is the person trying to do?" The assessor inductively arrives at a model or a "working image," a series of statements of recurring themes and relations. Murray and Adler and other theorists have used similar methods.

How does one know that the chosen interpretation is right? Allport (1961, p. 409) tries to answer this difficult question concerning what is largely subjective analysis. He lists six tests.

1. How certain does the investigator feel?
2. Does the interpretation conform to all the known facts?
3. Can one imagine the person's life without various crucial interpretive inferences?
4. Does the analysis predict subsequent personal events?
5. Do independent experts agree on the interpretation? (And, in some cases, does the subject agree with it?)
6. Are the parts of the interpretation logically consistent with each other?

These questions are a start in the direction of corroborating this complex task. Allport (1961, p. 410) confessed: "As yet we cannot honestly say that psychologists have learned to analyze documents or to write histories in a way that surely leads them beyond the level of accuracy achieved by unaided common sense." In the years since Allport's book, some additional techniques have been developed, but no great breakthroughs have occurred.

SYSTEMATIC USE OF BIOGRAPHICAL DATA ON APPLICATION BLANKS AND INVENTORIES

In almost every personnel office or clinical situation, the persons responsible for assessment use information about work experience, education, and other data related to life history. Many questions about present status also reflect past experience, such as marital status, number of children and their ages, and amount of income or debt. Such items can be treated either as informal background for interviews or other investigations, or as opportunities for systematic analysis.

One systematic approach to assessment is *weighting items on application forms*. For many decades, industrial psychologists have been applying psychometric principles to personal history data that applicants provide on application blanks (Webb, 1915; Guion, 1965). The psychologist simply correlates the answers on application blanks with a criterion such as success on the job. This process identifies which items predict success. They are then weighted according to each one's contribution to the prediction and totaled to give a composite score. The psychologist must, of course, cross-validate whatever scoring is obtained on the original investigation by administering the blanks to a new group and checking how well the formula works. Many such studies using weighted application blanks have reported positive findings. For instance, studies have shown, as one might expect, that among life insurance salesmen there is a correlation between amount of life insurance they buy for themselves and the amount of insurance they sell (Baier & Dugan, 1957). Other studies (for example Tiffin, Parker, & Haberstat, 1947) found that certain facts recorded on application blanks, such as older ages, being married, having relatively little education, and having children, predicted that unskilled factory employees would stay on the job longer than those not having those characteristics.

Instead of using the existing heterogeneous collection of items on the typical application blank, psychologists can go about specifically developing inventories that include life history data. In many personality inventories, such as the MMPI, there are items about personal history and background but there are very few instruments that are organized to systematically cover the course of development, crises, and other prominent issues of life history. One approach that addresses part of the area of concern would be an inventory *assessing developmental level*. A widely used example in the diagnosis of retarded children and adults is the Vineland Social Maturity Scale (Doll, 1953). Initiated in the heyday of intelligence testing in the 1920s and 30s, the Vineland is based on the idea that there are levels of development of social and personal competence that are normal for each chronological age. Most children can tie shoes without help by a certain age, for instance. Usually through an interview with parents, the psychologist gets answers to items covering skills like playing simple games, making change, taking a bath unassisted, using tools, and buying one's own clothing. The result of testing is a "social age" based on the ages when most children do these things that is comparable in concept with the mental age of an intelligence test. The Vineland is useful in describing adequacy for daily living tasks from birth to twenty-five years and is helpful in suggesting areas where training is needed. A newer test similar to the Vineland is the Adaptive Behavior Scale, or ABS, developed by the American Association of Mental Deficiency (1974). The Vineland and the ABS are tests that straddle the area between ability and personality testing, which we will discuss again in a later chapter.

Similar to the weighted application blank but more comprehensively related to life history is the *biographical information blank* (often abbreviated "BIB") or *biographical inventory*. A BIB does not refer to any one published instrument, but to a general approach. The test developer gathers a set of life history items, presumably related to a criterion such as job performance, or to a theoretical construct such as achievement motivation. The items cover relevant facts and past experiences and activities. In addition to *experiential* items such as number of schools attended and age of obtaining a driver's license, biographical data sheets often cover *demographic* items such as age, sex, and marital status, and *behavioral* items such as current leisure activities and number of miles traveled to work. These procedures do not directly ask for self-descriptions or attitudes and feelings that are more common to personality inventories. In various studies, large pools of items have been developed from which researchers have selected those items that correlate with criteria such as creativity, sales performance, military performance, leadership, and many other areas (Owens and Henry, 1966; Owens, 1971). A BIB has even been developed to detect faking on personality tests (Cohen and Lefkowitz, 1974). It is, of course, important that items found to correlate with a criterion on the original sample, be cross-validated on another.

In comparison with industrial work, clinical psychology has done less systematic research with life history items, although the importance of information about life history is continually emphasized. One direction of study has been the search for premorbid adjustment factors in schizophrenia—the histories of people before they developed this serious disorder of mental and social life that accounts for a large proportion of the psychotic cases in the world. Leslie Phillips and his associates (Phillips, 1968; Zigler and Phillips, 1960; Phillips and Draguns, 1971) have shown that impairments of social competence in early life, as revealed by data on employment, marital status, and education, is related to development of this disorder. The patients who have a better prognosis for recovery are those showing early signs of "turning against the self" rather than social withdrawal and turning against others.

Among the very few specific biographical inventories for clinical use is the M-B History Record. Developed by Peter Briggs, first as a form for obtaining history information from relatives of patients hospitalized for psychiatric disorders, it has been converted into a self-administered inventory (Briggs, et al., 1972). It consists of 127 items on which the person may record many facts about his past and present life, such as,

> As an adolescent, I was (1) "skinny"; (2) about average in weight; (3) over-weight.
>
> My parents (1) never to my knowledge considered divorce; (2) considered divorce but did not separate; (3) got a divorce.
>
> My mother drank alcoholic beverages: (1) almost daily and always to excess; (2) almost daily though moderately; (3) to excess only now and then; (4) only irregularly; (5) never.

The M-B History Record, among other things, shows differences between juvenile delinquents and nondelinquents and between different kinds of alcoholism. A factor analysis provided the basis for seven scales on the inventory: family disunity, conflict with parents, health awareness, introversion, school and job failure, social maladjustment, and breakdowns and addictions.

EVALUATION AND COMMENT
ON LIFE HISTORY ASSESSMENT

In many ways, the person's life history *is* the person. There is nothing more individual and "personally possessed" than the series of events through which a person has passed. Assessment can largely be seen as an attempt to obtain the relevant aspects of the person's experience, sometimes in a more economical way by tests than by means of a long investigation of life history details. A general guideline for assessment is the statement that the best predictor of the future is the person's past behavior in similar situations.

Life history assessment suffers from inadequate development of conceptual framework and methodology. Only a beginning has been made in the investigation of many important questions. What are the most efficient ways of collecting life history information? What sort of general developmental theory is most suitable for defining units and periods in a complex body of information? How truthful and accurate are respondents? Guion (1965) indicates that for the most part, truthful responses are given on application blanks but distortions do occur in some kinds of responses under some circumstances.

What is the validity, especially the predictive validity, of life history information? On this point Owens (1975) has reported that for employment situations, correlations of weighted biographical data with criteria of success usually range from .40 to .60, which is at least as high as the validities of good tests. However, changes in people's circumstances or in the social milieu can affect the predictive validities of particular life history instruments. Guion (1965) cites one study in which the coefficients for one instrument dropped from .74 to .07 over a period of years because of changes in the predictive power of some background data.

In clinical situations, how much does a case history add to the effectiveness of the services clinicians provide to clients and how do clinicians actually use the data to which they have access? Kostlan (1954) systematically gave different kinds of information on five psychiatric patients to twenty clinicians, varying the kind of information they received. The four kinds of information were the social case history, the Rorschach, the MMPI, and a sentence completion test. The clinicians' judgments were compared with judges' descriptions of the patients. Kostlan found that clinicians who did not have access to the social case history gave personality descriptions that were not significantly better than those made on the basis of minimal data alone such as age, occupation, education, marital status, and reason for referral. The case history did produce significant improvement beyond the basic identifying data, but it is surprising how powerful the minimal data is. Several other studies have yielded similar results (Soskin, 1959, Little & Schneidman, 1959, Sines, 1959, Golden, 1964). Potkay (1973), reviewing most studies to date, concludes (p. 208) that "personal history data as a source of clinically descriptive or predictive information is at least as effective as information derived from psychological test sources."

Why would the *basic identifying data,* the minimal demographic and historical characteristics, be so important in predicting behavior? Let us speculate a bit in terms of systems theory—speculations which take us toward the topics to be discussed in the next chapter. It would seem that the identifying data on job applications, hospital charts, journalists' reports, and other accounts of a person are powerful indexes of personal continuity. The surrounding social systems depend to a great extent on these continuities and statuses. They exert pressure on those who do not "act their age" or "keep their place." Sociocultural memberships, statuses, and roles are either *ascribed,* as in the case of sex, age, and ethnic groups, or *attained,* as in the case of occupations, education, and political affiliation. These sociocultural memberships are likely to have a great influence on a person's behavior and must be considered in assessment. Roger Brown (1965, p. 637) put it like this in another context: "A knowledge of social structure alone will take one smoothly through a large part of the day's routine." The social structure as it impinges on individuals is reflected in their simple and social structure as it impinges on individuals is reflected in these simple and readily accessible identifying data.

SUMMARY

In this chapter, we have looked at the major ways in which assessment attempts to cover long periods of a person's life. One common source of data is the biography or autobiography that psychologists usually analyze in an impressionistic fashion. Psychoanalysis has been the most common source of theory for such analyses. Erikson and Buhler have extended such developmental stages into old age and have incorporated strong psychosocial emphases. Few psychologists, however, have attempted to systematize these developmental levels psychometrically, although Loevinger's identification of ego development is one notable exception. Some longitudinal studies use repeated assessments of personality; Block has identified certain types of developmental change through a Q-sort technique applied to longitudinal data.

Another approach to the study of life history is to identify important crises and life changes. Holmes' research has scaled the number of recent life changes, weighted for judged seriousness of stress, and found relationships between these changes and the onset of physical and mental disturbance.

The most common method of obtaining life history information is the interview. Interviews can cover a wide range of topics including early memories, family experiences, education, work history, sexual history, and current family situation. Life history information is also available in personal documents and archives. Many personal products have the advantage of being unobtrusive measures in that the person being studied did not know that the products would be used for assessment purposes. Another method for obtaining biographical data is through application blanks and inventories. Application scores has been used successfully for several decades in personnel work.

Despite some problems in obtaining life history information such as poor memory and distortion from ego-involvement, biographical data have generally been a powerful predictor of future behavior. In statistically developed blanks and inventories and in clinical judgment studies the power of minimal demographic data has been demonstrated by research. This basic identifying data seems related to the surrounding society's need to preserve personal identity over time.

SUGGESTED READINGS

BALTES, P. B. & K. W. SCHAIE, (eds.) *Life-span developmental psychology: Personality and socialization.* New York: Academic Press, 1973. Although this book is not primarily oriented toward assessment, it has good examples of the use of assessment instruments, and provides a good background for developmental concerns from birth to death. Other books on development that provide helpful background and assessment examples include *From instinct to identity* by Breger (1974); *Life history research in psychopathology,* Vol. I by Roff & Ricks (1970) and Vol. II by Roff, Robins, & Pollack (1972); *Stressful life events* by the Dohrenwends (1974); *The course of human development* by Jones, et al., 1971; and *From thirty to seventy* by Mass & Kuypers (1974). These last two books are about the Berkeley Growth Project, which is also the setting for the study by Block, *Lives through time* (1971) reported in the text. Doob's *Patterning of time* (1971) was described by a reviewer as "the most important work that has been published on the subject of time." (Green & Knapp, 1973.) It contains many hypotheses and methods of value for measuring individual abilities and perspectives on time.

DAILEY, C. A. *Assessment of lives.* San Francisco: Jossey-Bass, 1971. Dailey severely criticizes present assessment methods and points out the many studies which show the advantages of using life history information. His major contribution is a process for training and improving clinical judgments based on life histories.

LIFTON, R. J. & OLSON, E. *Explorations in psychohistory.* New York: Simon and Schuster, 1974. For those readers interested in psychohistory, this book and that of Wolman (1971) provide a good beginning and a number of excellent examples. Another book the reader might like to explore is Mazlish's *In search of Nixon—A psychohistorical inquiry* (1972), an interesting book relating to later events in the life of the former president. Mazlish notes some of the deep feelings about his mother and father which Nixon later mentioned in his televised farewell to the White House staff in August, 1974. Another book of interest is Langer's *The mind of Adolf Hitler* (1972), which was a secret report during World War II showing how an attempt was made to analyze and predict the dictator's actions; the analysis predicted that he would commit suicide. Erikson's *Young man Luther* (1958) and *Gandhi's truth* (1969) are classics in psychohistory. The anthropologist Mandelbaum's comment (1973) on the latter may be of interest to the reader as well as Erikson's statement (1975) about his own identity problems and development of the psychohistorical method. Munter (1975) reviews psychobiography as an area of psychological assessment.

OWENS, W. A. A quasi-actuarial basis for individual assessment, *American Psychologist,* 26, 1971, 992–999. A well-known industrial psychologist whose particular specialty is the use of biographical information, Owens presents a "developmental-integrative" model of the use of biographical information. He recommends starting with biodata on a large pool of subjects and using factor analysis to sort subjects into subsets which are internally similar but externally different in their life history patterns.

chapter five

Assessment of Persons in Context

Nothing springs from me, and nothing from my environment, but everything from the interaction, the "life space" in which I, as a person, navigate. —Gardner Murphy (1958, p. 303)

Like people, environments have unique personalities. Just as it is possible to characterize a person's "personality," environments can be similarly portrayed with a great deal of accuracy and detail. Some people are supportive; likewise, some environments are supportive. Some men feel the need to control others; similarly, some environments are extremely controlling. Order and structure are important to many people; correspondingly, many environments emphasize regularity, system, and order. —Paul Insel and Rudolf Moos (1974, p. 179)

A common psychological statement is that behavior is a function of person *and* environment. In this chapter we will pursue questions such as: How might we conceptualize the environment and discern its important parts? How do we assess person–environment interactions? What weight should be given to individual and environmental characteristics in predicting human behavior? Before looking at ways of assessing person–environment relations, let us look at a narrative account of a family and its environment.

LILLY

Lilly Parvin headed one of several families intensively studied by David Schulz in *Coming Up Black* (1969), in research on socialization in the ghetto. Lilly lived in the Pruitt–Igoe housing project in St. Louis. This set of high-rise apartment buildings was originally designed to be a model for low-cost housing. It turned out to be a vertical slum, with rampant crime and little supervisable play space for children. Part of the project was eventually torn down. Below is Schulz's description of Lilly and the environment in which she and her children live (pp. 15–17).

At thirty-three Lilly Parvin has been hospitalized for mental illness. She craves companionship but fears men. She even at times fears her eight-year-old son, Jerry, whom she becomes convinced is spying on her. When her boyfriend comes to visit, he "rapes" her. He comes and goes as *he* pleases. The Parvin apartment is usually bleak and dirty. The hand prints of the six children (who are most often confined within the apartment because of Lilly's fear that they will be exposed to the wrong kind of children) create a dark messy stain all along the walls to a height of about four-and-a-half feet, the distance being higher above the sofa where the foothold permits further exploration.

When Lilly first came to the project after being expelled from her father's house by her "stepmother," she had but one bed, a dining room table, several dishes, an inadequate number of eating utensils and a few cooking pots. These were all in the living room, where the whole family slept. The older children shivered on cardboard pallets on the exposed concrete floor, the younger three huddled close to their mother on the single bed. The second-hand clothes picked up at churches or the Salvation Army store lay in piles in the closet when not in use.

The furniture, which is provided periodically by Lilly's welfare worker, is always quickly destroyed by the loud destructive activity of the children, who seem to be playing on the edge of anger that now and then erupts into violent outbursts against siblings, and occasionally against their mother. In her illness Lilly fears all of her children, who seem to take advantage of the situation and taunt their mother.

Ironically, Lilly's illness brings her into more "contact" with her kin than do her daily activities. She sees visions of dead and living relatives and is haunted by her mother. She married because of a pregnancy while her mother was on her deathbed; now she fears that her mother still believes that she deserted her. An older sister tantalizes her. She would like to emulate this sister's feminine ways and her greater moral perfection, and would even have joined the Sanctified Church but for the fact that she considers herself too depraved to be saved. Her husband, from whom she has been separated since shortly after the birth of Richard, joins her visionary world. She believes that while she lived with him, he tried to work voodoo on her and shrink her into a tiny doll. He taunts her by bringing his girlfriend into her visionary world. The characters of this visionary world are at times more real and threatening than her own rambunctious children.

This illness is most pronounced in Lilly, but it has also affected her children. Willie Mae (nine) was expelled from school and ordered to take a psychiatric examination because she would not talk to her teacher. Jerry is very aggressive, acting out his aggression in dramatic combat with unseen assailants. Richard, now five, has only begun to utter words. When he first came to the project he rarely made a sound. He endured his continual colds in silence. By contrast, the older two daughters appear quite normal. They are the most dependable contact that the family has with the world outside its apartment. They shop, cook, and take care of all members of the household, including their mother when she is ill, even though Kim is only eleven and Stephanie ten.

Aside from infrequent baskets of food from kin, the family's sole source of income is Lilly's ADC check, which brings them $2,428 a year. Even though few families could live very well on this amount (in this city in 1966), the Parvins' deprivation is much more extreme. Lilly's illness has cut them off from the help of a boyfriend, and her stepmother has succeeded in separating her from her father's help. Thus, the Parvins have not been able to accumulate any significant amount of possessions. While the disorganization of this family is undoubtedly extreme, it is nevertheless representative (in pattern if not in proportion) of problems common in the project.

A psychological examiner seeing Lilly Parvin or her children, would have more on his or her hands than a diagnosis of mental illness! Suppose that you were to assess the personality of Willie Mae, the nine year old girl who is mute in school. From traditional psychological tests and interviews under good conditions, you might get estimates of Willie Mae's functioning intelligence, her hearing acuity, attitudes toward school, the degree of abnormality of her behavior and thought, and other kinds of information that might be useful in advising the school. The most pervasive influences in Willie Mae's life are environmental—the crowded home, the quarreling siblings, and the mentally ill mother. If you decided that another home was necessary, it would be difficult to find one, but if you looked, what kind of environment would you look for? The changes that need to be made to help Willie Mae attain a normal life are monumental.

Lilly Parvin and her children provide a sharp contrast to an American suburban, middle-class family. Imagine the living situation of Wilma, a nine year old, who was born with the same abilities as Willie Mae, into a middle class family in the same city. Wilma would have a room of her own, to which she could escape from occasional quarrels with siblings. She would celebrate her birthday and Christmas with many presents. Though statistics show less likelihood of psychotic mothers among the middle-class than among the poor, even if she had a psychotic mother, treatment would be instituted early and someone might be hired to help take care of the rest of the family. Wilma's home would have many books, records, television, and visitors who could stimulate Wilma's intellectual and emotional growth. Wilma's school and her neighborhood companions would probably be very different from Willie Mae's. Though the contrast is great, there are some common elements to understand in the process of assessing the girls and their environments. They share similar psychological development patterns and many of their simple pleasures would be the same—food, warmth, play. Both living patterns relate to the social-political-cultural matrix of the American society. The girls would see the same advertisements in the mass media. Community laws and customs would be of relevance to both. Provisions for mass transportation might curtail or enlarge their mobility. Their economic conditions are influenced by the same laws regarding taxes and the distribution of wealth—the reward system of the society. Inflation would affect the way they both live, though the effect of high food prices would be much greater on Willie Mae's poor family than on Wilma's middle-class family. Ways of living are profoundly related to the surrounding context.

CONCEPTS FOR PERSON-ENVIRONMENT RELATIONS

Schultz's report about Lilly Parvin and her family was based on interviews and field observation. The narrative accounts produced by such information sources are impressively communicative, even if they are not quantitative. However, such descriptions are inexact and not readily reproducible or verifiable, and the psychologist should not be satisfied until he or she can define the environments well enough to assign numbers to their characteristics. Two of the most influential theorists in moving toward quantification of environmental forces are Murray and Barker. In this section we will look at their concepts and also the concepts of system and role.

The personality theorist who has most successfully included environmental considerations in his work is Murray (1938, 1959). His theoretical formulations included both environmental press and individual needs. A *press* is anything outside a person that can do something to or for that person. Both press and need have organizing and directional qualities. Murray (1938, pp. 118–119) clarified the concept press as follows:

> . . . a directional tendency in an object or situation. Like a need, each press has a qualitative aspect—the kind of effect which it has or might have upon the subject . . . as well as a quantitative aspect, since its power for harming or of benefiting varies widely. Everything that can supposedly harm or benefit the well-being of an organism may be considered *pressive,* everything else *inert.*

Murray distinguished between two kinds of press—the *alpha press* that is the environmental force which objectively exists, as far as scientific inquiry can determine it, and the *beta press* that is the subject's own interpretation of the phenomena that he perceives. For instance, walking along a strange street at night, I might think a dark object ahead is a crouching person (beta press), but on getting closer I see it is only a shrub (now my beta press coincides with the alpha press).

In assessment, one also must relate personal needs to press. Murray, of course, used stories elicited by pictures on his Thematic Appreception Test to discern both needs and press. TAT analysts look for need-press patterns; the conjunction of need and press is called a *thema,* a concept also mentioned in the last chapter in analyzing life history. George Stern (1970) and his associates (Stern, Stein, & Bloom, 1956) have carried Murray's ideas and the analysis of press further than anyone else in the field of assessment and their work will be discussed in a later section.

Barker (1968) has contributed useful concepts about situations. As mentioned earlier, he developed the idea of the *behavior setting,* a relatively stable pattern of activities appropriately related to the surrounding environment. Behavior settings are not specific to particular individuals; the case of participants may change, but the behavioral *pattern* continues. Examples of behavior settings are a football game, a worship service, a piano lesson, and a grocery store and its activities. These larger units of behavior are observable, bounded by space and time, and are usually well known in the community. Children are socialized from their early years for behavior setting programs; they can easily differentiate, for example, the appropriate behavior for a football game or a worship service. The stream of any individual's behavior flows through a number of these programmed settings during a day and conforms in its fashion to the expectations. In Barker's terminology the extraindividual influences are called *environmental force units,* "active efforts made by the child's social environment to penetrate his psychological world and modify his behavior." (Schoggen, 1963, p. 42). Behavior episodes mentioned in the chapter on observation show the directedness of the person, and environmental force units show the directedness of the surroundings. Knowing *where* the person is becomes important in understanding behavior.

A broad term related to Barker's theory is *ecology,* the study of organisms in relation to their surroundings or habitat. *Behavioral ecology* is the study of behavior in relation to environment. The whole interacting set of physical and living things in a certain area is called an *ecosystem.* A pond in the forest is a good example. Many natural processes are going on, organisms live in the pond, die, and are used by other organisms in their life cycles. The pond receives rain and sunshine and gives off evaporation and changes with the season. One effect of the ecological analogy is that it leads one to think of individuals and communities as resources for each other (Kelly, 1975).

Another concept is *systems,* the set of mutually interacting elements that was discussed in chapter one. Systems have boundaries, and the relations between internal parts are closer and different from the relations to external systems of the environment. All living systems are open to exchanges of energy and information across their boundaries. Human societies, organizations, groups, and individuals have evolved in environments which nurture and reward certain behaviors and not others. Adaptation is going on continuously, but in times of rapid and turbulent change like that in our mobile, computerizing, urbanizing, mass-communicating society, pressures for change and adaptation come more quickly than in former times. Within the personal system is a hierarchy of problem solving skills and behavioral repertoires that are used as situations call for them. As mentioned in chapter one, only a small part of the person's potential is activated at any one time. Depending on its purposes, assessment involves getting to know not only the present behavior but, as much as possible, the repertoire and the potential behavior that might result from situational change and learning. Discerning the kinds of situations that evoke such behavior potentials is thus part of the assessment process.

One of the most useful concepts in understanding persons in contexts is *role,* a term, like "personality," taken originally from the stage. A role is a set of recurrent activities expected in a particular position. For example, a woman may play the roles of store manager, president of a museum advisory board, and mother, along with many other roles. Sometimes conflict between roles occurs, and sometimes the person does not live up to the expectations others hold for occupants of a position. Tension and even breakdown can occur when one's roles are not managed successfully, and a person's organization for role management is an important aspect of assessment.

Figure 5-1 shows the principal settings and system relations that a hypothetical person possesses at different periods of life, by depicting the proportion of a twenty-four hour day spent in different roles. The preschool child interacts with only a few other people who are particularly significant. Growing older, the person enters more and different settings and has interactions with more people in varying degrees of involvement. Some of these friendships and some group relations continue later in life. As an adult the person has a family and work and leisure relationships. In old age, this immediate family diminishes and roles and relations tend to constrict as the person retires and energy diminishes.

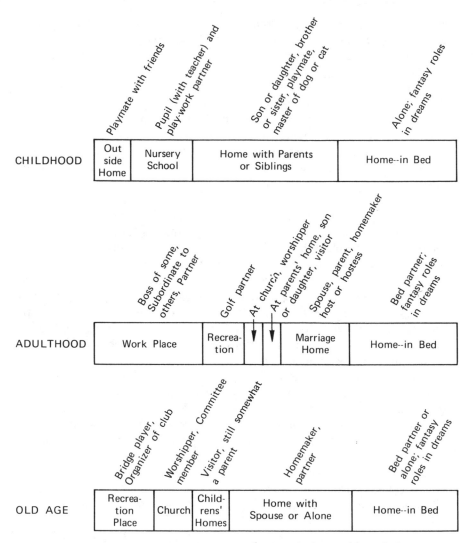

FIGURE 5-1 Hypothetical distribution of the twenty-four hour day into settings and roles at different times of life

SITUATIONAL ASSESSMENT

How does a person, then, to about assessing systems or environments in general, as they relate to personality? First it should be noted that the nature of the assessment task will vary with the needs of the person being assessed, the functions of the assessing agency, and the role of the assessor.

A psychologist may be involved in the vocational rehabilitation of a disabled person, trying to determine what kinds of work situations can be mastered by a former truck driver now paralyzed from the waist down. A social worker may face the question of how a patient's family can be helped to accept a patient when he comes home from the hospital. A psychiatrist has to analyze the living situation of an acutely depressed woman to determine if she needs to be hospitalized to prevent suicide. An educational counselor may be assisting high school students with decisions about what kind of college to attend and what sort of learning environment is likely to be most congenial. These examples are only a few of the occasions in which professional people must analyze the relations between persons and environments, whether they use exact assessment instruments or not.

Environments to be considered fall into three major classes each with their subsets: the *physical environment,* including the *built* and the *natural* environments; the *social environment,* including the small-scale, face-to-face, *interpersonal* environment and the large-scale, *organizational* environments; and the *symbolic environment* from the mass media, especially television.

The longest history of situational assessment is in industrial and personnel psychology. In factories and businesses, psychologists have had to relate individuals to the requirements of particular work situations and have developed procedures for *job analysis* (Dunnette, 1966). They obtain job descriptions from supervisors or others on the job. They may study training manuals and other job related material, use observational techniques to study the behavior of people at work, and develop checklists and tests covering the basic knowledges, abilities, and personal attributes which characterize the position.

Another source of information about directions in research is beginning to come from some psychologists (Fredericksen, 1972; Sells, 1973; Insel & Moos, 1974; Moos, 1975) who are developing taxonomies and other ways of describing situations. Sells, for example, proposes that the important aspect of the environment is *event structures,* the patterns of settings and action. These are thousands of different settings relating to the terrain, weather, and social institutions. Actions are occurrences such as banquets, church services, and classes. The event structure, like Barker's behavior settings, links actions with settings. Sells sees personality as a set of structures that determine the major ways people differ in carrying out the behaviors prescribed by the event structures. Fredericksen proposes that a form of factor analysis be used to define a taxonomy of situations using the kind of responses that they require. Price & Bouffard (1974) abstracted separate lists of behaviors and situations from diaries and used judges to develop indexes of the behavior appropriate to each situation. These various approaches to developing a classification of important situations in daily life are still at a very early stage, but they pose intriguing possibilities for future development.

In assessing the situation of a person whom one is trying to understand or help, the following five steps seem necessary: (1) Identify the *significant interactive systems* in the client's life, especially the primary (face to face) groups, such as the family and work groups. (2) *Study the characteristics of each of these systems,* especially as they relate to relevant role expectations and acceptance or rejection. In addition to identifying the major participants, the assessor should study the "rules of the game" and the kind of communication that goes on. (3) *Compare the characteristics of the client and the system.* Study what roles he or she typically plays, how the client's perception of the situation corresponds to that of others, and whether skills and resources are adequate for the tasks demanded. (4) *Plan for utilization of the situational resources or for change in the system, the client, or both.* At this point a clinical assessor would be involved in the design of the intervention to be used by the home, work place, hospital, or clinic. (5) Finally, *evaluate the on-going progress of the new person-situation interaction.* The assessor should study the effectiveness of the plan and make appropriate alterations.

IDENTIFYiNG THE PERSON'S SIGNIFICANT SYSTEMS

Let us look more closely at the first step in the person's continuous flow of energy and information transactions with the environment. The information the assessor can seek will be limited by the available time and the assessor's understanding of and relevance to the task at hand. Generally in the interview he or she will want to scan the daily life of the person, get a picture of the *daily round* in order to inventory the settings available to the client or subject and choose which of them should be studied in detail. The interview might be called a *situational survey,* with questions like: "Tell me about a typical day for you. When do you get up in the morning and what do you do first?" and "Tell me about each place you go to during the week." The assessor might ask the person to keep a diary or *daily activity record,* recording what he does every half hour. For behavioral therapy purposes, occurrences of specific problems are usually recorded, as will be discussed in chapter seven. The person's *distribution of time and energy* reveals his or her way of perceiving and interacting with environmental opportunities. Keeping environmental limitations and opportunities the assessor can evaluate the person's report as representing the *choice pattern* for daily living and might eventually assist the person in reorganizing his or her daily program.

One can also collect information from family members or others about their perceptions of the client's daily routine and distribution of time and energy, called a "behavioral-day interview" (Hoffman, 1957). Other assessment procedures might be devised to record the number and kind of behavior settings a person enters in a day, a week, or a month. Adaptations of instruments like Gough's Home Index (1971) could be used, not just for research showing socioeconomic status, but also for developing a picture of the kinds of objects and activities found in the home. Of special importance in the person's daily or weekly program is the amount and quality of mass communication to which he is exposed. Several studies have shown that American children spend as much time with the television environment as with the school environment. The child's personality related learnings from television might be assessed, as well as the learnings from school. In any case, the initial tasks are to scan the activities, places and persons in the person's world, and to select those interactional patterns of most relevance for assessment purposes.

ASSESSING INTERPERSONAL SYSTEMS

Of all these interactive systems, the situations of greatest importance for understanding personality are those involving combinations of persons who are in frequent and close contact. Face to face relations with family members and close friends are likely to provide the most highly charged emotional experiences, both positive and negative. In fact Harry Stack Sullivan, the eminent psychiatrist (1953, p. 110-111) defined personality as "the relatively enduring pattern of recurrent interpersonal situations which characterize a human life." It should be noted, however, that in Sullivan's view the term "interpersonal" included situations in which one person would be in interaction with his or her fantasies or illusions about other persons. The schizophrenic, a diagnostic type that particularly interested Sullivan, could be in communication with a hallucination of another person. Lilly Parvin, presented at the beginning of this chapter, not only reacted to her six children, but also to the relatives she had in her mind. Close interpersonal systems also need not be face-to-face. They can be maintained at a distance by letters and telephone calls.

Close family and friendship interactions, often called *primary relations,* are of great importance in understanding behavior and experience. However, less encompassing and intimate interactions can be of importance too. These *secondary relations* usually occur in organization-related activities, such as those between boss and workers or between members of an athletic team. Social workers and psychologists sometimes find interventions with secondary groups are more practical and effective than with primary groups.

An analysis of groups as interpersonal systems involves four kinds of questions. The first has to do with the *structure* of the group: What roles do the actors play? What are the power relations among them? What are the rules for interaction? In families, the mother may have the position of power in regard to the household activities and the father in regard to outside activities.

Both roles and rules present many possibilities for research (Sarbin & Allen, 1968). Role expectations can be assessed by various methods such as interviews, questionnaires, and observations. For instance, Sarbin and Jones (1956) found considerable agreement among respondents using an adjective checklist on the role of a daughter in the family. Violation of role expectations is one of the most frequent causes of embarrassment (Gross and Stone, 1964). Rules often account for the presence or absence of conflicts and frustration in a group. For instance, if several young children in a family are expected to get ready for bed and use the bathroom at the same time, there will be a piling up in this area of the house and squabbles are likely to break out. Gump, Schoggen, & Redl (1957) have shown the coercive effect of the structure of different camp activities. For example, free swimming allows great freedom for all to participate in some way, but rowing boats may cause conflict over who has the oars. Berne (1964) in *Games people play,* showed how people manipulate others and victimize them by misuse of implicit "contracts" or rules, and how people use unconscious rules as they interact with each other.

A second kind of question in group analysis has to do with the group's *processes.* How are decisions made and conflicts of interest resolved? How well do the members of the group communicate? How are emotions such as anxiety and excitement transmitted? How well does the group organize for a task? Each of these questions—group decision-making, communication, transmission of emotion, mobilization for action—are worthy of books in themselves, but here we can only raise them as topics that the assessor should remember in his or her observations and interviews. One technique used to discover family process is called *revealed differences.* Each family member fills out the same questionnaire individually, answering such questions as: Where should we go on a vacation? Who decides whether to buy a new car? and What does father do when his children bring home a poor report card? Answers may be openended, but frequently are in checklist form. The next step is to bring the family together and instruct them to compare answers and come up with a consensus for the family on a new answer sheet. The family can be observed through a one-way screen during the interaction and the answers can be checked afterward to see whose influence is strongest on the final report. Bodin (1968) reviews several other family assessment techniques.

A technique introduced by Bales (1950, 1970) called *interaction process analysis* is a widely used observational method for studying group interactions, such as problem-solving discussions. It can be used with natural groups, such as city council meetings, as well as laboratory groups. Figure 5-2 shows a form for checking the group related activities of individuals. The tabulation totals can be used to show the major kinds of interaction of each person or to characterize the groups as a whole. If repeated, the results show in the group with different leadership or different topics of discussion. Personality characteristics, which are relatively long lasting, obtained from other devices, can be compared with an individual's group role characteristics, which are related to interactions in specific groups (Bales, 1970). Using a somewhat different, earlier form, Bales (1968) reported that the most frequently used categories were "Gives orientation (information)" and "Gives opinion" and the least used are "Asks for suggestion" and "Shows

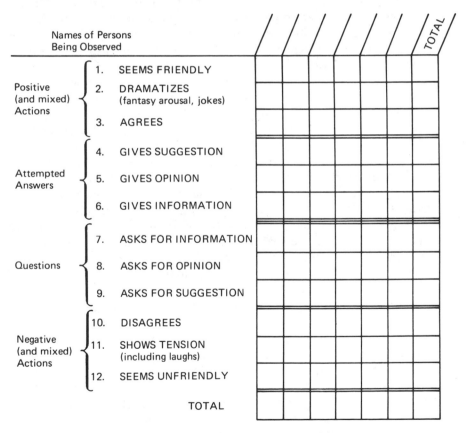

FIGURE 5-2   Checklist for Bales Interaction Process Analysis

antagonism (seems unfriendly)." It will be noted that Bales' system addresses itself to the two major interactional orientations—the task-oriented behaviors in the middle six categories and the social-emotional behavior in the top three and bottom three categories. The results from such a study of individuals and groups depend on the observer's perceptions, but good interrater reliability has been demonstrated with a little training.

A third general area of inquiry relates to *group development.* What are the directions of change over time? Is the group getting together or falling apart? What are the tasks it is dealing with now? What skills and knowledge are being used in meeting the task? Is the group attentive to the developmental needs of its members? What is the balance between task-orientation and socio-emotional orientation? The history of the group is important here. Like other relationships it has a beginning, a middle, and an end. The problems of a new family or a new work group are quite different from those of groups that have been interacting for a long time. Bales (1968) reports that groups tend to go through these phases in order—preliminary pleasantries, giving orientation, giving opinions and suggestions, some disagreement, then agreement. Typically socio-emotional aspects are mixed with task aspects, with jokes and laughter relieving tensions from time to time. Groups tend to start and finish on the positive side although there is great variation and some groups never enter the agreement phase.

The fourth kind of question in assessing a group concerns how the physical environment affects interaction. What effects are created by architectural or "micro-geographical" arrangements in the home or work place? Does the home or the surrounding neighborhood offer sufficient resources for the group's activities? What sorts of interests and activities are stimulated by the physical objects and the mass media available? As in a drama, action often requires certain "props." Psychologists in their concern for feelings and relationships often overlook the importance of the actual objects that people deal with in day to day behavior. Anyone who has watched a small child visiting a home with many breakable objects on low tables, appreciates the anxiety that is related to the environment.

Several assessment techniques for groups are included under the general topic of *sociometry,* which was developed by Moreno. A sociometric measure is "a means of assessing the attractions, or attractions and repulsions, within a given group" (Lindzey & Byrne, 1968, p. 455). Usually these measures depend on *peer nominations* or ratings, and they lead to a graphic portrayal of the relationships among group members, a *sociogram.* A common procedure is to request members of a group to indicate their choices for companions in a particular activity. Figure 5-3 illustrates the choices of ten college women for roommates in a dormitory. Each was told to give the names of two members in the group.

In the figure, Andrea, who receives many choices, would be called a *star.* Mary and Dorris, who are not chosen by anyone, are *isolates.* The

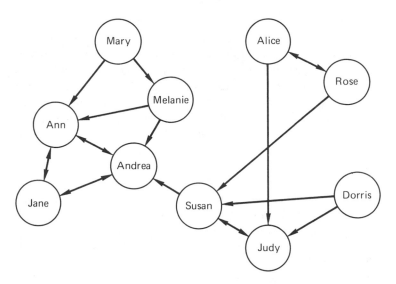

FIGURE 5-3   Sociogram of choices for roomates in a college dormitory

sociogram also reveals cliques of mutual choices, such as the isolated pair, Alice and Rose, and the trio, Andrea, Ann, and Jane. Melanie, Mary, and Susan's preferences are not accepted by the trio. Changes over time, and effects of different instructions can be studied. Choices for study partners would be different from choices for roommates.

   Quantitative indexes for individuals can be developed from choices or rejections and quite complex statistics can be used to reveal group cohesiveness and compatability (Lindzey & Byrne, 1968). Reliabilities and validities of sociometry compare very well with those of psychological tests. Gronlund (1959) concluded that sociometric choices are as stable as intelligence and achievement measures in elementary pupils over a one year interval, and Byrd (1951) reported a correlation coefficient of .80 between sociometric choices by school children and later actual choices for a play. Fiske (1971, pp. 253–254) nominated sociometric techniques along with tests of abilities as the only "fully adequate measurements" (indicators of one construct which differentiate dependably among subjects and which show the degree the construct characterizes the subject now). He says that they work because they are essentially operational definitions, that is, the sociometric procedure elicits popularity in the process of studying popularity. Lindzey & Byrne (1968, pp. 453–454) point out some advantages of sociometric techniques: "The rater is asked to apply exactly those particular, unique, and sometimes irrational criteria he has spent a lifetime developing. . . . Liking and disliking, accepting and rejecting are part of the process of daily living." However, sociometric assessment is seldom used except in research and training, because it can rarely be applied to a large sample of people.

One other successful form of group assessment should be mentioned: *Leaderless Group Discussion* (LGD). In this technique, observers rate defined aspects of the performance of strangers who are brought together to discuss a certain problem, such as how to market a product, or how to improve university-community relations. Raters typically score each person on prominence in the discussion, facilitation of movement toward goals, and sociability. Bass (1954), who developed the procedure, states that the process .measures tendencies for initiating structure in an unstructured social situation. Bass and his colleagues have reported some impressive evidence of validity and stability over short time periods. Vernon (1950) found that the LGD ratings correlated .33 with ratings of suitability for the British foreign service made after two years of duty. It is likely that much of the predictive validity of such situational tests resides in their similarity to actual life occurrences; that is, they are almost work samples.

ASSESSING PERSON-ORGANIZATION RELATIONS

Beyond the family and other small face to face groups, the individual relates to more impersonal systems. Particularly in highly bureaucratized and industrialized societies, the individual's behavior must be relevant to organizations much larger than the face to face primary groups. Workers in steel mills may never see the managers or labor leaders who make decisions about their salaries, benefits, and methods of evaluation that are of great importance to their personal behavior. Lawyers belong to the American Bar Association and respond to its decisions. A priest is shifted from one community to another as a result of decisions made by church superiors. Multinational companies move personnel around the world. Vance Packard's (1972) well titled book, *A Nation of Strangers,* takes as its topic the problems caused by the frequent shifts of the executives of large organizations from one place to another; this mobility prevents the benefits to communities that come from stable leadership, and the benefits to persons and families that come from having identifiable roots.

The concept *role* is useful here, as it was with interpersonal systems. The person is likely to occupy several roles in the organization, some formally assigned, such as foreman or secretary, others as members of working teams, committees, or informal groups around the locker or lunchroom. A role analysis of the relevant parts of an organization may be valuable. Another useful concent is that of *social norms,* or expectations about what is proper and improper behavior. These can be ascertained by interviewing and observing members of the organization. The degree to which an individual feels comfortable and adapts to the organization no doubt relates to these norms and to a sense of support. One study (Friedlander & Greenberg, 1971) showed that job performance of formerly hard-core unemployed workers related to their perception of support by their work environments.

Designing and "enlarging" the meaning of jobs is a challenging task that rests on a flexible and understanding view of individuals and organizations (Sandler, 1974).

In their analytic model of personality assessment, Stern, Stein, & Bloom (1956) present some important methods that can be related to organizations. They conduct a situational analysis, laying stress on the realistic methods by which people are judged in organizations. They seek to locate the significant people in the individual's progress or failure, and they study their opinions about good and poor performance. Biases and arbitrariness may be part of the way people are judged; these are realistic criteria which the assessor needs to recognize but may want to change. The end product of a situational analysis is an explicit statement of the psychological role requirements of the job and the operational procedures for studying these requirements in an individual.

Stern (1970) has contributed in another area of situational analysis. He is one of the few who have developed an objective measure for Murray's environmental press. Paralleling the thirty need variables in his Activities Index (AI) for measuring individual characteristics, the College Characteristics Index (CCI) measures thirty press variables appropriate to the academic setting. Data have been collected from almost 10,000 students in 100 institutions of higher learning. In the area of achievement, the AI asks a student to answer "like" or "dislike" to items such as "Taking examinations" or "Setting difficult goals for myself." In the same area the CCI asks a student to answer "true" or "false" concerning the applicability to his or her college of items such as "Examinations here provide a genuine measure of a student's achievement and understanding," or "Students set high standards of achievement for themselves." Other CCI items are "The students here represent a great variety in nationality, religion, and social status," and "Students are encouraged to criticize administrative policies and teaching practices." Studies suggest, as expected, that AI variance is mainly attributable to individual differences within colleges, and CCI variance is mainly attributable to differences between colleges. Pace has developed a similar and widely used instrument, the College and University Environment Scales.

There are other illustrations of person-organizational assessment (Moos, 1973, 1975). Classroom and home learning climates and mental hospitals have been studied. For instance, Marjoribanks (1972, 1974) found children's mental abilities to be more highly correlated with the home situation and parental behavior than with socio-economic status alone. Ellsworth and his colleagues (1968), in a significant and extensive study, have shown that adjustment in the hospital and adjustment in the community are two separate things. Using forms of the PARS (Personal Adjustment and Role Skill Scale), they found that relatives' ratings of mental patients were as useful as ratings by hospital staff members. They concluded that certain traditional assessment procedures, like the psychiatric interview on admission to the hospital, may not identify the patient's relevant problems because much symptomatology may be a function of the hospital setting. As policies for dealing with mental illness emphasize maintenance and care of patients at or near their homes, there is more need for assessment of persons relative to community life.

While identifying and analyzing the significant systems in a client's or subject's life, the assessor also naturally thinks about how well the person and those systems fit together. It may be useful to make this comparison explicit. One can compare at least four aspects of the personal system and the social system: boundaries, tasks, social-emotional characteristics, and exchange. Figure 5-4 shows these areas of concern.

PERSONAL SYSTEM CHARACTERISTICS	SUPRA-SYSTEM CHARACTERISTICS
Boundary Considerations	*Boundary Considerations*
e.g. possibilities for solving time and space problems, interest in joining, competing claims for time and energy.	e.g. physical location of organization, time requirements, criteria for membership, availability of positions.
Task Considerations	*Task Considerations*
e.g. interest and ability regarding field of effort, skills available or learnable, knowledge, ability to perform.	e.g. content of task, skills required, knowledge required, persistence, performance standards, productivity.
Socio-Emotional Aspects	*Socio-Emotional Aspects*
e.g. interpersonal expectations, role complimentarity, personal socio-emotional needs.	e.g. interpersonal expectations, role complimentarity, needs of co-workers.
Exchange	*Exchange*
e.g. what the person expects in terms of rewards and meeting personal needs.	e.g. what the organization can give in terms of financial reward, recognition, opportunity for self-expression, etc.

FIGURE 5-4   Comparing the person and the supra-system

Assessment often involves studying the process of creating or changing a system. The person being assessed may be joining or separating from another person (as in marriage), several persons (as in a work group), or may be taking or leaving a position in a large organization. Any change of systems involving boundary redefinition or boundary crossing involves extra energy and sometimes considerable stress to the organism involved. Working with a counseling client or a patient, the psychologist helps him or her see the characteristics of the suprasystem and personal system. Sometimes it is possible to try out activities in the new system before a final decision is made.

The assessor considers two major aspects of roles—the task and the socio-emotional aspects. Knowing something of the client's *role repertoire* he can judge whether the skills and social responses required are within his capabilities. The assessor will also compare the client's *perceptions of the system* with the perceptions of others, such as perceptions of the way decisions are made, the values of the significant participants, the exchange of affection, and the satisfaction with the physical arrangements.

Finally in this process the suprasystem and the person can be compared for the benefits and costs to be derived. The rewards for work done, the amount of recognition, the ability to satisfy security needs, and the potential for self actualization enter into the exchange. Completing the five steps listed earlier, the clinical assessor would utilize resources to improve the person-system interaction and evaluate the altered processes.

PERSONAL CHARACTERISTICS
RELATED TO SITUATIONS

So far we have primarily been considering interactional systems. In the previous section we began to look at personal characteristics that link a person to the environment or to people in general. We have taken two frames of reference—that of looking at the group as a whole and that of looking at individual roles within the group. The difference is like that between watching a team in a football game and watching one of the players in action. In the first case, we note the various formations the team takes in offense and defense and the pattern of roles (quarterback or right end) in teams; in the other case, we observe how the person plays a role such as quarterback or right end. We could ask the football player how many positions he can play on the team and what he sees as his responsibilities in various plays. This would be *role assessment.* Role assessment is transactional; a role is concerned with group behavior regardless of who occupies the position. We can, however, look at an individual's role repertory (ability to take different roles) and his or her expectations and perceptions of roles.

In contrast, we could focus on traits related to generalized role enactment in many situations; that is, we can look at long-standing characteristics like dominance or aggressiveness. *Trait assessment* focuses on the individual aside from immediate interaction. When we shift to individual characteristics supposedly related to social interaction, we find numerous assessment devices—perhaps the majority of personality inventories and projective techniques have socially relevant interpretations. We will select only a few explicit ones.

Research and theory in social psychology have pointed to two basic interpersonal dimensions that can be identified in individuals: dominance-submission and friendliness-hostility. In many studies of leadership (Petrullo & Bass, 1961; Gibb, 1969), these two aspects have been identified in various ways such as leadership by "initiating structure" versus leadership by "consideration of others," "task-orientation" versus "social emotional orientation" of people in problem-solving groups, interest in "production" versus "social awareness," and emphasis on "efficiency" versus "satisfaction." Similar dimensions of interpersonal characteristics have emerged from several different investigators (Leary, 1957; LaForge & Suczek, 1955; Foa, 1961; Rinn, 1965; Lorr & Suziedelis, 1969). Leary designates these dimensions as Dominance-Submission and Love-Hostility. The two dimensions show little or no correlation. The Interpersonal Check List (LaForge, 1963; LaForge & Suczek, 1955) is a convenient way for judges or subjects to rate others or themselves on these dimensions in the Leary system.

There are several other procedures for assessing interpersonal traits. Schutz (1958, 1967) developed the Fundamental Interpersonal Relations Orientation (FIRO) system of which the inventory, FIRO-B, is most widely used. It measures desired and expressed aspects of three kinds of interpersonal needs—inclusion, control, and affection. Gough's California Psychological Inventory (1968) measures such variables as socialization, responsibility, achievement, and capacity for status. George Kelly's Role Construct Repertory Test (Kelly, 1955; Bannister, 1970) takes a different approach. In this test the assessor first asks the subject to identify persons who occupy significant roles in his life, such as mother, or the most disliked student in high school and then the subject is asked to state similarities and differences between those role representatives. Tyler (1961; et al., 1968) has developed a similar method, the Choice Pattern Technique, to study how individuals view the world of work and leisure activities. A subject first sorts cards with names of occupations on them into "Would Choose" or "Would Not Choose" piles. Then for each pile the subject is asked to group those occupations which go together and give reasons for putting them together. In this way the assessor learns how finely the person makes distinctions about work and his or her ways of thinking about occupations. These last two procedures are ways of determining the thinking patterns regarding a person's relation to the environment. They are illustrations of the assessment of "cognitive styles," a topic to which we will return in chapter ten. There we will see some other relevant techniques such as the assessment of field dependence by Witkin et al. (1954, 1962), and internal vs. external locus of control by Rotter (1966) and his associates.

COMMENT ON THE ISSUE OF PERSON vs. SITUATION

In this wide ranging chapter a basic issue for assessment is the question of the relative importance of situational vs. personalistic data in explaining and predicting behavior. Strong stands have been taken on both sides of the issue. Note these two quotations:

The assessor who tries to predict the future without detailed information about the exact environmental conditions influencing the individual's criterion behavior may be more engaged in the process of hoping than of predicting. (Mischel, 1968, p. 140)

In the name of science, an enormous amount of poppycock has recently been expressed to the effect that (a) all behavior is "situational" in character, and/or (b) that psychometricians and/or trait theorists have never considered situational influences on human behavior. (Goldberg, 1971, p. 8)

Many sociologists and behavioral learning theorists contend that behavior is highly specific and that trait and factor theory is practically useless. Trait theorists, however, going back to Allport, argue that traits describe fundamental characteristics of human beings and the conceptions of traits which their opponents attack are superficial straw men. The argument is far from settled, but most of the work of personologists over the years has been on traits so it seems only appropriate that the other side now be given considerable attention!

What is the evidence that situational assessment is necessary and important? If we could be confident that individual traits were consistent and continuous, then our primary assessment effort should be the elucidation of those traits; however, such assurance seems unwarranted. The classic study in this connection is the Character Education Inquiry by Hartshorne, May and their colleagues (1928, 1929, and 1930) briefly mentioned earlier. This series of studies used quantitative methods to explore children's honesty and other traits of character and morality in several situations. For instance, one arithmetic problem involved the use of coins which the children could surreptitiously keep. Other situations allowed for cheating on tests or games. Harshorne and May found that the various tests of honesty produced only weak correlations and concluded that there was no generalized "good character" or general trait of honesty, but individuals were strongly influenced by the situations in which they found themselves.

Many subsequent studies of traits raise similar questions about their utility and consistency across methods and situations. Validity coefficients for personality trait measures usually range from .20 to .50 with a mean of around .30. Cognitive measures like intelligence tests tend to show more trans-situational consistency and trans-temporal continuity than personality measures. Mischel (1969, p. 1014) believes that "the observed inconsistency so regularly found in studies of noncognitive personality dimensions often reflects the state of nature and not merely the noise of measurement." An organism is in a state of relative flux. A particular need may be expressed only in certain situations. A person is romantic in some circumstances, hungry in others. The problem for assessment theory and research is the degree to which the features of personality should be attributed to the person or the context.

One of the most frequently quoted studies in this regard is the monograph, "An S-R inventory of anxiousness" by Endler, Hunt & Rosenstein (1962). These authors constructed a self-report device in an interesting way. The "S-R" in the title refers to the fact that they varied both the stimulus situation and the possible responses individuals could give to those situations. the inventory requires the subject to report the intensity of each of fourteen responses in each of eleven different situations. Situations include "You are going to meet a new date," "You are going into an interview for an important job," and "You are starting out in a sailboat into a rough sea." The subject indicated which of the following responses he or she would probably give in the situations, for instance, "heart beats faster," "perspire," "enjoy the challenge," or "become immobilized." Individual differences, as well as response and situational differences, were found, of course, so the test was measuring three major components relative to this issue. Endler & Hunt (1966, 1969) subsequently showed that the main sources of variance were not the individual differences, or the situational differences (each contributing only about 5 percent of the variance), but the interactions of subjects with situations and response modes.

Endler & Hunt (1969, p. 22) concluded that "the issue of the relative importance of individual differences and of situations is but a pseudo-issue. . . . These findings also suggest that personality description in general might be improved considerably by categorizing both situations and modes of response and then by describing individuals in terms of the kinds of responses they tend to manifest in the various kinds of situations." Endler (1973) buttresses the conclusions by referring to two reviews of person versus situation studies (Bowers, 1972; Argyle & Little, 1972), that found that the interaction accounts for more variance than either persons or situations alone. Cartwright (1975) asserts, however, that the experimental design used with Endler's S-R Inventory was faulty and concludes the findings do not have drastic implications for trait inventories; so the battle continues.

The Endler & Hunt work was based on self-reports of responses in situations. Psychologists need to study actual behavior in situations, and experiment with individual differences in different situations so that we can see the interaction in operation. For instance, Raush et al. (1959) observed children with different characteristics in different situations, and Eisler et al. (1975) varied role playing instructions with mental patients who differed in measured assertiveness and showed the importance of different role-played situations as well as individual differences. We need to be able to make conditional predictions such as if individual A is in situation M, he is likely to do Z; if A is in situation N, he will probably do Y; if B is in situation N, she will probably do W. Ultimately we need to conceptualize and assess the internal operations of the person in systems interacting with the environment—the Environment-Organism-Environment Arc, as Barker (1968) called it.

SUMMARY

In this chapter we have surveyed the relationship between the individual and the environment, and the possibilities for assessing situations. The illustration of Lilly Parvin and her family pointed out the complexity of the problem of environmental and community assessment as it relates to real persons. Ideas about environmental relations include Murray's press and needs, Barker's behavior settings and environmental force units, ecological and system theory concepts, and the widely used term, role. Other possibilities come from industrial job analysis and attempts to develop taxonomies of situations. For a psychologist or other person trying to help an individual there are five steps: identifying the significant interactive systems, studying the characteristics of each, comparing the personal characteristics and the systems, utilizing situational resources, and evaluating progress in the new person-situation interaction.

The identification of the significant systems usually leads to interviews with the person about his or her daily activities and distribution of time and energy among primary, closely interacting groups. When assessing the interactive systems, one looks at the structure of groups, including the roles and rules, the group processes, perhaps using a technique for interaction analysis, the group development over time, and the related aspects of the physical environment. The general term sociometry covers many ways of measuring and diagramming internal relations of groups, many of which yield high reliability and validity figures. The concept of role is also useful for assessing person-organization relations. Some questionnaires have been developed to measure institutional climates, for instance Stern's College Characteristics Index.

Looking at individual characteristics related to situations, we find considerable agreement on two major dimensions: dominance-submission and friendliness-hostility. Several personality tests and techniques measure these dimensions. Some of the cognitive style procedures to be discussed in a later chapter, such as field-dependence, also relate the person's characteristics to the environment.

Finally the chapter reviewed the controversy between the trait theorists and the situationalists and concluded that the interaction between person and situation is most important—but also most difficult to assess. The point to be remembered is that assessment of a person is incomplete if it does not include assessment of context. The next chapter will move from the external to the internal physiological systems of the person.

SUGGESTED READINGS

BODIN, A. M. Conjoint family assessment: An evolving field. In P. McReynolds (ed.) *Advances in psychological assessment,* Vol. 1. Palo Alto, Cal.: Science & Behavior Books, 1968. 223–243. Bodin classifies approaches to assessing family systems as individual, conjoint, or combined. He reviews the latter two categories, which require the families to be assessed together using both subjective and objective techniques. He gives a number of references to prior reviews and a useful commentary on the issues in assessing family units.

BRISLIN, R. W., LONNER, W. J., and THORNDIKE, R. M. *Cross-cultural research methods.* New York: Wiley, 1973. Another area we have slighted in this chapter is the effect of culture on individual and group behavior. Each culture, subculture, or ethnic groups rewards certain activities and ways of thinking and punishes others. No assessment procedure can be used across cultures with the assumption that it is free of cultural influences or is equally fair to persons of different cultures. Brislin and his colleagues provide an excellent review of the dangers and possibilities for assessment in a research context.

CRAIK, K. H. The assessment of places. In P. McReynolds (ed.) *Advances in psychological assessment.* Vol. 2. Palo Alto: Science and Behavior, 1971, 40–62. Craik covers one of the areas we have excluded or given short shrift in this chapter—the assessment of the physical environment. Environmental psychology developed rapidly from the late 1960s, spurred on by worldwide interest in ecological problems. There was also a growing recognition in architecture and urban planning of the importance of behavioral analysis. Craik's introduction discussed techniques for assessment such as the Landscape Adjective Check List. Craik's 1973 *Annual Review* chapter, "Environmental psychology," provides a broad overview of the emerging field.

INSEL, P. M. & MOOS, R. H. Psychological environments: Expanding the scope of human ecology. *American Psychologist,* 1974, 29, 179–188. Insel and Moos identify six different ways of conceptualizing human environments: ecological dimensions, dimensions of organizational structure, personal characteristics of inhabitants, behavior settings, reinforcement properties of environments, and psychosocial or organizational climate. They find that eight organizational climate scales consistently show three dimensions: relationship, personal development, and system maintenance and change. The article ends with some recommendations for optimal environments. Other related readings are "Toward a taxonomy of situations" by Frederickson (1972), *Issues in social ecology* by Moos & Insel (1974), and "Assessment and impact of social climate" by Moos (1975).

SARBIN, T. R. & ALLEN, V. L. Role theory. In G. Lindzey & E. Aronson (eds.) *Handbook of social psychology,* Vol. 1. (2nd ed.) Reading, Mass.: Addison-Wesley, 1968. 488–567. Sarbin and Allen provide a thorough review of such topics as the degrees of involvement of persons in role enactment, the dimensions and measurement of role expectations, skills related to roles and their assessment, and a taxonomy of roles and role conflicts. For two other approaches to roles and dramaturgical analysis see Goffman's *The presentation of self in everyday life* (1959) and Papajohn & Spiegel's *Transactions in families* (1975). Hogan (1976) relates personality to role theory and socialization. Ziller's *The social self* (1973) makes use of an interesting spatial technique to assess roles and relations between the self and others.

chapter six

Biopsychological
Assessment

Let me have men about me that are fat;
Sleek-headed men, and such as sleep o' nights;
Yond Cassius has a lean and hungry look;
He thinks too much: Such men are dangerous.
        —William Shakespeare, *Julius Caesar*, Act I, Scene II.

Personality may be biologically defined as the governing organ,
or superordinate institution, of the body. As such, it is located in
the brain. No brain, no personality. —Henry Murray (1951, p. 267)

Probably as long as human beings have been on this earth there has been
speculation about the relation of bodily characteristics to personality. The
importance of the physical state of the body to the functioning of a person
is obvious and within the experience of everyone—the daily cycle of fresh-
ness and fatigue, the periods of illness, the influence of handicaps, the
effects of drugs or alcohol, and the vibrant feeling of high energy and good
health. We notice in others great individual differences in attitudes toward
the body and reactions to illnesses or handicaps. We hear much about
psychosomatic problems, the misuse of drugs, the bad nutrition of many
people and the problems of physical development and aging. New ideas in
clinical psychology and psychiatry place emphasis on the body—bioener-
getics, biofeedback, and the differences in consciousness related to left and

right parts of the brain. Many of these concerns indicate the intimate relationship between physiological states and *emotions*—the basic glandular and nervous mechanisms which are active in joy, anger, and grief. Other concerns relate to the effect of physical condition on *behavior,* such as the limitations caused by injuries to the limbs or nervous system, or by disease, and the capabilities of people born with deviant bodies. The enormous amount of effort and expense put into health related professions and research reflects the fundamental importance of general assessment of the body. Part of that concern and effort is relevant to the psychological assessment of persons and personality.

ASSESSMENT OF THE BIOPSYCHOLOGICAL SYSTEM

One kind of assessment is a physical examination. The physician assesses each operating system of the body for evidence such as unusual coloring, growth, bilateral asymmetry, and reflexes such as the knee jerk following a tap on the patella tendon, or contraction of the pupil when light shines on it. He or she systematically asks the patient about complaints, obtains a history, and observes visible funcitoning of each set of interrelated organs—the respiratory, gastro-intestinal, genito-uninary, cardiovascular, and nervous system. The physician notes abnormalities of walking, speech, and flow of thought and also makes use of laboratory findings from blood and urine samples and from X-ray photography. If abnormal signs appear, there are specialists in any large community to examine and more carefully assess the condition. Among those health related specialists are clinical psychologists, psychiatrists, and social workers, who have particular responsibility for the diagnosis and treatment of socioemotional problems. However, the general practitioner is often the first professional to learn the meanings of the body's symptoms. The sensitivity of the physician or other first community contact person, such as a clergyman or teacher, to the bodily feelings and behaviors of the person and the images and misinformation about the body that a patient may have, is a significant factor in understanding and helping an individual. A thorough assessment would include an interview exploration of the person's worries and beliefs about the various organs of the body.

Some of the major diagnostic problems that concern psychologists are psychosomatic disorders, brain damage, mental deficiency, drug and alcohol addiction, vocational possibilities in relation to disability, and differential diagnoses of somatic versus psychological causes of disorder. This introductory book is not the place to describe any of these in detail. Psychologists have developed a number of tests and other procedures for these diagnostic problems, many of which are mentioned in later chapters, such as the MMPI and the Rorschach. Readers interested in more detail should see the suggested readings at the end of this and other chapters. Here we will simply consider one of these diagnostic problems at some length— the problem of assessing brain damage.

ASSESSMENT OF THE FUNCTIONING OF THE BRAIN

Injuries to the central nervous system (the brain and spinal cord) are fairly common. A survey of clients of the Division of Vocational Rehabilitation showed that 10 percent suffered from damage to the central nervous system (Lewinsohn & Graf, 1973). Among them, the incidence of personal and environmental problems was more than twice as high as among the other clients; they were a difficult population to rehabilitate. Brain damage can be due to cardiovascular disorders such as a "stroke," brain tumors, infections, toxic disorders, epilepsy, or one of a growing number of traumatic head injuries. Many victims of automobile and motorcycle accidents are young and potentially rehabilitatable. Military combat has also resulted in numbers of young brain-injured people who need assessment and assistance in re-entering occupations. The investment of professional resources and the human losses due to brain damage are very large. As medical science improves procedures for saving lives, the number of brain-injured persons needing an assessment of disorders and vocational potential will increase.

Working in the field called *neuropsychology*, a clinical and experimental psychologists try to discover the way damage to the central nervous system affect behavior. They have used intelligence tests like the Wechsler, and have developed many specialized procedures. This research has the persistent problem of the differentiation between decrement due to organic disruption, such as by a brain tumor or injury, and decrement due to motivational and abnormal personality patterns, such as depression and schizophrenia. It is now clear that brain damage cannot be considered a clinical entity or a unitary construct. Recent work gives more detail about the site of brain injury and its specific effects on functions. Researchers at least differentiate their subjects as to whether lesions are diffuse or localized, acute or chronic, and in the left or right hemisphere of the brain, and they seek to obtain for the neurologist or neurosurgeon as much information as possible about the exact area of the brain that is affected and the nature of the cerebral lesion. Here we are considering problems of intellectual *deficit*. Intellectual *retardation* or *mental deficiency* may also be organically caused, but this condition is ordinarily present from infancy onwards; by intellectual deficit we mean loss or impairment relative to an earlier level of ability.

Tests for the behavioral effects of central nervous system impairment may sample a limited area of functioning as does the Wechsler Memory Scale, the Benton Test of Visual Retention, the Graham and Kendall Memory-for-Designs Test, the Goldstein-Scheerer tests of abstract and concrete thinking, or the Bender Visual-Motor Gestalt Test. The instrument may be a group of tests that sample several diverse areas of functioning. Psychological measures like these are used to supplement the diagnosis that the neurologist makes by means of medical observation and specialized laboratory techniques like the electroencephalogram and X-rays of the head. Clinical psychologists are frequently called on by physicians to help detect border-line loss of functioning and to assist in differential diagnosis between brain damage and hysterical or psychotic conditions—that is, between physical and functional disorders.

Assessors need to be alert to suggestions of deficit as they take a case history or give tests. Any abrupt change in personality or problems of memory, thinking, or speech should alert the psychologist and physician to the possibility of brain damage. On any test of intellectual functioning a sharp difference between measurements of older knowledge, such as vocabulary or information, and measurements of new relationships or immediate memory, such as learning new pairs of words or repeating digits, has been considered suggestive of brain disfunction. Reitan (1955), Reitan & Fitzhugh (1971) and others have found that those with lesions of the right hemisphere of the brain did relatively poorer on Wechsler performance subtests, while those with left hemisphere lesions did better on performance subtests than verbal subtests. This finding matches the well known fact of cerebral dominance that language is controlled by the left hemisphere. Early differential diagnosis between physical and functional disorders is important, but in beginning stages it is difficult to tell whether symptoms like irritability, dizziness, and confusion are due to a hysterical disorder or a physical problem.

A short test that is frequently used as a rough screening measure for some forms of brain damage is the Bender Visual-Motor Gestalt Test. This procedure was published in the late 1930s by a psychiatrist, Lauretta Bender, who was interested in the way children matured in their ability to perceive and represent form. The German word for form or configuration is *Gestalt,* and the principles of perception were the primary concern of Gestalt Psychology. As had been known for some time, there is a progression in children's visual motor coordination in copying figures. The easiest thing for very young children to draw is a loop; angles come later. The square is easier to draw then the diamond, which is not mastered by the average child till age seven, at which age level it is found as a copying test on the Stanford-Binet. The Bender test uses nine geometrical figures, some of which are shown in Figure 6–1. Subjects are simply shown the figures one at a time and asked to copy them. With normal people the task takes only five to ten minutes. The

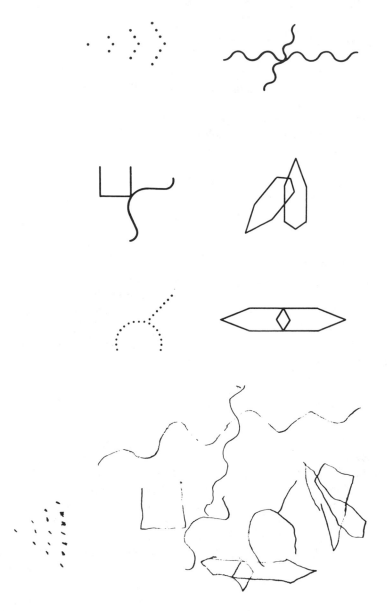

FIGURE 6-1 Six of the Bender-Gestalt figures-originals and copies by a sixty-two year old brain-damaged man. (From M. L. Hutt and G. J. Briskin, *The clinical use of the revised Bender-Gestalt Test,* New York: Grune and Stratton, 1969, pp. 3 and 170.)

Bender test has been used to study children's maturational level, indicating problems related to retardation in visual-motor coordination. She extended the use of the test to adults, as a test of brain damage she also found that the drawings seemed to relate to certain personality characteristics. Overly neat and small figures suggested compulsiveness, and sloppy, uncontrolled drawings suggested impulsive or psychopathic features. Distortions of male and female symbols in the process of drawing were also interpreted. The Bender has become a widely used projective technique. When employing the Bender for detecting brain damage, the assessor looks for rotations or shifts in directions of the figures, for difficulty with answers, and for general difficulty in copying and locating the figures. The copied figures at the bottom of figure 6–1 illustrate distortions often found in cases of brain damage. Reviews (such as Kitay's review in Buros, 1972) suggest that the Bender does not have high validity, but that it is often worth the short administration time to provide the clinician with an opportunity to observe this kind of behavior. Formal scoring systems have been developed for the test (Pascal & Suttell, 1951), but most experienced clinicians simply analyze the results by visual inspection, sometimes with considerable accuracy (Bruhn & Reed, 1975).

The Bender, however, is only one kind of behavior sample. A number of researchers of brain damage, including Reitan (1975), state that no single test for organicity is sufficient and that the intraindividual pattern must be carefully studied on a variety of tests and procedures. A person may have a visual perceptual problem, but not an auditory one; motor skills such as drawing may be affected, but not the ability to recognize correct answers among several choices; speech understanding may be poor but speech itself perfect. The disturbance depends on the location and nature of the lesion.

A widely used set of measures of intellectual deficit is the Halstead-Reitan Neuropsychological Test Battery, referred to in various forms as the Halstead, Reitan, or the Halstead-Indiana Battery. This procedure consists of an extensive series of tasks designed to cover various problems of auditory, visual, motor, and abstracting difficulties. For instance, one test asks the subject to select among multiple choice alternatives the word or syllable representing the sound that he or she heard from a tape recorder. Another test requires the person to differentiate between rhythmic beats which are sometimes the same and sometimes different. Another test involves tapping speed; the score is the number of taps made with the index finger in several ten second trials. The subject is also blindfolded and asked to fit blocks into a formboard by feel, and then to draw the outline of the blocks from memory. In another test, the subject indicates principle for grouping a set of objects such as shape, size, or color. In the process of testing the subject, the psychologist will also have the subject write his or her own name with the preferred and nonpreferred hand and perform a number of little tasks that test tactile, auditory, and visual abilities. The result of the Halstead battery can be represented by an Impairment Index showing the number of tests on which performance fell in the abnormal range, but the most useful results are from the comparisons a trained assessor can make among various parts of the battery to see where the person has specific problems. Lewinsohn (1971) has shown how students can be taught diagnostic skills in the use of the battery. Filskov & Goldstein (1974) demonstrated that the Halstead-Reitan tests surpassed physical measures as a screening battery for brain damage. The tasks on this battery have also been revised for use with children (Kilpatrick & Spreen, 1973).

Lewinsohn (1973) has also shown that an extensive set of tests, including the Halstead-Reitan measures, discriminated well between normals and brain-damaged patients‾ and between those brain-damaged persons who could resume gainful employment and those who were not able to do so. The survey mentioned earlier (Lewinsohn & Graf, 1973) of clients in the Division of Vocational Rehabilitation showed that the most frequently occurring problems in the brain-damaged sample were social immaturity, emotional uncertainty, slowness, depression, poor motor coordination, general inadequacy, short attention span, and speech difficulties, physical and financial limitations of the home. Therefore, a complete assessment requires many of the same procedures mentioned elsewhere for general personality evaluation.

ASSESSING PERSONALITY FROM GENETIC, ANATOMICAL AND PHYSIO-CHEMICAL CHARACTERISTICS

The search for indexes to personality in bodily characteristics has a long history. It would be simple and easy if we could literally "size up" a person—measure bodily dimensions, the symmetry of the face, or the chemistry of the blood, and then classify and predict behavior. As mentioned earlier in the book, the ideas of the Greeks and Romans about the pre-dominance of the four "humors" are still reflected in our language with such words as "sanguine" and "choleric." An Italian scientist of the late nineteenth century, Lombroso, believed that criminality was indicated by certain physical features, such as absence of ear lobes. In that century and into the twentieth, many people believed in phrenology, reading character from the bumps and shape of the skull. Similarly some people associate skin color and other racial characteristics with personality believing such notions as "all Negroes are musical." But things are not that simple, and such clearly identified bodily dimensions have not stood the test of scientific scrutiny. As with many other systems such as astrology, Tarot cards, and some prominent personality systems, careful definition of terms and careful measurement fail to demonstrate the relationships that have been con-fidently asserted. Still the search continues.

There seems to be no doubt that there must be some relationship between personality and the nature of one's body, but the relationship is complex. As an example, the psychodynamic theorist, Adler, asserted that people with organic inferiorities overcompensate for them. However though

Napoleon may have overcompensated for his shortness, few short men become Napoleons and there must be many other factors involved. Still the person's principle that the perceptions and attitudes about a bodily condition have profound effects on behavior and social relations seem an important one to keep in mind.

In looking for biological indicators of personality, we shall briefly cover four general kinds of assessment—genetic, anatomical, physiochemical, and neurophysiological. We shall take up the first three in this section and the last in the next section. First, how do *genetic factors* relate to personality and personality assessment? There are very few practical assessment techniques that can be recommended. Most procedures such as the study of identical twins and family records have been used only for research purposes. Recent developments in biochemical identification of genetic disorders offer promising possibilities. The disorder called phenylketonuria (PKU) has been shown to be due to a single recessive gene and is inherited from both parents in about one in 10,000 people (Vandenburg, 1971). PKU causes liver disfunction that in turn results in the production of blood-carried substances that cause severe subnormality as the brain develops. If it is discovered, through a simple urine test with a newborn baby, PKU can be prevented by dietary control and the child will not grow up mentally retarded. Another form of retardation, Down's Syndrome, commonly called "mongolism," is definitely related to genetic chromosomal abnormality but it is probably not inherited. An abnormal chromosome in males, the XYY chromosome, is hypothesized to be linked with aggressive and antisocial tendencies, but findings are inconclusive (Shah and Borgaonker, 1974). Some methods for detecting hereditary characteristics are sufficiently dependable so that couples can be told the probability that certain disorders will show up in children they may have; so *genetic counseling* for physical disorders is becoming possible. Some scientists believe that there is sufficient evidence from twin studies to assert that schizophrenia, and perhaps other psychoses, develop from inherited predispositions. Meehl (1972), for instance, hypothesizes a complex relationship between schizogenic inheritance and early life experiences that lead to inappropriate social behavior and eventually to clear-cut schizophrenic symptoms. Another investigator (Vandenberg, 1969) concluded that three personality traits are influenced substantially by genetic sources—activity level, emotional expressiveness and long-range planning tendencies. Eysenck (1967), the prominent British psychologist, asserts that there is considerable evidence that a basic dimension in his personality theory, extroversion-introversion, is inherited. However, at this time, the professional person assessing personality will seldom be able to make much practical use of genetic information. Eventually, it seems likely that early detection of genetic disorders affecting personality will provide a basis for more extensive preventive counseling and even biochemical intervention than is now possible.

Another area in which there has been much research, but few practical applications in assessment, is the relationship between *physique* or *anatomy* and personality. Obvious physical handicaps and extremes of physique and physical development are likely to expose the person to psychological and social stress. Studies show that ratings are affected, usually in a positive manner, by physical attractiveness (Cash et al., 1975; Dermer & Thiel, 1975). Assessors need to be attuned to the person's reactions to his or her physical conditions as they conduct interviews and other procedures. Longitudinal studies of adolescents show that the onset of puberty and the growth spurt have important effects on personality (Dwyer & Mayer, 1969; Tanner, 1970). Athletically able, larger boys tend to have prestige with their age mates. Boys that mature early are likely to become more sociable and less neurotic, and are more often leaders than late maturers, at least in American culture. Girls suffer somewhat the reverse effect; a large, early maturing girl may feel awkward, selfconscious, and unable to meet the challenging social situations that her maturity brings her. These research findings apply to groups, and do not necessarily hold in individual cases.

The most extended research program exploring relationships between personality and physique is that of Sheldon (1942). Building on concepts of ancient philosophers and the German psychiatrist, Kretschmer, Sheldon postulated three components in physique: *endomorphy,* the soft and rounded quality of a fat person, with underdevelopment of bone and muscle, *mesomorphy,* the hard and rectangular body of the athlete with a high predominance of bone and muscle, and *ectomorphy,* the linear and fragile aspect of the thin person with flatness of chest and delicacy of body. Figure 6–2 shows drawings of the extremes of these *somatotypes.* Sheldon differentiated eighty-eight body shapes varying in the degree to which they showed each of these three characteristics. Somatotyping methods were carefully developed and can be done quite reliably. There is a problem, however, when Sheldon tries to relate somatotypes to temperament. His theory is that endormorphy accompanies *viscerotonia,* or love of comfort, relaxation, and sociability; mesomorphy relates to *somatotonia,* that is vigorous selfexpression accompanied by insensitivity to others' feelings, and a liking for exercise and adventure; and ectomorphy involves *cerebrotonia,* which is characterized by restraint, intellectual interests and preference for solitude. (Shakespeare's Cassius was an ectomorph.) Research on these hypothesized relationships has produced mixed results. Some studies used ratings for temperament by judges who saw the subjects, thus confounding the results (Tyler, 1965). Several studies have shown that delinquents are much more likely to be mesomorphs than nondelinquents

(Glueck & Glueck, 1950; Cortes & Gatti, 1972). Though recently psychologists have tended to disregard Sheldon's work, many respect the classification of physiques that was developed, and most would agree that body build affects many aspects of everyday living and thus, indirectly at least, relates to personality.

Extensive research has demonstrated that there is an impressive degree of variability in physical and physiological characteristics. A person is biochemically and anatomically unique. Williams (1956) has shown that the organs of the body such as the heart, glands, and stomach, differ markedly in size and shape, and that the chemical composition of bodily fluids show great variability. Reactions to pain, stress, and drugs are also diverse. However, a person's behavior arises from both personal experiences and

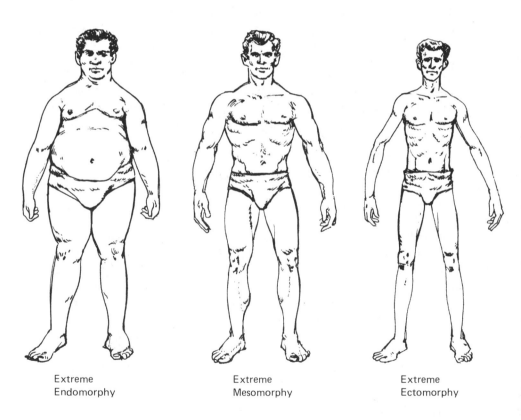

Extreme   Extreme   Extreme
Endomorphy   Mesomorphy   Ectomorphy

FIGURE 6-2 Sheldon's Somatotypes. (From D. Krech, R.S. Crutchfield, and N. Livson, *Elements of Psychology.* Knopf, 1969, p. 736.)

the social environment, and thus it is not to be expected that differences in behavior will be a direct result of somatic differences. Just as the degree to which a person gets "high" on drugs or drunk on alcohol depends partly on his or her expectations and on social stimulation, any other bodily function is influenced in its expression by the circumstances in which it occurs.

This discussion brings us to the third area of biological assessment that has implications for personality—the *physiochemical indexes*. As Milton and Diesenhaus (1972) point out, the aims of those people who are convinced that physiochemical abnormality lies behind all mental aberrations are very high; the great physiologist, Gerard (1956) coined the phrase "no twisted thought without a twisted molecule." Physiologists, psychopharmacologists, and physiological psychologists have carried out many studies, a large number of which have attempted to relate blood extracts and urine measures to schizophrenia and other disorders. Analyses of perspiration, saliva, and cerebrospinal fluid have also been made. It is well known that chemicals inserted into the body, whether prescribed or nonprescribed, have strong effects on behavior and it is also clear that body-produced chemicals are important. The endocrine glands secrete hormones in reaction to stress and anxiety and these hormones in turn have influences throughout the body. Sometimes investigators are misled by the so-called "grapefruit effect." The term derives from one study in which researchers found that blood or urine samples of schizophrenics showed significant differences from normals in certain chemical characteristics, and they excitedly reported their findings. Later, they discovered the hospital breakfasts had included grapefruit, which added the "significant" chemical to the body fluid being studied. Effects of differences in exercise, diet, and drug treatments must be carefully observed in such studies. Analyses of the blood and other fluids have been extremely useful in detecting organic or physical disorders but so far, despite periodic enthusiasms, there have been no breakthroughs in the understanding of personality or psychopathology. Barchas et al. (1971, p. 291) summarize as follows:

> In terms of psychological assessment, it is as yet too early to say what the role of these compounds and of the various means of measurement of them will be in assessing behavior of individuals. Nevertheless, it has become increasingly clear that these neuroregulatory agents are involved in basic forms of behavior and that investigation of their role in behavior is highly pertinent to a deeper understanding of severe mental illnesses. Over the coming years, one can expect that tests for these compounds and their metabolic products will be of potential importance in diagnosis and differentiation of severe mental illnesses. Hopefully, there will be increasing collaboration between investigators, biochemical and psychological, concerned with psychological assessment.

ASSESSING PERSONALITY WITH
NEUROPHYSIOLOGICAL METHODS

The final and most widely used category of measures is *neurophysiological procedures.* Within that category, the most common assessment device is the *polygraph,* popularly known as the "lie detector." The typical polygraph makes a continuous recording of three channels of physiological data—the galvanic skin response (GSR), heart rate, and respiration. Wires connected to the palm of the hand measure changes in skin resistance to a mild electrical current as perspiration increases or decreases. The "cardio" channel records changes in upper arm volume as the pulse affects a tight cuff (plethysmograph) around it. The third channel records changes in an expandable belt around the subject's chest. A recent innovation used with some instruments is a fourth channel that records certain low voice frequencies that are said to diminish under stress (Lykken, 1974).

In a lie detection interrogation, the subject is asked questions while he or she gives associations to a list of words. The assessor establishes at the beginning an individual baseline on the polygraph, after the subject has become used to the apparatus and the procedure. Deviations from baseline as the person answers certain critical questions are the usual basis for "lie detection." In addition, the assessor may insert some items in the series that he thinks are likely to have special meaning to the individual if he or she is guilty. In police interrogation, for example, words may be included that are related to the crime but unlikely to be of importance to anyone who does not know the details of the crime. Lykken (1974), in an excellent critique calls this latter procedure a "guilty knowledge test" and advocates much more extensive use of that technique rather than the "lie detection," which merely looks for unusual polygraph deviations in response to a series of questions. For instance a guilty knowledge test might involve showing an accused bank robber a series of photographs, one of which is of the teller at the window where the robbery occurred. In work with neurotics, items that relate to personal problems are included. The extent of deviation on the polygraph as well as the person's hesitancy in responding are useful for locating especially meaningful areas. It should be noted that the procedure does not reveal lying as such. It is simply a measure of emotionality. One clinician used the process to uncover hysterical repression. An adolescent girl, fearfully unable to cope with family problems, suddenly became deaf. The clinical psychologist gained the girl's permission to use the polygraph with the understanding that it would show emotional response to words if she could hear. Standing behind her, the clinician read a list of words, to which she did indeed respond with emotion. With this demonstration to herself that she could hear, the girl made a rapid recovery.

Measures of changes in the galvanic skin response, respiration, blood pressure, and heart rate may be used independently of the polygraph to study reactions to stress in connection with personality research. For instance, an interesting study of "interpersonal physiology" used correspondence between the client's and psychotherapist's heart rates as a measure of rapport. Attaching an apparatus to both members in the interview, DiMascio, Boyd, and Greenblatt (1957) found a tendency for their hearts to speed up and slow down together in discussions that were judged to express tension or tension release; however, when the client expressed antagonism, his heart rate decreased but the therapist's heart rate increased. In another study of heart rate, Darley and Katz (1973) found that fifth grade boys working on a quantitative estimations task responded differently when told that the task was a game (heart rate deceleration) rather than a test (heart acceleration).

There are several related measures. One unusual device is the penile plethysmograph, that measures the volume of the penis as a function of blood supply. This test has been used in the behavior therapies for sexual problems (Bancroft, 1971; Barlow et al., 1970). Freund, who was one of the first to use this instrument (1963, Freund et al., 1965), claims to have sorted out males who faked homosexuality to avoid military service by measuring reactions in viewing erotic stimuli. Other investigators (Cohen & Shapiro, 1971; Geer, 1975) have developed an index of female sexual arousal. The *pupillary response* (dilation of the pupil of the eye) has been mechanically measured as an indication of interest in what the person is viewing (Hess, 1968). Cattell (1965) has incorporated a wide variety of physiological measures in his factor-analytic studies of personality traits. For instance, he uses a perceptual phenomenon called *flicker fusion,* the point at which the nervous system integrates lights flashing at varying intervals into one continuous light. This procedure has been used in the diagnosis of brain damage, and there is a suggestion that high thresholds are related to impulsiveness and restlessness (Cattell & Warburton, 1967).

Electronic amplifiers are used to increase bioelectric signals so that they can be easily observed and recorded. One example is the electrocardiograph (EKG) that, like the polygraph, produces a record by the movement of pens over a running tape. To produce the EKG the operator attaches several pads with wires to different parts of the body near the heart and major arteries. These "leads" record differences in electrical activity as the heart beats and sends volleys of blood through the arteries. Similar procedures with leads placed on muscles produce electromyographic (EMG) records. A dramatic use of such physiological measurement in behavior therapy (aversive therapy, to be discussed in the next chapter) is reported by Lang (1971b, p. 76).

Recently I was asked to treat a nine-month old boy who regularly vomited his entire meal immediately after eating. When I first saw him he was in an advanced state of dehydration and malnutrition. He weighed less than 12 pounds, was being fed through a stomach pump, and was not expected to live.

Extensive medical tests showed that his condition was not organic. I'm still not sure how he learned this response, but we know that what is learned usually can be unlearned. I measured the muscle potentials along the infant's esophagus and found that on the graph paper I could detect the first wave of reverse peristalsis that just preceded regurgitation. I arranged an apparatus to give aversive electric shocks to his leg whenever his esophagus started to back up, which continued until vomiting had ceased. After only a few meals with this therapy the infant ceased to vomit. He is now a healthy toddler.

Another widely used physiological instrument is the *electroencephalograph* (EEG). In 1929 Berger discovered that electrodes placed on the human scalp would produce characteristic signals that could be amplified and recorded. There are several "brain wave" rhythms—alpha, beta, delta, and theta. The reading of the tracings, though sometimes assisted by electronic and computer analyzers, requires considerable training. Figure 6-3 shows an EEG tracing. Abnormal EEGs are most commonly found in cases of brain damage such as epileptics and persons with psychomotor seizures. They are also found in a sizable proportion of schizophrenics, mental defectives, and sociopaths. An abnormal brain wave pattern is not an invariable symptom of these functional disorders; many psychiatric cases have normal patterns. The EEG is useful for personality related research, for instance in studies of arousal or stages of sleep. It is also used to determine sedation thresholds in various psychiatric disorders.

One very interesting development in the late 60s and 70s arose from the discovery that cerebral electrical activity could be subjected to operant conditioning. For example, the EEG machine can be arranged to give the subject feedback, perhaps a "beeping" sound, when the alpha rhythm (an electrical pattern of eight to twelve cycles per second, predominant in a state of relaxed wakefulness) reaches a certain level. With relatively short practice, a person, by "looking in a physiological mirror" so to speak, can learn to increase the amount of time when alpha is dominant, producing a pleasant, relaxed experience. One study (Johnson & Meyer, 1974) found that subjects who scored high on a paper and pencil measure of their belief in being in control of themselves, learned control alpha rhythms better than those without that belief. This control is only one form of *biofeedback*. Other kinds of apparatus can be used for subjects to learn how to increase or decrease their own blood pressure, gastric secretions, and heart rate. The implications of this new technology for treatment of psychosomatic conditions such as ulcers are promising. There are reports (Lang, 1971) of cardiac patients reducing pathological arhythmias through feedback and conditioning, and of the use of feedback to treat cardiac neurosis (Wickramasekera, 1974). Though this is a new technical discovery, the process of self-control of breathing, heart rate, stomach contractions, skin temperature, and other bodily phenomena has been practiced by Hindu yogis for centuries, some of them have demonstrated great prowess to Western scientists (Green et al., 1970).

Another important area in the search for the relationship between psychological and physiological functions is the phenomenon of *stress*. Richard Lazarus and his colleagues (1965, 1966) have conducted a series of investigations on the effects of different defensive sets, or instructions, on psychophysiological reactions. One film entitled "Corn Farming in Iowa" elicited practically no emotional reaction. Another film "Subcision Rites Among the Arunta," showing the ritual genital mutilation of adolescent boys among aboriginals in Australia, elicited a strong reaction in blood pressure and GSR's. Lazarus et al. (1962) found that some subjects who verbally disclaimed disturbance showed it physiologically. In another study, Lazarus used different instructions to inculcate "defense mechanisms" against anxiety. He found that denial ("It does not actually hurt; these are very kind old men doing this") worked "better" with less educated workers than intellectualization. But intellectualizing sets ("Anthropologists have

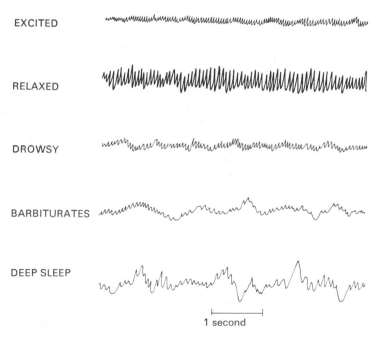

FIGURE 6-3 Normal EEG waveforms taken from the intact human skull during various states. (From Kleinmuntz, 1970, p. 175. Copyright © 1970 by Holt, Rinehart and Winston, Inc. Reprinted by permission.)

made numerous studies of puberty rites; this is how primitive people establish the new status of a young person"), reduced anxiety "better" with well educated students, Figure 6–4 (Taken from Lazarus et al., 1965) shows the modulating effects of suggested orientations on the galvanic skin response while subjects watched a series of bloody accidents. The three peaks come at times of most intense arousal. In trying to understand coping with the environment, Lazarus and his co-workers emphasize the importance of the assessment of the person's thinking processes that evaluate the significance of environmental events.

CRITIQUE

No one denies the importance of understanding the somatic system and its relationship to behavior and feelings. The close connection between organismic reaction and environmental events has been demonstrated in many ways. One important concept is the "orienting reaction" to novel stimuli or rapid change in stimulation (Sokolov, 1963). It is comprised of many autonomic nervous system responses, such as dilation of the pupils,

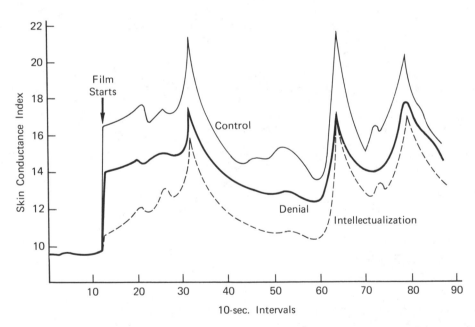

FIGURE 6–4 Effects of instructions for denial and intellectualization on GSR of subjects watching an anxiety-arousing film. (From Lazarus et al., 1965, p. 628. Copyright © 1965 by Duke University Press.)

breathing irregularities, increased palmar sweating, and increased blood supply to the head, accompanied by decreased blood to limbs and periphery. Some physiological psychologists also identify a defensive reaction that has other systemic effects and prepares the person for either a fight or flight. Such arousal patterns are multidimensional and complex (Lacey, 1967), and as yet are far from fully understood. It seems clear that these complex physiological reactions have served powerful adaptive purposes in the evolution of human beings. They cannot be looked at as simply negative indicators—measures of tension, stress, or anxiety. An extensive review of the applications of psychophysiological approaches to social psychology (Shapiro & Crider, 1969, p. 38–39) concludes that,

> The correlations among physiological variables show a great deal of variation across stimulus conditions. This single fact makes chimerical any notion of a unitary arousal dimension, and indicates that a single measure cannot be used to gauge the state of the organism. This necessary conclusion becomes a virtue, however, when it is seen that physiological processes are reliably patterned as a function of the environmental context. . . . The striking variability in physiological activity seen even in normal populations can certainly be partially attributed to the same socio-psychological processes that mold individual differences in overt behavior. If social setting modifies internal events, it is equally true that these events exert regulatory influences on the individual's social behavior. . . . At higher levels of analysis, a view of the continuous inter-relationship of systems should be possible.

The present picture of psychophysiological assessment procedures is both positive and negative. They are important and are likely to be of greater importance in the future, as theories and basic research clarify these complex connections, but the very complexity makes much of the research to date questionable and rudimentary, and makes practical application to individuals even more questionable. With the exception of a few techniques with a long history of use, such as the polygraph in lie detection, there are few procedures that are well enough developed to recommend them for individual applied usage. (And even the lie detector is very poorly used by many; see Lykken, 1974.)

Another conclusion that seems warranted from a review of the work in this area is that research on psychophysiological connections is becoming more specialized and technologized. Lang (1971) points out the advantages of polygraphic measurement, its continuous assessment record, and its many functions simultaneously recorded. He then adds (p. 94) that, "to the beginning investigator this asset often seems like a Pyrrhic victory over ignorance, as he faces the miles of paper or magnetic tape records that can result from a single experiment." However, technology is also coming to aid in the analysis, as on-line computers are attached to recording apparatuses.

One result of this increasing specialization is that gross concepts like "anxiety," "arousal," and "stress" are becoming less useful except as general "chapter titles" for an area of investigation. They are also being reformulated. Many psychologists had assumed that autonomic nervous system arousal was negative, and indicative of tension. Some investigators are now beginning to see that the *absence* of arousal may be pathological, and that so-called stress responses are really attempts to assist the person in coping with the environment. (Shapiro & Crider, 1969)

Finally, it is important to keep in mind that we should not attribute too much mystique to psychophysiological measures. Averill & Opton (1968, p. 288) conclude:

> Psychophysiological techniques possess certain unique advantages and liabilities, which can be, and often are, overemphasized. It sometimes seems that a physiological variable is recorded primarily because it lends an air of objectivity, or because it is considered to be somehow more "fundamental" . . . . One does not need elaborate recorders or massive computers to do meaningful research. Many important findings are amazingly simple, both conceptually and technically—once the appropriate question has been asked.

Somewhat similarly Millon & Diesenhaus (1972, p. 82) say:

> Psychological test users need not be intimidated; their "subject" matter is no less complex, and biophysical measures exhibit more, rather than fewer, shortcomings and limitations. Most biophysical instruments generate less discriminating data, have fewer norms to guide interpretation, exhibit lower reliability coefficients, rarely are subjected to validity studies, and involve considerable expense and professional time.

So, with this report of the state of the biopsychological assessment art, let us move on to the three major approaches to personality assessment in the next three chapters. Biopsychological assessment of personality is still in its infancy. But like most babies, it shows vitality and curiosity and promises much for the future.

SUMMARY

In this chapter we have first looked at the general problem of assessing the biological level as it relates to personality, with its important implications for feelings and behavior. We have taken special note of one major assessment problem—physical damage to the brain—and have seen its importance not only for the initial detection and treatment but also for the vocational rehabilitation of the person already brain damaged. A battery testing several different functions, like the Halstead-Reitan, seems to be most useful in this field, although the Bender is often used for a limited sample of visual-motor behavior, and intelligence tests and interviews often give important information.

The search for physical and psychophysiological measures of personality has a long history. It has led to four approaches: the genetic, anatomical, physiochemical, and neurophysiological. All these approaches provide interesting and promising research findings, but as yet, with possibly a few exceptions, they do not offer practical procedures for the personality assessment of individuals. They have made greater contributions in detecting organic problems, such as genetic inheritance of certain mentally retarded conditions, and electroencephalographic characteristics of epileptics and other abnormal brain conditions. Sheldon's somatotyping of general body form into degrees of endomorphy, mesomorphy, and ectomorphy has not been productive of clear connections with personality. The most widely used instrument for individual assessment is the polygraph or lie detector. A wide variety of other neurophysiological procedures is available for research by psychologists and others in the behavioral sciences. Among individual indicators, probably the most commonly used is the galvanic skin response, which shows differences in electrical conductivity between two electrodes, as sweat glands respond to emotional changes.

A number of experts, however, recommend that research be conducted on patterns of responses, not just single psychobiological indexes. Though the area is complex and present assessment devices are useful mainly for research, the promise for the future is intriguing. We can expect that a book like this one written ten years from now will have much clearer data about individual biopsychological assessment.

SUGGESTED READINGS

LANG, P. J. The application of psychophysiological methods to the study of psychotherapy and behavior modification. In A. E. Bergin & S. L. Garfield (eds.) *Handbook of psychotherapy and behavior change: An empirical analysis.* New York: Wiley, 1971, 75–125. Lang provides an excellent introduction to the methodology of biopsychological assessment. He explains the rudiments of physiological recording, provides background information on the functioning of the autonomic nervous system, and discusses the issues and evidence on response specificity. For a review of EEG literature and a critique of Eysenck's theories, see Gale in Kline (1974).

LAZARUS, R. S. Stress. In D. L. Sills (ed.) *International encyclopedia of the social sciences.* New York: Macmillan and Free Press, 1968, 337–348. Lazarus, who has probably done more research on stress than any other psychologist, discusses the concept of stress, its indicators, its relation to threat, frustration, and conflict and methods for measuring stress. He briefly explains his own cognitive approach to stress and the defense mechanisms which are used in coping with it. Those interested in biofeedback and the application of learning principles to reactions to stress, will find the articles by Kimmel (1974), Lazarus (1975), and Paskewitz (1975) helpful.

LYKKEN, D. T. Psychology and the lie detector industry. *American Psychologist,* 1974, 29, 725–739. Lykken states that several million polygraphic examinations are conducted annually not just in police interrogation but increasingly for employee screening. He explains how the polygraph works and critically examines interviewing and recording procedures. In addition to the usual "lie detection" methods whereby the assessor simply looks for deviations on critical questions, Lykken advocates the use of the Guilty Knowledge Technique. Lykken questions some of the reports of high validity for the polygraph and urges further study.

REITAN, R. M. Assessment of brain-behavior relationships. In P. McReynolds (ed.) *Advances in psychological assessment.* Vol. 3. San Francisco: Jossey-Bass, 1975. 186–242. This article by a leading expert in the field presents detailed neuropsychological examination procedures emphasizing the Halstead-Reitan battery. Saunders (1975) describes the contributions which psychologists can make to neuropsychological assessment.

chapter seven

Behavioral Techniques

> *If we are to use the methods of science in the field of human affairs, we must assume that behavior is lawful and determined. We must expect to discover that what a man does is the result of specifiable conditions and that once these conditions have been discovered, we can anticipate and to some extent determine his actions.* —Skinner, *Science and Human Behavior* (1953)

We are now entering the three core chapters of this book, in which we will examine the most commonly used techniques in personality assessment itself. The first method to be discussed, the behavioral techniques, is the newest and it is presently in a rapid stage of development. Coming from learning theory and behavior therapy, this approach rests on special assumptions, and concentrates on certain procedures. In fact, each of the three major assessment approaches looks for different things in the person, and records and emphasizes different aspects. They obtain, as a result, different assessment pictures of individuals—but how different is yet to be determined.

THE THREE MAJOR ASSESSMENT APPROACHES

Table 7-1 compares the three techniques—behavioral, objective, and projective—on their major "thrusts," their aims, the kinds of data and procedures they emphasize, and their theoretical underpinnings. In the following two chapters we will note the characteristics of the objective and projective devices described in Table 7–1. One central distinction to keep in mind is the different uses of the three primary modes of treating data mentioned in chapter one. Behavioral techniques look at obtained information as a *sample,* objective techniques look at behavior as a *correlate* of something else, preferably a useful criterion, and projective techniques see any obtained data as a *sign* of important personal characteristics and inner dynamics. As mentioned in chapter one, any observation and any piece of information about a person can be viewed in each of these three ways. Particular data collecting procedures do not necessarily have to be used by the three chief approaches, but historically they have tended to group around observation, inventories, and unstructured stimuli.

TABLE 7-1   Comparisons of the Three Major Assessment Approaches

	Behavioral Techniques	Objective Techniques	Projective Techniques
Primary Aim:	To determine antecedents and consequents of problem behavior (S–R)	To develop test scores that relate to criteria of problem or solution (R–R)	To elicit material of importance for inferring inner dynamics of person (R–O)
Construction methods:	Individually tailored data collection on problem behavior, counting, recording	Theoretical or empirical scale construction, norms, validity, reliability	Theoretical or impressionistic selection of ambiguous stimuli and classification of signs
Typical stimulus format:	Natural or contrived situations, interviews, report form for own behavior	Paper-and-pencil, self-reporting, verbal personality inventories, attitude scales	Ambiguous, open-ended stimuli, both verbal and non-verbal.
Typical data produced:	Observational reports, coded records, behavior counts	Choices on verbal items, scores, profiles	Perceptual reports, verbal narratives, observations, scores
Obtained data treated as:	Sample	Correlate	Sign
Level of subjective interpretation:	Low	Medium	High

	Behavioral Techniques	Objective Techniques	Projective Techniques
Time scale:	Here and now, plus follow-up of problems	Mixed; predictive	Concerned with childhood history, long range dynamics
Classifications and "language" used:	Behavioral excesses, deficits and inappropriateness; functional analysis; learning terms	Traits, diagnostic categories, psychometric terms, social psychological terms.	Psychodynamic terms; psychiatric categories; perceptual-cognitive terms.
Principal theoretical underpinning:	Behavioral learning theory, functional analysis, Skinner, Bandura, Wolpe.	Trait and factor theories, attitude theories; psychometrics, Hathaway, Meehl, Cronbach, Cattell, Guilford	Psychoanalysis, perceptual-cognitive theories, Freud, Murray, Rorschach
Examples of assessment instruments:	Few standard devices; Behavioral Coding System, Fear Survey Schedules	Many standardized inventories and scales, MMPI, CPI, Strong, EPPS, PRF, A-V-L, F scale	Great variety, Rorschach, TAT, Sentence Completion, Draw-A-Person, Bender, World Test, play situations

All assessment is, of course, assessment of behavior. Broadly defined, behavior includes verbal reports of feelings and thoughts, or the checking of answers on a questionnaire. This chapter will concentrate, however, on actions and motor performance observable from outside the person. It will necessarily include verbal behavior, too, but the concern rests with the way verbalizations relate to what a person *does,* not just his or her reported thoughts and feelings. One cannot change behavior, behaviorists aver, without changing the antecedent stimuli and/or the reward system external to the organism. Behaviorists, however, concentrate less on an analysis of groups interaction and the organization and the dimensions of social systems (which we covered in chapter five) than on individual behavior and its immediate environmental relations.

Many behaviorists also make use of the psychophysiological measures mentioned in the last chapter. Lang's treatment of the nine-month-old boy who vomited is an example. In general, as the number of behaviorally oriented clinicians has grown in the 60s and 70s, they have spread out to make adaptations and innovations with instruments and ideas used in other less action-oriented areas of psychology such as cognitive and self-talk therapies. The breadth of the spectrum of work included in behavior therapy and behavior modification is expressed by the statement of Davison & Neale (1974, p. 485) that "Initially the approach was restricted to therapy based on classical and operant conditioning, but today it is viewed more broadly as applied experimental psychology." In this chapter, we will explore the background of behavioral or functional analysis, present a variety of assessment procedures, and critique the behavioral approach.

ILLUSTRATION OF BEHAVIOR MODIFICATION

Behavioral assessment is intimately tied to treatment, as this case reported by Allen et al. (1964) will illustrate. Ann was an attractive and capable four-year-old from a well to do family. Her parents and teachers noticed that she had progressively isolated herself from other children and demanded attention from adults, usually successfully. Ann was slipping into a vicious circle where the more she failed to develop friendships with other children, the more she depended on adults. With the cooperation of the parents, the teachers at her nursery school developed a therapeutic plan. The plan involved rewarding Ann's behavior if it related to children but not if it related to adults. The plan followed operant conditioning procedure, which will be explained in the next section.

As part of the assessment, two observers sampled and recorded Ann's interactions with adults and children at regular ten-second intervals. They kept a record for five days to obtain a *baseline,* and then began the therapeutic activities. Whenever Ann started to interact with children, an adult quickly showed interest and rewarded her. Even going near another child was followed promptly by attention. The teacher might say "You three girls have a cozy house. Here are some more cups, Ann, for your tea party." On the other hand, whenever Ann started to leave her playmates or make solitary contacts with adults, the teachers stopped showing interest. Figure 7–1 shows the data that the observers collected on Ann's interaction with children and adults through several periods—the baseline, the reinforcement period, a "reversal" period (in which the effects of the reinforcements were tested by stopping them and Ann's behavior went back to baseline), continued reinforcement, and follow-up.

The chart shows that at the beginning Ann spent about 10 percent of her time with children and 40 percent with adults; in the follow-up period the rates were almost exactly reversed. Now Ann did not demand attention from adults and readily played with other children. The natural pleasures of play with others maintained her child contacts. Similar methods are used with problems of chronic schizophrenics in hospitals, college students with fears of giving speeches, stutterers, and in many other cases.

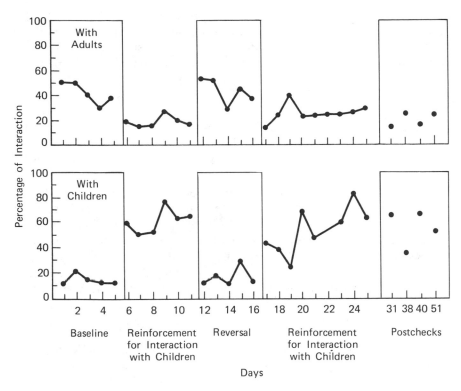

FIGURE 7-1 Percentages of time during morning sessions when Ann interacted with adults and children. (From Allen, K. E., Hart, B., Buell, J. S., Harris, E. R., and Wolf, M. M., "Effects of social reinforcement on isolated behavior of a nursery school child," *Child Development,* 1964, *35,* p. 515. Copyright © 1964 by The Society for Research in Child Development, Inc., The University of Chicago Press.)

CONCEPTS FOR FUNCTIONAL ANALYSIS
OF BEHAVIOR

In the 1960s a large group of experimenters and practitioners, basing their efforts on Skinner's research (1938 and later) and Wolpe's conditioning therapy (1958) developed what is variously called "behavior modification," "behavior therapy," or "behavioral engineering," under the conceptual frameworks of classical and operant conditioning or what is sometimes called "social learning theory." The term Bijou and Peterson (1971) use for assessment under this system is the term Skinner used in referring to analysis of behavior in terms of cause and effect—"functional analysis." Under this name they describe procedures of problem identification, planning treatment, and evaluation in clinical work with children. Using a different label, "behavioral personality assessment," Goldfried and Sprafkin (1974) summarize many of the same procedures, and expand on their applicability to adults. Kanfer and Saslow (1965, 1969) provided one of the first general guides for functional analysis in the assessment of adults in psychiatric situations, including such topics as analysis and clarification of the problem situation, motivation, development, self-control, social relations, and the social-cultural-physical environment.

Two major kinds of learning experiments have provided the scientific basis for behavioral treatments—classical and operant conditioning. *Classical conditioning* derives from the famous studies of Pavlov in which a bell (the conditioned stimulus) presented shortly before a morsel of food (the unconditioned stimulus) came to elicit salivation in dogs by itself. Applying this principle to a human situation, Watson found a rat (the to-be-continued stimulus) repeatedly paired with an unpleasant loud noise (the unconditioned stimulus) developed in a child a fear of rats and other furry objects in the famous case of Albert. Later, in 1924, Mary Cover Jones eliminated a fear of furry animals in another child by bringing furry objects gradually closer in the presense of pleasant stimuli, such as food (Jones, 1974).

The other kind of learning is *operant conditioning.* The Skinnerian term "operant," refers to behavior that is controlled by its consequences. The behavior operates relative to a following *reinforcement,* a reward or punishment that acts to increase or decrease the likelihood of the act's re-occurrence. Skinner points out that behavior is going on all the time, and much of it apparently random. It is not necessary to know the exact stimulus for any action. One identifies the situation in which the behavior occurs and the reinforcements that accompany it or may influence it. Then in the future the behavior in that situation and situations to which it will generalize can be controlled. Most behavioral clinicians use both classical and operant conditioning. Sometimes it is appropriate to teach new responses by repeated pairing of unwanted habits or fears with forceful stimuli such as electric shock or deep relaxation. Sometimes it is more appropriate to arrange environmental reinforcements for specific desired responses. In one case most attention is given to assessing stimulus conditions; in the other to reinforcement conditions.

In a complete behavioral assessment then, one is looking for stimulus-response-reinforcement relationships that are the conditions under which behavior occurs. It should be noted that the assessor is dealing with stimulus-response (S–R) predictions, not just response-response (R–R) predictions. In objective testing, the assessor obtains a person's responses to a personality inventory from which he or she tries to predict responses in other real-life situations such as response to drug treatment, occurrence of parole violation, or performance in college. In projective testing the assessor is interested in response-organism (R–O) connections, or the implications of responses for internal states of the organism. In functional analysis however, the assessor trys to say that if situation X occurs, the person is likely to do Y. For example, if children in a classroom situation are rewarded (by teacher's praise or some indicator on their desks) for staying in their seats and working rather than moving around hyperactively, they will increase the amount of time they do their schoolwork in their places. The specification of conditions involves both the ascertaining of *antecedents,* what went on before the critical behavior, and *consequents,* what happened afterward, especially with regard to positive or negative reinforcement. The *timing* of reinforcement is very important; immediacy is necessary, though it can be in the form of tokens for later rewards. Understanding of the *generalization* of a habit to similar situations is important because responses tend to be situation specific. Functional analysis is more situation oriented and treatment oriented than the traditional psychometric approach; assessment is intertwined with intervention or training processes. A treatment program of managing the nature of the stimulus situation or the *contingencies* of reinforcement (the timing and nature of reward or punishment) *shapes* the behavior gradually toward what is desired.

Most adherents to the Skinnerian approach deny the value of looking for hypothetical internal variables. Bijou and Peterson (1971) say that it is necessary to conclude that a child who typically hits other children has a "need for aggression." It is sufficient to simply state what kind of behavior occurred or to say that he or she is "aggressive," which is to use only a descriptive generalization about behavior. Behavior is treated as a *sample,* a selection from a larger number of events. Unlike traditional psychoanalytic thinking or much medical thinking, the "symptom" a patient or client brings to a clinic or hospital is not seen simply as the surface manifestation of an underlying cause. The manifest behavior is important in itself, and the object of assessment is to identify the important symptoms and plan their change.

While the assessment in Skinnerian behavior modification consists primarily of observations of behavior itself, the broader behavioral movement has stimulated a variety of approaches, some of which require that inner states and cognitive variables be assessed. Bandura (1969) and his associates have shown the value of *modelling* desired behavior. By observing others directly or on film, individuals learn what kind of behavior is rewarded and valued. The implication of this research, for television in relation to community mental health, and other applied psychology such as advertising, is considerable. Wolpe (1958) treats patients who have excessive fears by *systematic desensitization*. This procedure often involves *guided imagery*—the imagining of mildly disturbing scenes while the patient is encouraged to relax; as he or she becomes less anxious with repeated imagined exposures to one scene, the therapist asks the patient to move on to scenes that were originally more fearful, until he or she is able to practice new behaviors without agitation, first mentally and than actually. A. A. Lazarus (1971), who also has done a great deal of work with desensitization, has emphasized that in order to prevent relapses, the patient needs to develop more generalized self-concepts and social attitudes. Thus behavior therapy may merge into the cognitive concepts that Skinner scrupulously repudiated.

One other important clinical theorist is Julian Rotter (1954). He was an early proponent of the social learning approach to clinical problems. He and his associates (Rotter, Chance, & Phares, 1972) have developed extensive techniques for assessment and treatment which incorporate cognitive elements, such as *expectancies* for reinforcement, thus bringing hypothesized internal constructs to this field. One of their assessment procedures, a scale describing the locus of control of reinforcement, is briefly discussed in chapter ten.

A few more assumptions that underlie functional analysis should be mentioned. In this approach it is assumed that current problematic behavior was not only learned relative to an environment, but is *maintained* by conditions in the current environment, either external, internal, or both. Those conditions act to preserve even behavior that is consciously disliked by the client. Alcohol and heroin give temporary release to addicts. Sexual exhibitionism or sadism are stimulating for a time, though the person may have regrets later. A child throwing a temper tantrum may get some rare attention from his mother. Destructive behavior may proliferate in the absence of support for positive behaviors. The implication for assessment is that the assessor and client must look closely at both the immediate rewards and the potential for alternative responses in the client's behavior repertoire.

Another aspect of this kind of assessment is the emphasis on monitoring change over time, empirically recording increases and decreases in the target behavior relative to changes in the physical conditions or the behavior of caretakers and significant people in the person's environment. Thus observational procedures, as discussed in earlier chapters, must make provision for clearly specifying behavior, coding it, and checking on its reliability. If, as is often the case, these observers are people in the natural environment such as mothers in the home, teachers in schools, or psychiatric aides on a hospital ward, then considerable attention must be given to training them for the observational task. Some behavior or social learning therapists such as Patterson (1971) and Tharp and Wetzel (1969) design improvement programs specifically for *natural caretakers*. They train these mediators, who are often community members such as housewives, for the detailed recording of behavior and for treatment itself. As illustrated in Ann's case, presented earlier, observation typically takes place in several phases: before treatment to establish a *baseline* for further comparison; during *intervention*; often during a *reversal*, to check the effects of the program when the reinforcement contingencies are discontinued; and finally, during a *follow-up* after treatment. To make sure that the treatment program persists, the psychologist may arrange for a "booster shot" of behavioral training during the follow-up period.

Goal-setting for behavior change is a crucial part of functional analysis. The assessor must help decide which behaviors are to be reinforced and which ones are to be diminished or eliminated. Ideally this process involves close cooperation with the client. As the client reviews the symptoms and problems with the clinician or teacher, a decision is made as to what she or he would like to do—overcome a fear, lose weight, stop quarreling in the family, or develop good study habits. Sometimes the client is only minimally involved where the primary goal-setting is done by others. For example, parents work out desirable behaviors for a young child and institutional staff start a program for deteriorated psychotic patients or retarded children. Whenever possible, however, the program is developed *with* the client, and assessment procedures are clearly explained because the psychologist wants the client to be fully involved. To specify this involvement, initial assessment leads to a "contract" between the client and the clinician for the treatment program.

A particularly high degree of client responsibility is involved in behavioral *self-control programs,* another special development of the social learning approach. Thoreson and Mahoney (1974) present an excellent overview of how a person might apply functional analysis to his or her own life. This approach involves self-observation, self-reward, aversive self-regulation, and control through self-talk, and the comments made in an earlier section about the special difficulties of self-observation must be kept in mind. Figure 7–2, taken from Thorenson and Mahoney (1974, p. 15), summarizes the component processes of a systems model for self-control. The antecedent initiating stimuli (AIS) are cues in the situation that precede the controlled response (CR), that may be either positive or negative. For instance a person trying to control overeating comes to a candy machine in the hall; situational stimuli in this analysis include both internal hunger pangs and the sight of the candy. A positive controlled response would be behavior such as walking on down the hall or taking a drink of water; a negative controlled response would be the undesired behavior of taking the candy and over-eating. A conscious choice may be involved that is related to the SCR, or a self-controlling response (either an internalized thought or external action), which in this system has an influence on the consequences of

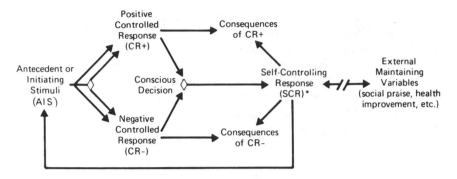

*Self-Controlling Responses (SCRs):

1. Environmental Planning

    a) AIS modification (stimulus control) and preprogramming of CR consequences
    b) Self-regulated stimulus exposure (e.g., self-administered desensitization)
    c) Self-instructions

2. Behavioral Programming

    a) Self-observation
    b) Self-reward (positive and negative, overt and covert)
    c) Self-punishment (positive and negative, overt and covert)

FIGURE 7-2 A systems model of self-control. (From Thoresen & Mahoney, 1974, p. 15. Copyright ©1974 by Holt, Rinehart and Winston, Inc. Reprinted by permission of Holt, Rinehart and Winston, Inc.)

the controlled responses and feeds back to the originating situation (AIS). For instance, one may regulate behavior through rewarding noneating by treating oneself to one's favorite music, punishing oneself for eating by taking an extra walk around the block, or avoiding the situation, not going by the candy machine, in the future.

Throughout this description of functional analysis, the reader will have noted that the persistent emphasis is on *specification* of behavior— exactly what is done when and where by whom. The assessment is also highly *individualized,* and reports in the literature are frequently on single cases. Assessment procedures are often custom-made for particular situations. As the reader might guess, high specification and individualization often make functional analysis of behavior very time consuming and expensive.

BEHAVIORAL ASSESSMENT TECHNIQUES

Despite the great concern for careful specification and objectivity, most people doing behavior modification are still quite "clinical." This is true particularly in the initial phases of assessment, when the assessor identifies the difficulty, examines the situation and the person's behavioral repertoire, and determines the plans for intervention. Thus the first step is likely to involve interviewing rather than observation. The assessor talks with the client and the informants, insisting not on trait descriptions, but on detailed reports of episodes and the surrounding conditions under which the problematic behavior occurred. As Peterson (1968, pp. 121-122) indicates in his guide to an interview, the assessor keeps trying to help the client carefully define the problem and its history. He asks questions such as "How long has this been going on?" "Where does the problem usually come up?" "When was it the worst, and what was going on then?" "When was it better?" "When it happened last time, were there other people around? Who? What were they doing?" "What were you thinking at the time?" "What happened afterward?" "You have thought a lot about the problem; what do you think might be done to improve the situation?" Most people can give considerable detail, but many have not observed very well and are so concerned with their own feelings that they have difficulty reporting their actions. Mischel (1968, p. 239) says "Just as the psychologist interested in identity, or ego strength or anxiety must find public referents to help specify what he means, so must the client find public referents for his personal problems and objectives." Differences in perceptions of action and situations also appear when several informants are interviewed. The interviewer will explore not only the present and past of the behavioral problems but also potential behaviors. She or he may test the client's ability to explore reactions to hypothetical situations, looking for clues as to what might be done in treatment. Morganstern (1976), in an excellent introduction to behavioral interviewing, advocates a multi-faceted strategy focusing on the antecedents, behaviors, and consequences (ABC's) of targeted problems.

Problem checklists can be a helpful supplement to the interview. They assist the assessor in reviewing all the behavioral domain and the person's disturbances and complaints. Peterson (1961) and Quay (1966) provided lists specifically for children. Lang and Lazovik (1963) developed a Fear Survey Schedule. Geer (1965) found that specific items, such as fear of snakes or public criticism, correlated well (.52 to .92) with fear reactions when subjects were placed in actual situations eliciting such fears. In medical settings, the Cornell Medical Index can be used to survey physical and psychiatric complaints, and in college settings, the Moody Problem Checklist and the Survey of Study Habits and Attitudes cover the many possible problems that young adults bring to a counseling center or mental health clinic. Goldfried & D'Zurilla (1973) have found the latter procedure particularly useful in research on freshman effectiveness in handling academic course material.

Behaviorists generally find psychiatric diagnostic classification of little use. Instead, they separate behavior problems into three general classes: *behavioral excesses,* which include such problems as overeating, hyperactivity, and compulsive hand-washing, *behavior deficits,* which include lack of social skills, poor study habits, or psychotic lack of ability to communicate or control oneself, and *behavioral inappropriateness,* which covers a large number of examples such as enuresis, talking to imaginary people, masturbation in public, and stealing. Each of these behaviors suggests somewhat different approaches to treatment. A behavioral excess suggests treatment through nonreward of the problem behavior and the setting up of a conflicting kind of activity; a deficit suggests a program of training; and inappropriateness suggests programs for differentiating proper from improper occasions for the activity, and obtaining more direct feedback from the environment. In addition the assessor surveys the client's behavioral repertoire of positive activities, or *behavioral assets,* skills, and achievements that might be more heavily emphasized in replacing undesirable behaviors. A more complete classification system would also take into account the stimulus control factors and incentives in the environment (Bandura, 1968).

It is especially important to determine what is reinforcing to the individual. The assessor often asks the person to make out or check a *reinforcement list,* indicating what he likes or would like to do. For instance, some psychologists (Lewinsohn & Libet, 1972; MacPhillamy & Lewinsohn, 1974) make use of a Pleasant Events Schedule, a long list of items that the beginning client rates to show how pleasant they are; items such as "Being with happy people," "Having spare time," "Taking a walk," "Having sexual relations," "Reading the newspaper," and "Taking a bath." This list produces a shorter list of the reinforcements most meaningful to the particular individual. In their study, Lewinsohn & Libet found that daily reports of enactment of these reinforcing activities correlated with reported mood in both depressed and normal people. Cautela & Kastenbaum (1967) have produced a more general Reinforcement Survey Schedule, that consists of over ten different factors of varying reliability (Thorndike & Kleinknecht, 1974).

Self-observation and record-keeping is another kind of behavioral assessment. Assessors often ask clients to keep a *daily record* of their problem behaviors, listing the exact conditions under which their anxieties change markedly (Wolpe & Lazarus, 1966). A person might be asked to make a *count* of the number of times he engages in a certain kind of behavior, using a golfer's wrist counter. For instance, every time he smokes a cigarette he pushes the counter. The sheer amount of problem behavior can be ascertained in this way, but in order to work with it, there needs to be more investigation of the preceding and subsequent conditions. Thus the person is often asked to notice or record the surrounding events as well as count the occurrences. Of course, one of the important by-products of self-observation is what one learns about oneself and one's adaptation to the environment;

this in itself may be therapeutic. For instance, McFall (1970) reports positive effects just from self-monitoring smoking behavior.

Observation in the natural environment by outside observers has been discussed in chapter five. The behavior is sometimes recorded by mechanical means. In a classroom, a television camera can be set to take time samples every few minutes, and sometimes cameras or audio-recorders can be used in work situations or at home. In any case the behavior has to be coded for use in functional analysis. Table 7–2 shows the code developed by Patterson, Ray, & Shaw (1968) for recording interactive sequences. Every two minutes the trained observer notes what is happening for fifteen seconds, assisted by a timing mechanism on a clipboard.

TABLE 7–2   Code for observation of parent-child interaction

AP	Approval	DS	Destrictive-ness	NR	No Response	SS	Self-Stimulation
AT	Attention	HR	High Rate	PL	Play	TA	Talk
CM	Command	HU	Humiliate	PN	Negative contact, Physical	TE	Tease
CN	Command (Negative)	IG	Ignore	PP	Positive contact, Physical	TH	Touching, Handing
CO	Compliance	LA	Laugh	PX	Proximity	WH	Whine
CR	Cry	NC	Noncompliance	RC	Receive	WK	Work
DI	Disapproval	NE	Negativism			YE	Yell
DP	Dependency	NO	Normative				

(From Sundberg, Tyler, & Taplin, 1973, p. 374) (based on Patterson, Ray, & Shaw, 1968).

The following sequence illustrates how this system is used. The observer witnesses the interchange between mother and eight-year-old John (taken from Sundberg et al., 1973, p. 373–374).

MOTHER: Please put your sweater on.	CM
JOHN: (Walks into next room, begins to play with toy)	NC, PL
MOTHER: (Ignores John's noncompliance)	IG
JOHN: (Continues to play)	PL
MOTHER: Please, John, put on your sweater, You've just had a cold.	CM
JOHN: So what?	NC, NE
MOTHER: You're the rudest little boy. How you hurt your mother!	DI
JOHN: Damned bitch.	HU
MOTHER: (Strikes at John)	PN
JOHN: (Yells vigorously)	YE

The actual way the coding is reported on the record sheet is:

CM–NC, PL–IG
PL–CM–NC, NE
DI–HU
PN–YE

Such a record can then be studied by the assessor-clinician in order to develop a treatment plan. The clinician reviews the record with the mother and instructs her in altering her behavior, and records will be used for comparisons after the treatment has been started. Patterson and his colleagues (Jones, Reid, & Patterson, 1975) have continued to carry out many research studies with this naturalistic observation technique—the Patterson Behavioral Coding System (BCS). Showing considerable psychometric sophistication, the BCS has good generalizability across occasions and raters, and outside reports of behavior confirm its validity.

Observation in contrived situations (or experimental set-ups analogous to real life) is also used in the functional analysis of behavior. A person or a family may be asked to role play a problem situation, or a child and his mother may be observed while they play together in a playroom with a one-way vision screen. Avoidance responses to feared objects such as dogs or snakes, can be directly measured by exposing fearful persons to these stimuli at various degrees of distance—the Behavioral Avoidance Test (BAT) (Borkovec & Craighead, 1971). A. A. Lazarus (1961) has measured claustrophobia by having a person sit in a room with large French windows on one end opening on a balcony; the assessor closed the windows and slowly moved a screen closer and closer to the person, shortening the space of the room. The assessor instructed the client to say when he felt too uncomfortable; the client could terminate the procedure at any point and open the windows. The closest distance which a fearful person will come to a feared object like a snake is another illustration of BAT. Bandura (1969) uses films extensively to expose people to anxiety-arousing situations in a graded series, teaching them to counteract anxiety by relaxation. The subject can control the film presentations so as not to experience too much anxiety too soon. Mischel (1968) suggests that films be developed concerning the prevalent maladjustments in the culture so that they can be used for preventive purposes.

Traditional psychological *tests* are rarely employed for functional analysis, although some special test-like methods have been proposed. Some assessors ask clients to tell stories in response to pictures of situations that are similar to those in which problem behavior occurs. Rating scales may be used to record characteristics of patients on wards and special testing apparatus has been developed to study reinforcement behavior. For example, Weiss (1968) has studied individual differences in responsiveness to a speaker; the subject is instructed to press a button to "maintain rapport" with a recorded speaker. Weiss has found some evidence for the validity of this procedure by correlating scores with peer ratings and personality inventories. With colleagues, he has also developed inventories of activities and spouse behaviors for use in marital therapy (Weiss, 1977). Another interesting procedure is the inventory by Endler et al. (1962) described in chapter five, in which subjects report the kind of anxious responses they give in different situations. Similarly, Goldfried & D'Zurilla (1969, 1972) asked for responses to verbal descriptions of situations, in their study of competence in college freshmen. From a survey of problematic experiences, situations were selected that had occurred at least once for half of the freshmen. An example of a situation reported by over 90 percent of the freshmen is (p. 175):

> A lengthy composition is due in your English class this Friday. It was assigned a week beforehand and is on a rather difficult topic, which you really don't understand.
>
> On Wednesday afternoon when you sit down to work, you find that you have absolutely no idea about what to include in the paper. You realize, however, that you must start writing the composition soon in order to have it in on time.

Goldfried & D'Zurilla obtained a set of responses for each situation that were rated on their degree of effectiveness, and provided a scoring key. The final questionnaire presented situations in which the subject was asked to imagine himself, and write an account of how he would react. Then judges scores these responses on effectiveness. This behavioral-analytic method of test construction appears to hold great promise. It seems likely that more, similar tests will be developed as time goes on and behavioral technology for handling particular problems becomes more standardized. However, as Mischel (1968, p. 257) points out in discussing the strategy of learning against a criterion,

> (Behavioral) assessment does not necessarily require comparisons between individuals. . . . Criterion-referenced assessments compare the person's performance against a performance standard; norm-referenced assessments compare people against each other [to] indicate the individuals *relative* standing. . . [but] give little or no information about how the individual's behavior compares with a performance standard.

The reader will recall that the movement away from norm-referenced tests and toward criterion-referenced (or performance, expectancy, and self-referenced) tests was discussed in chapter two.

Monitoring behavior during the intervention and the follow-up period involves extensive record keeping. The client frequently keeps a tally of his problem behaviors himself or is shown a chart of daily observations. Thus continuous feedback is provided to the client as well as to the assessor, encouraging motivation for his or her efforts. For example, Axelrod et al. (1974) report the results of a contract worked out with a man who wished to stop smoking. Recording the number of cigarettes smoked, the subject punished himself by tearing up a dollar bill each time he exceeded a determined daily limit, which was decreased steadily. After five days the subject had stopped smoking and still did not smoke at follow-up two years later.

CRITIQUE

There is no doubt about the generative character of the behavior modification movement. More experimentation with new treatment approaches, and more research can probably be credited to the ideas of Skinner, Wolpe, Bandura, and other behavioral and social learning advocates than to any other movement in psychology, with the possible exception of Freud and his followers. If we consider the stimulation of research to be the criterion for the success of a theory (Hall & Lindzey, 1970), then this general approach can be said to be highly successful.

As yet, most of the research on persons, however, has been an experimental, clinical, or educational process, and relatively little research has been devoted to assessment techniques per se. One finds few standardized techniques and little concern for the usual assessment concepts of reliability, validity, and norms. The same general psychometric concepts and principles apply to behavioral measures as to any other; the APA standards for tests (1974) need to be studied by behaviorists, too. Observations of behavior in natural settings come as close to having an intrinsic validity as is possible, but the observation itself, if by an outsider, may be confounded by social influences. If the observational record is kept by the persons themselves, they become conscious of their own actions and may alter them to fit their fears or wishes. Thus the behavioral sample may be biased and not a truly representative.

Behaviorists must also be concerned with validity under the question of generalizability. The problem is the extent that behavior modified in the home or clinic carries over to other situations and other times. Some research (Forsyth & Fairweather, 1961; Paul, 1966; A. A. Lazarus, 1971) suggests limited generalizability and the need to either carry out treatments in a number of situations or to teach the person to generalize. As mentioned before, Patterson includes ''booster shots'' of follow-up training to prevent back-sliding into undesirable behavior.

The most important value established by the behavioral approach is the demand for clear definition, for measurable data on observable behavior. The insistence on defining what people mean by their complaints and goals, and the search for reinforcements that alter behavior, force the researchers and practitioners to think more clearly than they ordinarily do in following other theories, in which there are more slippery concepts and less demand for specification. When assessors or clients lack clear definitions, they tend to use inference more and invent hypothetical causes.

The "proof of the pudding" that behaviorists demand is the usefulness of techniques in changing behavior. The purpose of this book is not to review therapy; let us simply note that some extensive reviews provide an optimistic view of therapeutic effects. One such reviewer (Bergin, 1971) concludes that future research should be directed toward assessing the style of the few practitioners who are very successful, assessing the personal and social problem-solving in natural life, and developing assessment techniques derived from experimental psychology and oriented to specific changes. Zifferblatt (1973) and Kanfer (1975) urge the development of social systems analysis. As noted before, most existing behavioral techniques, especially observation, are expensive in terms of time and training. Whether private individuals or public agencies are willing to shoulder those costs will depend on the demonstrated effectiveness of the whole treatment program and the future development of less expensive methods. (Interested readers are referred to books like Bergin & Garfield, 1971, Sundberg, Tyler, & Taplin, 1973, or Rimm and Masters, 1974, for discussions of behavior modification programs and therapies.)

Some attacks on behavior modification have come from the public, on moral and political grounds. The name has somehow become attached to the coercive manipulation of people and sometimes even to brain surgery to diminish aggressive criminality. The film "A Clockwork Orange" depicts a brutal young man conditioned to become severely sick when he sees sexual objects and violence; in the process he also becomes adversely conditioned to Beethoven's music and has a breakdown when later subjected to the music. Popular writings and newspapers have not adequately separated destructive and unethical "behavior modification" from the usual professional approach which involves close attention to joint formulation of treatment goals with the client and his or her informed consent about procedures. Morganstern (1976) discusses the ethical aspects of therapist influence in the determination of goals and in decisions about accepting what the client says she or he wants.

On the socio-political side of the question, there has been much debate over Skinner's views in *Beyond Freedom and Dignity* (1971). Some critics (Winett & Winkler, 1972) have pointed to the danger of using behavior modification simply to support traditional authority, saying that in the schools the aim seems to be to get children to "be still, be quiet, be docile." Braginsky & Braginsky (1974, pp. 72–73) have attacked behavior modification as a "scientized" version of "Protestant, capitalistic morality of our society-at-large . . . where man can be exploited, degraded, and duped under the name of science." In response, Kanfer & Grimm (1975) note that the application of any technology carries certain values, but "it is a monumental error to confuse and blur the line between technology and its application. To blame the abuses of behavior modification on its principles and techniques is as irrational as blaming airplanes for the napalm bombing in Vietnam." This controversy can be salutory if it reminds people—of any theoretical or technological persuasion—to examine deeply and carefully the goals and values to which they put their efforts.

The major theoretical opponents to a strict behavioral approach are those who prefer to hypothesize internal states and dynamics in personality. These people consider that assessing behavior alone is a superficial procedure that tells us little or nothing about the "real" person. Allport (1961) characterizes behaviorism as a typical American approach in that it views man as a *reactive* being, not as an active, creative organizer of himself and his world. He refers (p. 466) to John Dewey's criticism of the stimulus-response psychology as a "monstrous assumption" of American psychology, treating people as if they responded only to an external goal or an internal need. Allport and others claim that European and Asian psychologies look deeper and see more subtle and *active* aspects of persons. Perhaps behaviorists would respond that, yes, they are indeed attempting a limited task, dealing with observables, but they would challenge others to define just what they mean by their nonobservables. At any rate, behaviorists have become less dogmatic as time has passed. As we have seen, many of them are not averse to using self-observation, self-talk, and self-reinforcement. If we are willing to classify enough things as "behavior," all psychologists become "behaviorists."

SUMMARY

The "behavioral revolution" in the 60s ushered in a reassessment of assessment. Behavioral techniques differ in several ways from the two other major assessment techniques—objective and projective. Strongly oriented toward behavior change in individuals, assessment emphasizes clear definition of problem behavior and the antecedent and following conditions, especially as they relate to reinforcement. Data collected is treated as a sample, not as a correlate or sign of some inner personality trait or condition. Daily record keeping of problematic behavior before, during, and after therapeutic intervention is common. Deriving mainly from Skinner's theoretical position, a great many experimental procedures for behavior change have been developed, always accompanied by assessment, even if it is simple counting of behaviors. Procedures for selfmonitoring of behavior seem to be increasing.

Few traditional tests are used in behavioral assessment. The most common behavioral techniques are interviewing for problem behavior, observation in natural or clinical situations, problem checklists, reinforcement preference lists, and a few promising tests that describe situations and response alternatives. Behavior is classified into excesses, deficits, inappropriateness, and assets.

The behavioral approach has been very generative of research, though not yet of standard assessment measures. The training and use of observers, and the time used in behavioral treatment may sometimes make this form of therapy quite expensive. The relative costs and benefits of all therapies need evaluation. As the behavior modification movement has grown, a wide variety of techniques of assessment and treatment is developing, some of them very close to cognitive and perceptual procedures and suggesting a reapproachment with other wings of psychology. Some public criticism of behavior modification shows a lack of understanding of the joint goal setting and informed consent that behavioral psychologists advocate with clients. Some psychologists see the behavioral approach as assuming that the organism is only reactive and not an active, creative organizer of his or her own world.

SUGGESTED READINGS

GOLDFIELD, M. R. & SPRAFKIN, J. N. *Behavioral personality assessment*. Morristown, N.J.: General Learning Press, 1974. This twenty-seven page presentation in the series of University Programs Modular Studies is an excellent introduction and survey of behavioral techniques. Summarizing an earlier article (Goldfried and Kent, 1972), the authors point out the major distinctions between traditional and behavioral methods—the assumptions underlying the nature of personality, the selection of test items, and the interpretation of responses. The authors view personality as an abstraction involving "the likelihood of an individual manifesting certain behavioral tendencies in the variety of situations that comprise his day to day living" (p. 3). Under methods of behavioral assessment, they review direct observation, self-report measures, role-playing, physiological measurement and assessment of behavior change, and discuss the advantages and disadvantages of the various devices. Other useful reviews of behavioral assessment are "Functional analysis in the assessment of children" by Bijou & Peterson, 1971; "Behavioral assessment: A review of clinical methods" by Wolff & Merrens (1974); "Behavioral assessment in mental retardation" by Haywood et al. (1975); "Role of assessment in behavior therapy" by Dickson (1975); "A curriculum for the teaching of behavior assessment" by Evans & Nelson (1974); *Behavioral assessment* by

Hersen & Bellack (1976) and *Handbook for behavioral assessment* by Ciminero, Calhoun, & Adams (1976).

PATTERSON, G. R. A basis for identifying stimuli which control behaviors in natural settings. *Child Development,* 1974, 45, 900–911. Patterson, one of the leading researchers in applying behavioral techniques to the social interactions of children, describes how observational data are analyzed from family situations to identify networks of stimuli controlling the interaction. Empirical information about hostile actions are used to construct "probability trees" for individual children. The naturalistic observation method of Patterson and his colleagues, the Behavior Coding System is discussed extensively in an excellent review by Jones, Reid, & Patterson (1975).

chapter eight

Objective Techniques

> *A kind of lying or role playing (if we must use a euphemism) is inevitably a part of personality. . . . It is obvious that we provide a physician, a bartender, an employer, and a spouse with different views of ourselves. One cannot say which of us is the* real *person. The* real *person we speak of is usually a vaguely described confidential self that we see in ourselves or others. But such confidential selves are roles too and much less useful ones for most purposes than are the routine ones of our daily encounters. . . . I still feel, as I have for some time, that no subject is more important for our work with personality measurement than is role playing or, perhaps, better, multiple personality. We need to know the various personalities of an individual and the motivational factors influencing their appearance . . . interpretation of test data can proceed validly only when we can have an idea which personality the testee has presented.* —Starke R. Hathaway in the Foreword to the first (1960) edition of the *MMPI Handbook* (Dahlstrom, Welsh, & Dahlstrom, 1972, pp. ix–x)

The quotation from Hathaway is reminiscent of William James' description of the mind as a "theatre of simultaneous possibilities" in which one must choose which self to present (1890, p. 288). It suggests some of the important assumptions behind this second of the three major personality assessment techniques—a recognition that what a person presents on a test is only a part of the self and that detecting test-taking attitudes or manner of self-presentation is an important part of assessment. Hathaway warns that we cannot think of the content of self-report as "objective" as if it came from a dispassionate observer, but we must see it simply as verbal behavior. The meaning of what the person says involves learning the person's purposes and manner of self presentation and determining the relationship of obtained statements to outside criteria.

This chapter will discuss in more detail information about inventories and scales scattered earlier in the book, particularly in the discussion of tests in chapter two. These important procedures, that go back at least to Woodworth and Poffenberger in the first quarter of the century, are called *psychometric techniques* or *objective techniques.* In this chapter those terms will be used interchangeably. Like the terms "behavioral" and "projective," the words "psychometric" and "objective" have broad meanings that overlap with the other major approaches. The objective and data-oriented aspects are simply the most prominent characteristics of the kinds of tests discussed in this chapter. Objectivity is, of course, the goal of all scientific effort, and psychometrics in other contexts is used to refer to all psychological measurement.

In pointing to objective or psychometric techniques in the study of persons, psychologists are typically referring to reproducibility and minimal private subjectivity in the collection of data. Watson (1959, p. 16) quotes Hathaway, saying that the distinguishing characteristic of objective techniques is "the absence of an intervening interpretation between the behavior of the subject and the material available to a third person" (i.e., someone other than the subject or the test administrator). Data are objective when they are transmitted directly from the subject to others who may then interpret them. The responses the subject can make are limited to the choice among multiple answers, the marking of true or false, the matching of pairs of items, or the assignment of numerical weights. Counts of words in a recorded interview, self ratings, measurements of behavioral or physiological performance, and many intelligence test items would fit this definition. The results of some projective testing can be used in an objective way but the typical referent of the term psychometric or objective is the written, paper-and-pencil personality scale or inventory, and these techniques will serve as the main illustrations of this chapter.

The objective assessment device, then, typically requires a limited and structured response, either true-false or multiple choice. Answers are added to arrive at measurements of a dimension or trait that relates to a criterion. The responses or scores obtained are usually treated as *correlates* of something else. The scales measuring the dimension are not treated simply as samples of behavior but as indicators of a personal characteristic that has some relationship to other characteristics. While the data are sometimes used as signs of a construct, they are most often used for predicting other behavior. As Table 7-1 indicated, the tradition of the psychometric approach is one relating responses to other responses (R–R connections) rather than relating responses to antecedent stimuli or consequent rewards, (S–R connections), as is typical of behavioral techniques.

A great advantage of psychometric or objective techniques is that the procedures for data collection are clearly understood and inexpensive in terms of professionals' time. Even clerical workers with minimal training can score personality inventories and carry out the manipulation of data and the preparation of profiles. This characteristic of inventories makes them efficient and inexpensive. The subjectivity of the assessor enters only at the time the processed data are interpreted—not at the time that the information itself is collected. Extensive use of statistics, and even automation, are also hallmarks of objective techniques. In this chapter we will first examine some of the general characteristics of objective personality techniques and then look at several examples of this approach to assessment.

PSYCHOMETRIC ANALYSIS

A psychometric approach to assessment first involves the choice of the traits or dimensions to be measured, in order to describe some aspect of personality or predict some sort of behavior. The aim is to produce a set of items that combine into a *scale* measuring one trait only and having properties of reliability and validity. The basic unit is the test *item,* that in this approach is typically a verbal term, a statement, or question. There is, however, no reason why the test cannot use non-verbal stimuli requiring structured responses such as the choice between two drawings or the measurement of actions. Because test items provide the behavioral data on which the assessment rests, it is important that they be carefully selected and grouped in some reasonable way.

In collecting items for the construction of a personality inventory, one must define the content area, the *domain of interest,* in which items will be written. Some investigators are interested in producing only one scale to measure a single trait, such as introversion-extroversion, anxiety, or need-achievement. Other investigators plan to produce a multiple-trait scale to measure several traits at once. For example, the Allport-Vernon-Lindzey Study of Values covers six values, and the Edwards Personal Preference Schedule measures fifteen personal needs. In any case, the investigator collects a large body of terms, questions, or statements that appear to be related to the trait or traits being studied. There are many sources for items —earlier inventories, personality theory, interviews, observations, or just hunches and hypotheses the item writer may have.

The next step is to refine the *item pool.* Judges may be requested to eliminate duplicates or near duplicates. The investigator may wish the test to be below a certain reading level if it is intended for use with children; in this case he or she will analyze the reading difficulty of words and statements against standards available for different grade levels. The form of the item must be considered. Double negatives such as "I always try not to be unfair to others," tend to be confusing and it is best to eliminate them. Decisions must be made about whether to use the first or third person, whether to use questions or a check-list of terms, and how to arrange the items on the page. Items are often tested on pilot groups, to see how they respond and to find out if misunderstandings occur. A statistical procedure called *item analysis* may be used to screen out certain kinds of items, particularly those which do not contribute sufficiently to the total score. For instance, for each of fifty items used in a try-out of a preliminary single-trait scale, the correlation with the total score on the scale is computed. If items have low or negative correlations, they are dropped. Large sets of items must be pruned down in the interest of usefulness and economy. Some investigators start with a very large item pool. For instance, Cason (1930) reported that he first collected 21,000 items dealing with personal annoyances, such as false teeth, belching, particular kinds of clothes, or physical appearance. Ultimately judges and try-outs reduced this huge pool to 217 phrases. As another example, the developer of the widely used Taylor Manifest Anxiety Scale started with 200 items from the MMPI and cut the number down to fifty by using judges and pilot testing.

STRATEGIES OF SCALE CONSTRUCTION

There are three strategies for producing scales, or sets of similar items —one making use of judgment, the second using techniques to group items by internal consistency, and the third employing group comparisons to identify items. The *judgmental strategy,* sometimes called *rational-theoretical* (Lanyon & Goodstein, 1971), makes use of expert opinion to decide which items should be grouped together to obtain a scale. The basis for the judgement may vary from crude intuition and "common sense" to systematic deductions from personality theory.

Most early test constructors assumed that they could construct a scale by simply asking questions obviously related to what they were trying to measure. For instance, early questionnaires on adjustment had items such as "Do you make friends easily?"; "Have you had trouble with the law?"; "Do you drink too much alcohol?" Answers in the presumably abnormal direction were added up to produce a maladjustment score. Underlying much of this work was the assumption that what a person said on an inventory corresponded to what he or she did or would say on other occasions (Buchwald, 1961). This naive "correspondence" view of human verbal behavior led to tests much like those occasionally printed in popular magazines with titles such as "How Strong is Your Marriage," that list ten questions, such as "Do you go out to dinner with your partner once a week?" or "Do you remember birthdays and anniversaries?" While such items may actually be related to marital bliss, the only evidence presented for this is the writer's opinion.

Later on, test constructors used more subtle and theoretical approaches to the development of scales. Of particular importance in the history of test construction has been the personality theory of Henry Murray, which has led to scales such as the need for achievement and need for autonomy on the Edward Personal Preference Schedule, Jackson's Personality Research Schedule, and Gough's & Heilbrun's Adjective Check List, as well as a number of projective techniques. Many other general personality theories, such as those of Freud, Jung, Rotter, and Kelly, as well as more specific models and hypotheses such as models of repression-sensitization, anxiety, and depression have stimulated judgmental scale construction. Another large source has been attitude theories in social psychology.

After judges have selected and grouped items, a statistical item analysis may be used to eliminate any that are unrelated to the rest. It must be kept in mind that a personality test constructed in this way cannot be considered to have any empirical validity as a result of its construction. It has only "face validity" (or "faith validity" as some say); scales are dependent on the subjective judgment of the test developer. What such a scale accomplishes is a reflection of a coherent view about personality. It is a step toward the specification of a personality construct. Test theorists and investigators such as Loevinger (1957), Wiggins (1973), and Jackson (1970) have given judgmental activity an important place in personality procedures aimed at measuring constructs. For research purposes, the measurement of a theoretical construct is usually of foremost importance.

The second strategy for scale construction is *internal consistency,* or clustering. The method usually used is *factor analysis,* a technique for analyzing somewhat similar items, came out with only two dimensions. Raymond The test developer is interested in finding a systematic set of personality traits by identifying groups of items that correlate closely with each other but correlate little or not at all with other item groups as they are extracted from the item pool. Guilford was one of the pioneers applying factor analysis to personality inventories and produced the Guilford-Martin Inventory of Factors and the Guilford-Zimmerman Temperament Survey (Guilford, 1959a). The latter inventory provides scores for ten traits, such as General Activity, Restraint, Ascendance, and Sociability, each measured by thirty items that had been found to be internally related. One problem with factor analysis is that several different solutions of the problem embodied in a correlation matrix are possible. Thus different investigators using the same data do not always agree. Thurstone (1951) reanalyzed Guilford's original factorial data and concluded that seven major factors were sufficient to account for the intercorrelations. Eysenck (1953), analyzing somewhat similar items, came out with only two dimensions. Raymond Cattell and his colleagues (1946, 1965) have applied factor analysis in the construction of many tests, of which most widely known is the Sixteen Personality Factor Questionnaire. This inventory measures traits described as reserved vs. outgoing, trusting vs. suspicious, and practical vs. imaginative; in some cases Cattell has invented words or used unusual terms to name factors. One of Cattell's best established factors is "surgency," a term meaning cheerful, enthusiastic, and assured and a factor discovered independently in a large study (Meehl, et al., 1971) making use of a special method for reducing the highly subjective process of naming factors.

As with the judgmental strategy, it should be noted that internal clustering does not guarantee validity. So called "factorial" validity is only internal consistency. The relationship to outside empirical criteria remains to be demonstrated. In general, factor inventories have been found to be less useful in the practical clinical situation than other procedures derived explicitly to help make practical differentiations.

The third strategy for producing tests is to form scales by the *group contrast* method, sometimes called *criterion keying*. The test constructor administers a large set of items to two or more groups known to differ on some important characteristic. Any item that differentiates statistically between the two groups is a candidate for inclusion in the scale being constructed. The first important effort in this area was by E. K. Strong in his work on the Strong Vocational Inventory Blank. He first developed a form for men. On 400 items about interests, activities, and other preferences, Strong compared a group of men who were members of a specific occupational group, such as lawyers, physicians, or businessmen, with a large group of men from other occupations—"men-in-general." Each item that differentiated between the given occupation and men-in-general went into the scale that would be used to measure the interests of that particular occupation.

The advantage of group-contrast methods is that some empirical validity is built into the test itself. One disadvantage is that this method usually produces a heterogeneous mixture of items, sometimes difficult to interpret theoretically. It may also fix chance characteristics of the samples chosen in the empirical key that are irrelevant to the purpose of the test. For instance, if a group of disturbed adolescents answering some items intended to measure maladjustment happen to have many more members from lower socioeconomic groups than the comparison group has, such items as "I put on clean clothes every day," or "I enjoy going on long trips," may reflect social status, not personality disturbance.

Because each of these strategies produces somewhat different results, a test constructor may wish to incorporate the advantages of all three. He or she would like to have a trait measurement that is clearly related to theory, that is internally consistent, and that also separates groups and relates to external criteria. In the process of developing item pools and refining them, the psychologist may attempt to use several methods. Highly developed tests, as we shall see with the Strong and the MMPI, may have several different kinds of keys and scales, to be used flexibly for different purposes.

There have been only a few attempts to compare these three strategies to see which one works the best. Hase & Goldberg (1967) and Goldberg (1972a) carried out a complex and sophisticated investigation using several methods to produce several scales. They found that scales produced by four methods—rational, theoretical, factor-analytic, and contrasted groups— were equally effective in predicting external criteria, although the contrasted group method seemed to have some advantages over the others.

PSYCHOMETRIC INDICATORS OF TEST-TAKING ATTITUDES AND BEHAVIOR

As Hathaway suggests in the quotation at the beginning of this chapter, one of the important problems one encounters in interpreting the results of a personality inventory is the attitude with which the person took the test. Did he or she read the items carefully? Was there an effort to present a particularly good or bad picture of the self? Did the person have a tendency to agree readily to statements, or to disagree? These questions can be partially answered from evidence in the answers themselves. Over the years in which personality inventories have developed, several different procedures have been worked out to help the assessor understand what went on in the mind of the subject. In addition to these procedures, the sensitive assessor makes use of opportunities to discuss the person's feelings and attitudes about a test and perhaps supplement the test results with data from interviews. For example, the writer asked a class of medical students who were learning about the MMPI to take the test themselves and observed one very deviant profile in the results. The pattern suggested either a very high degree of psychiatric disturbance, which seemed unlikely, or some unusual way of taking the test. In an interview, the young medico confessed that he had been so busy that he had stopped reading the items about half way through the inventory and had finished by randomly marking true or false.

The issue is how much the test results are based on the content of the test items and how much they are based on the person's general style of responding. Controversy over *response style* was a major professional debate in personality assessment for over a dozen years (Wiggins, 1973). Some asserted that the content of tests is not important at all while others maintained that responses to such tests as the MMPI are so strongly biased toward giving "socially desirable" responses that little else remains in the resulting profiles (Edwards, 1957). Without discussing these extensive debates and the research they stimulated, we can conclude with Wiggins (1973) and Block (1965) that content remains a very important aspect of personality measures but that we must also continue to be aware of possible response sets and biases as we interpret results and construct new tests. The problem arising from test-taking behavior, and from human communication in general, is that content and manner of response are linked together. The tendency to give socially desirable answers is an important part of the content of personality for many people. For our present purposes it will suffice to note some of the main things assessors can study to get some idea of how an individual has approached the task.

One simple way to understand how a subject took the test is to note the number of *item omissions*. The scoring of several inventories involves a count of unanswered items. The distribution of such omissions is worked out for the normative sample, and one can judge then how unusual the person's behavior was. Items may be omitted for many reasons, such as low reading ability, carelessness, or indecisiveness. The assessor, seeing a large number of items unanswered, is alerted to look for evidence regarding these explanatory conditions.

Another simple indicator of a possible deviant test-taking approach is the *number of items answered in a manner rarely chosen* by the normative sample. The "F" (Frequency) scale of the MMPI and "Cm" (Commonality) on the California Psychological Inventory are examples. Though the titles suggest otherwise, the scales consist of items seldom answered in the scored direction. The results show a willingness to say some unusual things about oneself, such as "I see people around me that others do not see," or "I have attempted suicide." Even a few such scores alert the assessor to look for an explanation such as random answering, reading difficulties, true deviant experiences, or some other reason.

Another more complicated procedure is to develop scales based on *faking* or dissimulation. Subjects are asked to take the inventory as they would normally, and then to take it in order to portray either an overly good picture or an overly bad picture; for instance, instructions might tell the subject to imitate a neurotic or someone who is trying to get out of the military service. Then the normal and faked results are compared to see what items were changed. One can also compare the faked neurotic results with those of bonafide neurotics. The scale produced from such a dissimulation (Gough, 1952, 1957), after proper cross-validation and norming can be used to detect faking by individuals who take the test in the future.

Considerations of test-taking attitudes and response styles should enter the test construction itself. It is now common practice to make sure

that there are almost equal numbers of items phrased in positive and negative ways, so that persons with an *acquiescence set* do not obtain high scores
simply by their tendency to say "yea" instead of "nay" to any question put
to them. It is also becoming common to make a preliminary study of the
social desirability of items by having judges rate them. These ratings have
shown a surprising unanimity across groups as to the desirability of items
(Edwards, 1957, Crowne & Marlowe, 1964). Some test makers have worked
with *forced choice* formats. These require subjects to choose between
different items that have been equated on social desirability, such as choosing
whether they would prefer to be known as "competent" or "respectable."
In previous research the test developers would have found that one of the
pair of the equally desirable terms has criterion relevance but the other does
not. In this case, the answer "competent" might be scored on a scale
differentiating successful people from others, while "respectable" would
not.

PERSONALITY INVENTORIES

Two major streams in the history of personality assessment have been
the measurement of "negative" aspects such as maladjustment, mental
illness, and delinquency, and the measurement of "positive" aspects such
as interests, attitudes, and values. The first stream as it related to psychometric techniques will be represented here primarily by the Minnesota
Multiphasic Personality Inventory and the second topic primarily by the
Strong Vocational Interest Blank. Additional related techniques, scales,
and self-reports will receive brief comment later.

The problems of diagnosing mental patients and evaluating their treatment have been important spurs to the development of personality inventories.
The Woodworth Personal Data Sheet of World War I was followed by
several other measures. The most important of these has been the MMPI.
As mentioned earlier, Hathaway and McKinley originally devised the MMPI
to aid in psychiatric diagnosis. From the 550 items, which are answered
"true" or "false," they identified those that statistically differentiated each
diagnostic group of psychiatric patients from a large sample of the general
population who were not under psychiatric treatment. In all, they used results
from about 800 carefully selected patients and about the same number of
normal visitors to a hospital and other groups. Nine "clinical" scales
were originally developed, to which Social Introversion, based on an item
analysis of college student groups, was added. In addition there were
four "validity" scales measuring test-taking attitudes. Table 8–1 describes
the fourteen scales of the basic MMPI.

Reading the original items (from Hathaway & McKinley, 1951, and
Dahlstrom et al., 1972, 1975) or the simulated ones in Table 8–1, the

observant person notices that some of the items do not quite fit the description of the criterion group and that some items look as if they could be on scales other than the one on which they are listed. The items are a mixed lot on any of the scales, and an entire scale shows considerable diversity. As has been explained, this technique for constructing scales simply selects items producing significant differences between groups; these differences may be obviously related to the deviancy or may seem irrelevant. Some of the seemingly irrelevant items may stand up on repeated studies of normal and deviant groups. Both *obvious* and *subtle* items differentiate the two groups. In some ways the nonobvious items are more useful than the others, as they are less easily "faked."

The reader should not jump to the conclusion that a person is abnormal simply because he or she answers an item in the scored direction. Nearly everyone in the normal population scores a few points on these scales of psychiatric disturbance. It is only when comparison with the norms indicate a large deviation from the average that a clinical condition may be suggested. Clinical interpretation is quite complex, and considerable training and experience are needed to make skillful use of these personality inventories. Usually the patient or client is not shown his or her scores on the MMPI because these can be alarming and misleading. Even though a person may have an Sc score of seventy (which as the reader will recall is a T score two standard deviations above the mean of normal groups), a full understanding of the profile pattern may suggest that this score is not alarming.

Even though the scales were originally derived from the use of abnormal groups, they have now come to have a meaning of their own, in some cases different from the original meaning. Current practice is to refer to the scales by number rather than name to deemphasize the original diagnostic meaning.

It is important that the results be interpreted as a *pattern,* not scale by scale. In over thirty years of using the MMPI, experienced clinicians have built up a great storehouse of interpretive lore. For instance, when the scores on scales 1 and 3, both of which include many physical complaints, are high, but the score on 2, made up of items reflecting depression and discouragement, is low, the test interpreter will draw the tentative conclusion that the symptoms of the patient or client have a neurotic or hysteroid basis, particularly if the level of the whole profile is high enough to suggest psychiatric difficulties. Other combinations suggest other conclusions. To facilitate comparisons, the MMPI developers have invented a *coding* system that essentially involves listing the numbers of the scales from high to low and inserting marks to indicate the height of the scale score. (For details, see Dahlstrom et al., 1972.) Figure 8–1 is an example of an MMPI profile and its code, for which Dahlstrom et al. (1972, p. 295) give a blind interpretation.

TABLE 8-1   Scales of the MMPI With Simulated Items

Validity (or Test-taking Attitude) Scales

? (Cannot Say) Number of items left unanswered.

L (Lie) Fifteen items of overly good self report, such as "I smile at everyone I meet." (Answered True).

F (Frequency or Infrequency) Sixty-four items answered in the scored direction by 10 percent or less of normals, such as "There is an international plot against me." (True)

K (Correction) Thirty items reflecting defensiveness in admitting to problems, such such as "I feel bad when others criticize me." (False)

Clinical Scales:

1 or Hs (Hypochondriasis). Thirty-three items derived from patients showing abnormal concern with bodily functions, such as "I have chest pains several times a week." (True)

2 or D (Depression) Sixty items derived from patients showing extreme pessimism, feelings of hopelessness, and slowing of thought and action, such as "I usually feel that life is interesting and worthwhile." (False)

3 or Hy (Conversion Hysteria) Sixty items from neurotic patients using physical or mental symptoms as a way of unconsciously avoiding difficult conflicts and responsibilities, such as "My heart frequently pounds so hard I can feel it." (True)

4 or Pd (Psychopathic Deviate) Fifty items from patients who show a repeated and flagrant disregard for social customs, an emotional shallowness and an inability to learn from punishing experiences, such as "My activities and interests are often criticized by others." (True)

5 or Mf (Masculinity-Feminity) Sixty items from patients showing homoeroticism and items differentiating between men and women, such as "I like to arrange flowers." (True, scored for femininity).

6 or Pa (Paranoia) Forty items from patients showing abnormal suspiciousness and delusions of grandeur or persecution, such as "There are evil people trying to influence my mind." (True)

7 or Pt (Psychasthenia) Forty-eight items based on neurotic patients showing obsessions, compulsions, abnormal fears, and guilt and indecisiveness, such as "I save nearly everything I buy, even after I have no use for it." (True)

8 or Sc (Schizophrenia) Seventy-eight items from patients showing bizarre or unusual thoughts or behavior, who are often withdrawn and experiencing delusions and hallucinations, such as "Things around me do not seem real" (True) and, "It makes me uncomfortable to have people close to me." (True)

9 or Ma (Hypomania) Forty-six items from patients characterized by emotional excitement, overactivity, and flight of ideas, such as "At times I feel very 'high' or very 'low' for no apparent reason." (True)

0 or Si (Social Introversion) Seventy items from persons showing shyness, little interest in people, and insecurity, such as "I have the time of my life at parties." (False)

A blind interpretation is one made without the assessor knowing anything about the person except the test results and a few identifying facts like age and sex. In the case below the assessors had only the information given in Figure 8-1. The following excerpts from the two page analysis (Dahlstrom et al., 1972, pp. 296–298) will illustrate some of the inferences that a well trained clinician may obtain from the MMPI:

> All the indices of test-taking attitudes indicate that this man tried to comply fully with the instructions and describe himself as fully and completely as he was able . . . . At this time he appears to be highly tense, anxious and agitated . . . . He feels greatly overwhelmed and hopeless with feelings of personal inadequacy and worthlessness. . . . This man is an idealist and perfectionist. He is probably raising his own family in a way similar to his own background with strictness, excessive protectiveness and emphasis upon duty and self-abnegation. When things go wrong, he is prone to blame himself, even for inadequacies in others . . . . In addition to a long-standing pattern of personal integrity and mature (perhaps overly mature) responsibility, he has some important conflicts over his sexual identification . . . . He is not a joiner or a participant in the usual round of social activities in his neighborhood or professional group . . . . His hobbies are likely to be solitary pursuits . . . . The pattern is . . . consistent . . . with some acute disturbance. These reactions can stem from a depressive condition secondary to the loss of a loved one, to panic arising from facing new responsibilities, such as a promotion, new additions to the family, or a move to a new community, or, less likely, to some internal conflict over sexual adequacy or other masculine identification problems . . . . Among these various alternatives some reactive depression is the most likely possibility with favorable reaction to therapy to be anticipated.

This blind interpretation was prepared for research purposes. In the actual clinical situation, the diagnostic study involved the administration of several other tests. The full psychiatric and psychological examination and history revealed additional information and impressions. The facts of the case were that the patient was a minister who had engaged in transvestite and homoerotic practices that had gotten him in trouble and that he wished to change. The MMPI interpreter did pick up the patient's anxiety, depression, social introversion, guilt, obsessive-compulsive trends, and his struggle with passivity and femininity. His vocational dislocation and possible suicidal preoccupation were also noted (p. 306). In general we conclude that the interpreter was able to propose several hypotheses that were borne out by further study.

There has been more attention given to systematizing and automating the interpretation of the MMPI than to any other test. The coding of MMPI profiles by their high and low points has made it possible to compare results of individuals. Over time, quite extensive files of clients and patients were established and hypotheses about patterns could be tested (e.g. Marks et al., 1974). For instance patients with the "neurotic V"—that is, 1 (Hs) and 3 (Hy) high and 2 (D) low, were often diagnosed as hysterics. In 1956 Meehl suggested the possibility of using a "cookbook" for interpretation. Subsequently research began to relate MMPI patterns to clinicians' or other judges' personality descriptions. Thus a number of the interpretive aids were developed, among them computerized interpretation. Several services providing computer print-out descriptions of clients and comparisons with results from various kinds of disturbed people now exist (see Buros, 1972; Dahlstrom, et al., 1972; and Manning, 1971). Their effectiveness needs to be carefully studied and the ethics of their use held to high standards. Some investigators (Lushene et al., 1974) have found the MMPI can be effectively administered by machine, so that it is possible to automate the entire process from the stimulus presentation to the final personality description.

Our discussion of the MMPI is only introductory. Many volumes have been written about the inventory and hundreds of additional scales have been developed beyond the basic scales described here (Dahlstrom, Welsh, & Dalhstrom, 1975). Since the early 1940s the MMPI has been extensively used for practical clinical purposes, and it has also stimulated prolific research on nonclinical as well as clinical populations and improvements in psychometric methods in general. In the critique at the end of this chapter we will consider a number of limitations and problems with the MMPI.

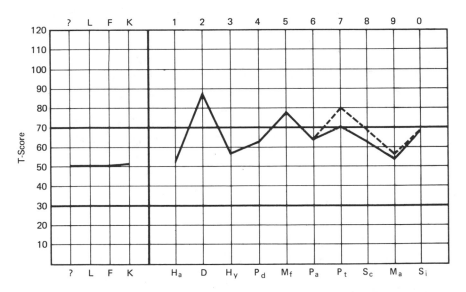

FIGURE 8-1 The uncorrected (solid line) and K-corrected (broken line) profiles of a thirty-four-year-old married professional man seen on an outpatient pscyhiatric referral. Uncorrected code = 2″57′0648—391/—?LF/. K-corrected code = 27″5′8064—391/—K?LF/. From Dahlstrom, W. G. Welsh, G. S. and Dahlstrom, L. E. *An MMPI Handbook Vol. 1: Clinical Interpretation.* (Rev. ed.) Minneapolis: Univ. of Minnesota, 1972.

A number of additional personality inventories deserve mention but space precludes extensive reporting. The reader is reminded that the several Buros *Mental measurements yearbooks* and Buros' *Personality tests and reviews* provide excellent opportunities to identify and obtain evaluations on all published tests. Especially important is the California Psychological Inventory by Harrison Gough (1957, 1968; Megargee, 1972). The CPI contains 480 true-false items, and is designed for the diagnosis and evaluation of interpersonal behavior and concepts of social living. Scoring leans toward the positive rather than the pathological end of the scales. Like those of the MMPI, most of these scales were developed by the strategy of comparing the responses of defined groups. The scales are based on "folk concepts" that Gough considers to be basic dimensions in psycho-social relations, demonstrable in all cultures. Gough and his colleagues have shown that some CPI indicators have this sort of cross-cultural validity; for instance, the Socialization scale and a Social Maturity Index differentiate delinquents from nondelinquents *within* several countries (e.g. Gough & Sandhu, 1964; Gough & Quintard, 1974). Altogether the CPI provides eighteen scales such as Responsibility, Social Presence, Tolerance, and Achievement by Independence. These are portrayed in a profile form, which was presented in chapter two. Associated adjectives assist in interpretations. Another inventory, the Personality Research Form (PRF) by Jackson (1967; Siess & Jackson, 1971) illustrates the conscientious development and complex sequencing required to develop a personality inventory that measures constructs. The final inventory comes in two forms of fifteen twenty-item scales each, reflecting the theory of Murray from which the test started, with scales such as Impulsivity, Order, Achievement, Dominance, and Affiliation. Other inventories such as Edwards' Personal Preference Schedule, the Sixteen Personality Factor Test, the Eysenck Personality Inventory, the Myers-Briggs Type Indicator, and the Personal Orientation Inventory are some prominent procedures that the reader might want to investigate further.

INTEREST INVENTORIES

In contrast with many of the personality inventories measuring maladjustment, interest inventories look for directions of positive effort. Interest inventories usually concentrate on the relationship of the individual to the world of work. Psychologists developed them to help counsel people in their vocational and educational decisions. Choices along these lines are particularly salient in high school and college, when important career decisions are often made—decisions which affect the whole subsequent course of one's life. The significance of occupation is described eloquently by David Campbell (1971, p. vii.):

> Under the guise of employment, men allow themselves to be manhandled physically (professional football players), to be subjected to public ridicule (politicians), to be displayed publicly (cocktail waitresses, Bunnies, and strippers) or to be deprived of all material possessions (priests and monks). The excitement of occupation has led men into more risks—undercover espionage, space travel, Antarctic exploration—than could money or fame; the fanatic commitment of some men to their jobs has probably caused more divorces than has marital infidelity; the possibility of better employment has created larger mass migrations than has religious fervor, and the absence of meaningful work has likely created more mental depression than any other single factor. For most people, where they work is where the action is.

Young men and women want to explore themselves in relation to the many and various possibilities for rewarding activities, asking themselves "What do I want to do in life? How can I begin to support myself in a way that I also enjoy? With what kinds of occupations and organizations do I want to be associated?"

The two major questions that arise in making vocational plans have to do with abilities and interests. Surprisingly, the two are not highly correlated. A person can have a high interest in something but achieve in only a mediocre way. In the same way a person may have a high degree of ability to do something, but not be interested in it. Interests stake out a domain of preference such as medicine or carpentry, and abilities point to the potential level of skill or attainment, whether the person may become a medical assistant or a highly specialized neurosurgeon, whether a carpenter eventually works only on rough framing or in skilled cabinet making. Of course abilities and interests interact. Abilities certainly are not fixed for all time by the age of twenty, but depend on experience, new learning, and changing job needs. Individual shifts in occupations, or specialities within occupations, are quite common. Nevertheless research has shown that within broad categories of interest such as medicine, business, and engineering, interests do settle down typically in young adulthood and with most people do not shift radically for the rest of their lives (Strong, 1955; Campbell, 1971).

Interests have been measured primarily by verbal inventories. Two methods have been used to produce useful scales; criterion keying based on group comparisons, pioneered by E. K. Strong, Jr., and internal consistency, or clustering of related items, used by G. F. Kuder. As mentioned before, the Strong Vocational Interest Blank for Men, first published in 1927, selected items for occupational scales by comparing responses of successful men in the given occupation with those of men in general. For instance, if a group of engineers stated that they liked "working with figures" and disliked "painting flowers" more frequently than the men in general did, then those two items would be included on the Engineering scale. In this way many scales were developed for many occupations.

The Kuder Preference Record-Vocational, first published in 1934, began with the idea that items of similar content should be grouped together. Through item analyses, items that correlated with each other and not with items on other scales were sorted out. In this way ten general areas of interest were differentiated—Outdoor, Mechanical, Computational, Scientific, Persuasive, Artistic, Literary, Musical, Social Service, and Clerical. The Kuder inventory uses a forced choice format in which the respondent is asked to choose the most liked and most disliked activity within each triad, for example:

1. Visit a forest lookout station.
2. Go to a concert.
3. Visit a children's hospital.

One advantage of the Kuder is that the subject can score his or her own paper. He simply removes the back of the answer sheet and counts the number of marks within the guidelines shown. Numbers can be plotted on a profile and a Verification score helps to detect carelessness in responding.

The homogenous keying, which the internal consistency strategy produces, provides some clear interpretative advantages. Broad categories are easy to talk about in a general way. Patterns have been identified and norms developed to aid in the interpretation. However, scales like those of the Strong, which are based on actual responses of people in the occupations, have the advantage that they allow the individual to compare his or her interests with those of people in the field. In order to provide both kinds of advantage, new forms of the Kuder and the Strong are now using both kinds of scales. The Kuder Occupational Interest Survey provides empirically based scoring keys for a considerable number of occupations and college majors. The Strong Basic Interest Scales are made up of clusters of related items.

One of the present controversies in interest measurement revolves around the question of sexism. This problem flared up as women's organizations began protesting against discrimination in the late 60s and 70s. Interest tests were said to have perpetuated sex discrimination. The Strong Vocational Interest Blank then had separate forms for men and women. David Campbell (1972), who was then in charge of the research on the instrument, felt the full brunt of the feminist attack. As a result, Campbell made a thorough revision of the test. The Strong-Campbell Interest Inventory (SCII) is a combination of items from the two earlier forms, with sex-oriented items eliminated and the Masculinity–Femininity scale dropped. The SCII profile provides information based on norms for both sexes separately and uses three types of scales: six general occupational theme scales based on Holland's theory that occupations and individuals can be categorised as realistic, investigative, artistic, social, enterprising and conventional: twenty-three basic Interest Scales based on homogeneous items; and 124 occupational scales, including many new ones developed by the original contrast-group method. The SCII thus provides a great deal of information to the counselor. Results from interest tests, unlike those from personality inventories, can be openly and readily shared with a client. A copy of part of the SCII profile form for a student in business is shown in Figure 8–2.

As with personality inventories, there is much more to interest measurement and career planning than can be described in this introductory section. Vocational choice is intertwined with personality and environment (Holland, 1973). Exploration of directions for personal effort that society will reward is a life-long task. Students in high school and college need to know their interests in order to make wise decisions for beginning studies and careers. Throughout life, changing personal needs and environmental opportunities bring repeated questions about life satisfactions and personal directions. Career change in middle age is no longer uncommon as mature women with grown children take jobs, and many mature women and men seek different life styles. Changes in the nature of jobs and retirement also offer opportunities for re-thinking directions. In affluent countries interest assessment for life planning seems to have a promising future. Among many poor people, and in developing countries, however, there is little opportunity to follow one's interests.

ATTITUDES, OPINIONS, BELIEFS AND VALUES

The measurement of attitudes, opinions, beliefs, and values provides a rich and extensive literature. These procedures have generally been addressed to purposes of research, or used in organizational or sociopolitical projects rather than in work on individual differences. Measurement of attitudes and attitude change occupies a central position in social psychology, and public opinion polling is important in applied work in politics and marketing, but clinicians, counselors, and personnel workers seldom administer attitude or opinion questionnaires to clients. Still, attitude and opinion items are often found in personality and interest inventories without being labelled as such. Values inventories are occasionally used in vocational counseling and personality research. William Scott in the *Handbook of social psychology* (1968, p. 204) has written "The construct *attitude* falls, by historical accident, within the domain of social psychology. It might more reasonably have been elaborated within general personality theory,

SVIB-SCII Profile for

Sex	Age	Date Scored ▶
M	21	Date Adm. ▶

General Occupational Themes

Theme	Std Score	Result
R-THEME	43	This is a LOW Score.
I-THEME	54	This is a AVERAGE Score.
A-THEME	50	This is a AVERAGE Score.
S-THEME	34	This is a LOW Score.
E-THEME	57	This is a AVERAGE Score.
C-THEME	38	This is a LOW Score.

Administrative Indexes

(for the use of the counselor)

TOTAL RESPONSES		32
INFREQUENT RESPONSES		1

Response

	LP	IP
OCCUPATIONS	24	28
SCHOOL SUBJECTS	47	17
ACTIVITIES	35	25
AMUSEMENTS	36	28
TYPES OF PEOPLE	54	17
PREFERENCES	53	0
CHARACTERISTICS	64	7

Special Scales: AOR: 37 IE:

Basic Interest Scales

	Scale	Std Score
R-THEME	AGRICULTURE	65
	NATURE	63
	ADVENTURE	38
	MILITARY ACTIVITIES	45
	MECHANICAL	35
I-THEME	SCIENCE	46
	MATHEMATICS	35
	MEDICAL SCIENCE	58
	MEDICAL SERVICE	40

Chart columns: Very Low | Low | Average | High | Ver(y)

Occupational Scales

Code	Scale	Sex Norm	Std Score
AE	INT. DECORATOR	m	53
AE	ADVERTISING EXEC.	m	52
A	LANGUAGE TEACHER	f	28
A	LIBRARIAN	f	35
A	LIBRARIAN	m	22
A	REPORTER	f	43
A	REPORTER	m	41
AS	ENGLISH TEACHER	f	25
AS	ENGLISH TEACHER	m	31
SI	NURSE, REGISTERED	f	29
SIR	PHYS. THERAPIST	m	17
SRC	NURSE, LIC. PRACT.	m	23
S	SOCIAL WORKER	f	35
S	SOCIAL WORKER	m	30
S	PRIEST	m	34
S	DIR. CHRISTIAN ED.	f	7
SE	YWCA STAFF	f	45
SIF	MINISTER	m	22
SEA	ELEM. TEACHER	m	31
SC	ELEM. TEACHER	f	7
SCE	SCH SUPERINTEND	m	38
SCE	PUBLIC ADMINISTR.	m	46
SCE	GUIDANCE COUNS.	m	28
SER	RECREATION LEADER	f	34
SEC	RECREATION LEADER	m	37
SEC	GUIDANCE COUNS.	f	29
SEC	SOC. SCI. TEACHER	f	35
SEC	SOC. SCI. TEACHER	m	38
SEC	PERSONNEL DIR	m	55
ESC	DEPT. STORE MGR.	m	37
ESC	HOME ECON. TCHR.	f	12
ESA	FLIGHT ATTENDANT	f	35
ES	CH. OF COMM. EXEC.	m	48
ES	SALES MANAGER	m	45

Chart columns: Very Dissimilar | Dissimilar | Ave | Similar | Very Similar

A-THEME

Theme	Score
MUSIC/DRAMATICS	54
ART	56
WRITING	43

S-THEME

Theme	Score
TEACHING	33
SOCIAL SERVICE	35
ATHLETICS	38
DOMESTIC ARTS	49
RELIGIOUS ACTIVITIES	33

E-THEME

Theme	Score
PUBLIC SPEAKING	61
LAW/POLITICS	59
MERCHAND'NG	58
SALES	57
BUSINESS MGMT.	66

C-TH

Theme	Score
OFFICE PRACTICES	39

Code	Occupation	Sex	Score
ES	LIFE INS. AGENT	m	37
E	LIFE INS. AGENT	f	52
E	LAWYER	f	49
E	LAWYER	m	47
EI	COMPUTER SALES	m	36
EI	INVESTM. FUND MGR	m	50
EIC	PHARMACIST	m	31
EC	BUYER	f	39
ECS	BUYER	m	41
ECS	CREDIT MANAGER	m	28
ECS	FUNERAL DIRECTOR	m	40
ECR	REALTOR	m	35
ERC	AGRIBUSINESS MGR	m	18
ERC	PURCHASING AGENT	m	37
ESR	CHIROPRACTOR	m	45
CE	ACCOUNTANT	m	12
CE	BANKER	f	20
CE	BANKER	m	35
CE	CREDIT MANAGER	f	38
CE	DEPT. STORE SALES	f	13
CE	BUSINESS ED TCHR	f	6
CES	BUSINESS ED TCHR	m	30
CSE	EXEC. HOUSEKEEPER	f	20
C	ACCOUNTANT	f	12
C	SECRETARY	f	26
CR	DENTAL ASSISTANT	f	19
CRI	NURSE, LIC. PRACT.	f	10
CRE	BEAUTICIAN	f	26

FIGURE 8-2 A profile form for the *Strong Campbell Interest Inventory*. © Consulting Psychologists Press, Palo Alto, Calif.

for an attitude is always formulated as a property of an individual personality.''

Those who wish to understand personality would do well to be aware of attitudes, opinions, beliefs, and values. These constructs refer to important connections between the individual and society, and they often have practical implications for economic, political and social behavior. Nearly all theories about interpersonal attraction and group functioning are concerned with attitude congruity or consistency between the persons involved. For example, one of the consistency theorists, Newcomb (1953), states that people talking with one another seek to *establish a symmetry of orientations,* to bring their attitudes in line with each other, or to find areas of common belief and experience. Notice your next conversation with a stranger; you are likely to search for mutual acquaintances or experiences. Shared orientations make interpersonal communication easier, and for this reason people tend to like those individuals who share their opinions and values. This theory in expanded form has led to many studies of attitude change and interpersonal attraction. Rokeach (1960, 1968, 1973) states that intergroup hostility and race prejudice can be analyzed as an instance of perceived dissimilarity or "imbalance" of beliefs and values. A number of studies (e.g. Secord & Backman, 1964) show that perceived similarity in beliefs can cause increased liking. Another influential cognitive consistency theory is Festinger's theory (1957) of *cognitive dissonance,* which states that a person possessing two or more elements of contradictory knowledge experiences a state of tension or dissonance and is motivated to attempt to reduce that tension by changing his or her attitudes and beliefs.

The concepts of attitude, opinion, belief, and value overlap a great deal. McGuire (1969) states that Allport as early as 1935, mentioned seventeen different definitions of attitude, and McGuire himself adds other surveys that report at least thirty. A commonly accepted definition, as good as any other, is that of Katz (1960, p. 168): ''*Attitude* is the predisposition of the individual to evaluate some symbol or object or aspect of his world in a favorable or unfavorable manner.'' Attitude scales have been developed regarding almost anything one can think of—war, religion, race, legislative reapportionment, sports, sexual customs, foreign nations, and specific persons, institutions, or products. Attitude scales often have ten or twenty items that are added to give a score that represents the degree of favorable feelings toward the object.

Opinions are similar enough to attitudes so that the terms could be used interchangeably, but custom has led to the use of the term "opinion poll" for a technique in which a person is asked to express favorable feeling on one item at a time, rather than answering several items of a scale. An opinion poll item could be "How do you rate the success of the current president in running the government—outstanding, good, about average, poor, or extremely poor?'' Opinions are thought to be less emotionally tinged and more objective than attitudes, and they often relate more to knowledge and facts than do attitudes.

A *belief* is ''an emotional acceptance of a proposition or doctrine upon what one implicitly considers adequate grounds'' (English & English, 1958, p. 64). An early psychologist said that the human ''mind is a belief-seeking rather than a fact-seeking apparatus'' (Rokeach, 1968, p. 113). The bases for beliefs are often not examined, and are considered to be deeper and less subject to change than opinions or attitudes. Many beliefs are personal assumptions that are never consciously examined or checked for proof. Examples are beliefs in God, patriotism, the perfectability of man, and the flatness or roundness of the world.

Values are ''personal conceptions of the desirable that are relevant to selective behavior'' (M. B. Smith, 1963, p. 332). Like belief, value is considered more basic and central, less superficial, than attitudes and opinions. Belief refers to assumptions behind behavior, and value refers more to the future—the ends or the means to an end that are to be sought, or one's notion of the desirable in life. Examples of items from one study (Sundberg, Rohila, & Tyler, 1970) are: ''I try to have religious ideas enter into every choice I make in life,'' ''I judge a job by how much money it brings in,'' and ''It is important for me to get all the schooling and learning that I can.''

Much of the work on attitudes grew out of experimental psychology, and perhaps this emphasis on prediction of measurement is the major reason for our slowness in applying this area of measurement to individuals. An early and very influential paper by Thurstone (1928) applied the processes of psychophysics to the development of attitude measurement by asking people to compare different statements and arrange them on a scale of noticeable differences in magnitude of favorableness. Figure 8–3 shows the results of comparing the severity of crimes as judged in 1927 and 1966 (Dawes, 1972, p. 7).

It is interesting to note that sexual crimes were being judged less severely in the later year, while crimes involving bodily injury were being judged more severely.

Later techniques for attitude measurement, such as those of Likert and Guttman (see Scott, 1968) also used the reports of judges in assigning values to statements. Although statistical refinement has been emphasized, empirical validity has not; this emphasis has made these scales less usable for practical purposes and everyday decisions than tests. Their principal utility has been in research.

One attitude scale that has been involved in much psychological research is the California F Scale. This F scale (not to be confused with the MMPI F scale) was used in a large program of investigation of authoritarianism and prejudice against Jews and others (Adorno et al., 1950). The F

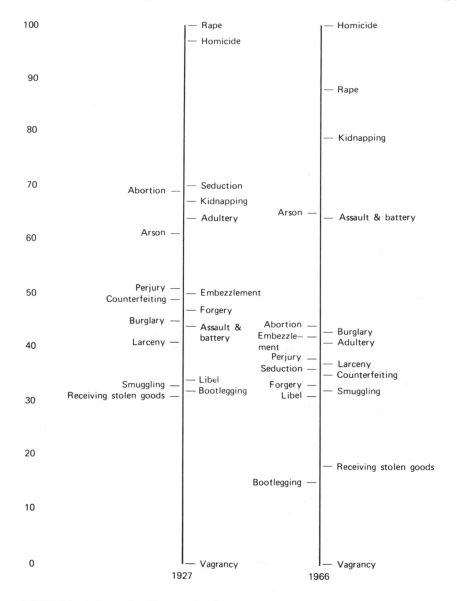

FIGURE 8-3 Judgements of the severity of crimes in 1927 and 1966 (From Dawes, R. M., *Fundamentals of attitude measurements,* New York: Wiley, 1972, p. 7. © John Wiley & Sons, Inc. Reprinted by permission of John Wiley & Sons Inc.)

(Fascism) scale is composed of subtle items like "Sciences like chemistry, physics, and medicine have carried men very far, but there are many important things that can never possibly be understood by the human mind;" the subject is asked to indicate the extent of agreement on a six point scale. Other items deal with attitudes toward conformity and "law and order." The scale was found to differentiate between those who are racist, totalitarian, and prejudiced on one hand, and those who are equalitarian and liberal on the other. One criticism of the scale is that the response format easily permits an acquiescence set to operate. There are other criticisms (Christie & Jahoda, 1954), including the fact that the test can be easily faked (Sundberg & Bachelis, 1956). The F scale has generated much research and is still widely used in this country and elsewhere (Gough & Lazzari, 1974). Other examples of extensively used attitude instruments are the Parental Attitude Research Instrument (Schaefer & Bell, 1958; Paulson et al., 1974) and the Opinion About Mental Illness Scale (Cohen & Struening, 1962; Rabkin, 1972; Levine, 1972).

The most widely used measure of values is the Allport-Vernon-Lindzey Study of Values (A-V-L). The items were formulated on the basis of the theoretical framework of the German philosopher Spranger. The final item selection was based on internal consistency within each of the six areas— theoretical, economic, aesthetic, social, political, and religious. The areas are not highly correlated either positively or negatively and the items are arranged so that the subject is forced to choose between statements representing different values. Figure 8–4 illustrates the format in which the items are presented, a format that conveniently allows the subject to total up his or her scores at the end and compare them with the norms provided. The forced choice format, of course, means that if a person is high on one score, he or she must be low on some others. A person cannot be high on all of the six values. Another value instrument widely used for research purposes is Rokeach's values survey (1973).

Part I

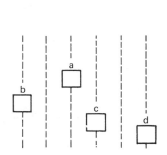

8. When witnessing a gorgeous cermony (ecclesiastical or academic, induction into office, etc.) are you more impressed: (a) by the color and pageantry of the occasion itself; (b) by the influence and strength of the group?

Part II

10. Which of the following would you prefer to do during part of your next summer vacation (if your ability and other conditions would permit)
   a. write and publish an original biological essay or article
   b. stay in some secluded part of the country where you can appreciate fine scenery
   c. enter a local tennis or other athletic tournament
   d. get experience in some new line of business

FIGURE 8–4 Sample items from *A study of values* (G. W. Allport, P. E. Vernon, G. Lindzey, Boston: Houghton Mifflin, 1960).

Many additional self-report techniques could be mentioned, including not only those in Buros' books, but also many specialized techniques. A number of verbal-paper and pencil procedures are similar to scales and inventories and are easily subjected to psychometric methods. Persons can describe themselves by means of the adjective checklists, ratings, and Q-sorts described in earlier chapters and in chapter ten. Many of these tests are also used in the description of others and in research on the cognitive processes or the language of personality description.

CRITIQUE

Objective techniques have been the most powerful long-run force in personality assessment. The *Seventh Mental Measurements Yearbook* (Buros, 1972) lists 180 objective (nonprojective) tests and forty-six projective ones. But how successful have individual objective techniques been? This question has to be answered for each test, but it may be sufficient here to take the MMPI as an example because it is the personality inventory about which most has been written and researched. In 1972 Buros reported that the test was then annually responsible for more publications than any other test—240 references annually, or twenty per month. Kleinmuntz (1967, pp. 334–337) reviewed MMPI publications and summarized its advantages: reported widespread use in many different situations; evidence of validity as an aid in screening and selection of emotional and adjustment problems in high schools, college, the military, medical situations, and industrial work; usefulness in the appraisal of severity of psychiatric symptoms, contact with reality, extent of patients' anxiety, and benefit from treatment. The MMPI's large and varied item pool has offered a common reference point and an opportunity for much research on new scales. Kleinmuntz points out that although validity of specific MMPI scales and indexes has fallen short of expectations, the willingness of those who developed the MMPI, especially Hathaway and Meehl, to publicize the test's inadequacies, has contributed to the test's current success. On the debit side, the MMPI can be strongly criticized for the unreliability of several of its scales, which in turn affects the realiability of patterns and of interpretations. Reported reliabilities have ranged from near zero to .96 with different scales over different time periods and in different populations. Since the group contrast strategy used in construction of the MMPI does not produce scales of theoretical or factorial purity, a number of problems of interpretation arise. There are high intercorrelations between several scales, which when added to the variable reliability, makes profile interpretation unclear. Another problem is the normative data available; the MMPI norms were developed largely on visitors to the University of Minnesota Medical School hospital in the late 30s and early 40s. There have been many changes in lifestyles and attitudes since then. There are also questions about using the test with people of different ethnic backgrounds. Opinions differ on the appropriateness of norms with blacks (Gynther et al., 1971; Strauss et al., 1974; Davis, 1975). Much criticism can also be made of the original criterion groups used for producing the scales; psychiatric diagnosis of schizophrenia, psychopathic deviation, and other disorders are notoriously unreliable and the size of the criterion groups was often small.

Why then has not a new improved personality inventory taken the place of the MMPI? At a conference largely devoted to the MMPI (Butcher, 1972) this question came up repeatedly. One chapter in the conference report by Hathaway is entitled "Where have we gone wrong? The mystery of the missing progress." He concluded pessimistically that personality is so complex and psychologists are so wedded to old techniques that the near future will see little fundamental improvement in personality testing. The complexity of the criteria that we wish to predict was part of the difficulty. The enormous expense of test development and of retraining users of new tests tends to retard change. Along with a great deal of criticism of the test, Meehl (1972, p. 146) sums up his point of view as follows:

> A device that takes a negligible amount of time for the skilled clinician to administer or interpret is often worth using even when the inferences it permits are of only moderate validity.

Meehl indicates his conviction that tests like the Strong, MMPI, and CPI possess, even now, sufficient construct, concurrent, and predictive validity to justify their use, a statement he feels cannot be made about projective devices that are more costly in clinical time.

In a more general way, let us look at the nature of objective techniques and try to discern directions for their future development. The overall assumption behind objective techniques is that verbal behavior is not random or purely situation-related; instead verbal behavior relates to long-term personal characteristics. Traits, or sometimes types, or some variant of these terms, signifying some persistence of personal differences in behavioral dispositions, are essential for this approach. The task for objective techniques, then, is measuring these individual predispositions and applying psychometric measures for consistency, predictability, and so on. The most important questions for the objective test are how this little sample of verbal behavior, these test responses, describe or predict important life events or represent a theoretical construct. The task is not directly one of measuring situational variables (although objective assessors do not object to their measurement), nor is the task the high use of theory for inference as in projective techniques. The limitations of this aim also impose some limitations on the results. Inventories have been used mainly for diagnosis, not for therapy or behavior change, because their construction has not been oriented toward that process.

It is important that any practical test relates not just to diagnosis and labelling, but to therapy and other activities of assistance to clients. Several trends seem to make objective techniques more amenable to direct use in treatment. One is the concern for *trait-state differences*. As mentioned before, traits are relatively enduring aspects of personality and states are relatively temporary conditions. For instance, one might measure anxiety as a trait or as a state (Spielberger, 1966). Trait anxiety is the individual's predisposition to be tense and upset under any given stress situation, and state anxiety is characterized by consciously felt periods of tension and apprehension and physiological upset. Measurement of the temporary condition will allow for "finer tuning" in relating treatment activity to individual changes (Stroudenmire, 1972). A second direction is the development of devices for measuring *response differentiation in different kinds of situations,* as the work of Endler and Hunt (1966) mentioned in chapter five, has begun to do. A third possibility is to apply objective test procedures to *different content,* such as choices of different pictures showing different situations, other nonverbal stimuli like the Welsh Figure Preference Test or biographical data of relevance to treatment. A fourth direction that will facilitate the use of objective measures in therapy is the development of *content scales* and other devices that allow the assessor to relate findings directly to what a client can understand. As with the Strong and the Kuder, some workers with the MMPI (Wiggins & Vollmar, 1959) are developing a variety of scales that can assist the therapist in talking with the client about what he or she has said on the test. Objective assessors might also exploit attitude change theories in psychotherapy in a fashion paralleling the use of behavioral assessment techniques with behavioral therapy. A fifth direction is the elaboration of *actuarial interpretation systems.* Such automated or semiautomated systems could include data in addition to personality inventory information such as influential variables like socioeconomic status, age, intelligence, and treatment settings. The amount of data to be collected makes such a task formidable. Finally a sixth and very important direction is the development of *theoretical models* to guide research. Inadequate theory is no doubt the greatest deficiency in personality assessment at the present time.

SUMMARY

The second major assessment technique is called objective because the subject's answers are transmitted directly for analysis, without intervening interpretation. In practice, objective techniques are structured according to possible answers (usually true-false or multiple choice) and written paper and pencil format. Data obtained are typically treated as correlates, not samples or signs.

Constructing an objective test starts with the collection of an item pool in a defined domain of interest. There are three general strategies for grouping items to produce scales—the judgmental or rational-theoretical strategy, the internal consistency or factor analytic strategy, and the group-contrast strategy. Research has indicated that all three methods have some value, and sophisticated test construction usually involves a combination of the three.

One of the important aspects of interpreting objective tests is the detection of test-taking attitudes. The developers of the Minnesota Multiphasic Personality Inventory (MMPI) have been prominent in the development of such procedures. Research suggests that subjects use both the item content and their own response styles in answering an inventory.

Objective inventories can be divided into two classes, those aiming to reveal maladjustment, and those concerned with interests and values. The MMPI, an example of the first kind, contains 550 items from which ten clinical scales, originally named for neurotic and psychotic diagnoses, and four so-called "validity" scales to detect test-taking attitude, have been derived. The principal interest inventories are the Strong Vocational Interest Blank and the Kuder Preference Record. Both the MMPI and the Strong were developed by group-contrast method, and the Kuder was developed by internal consistency. In subsequent revisions both interest tests have developed scales like those used in the other one. Strong has produced impressive data about the persistence of interests over several decades in adult life.

Another area of objective techniques is the measurement of attitudes, opinions, beliefs, and values. These measures are more often used for research than for applied or clinical purposes. The California F (Fascism) Scale is probably the most widely used attitude scale and the Allport-Vernon-Lindzey Study of Values the most common measure of values.

In comment, we noted that the psychometric tradition requires careful attention to reliability, validity, and other technical test qualities, but even the most widely used personality inventory, the MMPI, falls short on many points. However, because the MMPI requires little professional time and because it has amassed so much information for use, it is widely administered by psychologists. Objective techniques will probably continue to be prominent in assessment. Several possibilities for improving their relationship to therapy and other assistance were briefly discussed.

SUGGESTED READINGS

BUTCHER, J. N. (ed.) *Objective personality assessment.* New York: Academic Press, 1972. This collection of papers is from a series of symposia on the MMPI, but its principles apply to all objective techniques. The level of discussion assumes considerable knowledge about the MMPI, and the beginner would probably find it helpful to read introductory material first, such as the MMPI Manual or introductory parts of Dahlstrom, Welsh, & Dahlstrom (1972, 1975). On a more general level two articles by Lewis Goldberg (1971, 1974) provide excellent reviews of objective tests.

CAMPBELL, D. P. The Strong Vocational Interest Blank: 1927–1967. In P. McReynolds (ed.) *Advances in Psychological Assessment,* Vol. 1, Palo Alto: Science and Behavior Books, 1968. pp. 105–130. Campbell provides an excellent review of the development of this best known vocational interest test. Readers may also be interested in Vinitsky's article (1973) which is "A forty-year follow-up on the vocational interests of psychologists and their relationship to career development." With the thirty-two psychologists who completed the Strong at ages sixty-three to eighty-five, all have become significant contributors to the field. This is another illustration of the surprising consistency of interests over long periods of time.

CATTELL, R. B. How good is the modern questionnaire? General principles for evaluation. *Journal of Personality Assessment,* 1974, 38, 115–129. Cattell, a long-time, ardent advocate of the factor analytic approach to test construction, outlines eight basic requirements for factor-true scales that are often missing in published studies. For a more extensive presentation of the factor analytic approach, see Cattell's *Personality and mood by questionnaire* (1973), which one reviewer (Damarin, 1975, p. 453) describes as "one of the most important general treatises on personality assessment ever written."

GOUGH, H. G. An interpreter's syllabus for the California Psychological Inventory. In P. McReynolds (ed.) *Advances in psychological assessment.* Vol. 1. Palo Alto: Science and Behavior Books, 1968. Gough clearly describes the eighteen scales of the CPI and their interpretation. He discusses the interactions among the scales and interpretation of the profile and suggests some possible research applications. Megargee (1972) presents an extensive discussion of this important test.

KELMAN, H. C. Attitudes are alive and well and gainfully employed in the sphere of action. *American Psychologist,* 1974, 29, 310–324. Starting by quoting Allport (p. 310) "The concept of attitude is probably the most distinctive and indispensable concept in contemporary American social psychology," Kelman discusses the meaning of attitude and the problem of attitude-action consistency and suggests ways to relate attitudes to action. Of additional value for readers are the books by Rokeach (1968, 1973). Wilkinson's *The broken rebel* is a study of authoritarianism and the F scale, and Rabkin's review (1972) covers the Opinions about Mental Illness scale. Christie & Geis, in *Studies in Machiavellianism* (1970), report the development of a very interesting scale for measuring tendencies toward power-seeking manipulation.

chapter nine

Projective Techniques

When the subject is asked to guess what the examiner is thinking, we call it an objective test; when the examiner tries to guess what the subject is thinking, we call it a projective device. —George Kelly (1958, p. 332)

In the last two chapters we have considered behavioral and objective approaches to assessment. The third major conceptual approach for systematically producing personality data is called the projective approach. Like many other psychological phenomena, projective assessments have a long past as astute observations about human beings, but a short history as regularized devices for examining individuals. Sarma (1974) reports a tale from the Hindu Upanishads about the different interpretations three people gave in response to a single syllable spoken by their guru. Shakespeare's Hamlet led Polonius into agreeing that a cloud was shaped first like a camel and then like a whale. Alexander Pope wrote, "All seems infected that the infected spy, as all looks yellow to the jaundiced eye." (Allen, 1958, p. 154). Binet in 1895–96 used inkblots and storytelling in response to pictures, but his concern was with ways of testing imagination and intelligence.

The difference between simply eliciting individual differences in response to ambiguous stimuli and the development of projective techniques was the use of theory with standard materials in the interpretation of those individual differences. Investigators used inkblots before Rorschach, but there was no widespread acceptance of a standard set and a known framework of usage and interpretation. Development of systematic knowledge depends on acceptance of standard procedures by many investigators so that a common frame of reference and a common language can be constructed.

Three landmarks in the history of projective techniques were Jung's systematic use of word association beginning around 1905–1910, Rorschach's publication of *Psychodiagnostiks* in 1921, and Murray's publication of *Explorations in personality* in 1938. Jung used word association to identify unconscious conflicts and complexes. Rorschach tied inkblot responses to psychopathology and to modes of thinking and perception. The book by Murray and his colleagues was important for its presentation of his personality theory, a comprehensive assessment program, and one of the most important projective techniques, the Thematic Apperception Test.

Murray used the term "projection tests" in his book, but the accepted title for such procedures came from Lawrence Frank (1939), who called them "projective techniques." Frank argued against the then dominant use of personality inventories and enthusiastically promoted indirect methods of eliciting the pattern of internal organization, comparing them to X-rays of the person's mind. Frank denied that the task of studying personality is to measure separate variables on a large group of people and derive statistical characteristics. He felt that the task calls for the use of multiple methods "which will reveal the many facets of personality and show how the individual 'structuralizes his life space' or organizes experience to meet his personal needs." (Frank, 1939, p. 410) The most important period for projective techniques was in the 1940s and 50s, when psychoanalysis was a predominant force in thought about personality. Many new ways of presenting and recording ambiguous stimuli were developed in Europe and America. In the 60s Buros (1965) reviewed seventy-seven projective techniques published in English, and there were hundreds of similar devices in unpublished clinical or research usage. By the late 1960s and 70s projective techniques were still widely used, but they had also been profoundly criticized and their development appeared to reach a plateau.

RATIONALE OF PROJECTIVE TECHNIQUES

The driving force behind projective techniques has been Freudian theory and psychoanalytic approaches to understanding the unconscious (Lindzey, 1961). The belief that the most significant aspects of personality were not open to self report made many conclude that questionnaires and inventories had little value. The psychoanalytic idea of personality is that it is a dynamic whole with ideas and behaviors arising from strong but hidden sexual and aggressive urges connected with persons and objects encountered in childhood. This theory led to a search for methods for eliciting important material that would circumvent the strong defenses against threatening ideas and urges. These considerations are revealed in the definition by Lindzey (1961, p. 45):

> A projective technique is an instrument that is considered especially sensitive to covert or unconscious aspects of behavior; it permits or encourages a wide variety of subject responses, is highly multidimensional, and it evokes unusually rich or profuse response data with a minimum of subject awareness concerning the purpose of the test.

In addition to the intention to reveal unconscious psychic material while keeping subjects unaware of the purpose, this definition emphasizes the open-endedness and multiplicity of responses possible with the test stimuli. The variety of responses is related to the ambiguity and lack of structure in the test stimuli. The subject is told little more than to describe what something looks like or tell a story or draw a picture. Many projective techniques use nonverbal stimuli or call for nonverbal responses, though few are completely nonverbal, because words are used to give instructions or record responses.

In contrast to behavioral techniques, which treat obtained information as a sample, and psychometric techniques, which primarily treat data as a correlate, projective techniques emphasize that obtained material is a *sign* of underlying personality structure and dynamics. They are *indirect* attempts to probe personality. Their intention is to obtain hints of unconscious forces and conflicts at work. Projective techniques put a heavier burden on the skill of the interpreter than do any other kind of test; the psychologist must bring theory and intensive knowledge of the person together in understanding the often vague and idiosyncratic signs which are elicited by the testing situation.

The rationale behind the sign approach of projective techniques relates to the basic assumptions of psychoanalysis. One such assumption is Freud's dictum of *psychic determinism,* that is, that any person-emitted behavior or report is not random or accidental but is determined by psychological processes that are often unconscious. Thus, a slip of the tongue or a joke may tell of the speaker's hidden wishes or impulses. An aim of analytic psychotherapy is to bring highly emotional material past the censorship of the Super-Ego, or conscience, and to bring conflicts and strongly emotionalized images up for consideration by the conscious. Freud himself used *free association,* a kind of projective technique itself. He asked the patient on the couch to tell everything that came to his or her mind. The therapist even sat behind the couch to make the situation more ambiguous.

A further assumption in psychoanalysis and projective interpretation is that acts and utterances are *over-determined*. What a person says or does reflects many aspects of the total personality, and all behavior should be studied to discern the many motives it expresses. Slips of the tongue, drawings, and responses to inkblots show many sides of the personality. For instance, in giving a speech a businessman intending to use the word "represent" says, "I resent the Kute Klothes Company." Careful examination of the man's feelings and unconscious motivations reveals several determinants: He does resent the company; he also feels inadequate as its representative; he senses that the name of the company reflects on his masculinity, and furthermore he is considering an offer with another company. Janis and others (1969, pp. 625–626) list many possible influences on the response to a projective technique that must be considered in interpretation, the immediate situation including the impact of the person giving the test, the subject's identification with the figures perceived in the test stimuli, the many motives active in a person at one time, defenses that control expression of motives, the cognitive elaboration of the response from memories, the enabling or limiting effects of abilities to express oneself and moods and personal style. This untangling of complex, often unconscious motives and characteristics of which the projective responses are only outward signs, requires a considerable understanding of psychoanalytic theory and much experience with such testing.

Another conceptualization of Freud that is relevant to projective techniques is that of *primary and secondary processes of thinking.* Primary process is the primitive mode of thinking with which we are born; it is illogical and dominated by the seeking of gratifications and relief from tensions— the Pleasure Principle, as Freud called it. Such mental functioning is common in early childhood, drugged states, and during psychotic thought and hallucinations. Primary process is also characteristic of dreaming, and it has an important, perhaps even necessary, role to play in the loose exploratory thinking of creative problem solving. Secondary process is the form of thinking involved in adapting to reality; it is dominated by the Reality Principle. This mode is characteristic of the way we usually think when we are awake; it is verbal, logically organized, relatively unemotional, and related to the objects and environmental conditions around us. In some projective techniques, notably the Rorschach, some theorists (Holt, 1956) believe that the usual reality controls are somewhat lessened by the ambiguous nature of the stimuli and the instructions to give first associations or to fantasize. Some research (Goldberger & Holt, 1961) suggests that the shift toward the primary process form of thinking on the Rorschach is related to the ability to tolerate reduced environmental stimulation and the ability to go to sleep easily. This interesting finding needs further investigation.

A final concept from psychoanalysis is *projection.* There are two important ways in which the term is used (Lindzey, 1961, p. 31). *Classic projection* is the defense mechanism described by Freud, and refers to an unconscious and pathological process when the person rejects unacceptable impulses or qualities in himself but attributes them to individuals or objects in the environment. Freud's analysis of the case of a paranoid man named Schreber showed how he could not admit strong homosexual attachments and instead came to see other men as hating him, thereby justifying his own anxiety and suspicion about other persons; this reversal transformed Schreber's feelings so that they were acceptable to him. However, as the term projection is used with projective techniques, it does not necessarily have an abnormal or even completely unconscious connotation.

The second usage of the term, *generalized projection,* refers to the normal process whereby the person's perception and interpretation of the outer world is influenced by inner qualities and forces. Freud apparently used the term in both ways. In projective techniques then, the basic assumption is that the person "throws out" his or her own private views onto the object of attention. Because so much emphasis is placed on deviant responses, Cattell (1951) has argued that these procedures should be called "misperception" techniques. The *projective hypothesis* is a statement of this second view of the term, that the responses of an individual to a relatively unstructured situation reveal his or her inner predispositions, conflicts, and dynamics—the private world. Projection is seen as a general phenomenon occurring all the time with everyone, but varying in the degree with which it fits "reality" as perceived by others.

The analysis of *test protocols,* as the original records are often called, may involve quantification before the final interpretation, although those who use projective techniques often use only impressionistic interpretation. As with interview reports or autobiographies, aspects of the protocol can be categorized and counted. Thus assessors can develop norms, validity coefficients, and other forms of psychometric study.

Lindzey (1959, 1961) has categorized the great variety of projective devices into five groups, based on type of response required of the subject. (1) *Association techniques* ask the person to respond to some stimulus with the first word, image, or percept that comes to mind. Examples are the Rorschach and word association. (2) *Construction techniques* give the subject the task of producing something, usually a story or a drawing, such as the Thematic Apperception Test. (3) *Completion techniques* require the subject to finish an incomplete task in any manner he wishes, such as the sentence completion procedure. (4) *Choice or ordering techniques* merely involve a selection among alternatives, sometimes with instructions to rank the possibilities in order of preference or attractiveness, such as the Tomkins-Horn Picture Arrangement Test (Tomkins & Miner, 1957), which consists of sets of three line drawings depicting activities to be arranged by the subject to make a story. (5) Finally, *expressive techniques* are oriented toward revealing personal manner and style in the process of performing some activity, such as play situations with children, or the Draw-A-Person Test. We will consider the most common procedures in more detail.

THE RORSCHACH TECHNIQUE

The young Swiss psychiatrist Hermann Rorschach died shortly after publishing his now famous test, but others saw its potential. Beck and Klopfer were particularly influential in bringing the test to America, each of them developing systems of scoring and interpretation that are now widely used (Beck, 1972).

From the late 40s to the 60s, the Rorschach was the undisputed leader in test publications and use in clinical situations. It averaged over three English language publications per week for at least a decade (Sundberg, 1961). Since that time, the test's popularity has declined, but it is still an important part of the clinical testing scene (Reynolds and Sundberg, 1976). The 1972 Buros *Mental Measurements Yearbook* listed over 4000 publications on the Rorschach. In the popular mind the ten inkblots came to symbolize much of what a psychologist does, and implied a mysterious and magical image of the profession. In a different sense we still need to view the ink-blots as mysterious, because they continue to present many perplexing problems of interpretation.

The stimuli themselves are fairly simple—just ten symmetrical ink-blots originally produced by pressing together the sides of a folded paper with spots of ink on it. Half of the cards are black or gray, and half are colored. Figure 9–1 shows an inkblot similar to the Rorschach. Although many books do show Rorschach blots in reduced or distorted form, psychologists are generally reluctant to print the original blots because familiarity changes the meaning of a test. The influence of prior knowledge and suggestion can be great with an ambiguous figure. Notice later how hard it is *not* to see some of the things reported by the persons in Figure 9–1; it is difficult, if not impossible, to recapture the naive view of a figure already seen. The responses of two normal young people to the inkblot are shown in Figure 9–1. They gave two responses each, all of them different—a man's head in the central white space, an airplane, a decaying tree stump, and a pair of boots. Except for one, all the responses incorporated the whole blot, and all of the responses predominantly made use of form. One showed inanimate movement. The reader can easily guess which of the two people had recently been on a hike in the forest and which one had lived near an airbase.

FIGURE 9-1   Inkblot and responses from two persons

Responses of a 21-year-old carpenter:
1. It's like a stump of a tree with roots coming down. (Later inquiry: Q1, Where is the stump?) The whole thing. An overturned stump, jagged, with the center decayed, eaten away and maybe ferns growing on it. (Q2 : What is it about the blot that made it look like that?) The roots, the shape; it's a separate stump.
2. A pair of shoes, facing in the opposite direction, and these could be the shoestrings (pointing to the lower thin projections) (Q1) A pair of boots with shoestrings. (Q2) the shape.

Responses of a 16-year-old high school boy:
1. It looks like a man's head; he's bald on top and has a big moustache and sideburns and a goatee. (Q1) In the center (pointing to white space) These are his eyes (point to dark spots). His bald head is tall. (Q2) It's the dominant part of the blot—the center—surrounded by black. The shape.
2. Looks like an airplane with a blunt nose and a thin vapor trail behind it. (Q1) The whole thing. It's flying over you (Q2) The long protrusive sides, the thin trails behind, the slur made as it flies by.

The Rorschach examination has two parts. First the assessor presents the cards one at a time in order until the person has responded to all ten. He instructs the person to say what he or she sees or is reminded of. After writing down the subject's responses or "percepts" on all the blots, the examiner goes through the cards again, asking the subject (Q1) where he saw the things he reported and (Q2) what is was about the blot that made it look like what he saw. The results of this inquiry stage are used by the examiner to score the test. The Rorschach administration produces the following three kinds of scorable information: the *location* (whether the subject uses whole blot, large details, or small details), the *determinants* (the aspects of the card that the subject states are suggestive of the percepts, such as form, color, texture, and apparent movement), and *content* (the nature of the percept, such as human, animal, clothing, building, or water). In addition the assessor may judge the degree of *originality* of responses; "populars" are frequently reported percepts, and normative data may be available.

The use of scoring by practicing Rorschach specialists varies a great deal. There are several different scoring systems, although the ones by Klopfer and Beck are the most commonly used (Exner & Exner, 1972). For some of the scores normative data are available showing common responses, the average range of good form (responses that realistically fit the shape of the blots), the expected range of total number of responses, and so on. The assessor may draw a graph or profile from the resulting scores. A large number of psychologists do not, however, make much use of scoring. After having scored responses from many clients, a clinician develops internalized expectations and may not take the time for detailed scoring.

Interpretation of the Rorschach proceeds from many assumptions about location, determinants, and content. Using the whole inkblot suggests integration and organization; many small details indicate compulsiveness and over-control, and use of white space suggests oppositional and negativistic tendencies. The presence of much poor form, uncommon responses, and confused thinking suggests a psychotic condition. Responsiveness to color is supposed to represent emotionality, and in the absence of good form, it suggests uncontrolled emotions and impulsivity. Responses mentioning human movement indicate imagination, intelligence, and a rich inner life. A high ratio of movement to color responses suggests an introversive tendency, while if color is dominant, extroversion is likely.

Content also has much potential for interpretation, as might be supposed from the psychoanalytic connections with projective techniques. Knives, guns, mutilated bodies, and angry interactions suggest strong hostility. One Rorschach card is supposed to "pull" attitudes toward the father, and another toward the mother. The assessor must consider the pattern of determinants and the sequence of perceptions. She or he also must take into account such test-taking behavior as speed of response, manner of handling the card, and attitude and interest in the test. The complexity of relating these many features to each other and to other information about a patient or client make training and experience absolutely necessary before assessment results can be accepted with confidence. Some experts have devoted the bulk of their professional lives to these famous inkblots.

Much of Rorschach's original procedure and interpretive framework is still intact, many decades after his original publication, though Rorschach himself viewed his formulations as tentative and experimental (Zubin, Eron, & Schumer, 1965). Those who read reviews of the Rorschach technique in successive editions of Buros' *Mental Measurements Handbooks* will find increasingly critical and negative views because its psychometric properties leave much to be desired. Reliability of scores varies widely, partly because of the infrequency with which some of the scoring categories occur. Reliability of interpretation is another important problem. Jensen (in Buros, 1965, p. 506), reviewing several studies, concluded that "at least as much of the variance in Rorschach interpretations is attributable to differences among the interpreters as to differences among the subjects." With variable and poor reliability, it follows that validity cannot be high. Little & Shneidman (1959) compared twelve Rorschach experts' judgments recorded as Q sorts, with those of psychiatrists who read a comprehensive psychiatric case history. The validity coefficient was .21. Like Jensen, the investigators concluded that as much variance is attributable to differences among the interpreters as to differences among the subjects. Jensen (in Buros, 1965) ended his review by saying that the massive effort lavished for forty years on this technique has proven unfruitful, and the training and clinical usage of the Rorschach should be abandoned.

In contrast, Burstein (in Buros, 1972) is enthusiastic in his review about the prospects of validity through specialized ways of scoring content. He believes the status of the Rorschach will depend on what psychologists consider important, and says (p. 434) "The view that recognition, the act of construing an unfamiliar stimulus, taps central components of personality function is one that will remain crucial in any psychology committed to the understanding of human experience."

As these quotations illustrate, the research findings do not settle basic questions, and the assessment field is split between Rorschach believers and nonbelievers. The extensive review by Goldfried, Stricker, & Weiner (1971) strikes a level-headed medium. These authors attempt to find in the areas in which the Rorschach is valid. They carefully look at the evidence for the major indicators of specific personality conditions or problems, such as scoring systems for hostility, anxiety, body-image boundaries (barrier scores), homosexuality, schizophrenia, and prognosis for psychotherapy. They note that many studies have methodological flaws and that criteria for these clinical conditions are often imprecise. They state (pp. 380–381):

> It cannot be denied that the majority of the studies in the Rorschach litera-
> ture have yielded negative or ambiguous results, and a superficial appraisal of
> these data could easily lead clinicians and researchers to despair of pursuing
> Rorschach applications . . . the likelihood of outcomes favorable to Rorschach

indices seems directly related to the care with which assessment studies have been designed, and impressive positive data have emerged from studies in which appropriately derived Rorschach indices have been assessed with appropriate samples against appropriate criteria and with appropriate requirements for making concurrent or predictive judgments.

Goldfried and his colleagues note that expecting any test, especially just ten inkblots, to assess all of personality is unrealistic. They indicate that the Rorschach appears to be most valid for assessing functions close to the behavior it elicits. They note that the Rorschach can be approached in three ways—as a perceptual-cognitive task; as a structured interview; and as a stimulus to fantasy productions. The indexes derived from the first two approaches are directly representative of Rorschach behavior and offer more promise than the symbolic approach. They state that (p. 395) "The more numerous and complex the levels of inference necessary to provide a rationale for (an index), the greater are the possibilities for errors of measurement . . . Since each level of inference in constructing a hypothesis involves some possibility of error, each additional level of inference adds to the total degree of error." The reader will note the similarity of this conclusion to the discussion of levels of inference in chapter one.

There have been many variations on the Rorschach such as alternate sets of inkblots, methods for administration to large groups, multiple choice response forms, and ways of obtaining conjoint or consensus responses from interacting groups. One of the most promising variations is the Holtzman Inkblot Technique (Holtzman, et al., 1961; Hill, 1972; Holtzman, 1975). Developed over many years, the HIT is an attempt to retain most of the projective and theoretical advantages of the Rorschach in a form that is psychometrically sound. Many of the objections to the Rorschach stem from the lack of reliability inherent in the use of only ten stimuli and the wide variability of subjects in their responsiveness to the task. All of the scores on the Rorschach are affected by the productivity variable. If one person gives fifty responses to the ten cards and another person only nine, the chances of the first person having a variety of determinants and content is naturally much greater. Holtzman and his colleagues solved the problem by using forty-five cards, and restricting the subject to one response per card. In addition, a parallel set of forty-five cards is available, and good equivalent reliability has been established. The HIT scoring system covers twenty-two variables such as Reaction Time, Form Definiteness, Shading, Movement, Pathognomic Verbalization, Anatomy, Hostility, and Popular. Norms are available on subjects of differing ages, psychiatric conditions, and backgrounds, and investigators have carried out several cross-cultural studies. The authors report many substantial correlations between similar scores on the Rorschach and HIT. Few significant relationships are found with personality inventories. Holtzman (1975) indicated that few of the 300 publications on the HIT to date had studied validity, but there was good research evidence for the Movement score as a measure of imaginative capacity and ideational maturity, and for the ability of the HIT to differentiate between diagnostic categories such as schizophrenia and depression. Configural scoring methods and computerized processes are being explored with the HIT. The researchability of the test bodes well for the future; it is more likely that hypotheses can be proved or disproved with the HIT than with the Rorschach.

THEMATIC APPERCEPTION TEST

Second only to the Rorschach in importance as a projective technique is the Thematic Apperception Test. Christiana Morgan and Henry Murray elaborated on the relevant personality theory and important research in 1938, and the test was published in 1943. The 1972 Buros lists over 1500 publications about the TAT, and there are hundreds more about similar techniques that have derived from it. The TAT, like the Rorschach, is normally administered in an interview situation with one individual. It provides more structured stimuli than the Rorschach and is more obvious in intent. The test stimuli are a series of pictures, most of them of individuals or persons in interaction although some portray fantastic scenes. The full series would be twenty pictures selected from the thirty pictures available for boys or girls, women or men. Some pictures are used for all subjects, such as the first card, which shows a young boy contemplating a violin that rests on a table in front of him and the blank card for which the subject is to imagine a scene. Figure 9–2 shows a girl responding to a TAT card. The assessor introduces the TAT roughly as follows:

> This is a test of imagination. I am going to show you some pictures, one at a time; and your task will be to make up as dramatic a story as you can for each. Tell what led up to the event shown in the picture, describe what is happening at the moment, what the characters are feeling and thinking; and then give the outcome. Speak your thoughts as they come to your mind. Do you understand?

The examiner records the person's story by writing or tape recording. Sometimes the subject is asked to write the stories himself. If the full set of twenty pictures is used, they are usually broken into two sessions, each of which may take an hour. However, in practice clinical psychologists usually use only a few pictures, perhaps five or six selected to elicit themes of interest in the analysis of the case such as the person's perceptions and fantasies about mother figures or aggression. Many research psychologists have devised sets of cards for special purposes, such as cross-cultural studies or investigations of special personality characteristics like achievement or power needs.

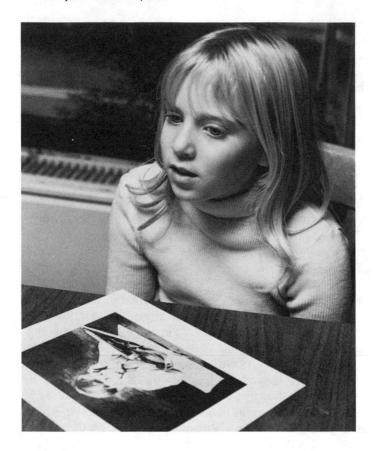

FIGURE 9-2

Stories told by two of the subjects to Card 1 reported in William Henry's *Analysis of fantasy* (1956, p. 140–141) follow:

> *Person A* (A woman, 22 years old): "A young boy looking at the violin on the table. His expression is one of tiredness and not much interest. It seems to me that he is too young to be forced to take violin lessons, at an age that he would have no love of the instrument or music. It is possible that his mother either believes that it is *good* to have a child 'play something,' or has visions of his becoming a great violinist. All of this might lead to the child's dislike of the whole thing.
> *Person B* (A woman, 33 years old): "First impression is the staged effect—child does not look at an unfamiliar object so quiescently. The child's facial expression is one of melancholy. The appearance somewhat—the bow is not clear-cut. Emotions as strong as this probably meant to be indicated here not in context with quietness of subject-coloring and delineation of individual and violin."

These responses show sharp individual differences. One of the first things to note in interpretation is the manner with which the subject responds to the task. A and B produce approximately the same number of words, about the average length for adults. Person A gives a standard plot and characterization consistent with the instructions, but B does not create a plot to give an outcome, though she describes the stimulus picture in such a way that she seems to perceive the same objects and sense the same general negative quality seen by many people. The kinds of words and sentences and the organization of the two responses differ markedly. The first is well organized and clearly moves from topic to topic. The second is unusual in its use of words, and the sentences are disconnected and incomplete, leaving the reader with a sense of bewilderment, wondering just what she said. This feeling engendered in the reader or clinician-interpreter is an important signal for the impressionistic interpreter.

The following passages slightly abbreviate Henry's interpretation (1956, p. 143) of the story from Person A:

> The woman of twenty-two moves with vigor into the heart of the matter. In the first two sentences she introduces the basic identification of the stimuli and relates them satisfactorily. She notices relevant details and sees things in good spatial terms (*boy* looking at *violin* on the *table*). She next indicates directly the emotions of the boy (tiredness and not much interest). She sympathizes in an active fashion with him and attributes his plight to a mother who is similarly real and has strong motivations. It is an interesting note that she has specially marked for us her notion of the social mobility goals of the mother in her emphasis on *good* and on "play something." All of this pressure, she says, might lead to complete rejection. Her story is well marked with motives and feelings; her plot is lively and shows time sequences.
>
> Person A's resentment of her mother, whose goals are forceful and ambitious, and the girl's intentions to rebel completely are marked. It should be noticed, however, that she does not basically reject the plot as untenable or inappropriate and she does not reject the values involved. This is a saga of a young woman resenting her mother's control, rebelling, but laying the groundwork for a return to the middle-class values represented.
>
> The woman comes from an upper middle-class suburb and has long resented her mother's desire to turn her into a matron. She fled to the university, moved into a Bohemian set, stored her suburban clothes, and for a period made great fun of the solid middle-class virtues represented by her mother. She has since, however, married a most respectable young man and is herself developing the symptoms of respectability.

The reader will note that the first paragraph describes and elaborates on the nature of the presentation, but the second paragraph moves to the projective hypothesis. The interpreter is connecting the TAT story with the intentions and life values of the subject. The third paragraph, then, gives a narrative confirmation of these basic personal conflicts and directions through some follow-up information.

Henry's analysis of Person B (1956, p. 144), slightly modified, is as follows:

> The record of the woman of thirty-three is clearly that of a disturbed personality, though at the time of the test her overt behavior was socially acceptable. She does sense and respond to the basic stimuli, though most certainly she does so in a unique fashion. From the opening phrase on, the form of the story is barely relevant, and organizational qualities and time sequences are at a very low level. Her content is presented in disjunctive form, a series of firm but logically unconnected associations. However, she says several things of great importance. In an interpreted form she says: (1) Reality is a fake; she rejects the picture as unreal—a "staged effect." (2) There is a disjunction between emotions and environment. While she senses some emotion and inner feeling, she is aware of a sense of misfit between these emotions and their stimuli. At one moment she focusses on the emotion, taking it as a firm reference point (child . . . quiescent) and accuses reality of misfit (unfamiliar object). At another, she claims that reality is the base (color and delineation of individual and violin) and that the emotions are inappropriate. Unable to be sure whether she or the outer world is out of focus, she vacillates, sensing primarily her feeling of inappropriateness and disassociation. (3) Her emotional orientation is one of melancholy. She cannot be sure even of this, however, since she sees it both as "quiescent" and "strong." In either state, she is unable to relate to reality.
>
> In spite of these many signs of acute disturbance, she is actively struggling with the fit of inner state and reality; she has not given up nor accepted her inner state as the only reality. She acknowledges the basic content demand of the picture, though she is unable to give it the form and organization required by the instructions.
>
> The week following this test, she was hospitalized following a break of a schizophrenic nature. She has subsequently recovered quite well after a period of hospitalization and psychotherapy.

The basic assumption underlying the interpretation of the TAT is that the stories reflect the subject's internal needs and the perceived external press. These needs and press are particularly apparent in the way the subject talks about the "hero," that is, the main person with whom he or she seems to be identifying in each story. Other persons in the pictures reflect attitudes toward significant people in one's experience. For instance, an older man in a story is presumed to portray feelings about the father, and figures of the opposite sex about the same age call forth heterosexual needs. In addition to looking at the hero and other major characters, the assessor notes the theme of each story—whether the plot reflects success or failure, how problems are resolved, and what topics the story deals with. Presumably these themes reflect the person's views about his or her own life. The assessor's purposes are to develop and check hypotheses about why the person tells the story, what personality determinants seem to be significant, and how the person copes with different kinds of situations. As with other projective techniques, the assessor particularly notes productivity, reaction times, signs of strong emotion, unusual words or expressions, repetitions, the intellectual quality of verbal response, and attitude and interest in taking the test. The interpreter may try to empathize with the subject, putting himself or herself in the place of the person and attempting to feel as he or she feels. The assessor may also use statistical information if that is available.

The TAT has no single accepted procedure for scoring and interpretation. In fact, for clinical purposes, it is scored much less frequently than the Rorschach; but elaborate systems do exist, especially for research programs. For example, one can count the number of words or the number of stories with positive outcomes vs. negative outcomes or one can rate the stories on a wide variety of attributes. Needs have been given the most attention, but as mentioned in chapter five, presses, such as perceived dangers, non-support of family, loss, and external dominance or aggression, can also be rated. Murray (1938, pp. 291–292) labelled twenty needs (using "n" for need) such as nAbasement, nAffiliation, nDominance, nNurturance, and nOrder. These dimensions of personality have provided a vocabulary and stimulus not only for TAT scoring systems but for several objective techniques mentioned in the last chapter.

McClelland and his colleagues (1961, 1975) selected certain of these needs, especially nAchievement, nAffiliation, and nPower, and have constructed reliable scoring systems for many research studies. They apply these scoring systems not only to stories told in response to pictures but also in content analyses of children's reading primers, popular literature, and films in various countries. One of the fascinating results has been the discovery of a cyclical character in the content of popular literature over time. They found the balance between ratings of power and affiliation themes in popular plays and songs and children's stories has a relationship to historical epochs of reform or war. From the beginning of the United States, strong themes of power accompanied by a drop in affiliation preceded wars by about fifteen years until recently when the rate became faster (McClelland, 1975). On the basis of these findings, McClelland predicted a war in the late 1970s. Earlier studies of achievement, in which raters scored any indication of competition against standards of performance in Chinese children's stories showed about a twenty-five year period of change before major changes occurred in China. As McClelland says (1975, p. 44), "Motivations . . . seem to run before events."

How should we evaluate the TAT? Certainly the technique has provided the vehicle for a great deal of clinical and research analysis. As with the Rorschach, one can find in the Buros Yearbooks applications to a variety of problems, such as delinquency, brain damage, asthma in children, bilingualism, mental retardation, obesity, phantom pain, achievement, affiliation, sexual identity, power, schizophrenia, and on and on. The quantity and quality of research stimulated by the TAT marks it as a highly successful contribution to the search for knowledge about personality.

From other standpoints, however, the TAT cannot be judged successful. Studies of psychometric qualities raise many questions about its use for clinical or other applied purposes. Eron's study (1950) illustrates several points. He administered the twenty card TAT to 150 American male veterans, some in Veterans Administration hospitals and some in college, obtaining 3000 stories. With generally high interrater reliability, the stories were scored for such characteristics as emotional tone, outcome, misidentification of the sex of person pictures, and themes. The results provide good normative data for those who wish to use the scoring system (which is unfortunately quite time-consuming). Eron compared the various clinical and nonclinical groups statistically, and concluded that TAT fantasy productions do not show differences between normals and patients or between different kinds of psychiatric patients, that stories are affected by the external environment of the hospital or other place where they are administered, and that the TAT should not be used for psychiatric diagnosis. Eron's study is one of many that threw cold water on the early enthusiasm for projective techniques in clinical work.

An important question for this test is how the personality needs or characteristics revealed in TAT fantasies relate to actual behavior. What is the correlation between projective expression and overt expression? Murstein (1963, 1965) has been particularly concerned with this problem. His conclusion in regard to fantasized and overt aggression is that the relationship is positive, but involves a number of complex relations with other variables such as guilt over aggression, upbringing and family attitudes and the specific areas in which the aggressive act is to be committed. For instance, one study (Purcell, 1956) comparing antisocial, "acting out" soldiers with others, showed that impulsive, antisocial men expressed more direct aggression on the TAT, telling stories of fighting, lying, stealing, and getting angry, and showed less internalized inhibition as revealed by stories with feelings of guilt or shame or self-deprecation. The author concluded that behavioral prediction from projective material must take into account inhibitory as well as impulsive forces. The investigator also noted differences in TAT reactions between lower and middle class subjects. Murstein emphasizes the need to know the background and environment of the person when one is interpreting the meaning of the TAT. In an excellent study of several influences on the TAT, Murstein (1968) also confirmed the obvious hypothesis that more hostility is reported for pictures with more objective hostile content.

Studies of experimentally induced needs have led to similar conclusions about the importance of knowing intervening control mechanisms between needs or impulses and expression in real life. In an interesting study that lends some validity to the importance attributed to the "hero" in TAT interpretation (Lindzey & Kalnins, 1958), it was shown that aggression attributed to the hero in the story increased following experimentally induced frustration, but aggression in other characters did not. Another study (Clark, 1952) counted the sexual themes in stories by an experimental group of men who had just looked at slides of nude females as compared to a control group of men who had seen slides of neutral scenes like landscapes. The experimental group showed less projection of sexual themes. The author attributed the diminished projection to arousal of defenses against the expression of sexuality. Another experimental group, however, after drinking alcohol, did show many expressions of sexuality on their TAT stories.

Based on long acquaintance with TAT research and clinical usage, Eron (in a review in Buros, 1972) made several points: (a) TAT responses are subject to conscious control by the subject; (b) although the predominant effect seems to be a direct relation between TAT fantasy and behavior, no conclusions will hold for all motives and subject backgrounds, and (c) higher ambiguity of the picture relates to a smaller relationship between story content and overt behavior. Eron (p. 460 and 462) concluded the TAT is a useful indicator of general interest, motives, and areas of emotional disturbance, but is not a specific measurement device for personality traits of individuals. He notes its wide acceptability for research purposes.

Many of the same conclusions would apply to the offspring of the TAT idea—projective techniques such as the Children's Apperception Test, the Thompson TAT, the Michigan Picture Test and Adult-Child Interaction Test, the Make-A-Picture Test, the Symonds Picture-Story Test, and the School Apperception Method. All of these are story telling proccedures for children. None of them have had the amount of work done on them that the TAT has, and some have had practically no research at all. One picture story test that has received considerable investigation and provides a clear scoring system is the Blacky Pictures, developed by G. S. Blum (1950, 1962, 1968). This technique, which is used with both adults and children, consists of a series of cartoons about a dog, Blacky, and its parents and sibling. The cartoons explicitly try to elicit aspects of the psychoanalytic theory of development. One, aiming at problems with oral sadism, uses a drawing of Blacky biting on Mama's collar, another, concerned with Oedipal feelings, has Blacky watching loving parents from behind some bushes. One of the most interesting aspects of the technique is that it combines both projective and objective aspects. After the subject tells a story about the picture, the examiner conducts an inquiry using questions with multiple choice answers. (It is surprising that more use has not been made of procedures combining projective and objective methods.) The scores for the Blacky test are on thirteen dimensions, such as oral sadism, anal retentiveness, and masturbatory guilt. A special inquiry provides scores on the subject's preferences for defense mechanisms. As to Blacky itself, reviews point out many of the same problems found for other projective techniques; in addition, its close relation to psychoanalytic theory makes it vulnerable to the problems in validating and using that theory.

SENTENCE COMPLETION METHODS

Another widely used and useful projective technique is the sentence completion method. Its use in personality assessment goes back to 1928 (Payne). As the term implies, this procedure consists of a set of uncompleted sentences that the person is asked to finish, such as "I worry a great deal about _____" or "In the future, there are going to be _____." The number of introductory "stems" to be completed may range from twenty to 100 in a standard test. This flexible and simple procedure has been adapted to many purposes and used in many forms.

The best known published form is the Rotter Incomplete Sentences Blank (ISB), which has forty short stems mostly in the first person. A manual (Rotter & Rafferty, 1950) gives examples as guides for scoring the responses as Conflict, Neutral, or Positive reactions. For instance, to the stem "My father _____," responses such as "is an alcoholic," "and I have many arguments," or "still frightens me" would be given a high score on Conflict, and "is very nice," "has a wonderful sense of humor" or "has a complete head of hair—hurrah!" would be scored high on Positive (Rotter, 1951, pp. 303–304). ISB scores add up to an overall adjustment total. Interscorer reliability is good, and normative data on college samples are available. Several validation studies are positive. For example, one study (Getter & Weiss, 1968) showed that maladjustment scores on the ISB differentiated between university students who made many visits to the college infirmary and those who did not. Other sentence completion forms have been developed for many special purposes. For instance, the Miner Sentence Completion Test is used to study attitudes of managers and management trainees. Other forms elicit specialized personality characteristics related to such topics as black-white differences, attitudes toward mental hospitals, old age, and school life.

Interpretation varies from a thoroughgoing impressionistic approach, to the use of norms based on length of completions, grammatical errors, use of personal pronouns, reaction times, and verb/adjective ratios. The interpreter does need to be very sensitive to test-taking attitudes, since this verbal method has little disguise. Philip Goldberg (1965), in an excellent review, summarized the results of fifty validity studies using a variety of forms. He concluded that the sentence completion technique is a valuable instrument justified for wide clinical and research usage, even though why and how it works is not yet clear. The best validities occur when standard objective scoring systems are used, and the most consistent success has been in assessing the psychological adjustment of adults and the severity of psychiatric disturbance. The technique has not worked well in certain areas, such as in the prediction of academic success. Murstein (1965, p. 777) called this method "probably the most valid of all projective techniques" due to its use in predicting selected criteria consistent with the test—verbal and consciously controllable behavior. In addition it is an easy procedure to administer and takes less of the assessor's time than many other projective techniques.

DRAWINGS AND OTHER TECHNIQUES

Another widely used projective method is drawing. The projective possibilities are strikingly expressed in the quotation (used by Hammer, 1958, p. 8): "When an artist paints a portrait, he paints two, himself and the sitter." The procedure is simply to give a person a blank sheet of paper with instructions to draw a person. Many variations in instructions exist, such as requests to draw one's family, one's internal organs, or objects like houses or automobiles. Drawings are fascinating products about which to speculate, and the simplicity and intrinsic interest to most subjects has made the drawing of a person a popular clinical procedure. After the drawing is finished, the psychologist usually interviews the client concerning the age, background, thoughts, and best and worst parts of the figure drawn.

Psychologists use drawings for two distinct purposes—as a quick and rough estimate of intelligence and as a projective guide to personality. The first usage has proved to be much more reliable and valid than the second. Florence Goodenough's Draw-A-Man test, originally published in 1926, was updated and given a much more extensive scoring system by Dale Harris (1963). Harris and others have shown that growth in intellectual maturity from age four to fourteen is closely related to the improvement of scores based on the number of details and proportion of figures. Many studies have also shown this progression in other cultures. The interpreter of intellectual maturity and details of drawing must be careful to relate to the background and educational opportunities of the children. Figure 9–3 shows the drawings of two Nepalese children and their Goodenough IQ's (from Sundberg & Ballinger, 1968, pp. 977 and 978). The reader will note many details that would not be found in drawings obtained from a child of the same age who has grown up in America or Europe. The two Nepalese drawings suggest considerable difference between the boy and the girl in sophistication and maturity.

Drawing of a man by a Nepalese boy (age 10   Drawing of a man by Nepalese girl (age 10½
years; IQ, 102).   years; IQ, 88).

FIGURE 9-3   Drawings by Nepalese children. (From Sundberg and Ballinger, 1968, pp. 977-78).

The widespread use of drawing for personality description and psychiatric diagnosis has run into much skepticism by researchers and reviewers (Swenson, 1957, 1968; Roback, 1968). The most frequently used clinical drawing methods are the Machover Draw-A-Person (DAP) and the Buck House-Tree-Person (H-T-P). Psychoanalytic speculation thrives on figure drawings, with the many possibilities for distortions of parts of·the body and choices about what to include or exclude. For instance, over-emphasis on the eyes is supposed to be suggestive of paranoia (indicating hypersensitivity to people looking at one), erasures and redrawings of the nose may indicate castration anxiety (the nose being a phallic symbol) and messy hair suggests sexual immaturity and immorality (hair representing virility strivings). Machover (1949) relates the sex of the first figure drawn to psychosexual identity; a first drawing of the opposite sex suggests homo-sexual tendencies.

Such specific interpretative principles do provide hypotheses that can be checked by research. For instance, one study (Roback et al., 1974) tested the last hypothesis mentioned. The investigators obtained first drawings from samples of both male and female homosexuals and heterosexuals and found no significant differences in sex of first figure drawn. Another study

(Heinrich & Triebe, 1972) of German school children found self-sex drawings predominant only after eleven years of age. In general, Swenson (1968) concluded, most of the alleged specific signs have proven unreliable or invalid, and global ratings of adjustment are more fruitful. One important complication in interpreting drawings is the artistic skill and training of subjects, which affect the quality of the drawing (Cressen, 1975). The testing situation can also affect drawings. For instance, induced anxiety or criticism may make children's drawings less free and spontaneous. Despite the negative psychometric evidence, drawings continue to be fascinating for those interested in personality, and it may be that over time techniques will be developed for analyzing details more usefully.

Another frequently used drawing procedure is the *Bender Visual Motor Gestalt Test.* As has been mentioned in chapter six, the Bender is widely used for indications of problems in visual-motor coordination due to brain damage and indications of personality problems. It will be recalled that the examiner presents a series of nine cards showing simple figures consisting of dots, curves, or lines, one at a time. The task is only to copy the figures on paper. Sometimes the examiner asks the subject to draw them again from memory. The projective analysis of the reactions primarily involves the study of the symbolic and expressive implications of the distortions, aside from visual-motor ability. One notes any kind of difficulty in copying the figures and whether the drawings are made carelessly or compulsively. Drawing problems and distortions of what might be male and female symbols in the figures are particularly important (Lerner, 1972; Hutt, 1969, 1970). The personality interpretations are particularly suspect and reviewers' reactions are mixed. One reviewer (Kitay in Buros, 1972, p. 395) states "The Bender-Gestalt should be included in every diagnostic examination of adults and of children from age five because of the unique contributions to the evaluation of perceptual motor functioning, neurological impairment, expressive styles and maladjustment. Elaborate projective use of the instrument should be employed with caution." In contrast, another reviewer (Blakemore in Buros, 1965, p. 414) states that "research has been carried out, but from it has emerged little in favour of the test as a valid and useful clinical tool."

The variety and richness of ideas about eliciting and studying behavior with projective techniques is impressive. The reader is encouraged to read in the *Mental Measurements Yearbooks* (Buros, 1965, 1972) about such techniques as the Color Pyramid Test, which asks the subject to use 200 color chips, making three "pretty" pyramids and three "ugly" ones, and supposedly reflects emotional expression and control; the Four Picture Test, which requests one written story based on a set of colored pictures representing the "fundamental existential situations;" the Group Personality Projective Test, which consists of ninety simple drawings about which the subject must make a choice among five alternative explanations of what is going on; the Rosenzweig Picture Frustration Test, which uses cartoons on which the subject must make a choice among five alternative explanations of what is going on; the Rosenzweig Picture Frustration Test, which uses cartoons on which the subject writes responses in balloons above the characters' heads; the Hand Test, in which the subject tells what the hands are doing on nine drawings of various ambiguous poses; the Kahn Test of Symbol Arrangement, which requires the individual to give meanings and make arrangements among a set of plastic objects; the Lowenfeld Mosaic Test, in which the subject is to "do something" with 456 small colored pieces; and Structured Doll Play, which provides a kind of structured interview technique for children.

These are only a few of the published techniques. There are many other projective techniques such as those that ask the person to interpret indistinct sounds, to play with puppets, to carry out a psychodrama or role playing, to do finger painting, or to state "three wishes" or "what animal would you like to be." As we know, almost any kind of behavior can be interpreted projectively. One reviewer says (Lee, in Buros, 1972, p. 397):

> It is always easy to set up stimuli which will evoke varied responses from human subjects—so complex are the minds of men—and it is a truism that behavior so elicited is a reflection of the personality of each subject. It is in the *interpretation* of these acts that false conclusions can be drawn. In the past, most of the attacks on projective techniques as such might more profitably have been levelled first against the theoretical beliefs that caused the test stimuli to be constructed in any particular way, and then against the same theoretical biases that distorted the conclusions drawn.

CRITIQUE

Three major conclusions about the projective hypothesis are warranted: (a) An individual's responses to ambiguous or unstructured stimuli are influenced by many factors other than the person's inner needs and conflicts, such as the test-taking attitudes of the person, the characteristics of the examiner, and the previous experience of the person with similar situations. (b) The skill and characteristics of the interpreter of the responses to the projective situation are, to a large extent, inseparable from the results of assessment. Subjectivity is doubled coming from both the subject and the assessor. The assessor's task is a particularly difficult one. (c) The relationship of reported perceptions and thoughts to behavior is far from clear; the correlations between projective test results and action (such as between aggression on TAT stories and aggression in daily life) are dependent on many variables, such as the immediate situation and the background of the person. The enthusiastic belief of Frank and other early proponents has not been maintained. Projective techniques do not provide an X-ray of the personality nor a "royal road to the unconscious," as Freud described dreams to be. The Rorschach and other procedures are not magical, any more so than other personality assessment devices.

Any evaluation of projective techniques as a whole must be general and theoretical. Individual devices need to be precisely compared with other procedures to discern what special tasks can be accomplished *in combination with* other procedures. Projective techniques are not tests in the strict psychometric sense; they are *techniques,* or tools for an expert in assessment, to explore and expose aspects of personality.

In assessing the status of projective techniques, we should make a distinction between their use as *exploratory procedures* for generating information and hypotheses about a person and as *psychometric tests* for obtaining quantitative information on a definite characteristic. Projective devices are used both ways. The use of the word *technique* implies the former usage and relates to the intention of their originators to break away from inflexible and atomistic psychometric approaches (Murstein, 1968). As to their use as exploratory techniques on an individualistic basis, it is difficult to condemn any approach. Any assessor should be free to pursue information that will help him clarify a client's problems and conditions. Interviews serve this flexible purpose and projective techniques can be seen as extensions of interviews. However, whether that kind of use of the assessor's time is as useful as an interview is very questionable.

Projective techniques can also be judged as psychometric tests and the utility of projective techniques is subject to the same questions of validity and reliability and other technical questions as other personality measures are asked. In general, the results of psychometric studies do not generate high enthusiasm.

The research on projective techniques is so voluminous that it is difficult to find a comprehensive review, although some publications approach this (e.g. Murstein, 1963; Zubin, Eron, & Schumer, 1965; Molish, 1972). Validity coefficients are usually positive but low—from .20 to .40. (For a review of predictive validity see Suinn & Oskamp, 1969.) Many of the studies are marred by methodological flaws, such as poor samples, poor validity criteria, inadequate control groups, failure to control for protocol length, and lack of recognition of clinical rater unreliability. Horowitz (1962) and others have shown that judges using the Rorschach, TAT, and sentence completion tests could not improve the validity of the base rate descriptions on a group of patients in psychotherapy. Of the many projective techniques, the one that seems to be considered most valid in studies is the sentence completion technique.

The decline in the popularity and clinical usage of projective methods since the 50s and early 60s can be related to several factors—the research producing unexciting results, even from well designed studies; the general decline in psychodiagnostic testing other than that using behavioral methods; and the decreasing belief in psychoanalytic theory. The 1960s, both in the sociopolitical arena and in psychology, ushered in a much greater concern with situational rather than individual influences on behavior. The time demands from the Rorschach and TAT (two to four hours each, including interpretation time) also make them quite expensive, and people began to doubt that their clinical benefit was worth their cost. Still the various projective techniques are quite widely used for clinical purposes and the research use of projective devices is likely to continue to be high, especially in modified scorable forms. It is interesting that some behavior therapists (e.g., Lazarus, 1971) include projective stories and sentence completions in their assessment repertoire. The phenomena that the projective techniques are attempting to assess—imagination, misperception, unconscious conflicts and needs, expressiveness to unstructured stimuli, coping styles, and the "whole person"—are important for understanding personality. An integrated theory must include these phenomena, though they may be given different labels. In their review of projective techniques, Klopfer & Taulbee (1976, p. 563) conclude:

> The most distinct contribution that projective tests continue to make . . . is in revealing aspects of motivation and personality that do not fit neatly into either the self-concept or behavioral category. Creative capacities, hidden resources, potentialities that currently are not in use are variables that sometimes emerge better in projective test performance than through other sources of information. Until clinical psychologists give up an interest in the inner person and abandon their search for probing the depths of the psyche, they probably will continue to use, improve, and rely upon the data derived from projective techniques.

SUMMARY

Projective techniques are relatively disguised and ambiguous procedures using a great variety of stimuli and eliciting a variety of responses. They rest largely on a base of assumptions related to psychoanalytic theory or modifications of it, and the typical projective technique requires the interpreter to view the results as a sign of underlying personality dynamics. According to the type of response, one can identify five kinds of projective techniques: association, construction, completion, choice or ordering, and expressive techniques.

The Rorschach has been the most widely used and published projective personality test. The subject first responds freely by saying what he or she sees on the ten inkblots, then the examiner asks for the location of the response on the blot and an explanation of what made it look that way. Rorschachs are scored for location, determinants, and content. Several elaborate scoring and interpretation systems have been developed. Research evaluation of the Rorschach shows variable reliability in the scores and questionable validity in many studies. Among many adaptations of the Rorschach approach, the Holtzman Inkblot Technique stands out as the most promising for the development of psychometric sophistication.

The Thematic Apperception Test is the second most prominent projective device. Its full administration involves obtaining stories in response to twenty pictures, but most clinicians and researchers use only a few selected ones. Many varieties of the TAT have also been developed. Scoring is done for research purposes but seldom for clinical purposes. The interpretation concentrates on the identified hero in the story and assumes that the hero's needs and environmental presses represent those of the subject. Murray's system of needs is often used to organize the content obtained, and some of the large research projects have specifically dealt with needs for achievement, affiliation, and power.

There are a wide variety of additional projective techniques beyond the two most common ones. Among them the sentence completion method is probably most promising. There is considerable evidence for its validity, and the professional time it takes is not great. Techniques for drawing a man or a person have shown good validity for intellectual maturation in children but are very questionable as personality indicators. The Bender-Gestalt test is also probably most useful as a rough indicator of intellectual maturity or deficit than of personality.

Some major conclusions about projective methods are that responses are influenced by many variables, not just inner dynamics, that they depend heavily on the skill and biases of the interpreter, and the relationship between reported perceptions and behavior requires conceptualization and measurement of moderating and situational variables. Projective techniques declined in popularity in the 60s and 70s due not just to research findings but also to a shift from psychoanalytic to behavioral therapy and lessened concern for psychodiagnosis. Many of the questions about the perception of ambiguous forms and the manner in which people express inner states still remain fundamental problems for understanding personality.

SUGGESTED READINGS

GOLDSTEIN, L. D. & LANYON, R. I. (eds.) *Readings in personality assessment.* New York: Wiley, 1971. This collection of articles has wide applicability to chapters throughout this book. Of most value to this particular chapter are Frank's

1939 article on projective methods, Goldberg's review of sentence completion methods, Swenson's survey of figure drawings, Murstein's study of variables affecting the expression of hostility on the TAT, and the excerpt from *An experimental approach to projective techniques* by Zubin, Eron, & Schumer (1965). Another good collection of articles is *Projective techniques in personality measurement* by Rabin (1968).

GOLDFIELD, M. R., STRICKER, G. & WEINER, I. B. *Rorschach handbook of clinical and research applications.* Englewood Cliffs, N.J.: Prentice-Hall, 1971. For those interested in some reading in depth about the Rorschach, this overview of the major scoring systems is excellent. Readers interested in the Holtzman Inkblot Technique are referred to excellent reviews by Gamble (1972) and Holtzman (1975).

PROLA, M. A. Review of the Transcendence Index. *Journal of Personality Assessment,* 1972, 36, 8–12. This article is interesting because of the importance of understanding and measuring the degree to which projective techniques stimulate fantasy. The Transcendence Index shows how much subjects go beyond simple description of the stimulus.

VARBLE, D. L. Current status of the Thematic Apperception Test. In P. McReynolds (ed.) *Advances in psychological assessment,* Vol. 2. Palo Alto: Science and Behavior books, 1971. Varble reviews scoring systems, reliability, validity, major areas of research, and factors shown to affect TAT performance. He recommends that the TAT be developed as a structured and standardized test suitable for self-administration and computerized scoring.

chapter ten

Assessment
of Cognitive Abilities
and Competence

When for any individual we have answered the two major questions, "What can he or she do?" and "What does he or she want?", we have sketched the main outlines of his or her individuality. —Leona Tyler, *Individual Differences*, 1974, p. 219.

In the first chapter of this book we noted the distinction between maximum performance, which is associated with ability testing, and typical performance, which is associated with motivation and personality testing. We have also realized that abilities are interwoven with personality and their assessment is necessary to achieve a picture of the whole person and to predict or explain behavior. This chapter will discuss the relationship between personality and tests of ability, especially cognitive, or thinking, abilities. We will also look at methods of measuring the related concepts of cognitive styles and creativity, and examine the place of competence in a view of personality. Finally, since this is the last chapter on assessment techniques, we will touch on some miscellaneous instruments of personality study that do not fit readily into other parts of the book.

What are the cognitive aspects of a person? Philosophers and psychologists for centuries have been analyzing the functioning of people into three major components: cognition (thinking), affect or emotion (feeling), and conation or motivation (willing). In any particular behavior episode, thinking cannot be neatly separated from feeling and willing, but we can point to certain acts where thinking aspects dominate or in which we purposefully observe and record only the products we define as cognitive. Cognition is a general term for any process for becoming aware of an object or thinking about an object or a situation. The term includes sensing, perceiving, remembering, recognizing, differentiating, developing concepts, and judging or reasoning about something. Cognitive assessment procedures may ask the person to define a word, solve a problem, sort objects into groups that go together, list ideas for a topic, make drawings, or perform almost any other kind of mental activity.

One can contrast cognitive assessment with other techniques in that cognitive techniques are concerned with thought and information processing. Behavioral techniques concentrate on observable activities and the surrounding situation. Cognitive techniques do not directly ask a person for self description as objective techniques do, and unlike projective techniques, they do not usually presume the projective hypothesis or use ambiguous tasks. There are, of course, areas that overlap with the three primary personality assessment procedures described in the last three chapters. The most highly developed and widely used cognitive assessment procedures are intelligence tests, but they are only one part of a broad spectrum that covers ability and achievement.

THE SPECTRUM OF ABILITY, APTITUDE, AND INTELLIGENCE TESTS

The many tests of ability and aptitude cover a broad array of specificity and generality. *Ability* is the currently available power to perform something and *aptitude* is the potential for performance after training. Both concepts have similarities with *achievement,* which is a measure of successful performance in the past. The typical college aptitude tests, for instance, are close to the achievement testing in high school and college courses; they may depend on specific knowledge of English, chemistry, social science, and so on. At the other extreme, many intelligence tests try to measure general problem-solving ability and consist of tasks that are abstract and depend little on specific information. Cronbach (1970, p. 282) has noted the relationship of these various tests in a chart, presented in *Figure 10-1*. Some college entrance tests, like the Scholastic Aptitude Test of the College Boards, mainly cover level C; some go lower into Level D. Other tests, like the Wechsler Performance Tests and the Progressive Matrices, concentrate on Level A. The reader will note on Figure 10-1 that the A level measures "fluid" ability or intelligence, and at the other extreme the D level measures "crystallized" ability. These terms, elaborated by Cattell (1963) refer to the relative reliance on flexible problem-solving and seeing of new relationships (fluid ability) versus the relative reliance on specific remembered information (crystallized ability). One important finding based on research over the life span is that young people are likely to depend more on fluid intelligence and older people on crystallized intelligence, though the general level of intelligence in longitudinal studies does not decline greatly until quite advanced years (Schaie, 1974).

Another way of conceptualizing the array of abilities covered by tests that are aimed at measuring cognitive abilities is shown in Figure 10-2. This figure by Cronbach (1970, p. 332) derives from factor analytic research. The top level is the most general and pervasive intellectual ability (called

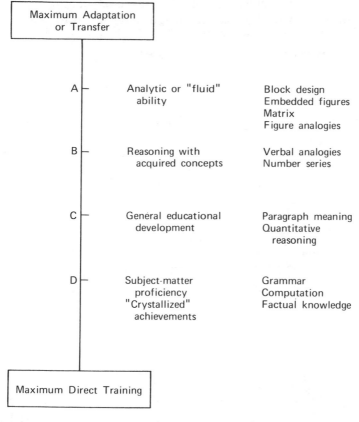

FIGURE 10-1   A spectrum for comparing tests of scholastic aptitude and general ability. (From Cronbach, 1970, p. 282. Copyright © 1970 by Lee J. Cronbach. Reprinted by permission of the author and Harper & Row Publishers, Inc.)

"g," fluid, or analytic). In successive levels going down the hierarchy other more specific measures are mentioned.

Still another way of conceptualizing the specific abilities that make up the general construct of intelligence is that of Guilford (1959b, 1967). He identified 120 different components that he neatly composed in his cubical Structure of Intellect model shown in Figure 10-3. Guilford posits five types of mental operations such as remembering and evaluating, each of which may use four types of content such as the behavioral and symbolic, and result in any of six classes of products such as units, relations, or transformations. These are all properties of thinking, and Guilford and his colleagues have developed tasks to measure many of the 120 possibilities. Box NFU in Figure 10-3 would be a task involving convergent thinking (giving one acceptable solution for a problem) about figural content (such as abstract drawings) that is presented as one unit (rather than several units in relationship). The correlations between many of the tests are high, and it remains to be seen how practical such fine distinctions are, but this conception of intelligence has generated much research.

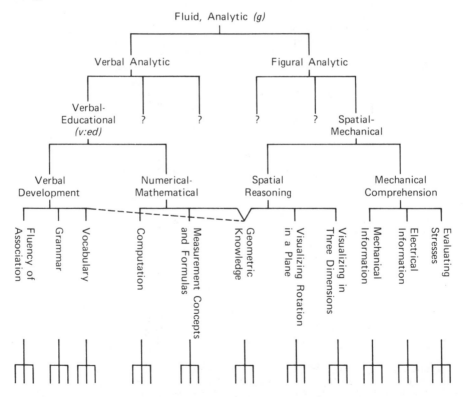

FIGURE 10-2 A possible hierarchical structure of abilities (From Cronbach, 1970, p. 332). Copyright © 1970 by Lee J. Cronbach. Reprinted by permission of the author and Harper & Row Publishers, Inc.)

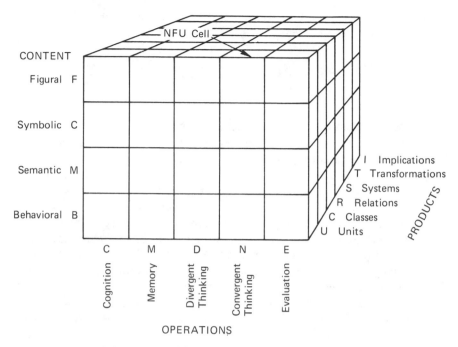

FIGURE 10-3   Guilford's structure of intellect model.

What we usually think of as intelligence tests fall near the upper end of the spectrum in Figures 10–1 and 10–2. Intelligence is a broad concept presumably generalizing across many domains of human functioning. It has to do with a person's repertory of ways to deal with tasks involving discriminations, abstractions, and problem-solving. Fischer (1969, p. 699) states that "intelligence refers to the effectiveness, relative to age peers, of the individual's approaches to situations in which competence is highly regarded by the culture." This definition points to the importance of "competence" as defined by the culture, a concept we will return to in a later section, and to the comparisons with others in one's age group, now the common basis for test norms.

Intelligence measured at the high general level may not say much about detailed cognitive operations, which must be measured by more relevant tasks. In addition, intelligence tests do not cover specific skills or talents. The more common practical ability tests that have been developed include measures of clerical ability, where a person might be asked to check pairs of words to see if they are spelled the same; tweezer dexterity, where a person uses tweezers to put small metal pegs in holes; reading comprehension, where the subject answers questions on a paragraph just read; or musical ability, where a subject differentiates between tones of different pitch. There are many other examples of such tests in education and industry, many of them described in the Buros yearbooks or such textbooks as Cronbach (1970) and Guion (1965).

PERSONALITY AS REVEALED
IN INTELLIGENCE TESTING

Since problems of reliability, validity, and norms have been discussed elsewhere, often using examples from ability tests, we will not go into them here in detail. We might, however, mention some warnings. Since the words "IQ" and "intelligence" are so value-laden in our society, it is important not to stigmatize a person by labelling him or her on the basis of a small amount of evidence. Interpretation must be very cautious with persons from minority groups or others on whom tests were not standardized (Sattler, 1974), and in some cases it might be better not to give the test at all than to create a misleading impression. We shall take up such problems about intelligence testing at length later in this chapter and in chapter twelve. It is true, however, in many studies on samples relevant to the tests, that recently taken general intelligence tests do predict the likelihood of success in academic work and many jobs. For instance, a correlation between college entrance examination scores and grades in the freshman year typically have been around .50. General intelligence enters into many activities so potently that it should always be considered as a possible confounding factor in results on most psychological studies of individual differences. In work with individuals, an assessor should always consider the possible influence of general ability on the results obtained.

There are a large number of published intelligence tests. Buros (1972) lists seventy-four group intelligence tests, of which the California Test of Mental Maturity, the College Board Scholastic Aptitude Test, the Cooperative School and College Ability Tests, the Goodenough-Harris Drawing Test (which was discussed under projective techniques, though it is usually used as a rough measure of intelligence), and the Progressive Matrices have over 200 publications. He also lists thirty-three individual intelligence tests, of which the Peabody Picture Vocabulary Test, the Stanford Binet, the Wechsler Adult Intelligence Scale, and the Wechsler Intelligence Scale for Children have over 200 references. Buros also has a category he calls specific intelligence tests where he lists fourteen tests of particular abilities, some of which we will be discussing under cognitive complexity, creativity, and concept formation; two have over 200 publications, the Illinois Test of Psycholinguistic Abilities and the Torrance Tests of Creative Thinking. Thus, there are many possible testing tools available to the assessor.

As an example of one intelligence test and its relationship to personality we will look at the Wechsler tests, or more specifically the Wechsler Adult

Intelligence Scale (WAIS), for which there is an excellent and thorough handbook by Matarazzo (1972). Wechsler (Matarazzo, 1972, p. 79) stated that intelligence is a hypothetical construct, "the aggregate or global capacity of the individual to act purposefully, to think rationally, and to deal effectively with his environment." Wechsler was interested in the practical aspects of intelligence, and his tests were developed for clinical use with individuals. He saw intelligent behavior as a result of many non-intellective aspects of personality such as emotional states, and believed that such behavior represented a broad concept still inadequately measured. Wechsler's original intention was to be able to identify clinical problems that affected intellectual functioning. He hoped that a pattern analysis of subtests within the test would show characteristic thinking patterns for the schizophrenic, the organically impaired, and the neurotic, and could thus help in the psychiatric diagnosis of personality disorder.

Wechsler developed his first intelligence test, the Wechsler-Bellevue, in 1939 just before World War II, during which it came into very wide use in military hospitals and clinics. Wechsler used three innovations not commonly found in other intelligence tests at that time: (a) the grouping of items of similar content into subtests, (b) the comparison of results on adults with others of the same age, and (c) the use of the deviation IQ, which is a standard score based on a mean of 100 for an age group, and a standard deviation of fifteen. The Wechsler Adult Intelligence Scale, published in 1955, was similar to the Wechsler Bellevue but with improved items, norms, and statistical characteristics. The WAIS consists of eleven subtests, including six verbal subtests and five performance tests, whose standard scores are added to produce Verbal, Performance, and Full Scale IQs. The subtests of the WAIS with illustrations of items similar to the actual ones are:

VERBAL
Information: What is the distance between Montreal and New Orleans?
Comprehension: Why do most women go to a hospital to have a baby?
Arithmetic: If an airplane flies at 500 miles an hour, how long will it take to go
    3000 miles?
Similarities: In what way are a hammer and an automobile alike?
Digit Span: (Examiner's instructions) After I say these numbers, repeat them
    after me: 7–4–3–9–2–5–1.
Vocabulary: What does "parallel" mean?
PERFORMANCE
Block Design: (The subject uses a set of blocks painted with different colors
    and diagonals on different sides to copy pictured patterns presented one
    at a time.)
Object Assembly: (The subject puts together separate pieces of a flat wooden
    hand or other object.)
Picture Arrangement: (The subject is given three or more cartoon panels that
    must be arranged in sequence to make a story.)

Picture Completion: The subject tells what is missing in a picture, such as the
    smokestack of a ship.)
Digit Symbol: (The subject fills in a code mark for each number in a list, using
    a master guide.)

Figure 10-4 shows the administration of part of the Wechsler test. All of the performance tests have time limits and the time required to complete the task is used as a score on several tests. The person's response to such speed situations is one of the clinical observations that Wechsler would have assessors make.

As personality tests, the Wechsler and most other intelligence tests are crude devices. Wechsler's original hope that the scatter of the subtests into patterns would clearly distinguish different psychiatric disorders has not been fulfilled despite much research and occasional positive results. However, any clinical testing gives rough information that can be checked by other assessment procedures. Matarazzo (1972, p. 435) reviews many studies that culminate in the conclusion that sociopathic persons (individuals who abnormally violate social norms and have difficulty learning from experience) tend to have higher Performance IQs than Verbal IQs. Among verbal subtests, Similarities seems to be particularly low in violent sociopaths (Kunce, Rayan, & Eckleman, 1976). Yet a study by Henning & Levy

FIGURE 10-4

(1967) has raised questions about this differential when applied to age and ethnic groups other than those used in the original studies. The authors point out the possibility that results may be related to reading ability, that would affect vocabulary, information, and other verbal scores. So the analysis of Matarazzo's conclusion becomes rather complex.

Standardized procedures such as the Wechsler tests do provide good opportunities for informal observation of personal behavior, particularly when tests are administered individually. The assessor obtains a sample of how a person copes with problems of varying structure and difficulty and how he or she expresses individuality and personal style. A clinician may find useful indications of thought disorders. A depressed person is likely to react slowly, to claim incompetence, and to demean his or her results. A paranoid person is likely to be hesitant and suspicious and see personalized meanings in the test. Psychopaths (sociopaths) often give flip, self-centered responses. Bizarre and over-inclusive responses may be indicative of schizophrenia. Here are some examples of responses given by psychiatric patients (Matarazzo, 1972, pp. 486–487):

    Q: What is the distance from Paris to New York?
    A: I don't know. I never walked that far. (By an adolescent psychopath.)
    Q: What is the population of the United States?
    A: The population is 10,000. (Involutional depression, IQ 96)
    Q: What is the capital of Italy?
    A: Rome, but it could have changed. (Manic-depressive)
    Q: In what direction would you travel if you went from Chicago to Panama?
    A: I'd take a plane and let the pilot worry about the direction. (Psychopath)
    Q: Define "cushion."
    A: To sleep on a pillow of God's sheep. (Schizophrenic)
    Q: Why are shoes made of leather?
    A: Because leather has undoubtedly proved to be the most durable that has been utilized for the preservation of the feet and to continue the comfort of those, that is, the people who have chose to wear shoes. (Schizophrenic)
    Q: What is a "guillotine?"
    A: Part of law subject only to those without call to stay on earth. (Schizophrenic)

The reader could probably imagine that the first four of the above responses might have been made by normal people. The last three, however, clearly reflect the distortion of thought that is the distinguishing mark of schizophrenia. A psychologist would never base a diagnosis solely on one response, of course, but would only use such responses to formulate hypotheses to be checked by other means.

Even within the normal range, the various ways that individuals cope with the tasks tell something about them and generate hypotheses for checking. Consider the impressions about personality you might receive from testing three five year old children in response to the question: "What is an orange?" The first child quickly answers "a fruit." The second says "It's something my mommy gives me when I get home. It's good to eat. I like apples, too, but oranges are juicy and sweet." The third child, squirming all the while, replies "Maybe, it's—uh—What? A thing to eat." All three receive a passing score as to cognitive ability, but the personality differences are striking. The manner of responding, the feeling of certainty, the amount of elaboration, the degree of ease with the task, and the relationship with the examiner are all "readable" as important personality differences.

COGNITIVE STYLES

In the borderland between ability and personality there has arisen a set of assessment devices that came largely from experiments on cognition and perception. Psychologists noticed that experimental subjects showed individual differences in studies of information-processing and attention. The psychologists have labelled these differences in various ways, but they all seem to point to personal differences in strategies of control. A frequently used term is *cognitive styles,* that refers both to ability and motivation. Whatever pattern of abilities the person has inherited or developed up to this time seem to be controlled or "programmed" for expression in distinctively different individual ways. We have mentioned some of these procedures in chapter five when discussing a person's linkage with the environment. Here we will briefly look at some of them again as assessment devices for individual differences in cognitive style.

Herman Witkin and his colleagues (1954, 1962, 1967, 1975), over a long series of studies, have identified one of the prominent dimensions of cognitive style. At first they called it *field dependence vs. independence*; later they have been using the term *psychological differentiation*. Either term refers to the differences among people in the ways they select and organize a complex situation or field to produce a requested cognitive response. The field independent or differentiated person is able to separate the required parts from the confusing display presented, but the field dependent or undifferentiated person reacts to the whole situation without analyzing it, seemingly dominated by the situation. Witkin discovered this basic cognitive dimension through a series of ingenious tests. In the Rod and Frame Test, the person's task is to adjust a luminous rod so that it is upright. What makes the job difficult is that the room is completely dark and the luminous square outline around the luminous rod is tilted at various angles as he or she sets or resets the rod. The subject is supposed to remain undistracted by the frame's different positions and must determine the upright position only by his internal bodily feelings. Field dependent or less differentiated people are more responsive to changes in the experimental surroundings than the field independent people.

Witkin and his co-workers have demonstrated this cognitive control characteristic in many studies and have related it to important personality variables. People who are accurate in this task, that is, they manipulate the controls so that the rod is truly vertical despite the position of the frame or chair, tend to be accurate on other tasks of differentiation. They are likely to be quick in identifying figures in a complex design (on the Embedded Figures Test) and in demonstrating a knowledge of body parts on drawings. The differences in psychological differentiation are also stable over long periods of time. Field independent or differentiated people are more active in dealing with their environments, more in control of impulses, and more aware of their inner experience. Moderate correlations with intelligence test results are often reported, but Witkin rejects the idea that these differentiation tests are merely measuring intelligence, and has demonstrated that on one of the Wechsler tests only three of the performance measures correlate significantly with his test results.

Field independent people tend to use the defense of intellectualization, and field dependent people tend to use repression and denial in situations where they are under attack. Alcoholics are likely to be field dependent. Delusions are more common among field-independents. One interesting cross-cultural study (Berry, 1966) found that Eskimo children, who live in a hunting culture and an environment that requires considerable self-reliance, show strikingly more field independence than the Temne children of West Africa, whose environment is less mobile and requires less independence. In general, hunting cultures are associated with more field independence than sedentary, agricultural cultures (Witkin & Berry, 1975). Eskimo boys and girls did not show sex differences in field dependence, though most studies elsewhere show that males tend to be more field independent than females; socialization practices are probably important in developing this cognitive personality trait.

There are a number of assessment procedures that explore other cognitive styles. The Conceptual Style Test (Kagen, Moss, & Sigel, 1963) asks children to pick from a set of pictures, two that go together and to state the reason they are alike. One set shows a watch, a man, and a measuring stick. Kagan and his colleagues find that children tend to use either an *analytic* or *global* (relational) categorizing style. When describing differences and similarities between pictures, some would note parts of objects in the picture and make comparisons while others would use relationships or other global concepts. (This distinction is reminiscent of the focusing and scanning operations recommended in the general strategies of assessment of persons discussed in chapter one.) Other studies have identified an important difference between children's impulsiveness-reflectiveness in carrying out perceptual tasks. Impulsive children are quick and inaccurate; reflective children are slow and make few errors. Reflective children do better on intelligence and achievement tests, because they "look before they leap," paying attention to distinctive features in the tasks.

One of the most interesting assessment procedures related to cognitive styles is that developed in connection with the personality theory of George Kelly (1955) and elaborated by his students and others (Bannister, 1970), called the Role Construct Repertory Test (RCRT, or Rep test, for short). Wiggins (1973, p. 494) states that "the Rep test approach advocated by Kelly appears to be the most sophisticated and convincing example of 'idiographic measurement' in the sense in which Allport (1961) employed that term. Personal construct theory is by assumption idiographic in *content* since each individual is held to construe the world in a unique fashion." The Rep test has taken on several forms, but in all of them the basic idea is that the person selects his or her own ways of comparing people rather than using the conceptual system of the test maker. Following the original method the tester presents the subject with a list of twenty-four role titles such as "your favorite teacher," "spouse or closest opposite-sexed friend," and "the most successful person you know personally." The subject writes the name of the person for each role on a separate card. Then the examiner takes three of the cards and asks the subject to say in which way two of them are alike and different from the third. The subject may say that his or her teacher and spouse are "kind" but the successful person is "hard-hearted." Making triads of the cards, the examiner goes through them all, asking the subject to explain the similarities and differences. By studying the results, a clinical assessor can determine the construct system of a client and the dimensions along which he or she thinks about other people. This analysis suggests how a client may most readily develop in psychotherapy and what new dimensions the client might need to learn in order to see other people differently.

Though the Rep test was first formulated as an idiographic, clinical assessment device, some nomethetic and general procedures and concepts have developed. For example, Kelly's concept of *cognitive complexity* refers to the total number of different constructs or dimensions a person uses in thinking about other people. One person may use only a few, like "intelligent-stupid" and "kind-cruel," but another person may construe people in many additional ways. There is, then, a general consensus of the number of personal constructs along which people can be placed, from the cognitively simple to the cognitively complex. Group forms and quantitative recording systems have been developed. Levy & Dugan (1956) for instance originated a system for factor-analyzing ratings of all the persons listed on each of the constructs chosen. As mentioned in chapter five, Tyler's Choice Pattern Technique (Tyler et al., 1968) similarly examines cognitive styles and complexity in the realm of occupations and leisure activities.

Finally, we should note an important assessment concept that is related to cognitive control and to beliefs—Rotter's internal vs. external *locus of control* of reinforcement (Rotter, 1966). Locus of control is measured by a set of item pairs, one of which related to expectations that a person can control his or her life (e.g., "A person gets about as much out of life as he puts into it"), and the other to expectations that outside forces or fate are in control (e.g. "Getting ahead is mostly a matter of luck"). A number of studies have shown significant relationships with other personal characteristics. Student activists, for instance, tend to be internal controllers, and smokers feel less in control than nonsmokers. Rotter's technique and his social learning theory of personality have generated hundreds of studies (Rotter, Chance, & Phares, 1972).

ASSESSMENT OF DIVERGENT THINKING AND CREATIVITY

Guilford's Structure of Intellect model (shown in Figure 10–3) contains two types of thinking operations that have been of particular interest to assessment specialists—convergent and divergent thinking. Guilford pointed out that most of our intelligence, aptitude, and achievement tests call for *convergent thinking.* The subject is presented with a problem or a set of stimuli and required to give the one correct answer. Arithmetic problems are a good illustration. Another kind of thinking, however, could be called *divergent,* where the subject is given a problem and asked to think of all the different possibilities that might happen. Some divergent problems are "What are the uses of a tin can?" or "Name all the places you can reach walking from here in an hour." The subject then may list many ideas. The convergent style of testing is close ended; the divergent style is open ended, calling for all the imagination and flexible thinking that the person can muster at the time. The idea of divergent thinking became one of the stimulating concepts that generated many new tests of creative thinking. Torrance (1962) was particularly involved in applying these and related ideas to school children. The Minnesota Tasks of Creative Thinking were the result. Tests of creativity based on divergent thinking give scores for *fluency* (for instance, the number of uses a person lists for a tin can), *flexibility* (the different kinds of uses given), and *originality* (the rarity of a response in a tested group). There are a number of other kinds of tasks from which creativity ratings and scores can be obtained—drawings; stories in response to TAT pictures; preferences for simple, symmetrical drawings vs. complex, asymmetrical ones; and many other activities calling for imagination.

The relationship between this kind of mental activity—divergent thinking or ideational fluency—and some aspects of creativity, raise many questions about the traditional tests of intelligence. One does not expect a retarded person to make a great scientific breakthrough, yet on the other hand many intellectually capable people lead unproductive lives. Getzels & Jackson(1962) found little relationship between IQ and creativity in a high school composed chiefly of capable children. The extensive work of the Institute of Personality Assessment and Research at Berkeley (MacKinnon, 1962, 1965) frequently showed that the intelligence measurements of highly creative people were scattered over a wide range. After reviewing many studies relating creativity to intelligence, MacKinnon & Hall (1972, p. 1888) concluded that,

> Creative persons in the professions tend to be highly intelligent. In such professional groups as we have studied, however, what differentiates the more creative members of the groups from their less creative peers is not a higher level of intelligence than theirs, though they may often possess just that, but rather distinctive patterns of interests, values, personality traits, and perceptual and cognitive preferences. Above a given minimal level of intelligence required for the successful practice of one's profession, which in the groups we have studied is quite high, what is most importantly determinative of creative performance is not a higher level of intelligence *per se* but particular constellations of non-intellective traits.

Reviewing research on the identification of creativity, Dellas & Gaier (1970) conclude that creative people appear to be distinguished more by interests, attitudes, and drives than by intelligence. Tests of scholastic achievement also seem to bear a limited relation to creativity, though extreme divergencies are rare. There are examples of very intelligent youngsters, like the young Albert Einstein, who had trouble with school work. Reviewing studies of creativity and intelligence, Tyler (1974, p. 104–5) points out one implication: "To evaluate the overall ability of individuals in terms of typical tests of scholastic aptitude alone is an unsound procedure. To 'type' a child as promising or unpromising on the basis of IQ alone is unfair to him and to the society in which he is a contributing participant."

A COMPETENCY-BASED VIEW OF PERSONALITY

Our discussion of creativity moves us toward a view of personality based on effectiveness. The concept of *competence* (or competency) is relevant when we are talking about abilities, and it sheds considerable light on certain attempts to assess and improve the functioning of people. The term carries two connotations. Competence is *ability-oriented*, not disability-oriented; it points to the opposite of maladjustment and disorder and emphasizes positive, coping skills. The concept also is *situation-oriented* in that it relates to the mastery of situations, or the ability to function in environmental interaction. Competence as high level functioning is then more than the inner motivation to explore and master, a view which has been well supported by White (1959). It is also the ability to deal effectively with the requirements and possibilities of different environments. Some of the pioneers in work on intelligence saw that concept as very close to a general competence. Binet considered tests requiring "judgment" to be of core importance. Wechsler (1975, p. 139) states "What intelligence tests measure, what we hope they measure, is . . . the capacity of an individual to understand the world about him and his resourcefulness to cope with its challenges."

This emphasis on ability is also found in the *competency-based* approach to education and training. Anderson & Messick (1974), for instance, discuss the problems of preschool programs like Headstart. They argue that the aims of such programs should be the development of social competence, not just improvements in IQ or scholastic ability. They list twenty-nine components of social competency related to the goals of early intervention programs; among them are a differentiated self-concept and consolidation of identity, perception of self as an initiating and controlling agent, realistic appraisal of self accompanied by a feeling of personal worth, interpersonal sensitivity and understanding, appreciation of different roles relevant to the child's situation, morality and prosocial tendencies, curiosity and exploratory behavior, and enjoyment of humor, play, and fantasy. An educational program based on such goals would be dealing with matters of personality and would be viewing personality as strongly infused with abilities.

With adults, similar considerations enter when one starts analyzing needed skills in human services or in business, for instance. Some effects are being made to develop competency-based training programs for social work, engineering, and other fields. In *functional job analysis* (Fine & Wiley, 1971), occupational roles are broken down into skills such as observing, listening, instructing, and leading. In each such function the specific tasks are identified, and assessment and training for those tasks is developed. Many of these skills are closely related to personality characteristics and interpersonal functioning.

A full-fledged competency-based view of personality would require an analysis of the functioning of people in the major roles of life, and the development of tasks to measure the components of those roles. Part of such an endeavor is already begun under such research efforts as the measurement of the ability to empathize in two-person situations, the ability to be sensitive to implied meanings in speech, a knowledge of others, effectiveness in responding to social situations, and other related work (Arkowitz et al., 1975; Carkhuff, 1969; Glasgow & Arkowitz, 1975; Goldfried & D'Zurilla, 1969; McQueen et al., 1975; Sundberg, 1966). One factor analytic study of the role of the counselor identified twelve basic competences such as social awareness, self awareness, listening, tutoring, and testing skills (Menne, 1975). A full program would be an extremely ambitious attempt, but it seems likely that such an effort joining ability and personality assessment would be profitable for both practice and theory. Such different personality theories as client centered (Rogers, 1957; Truax & Carkhuff, 1967), ego psychology (A. Freud, 1946; Hartman, 1958), and the behavioral approaches (Wallace, 1966) all seem to call for attention to an assessment of interpersonal skills.

SPECIAL PROCEDURES
FOR DESCRIBING PERSONALITY

Finally at the end of our discussion of techniques we need to mention a class of assessment procedures that are used by judges and observers in attempting to describe and portray personality as a whole. These are instruments that cover a wide range of items or phrases and are useful to summarize impressions of individuals. They are often used in the large research projects on personality that are described in the next chapter, and in research on personality change. The major instruments, some of which have been mentioned previously in other contexts, are adjective check lists, Q sorts, and rating scales.

One instrument frequently used in personality research is the Adjective Checklist (ACL) by Gough & Heilbrun (1965). This simply consists of 300 adjectives beside which are spaces for people to check the words they consider to be descriptive of themselves. The ACL can be scored like an inventory on keys for such traits as self-confidence, achievement, dominance, heterosexuality, and autonomy. The ACL is probably more useful for research than for practical purposes. The words can be used as a pool for finding adjectives that correlate with another instrument or scale. For instance, Gough and others have used the ACL in identifying how high scorers on CPI scales describe themselves or are described by others.

The Q sort technique has been widely used for a variety of purposes, although mostly for research. One of the few published forms is the California Q-Set (Block, 1961), which provides 100 statements to be sorted into a specified number of piles. It is to be used for the description of personality and psychodynamics by experts. As another example, study of values one (Sundberg, et al., 1970) asked ninth graders in India and America to sort forty statements (such as "My first duty is to myself," "I judge a job by how much money it brings in," or "I like beautiful things even if they are not useful,") into seven piles with a certain number in each pile.

Pile 1	Pile 2	Pile 3	Pile 4	Pile 5	Pile 6	Pile 7
Most Strongly Disagree	Strongly Disagree	Moderately Disagree	Neutral or Mixed	Moderately Agree	Strongly Agree	Most Strongly Agree
3 cards	6 cards	10 cards	12 cards	10 cards	6 cards	3 cards

The average scores given by groups can be correlated. For instance, in this values study the correlation between Indians and Americans was .55 for boys and .44 for girls. These cross-cultural correlations were lower than the intracultural, cross-sex correlations of .85 for Americans and .78 for Indians. In addition the use of a fixed number of cards distributed over the piles to form a symmetrical series makes it easy to apply correlational techniques between different sorts by the same person or between sorts by different persons (Block, 1961); Stephenson, 1953). Carl Rogers and his colleagues have used this technique extensively in comparing individuals before and after psychotherapy (e.g. Rogers & Dymond, 1954).

Another interesting and important rating technique is the *Semantic Differential* developed by Charles Osgood and his associates (1957, Snider & Osgood, 1969). This procedure starts with ratings of any target (such as self, father, wife, or an abstract concept like "mental illness" or "community") on a set of bipolar scales such as cold-hot, strong-weak, clean-dirty, and tense-relaxed. The subject checks whether the target seems to be like one end or the other of the dimension by checking on a seven point scale that is placed between them. A number of factor analytic studies using this instrument in a large number of different cultures have revealed three basic factors: evaluation (good-bad or like-dislike), potency (strong-weak) and activity (active-passive). Usually the concepts being investigated are located by averaging the ratings on three or four bipolar scales on each of the three dimensions.

RESOURCES FOR MISCELLANEOUS
ASSESSMENT PROCEDURES

Since this is the last chapter specifically devoted to assessment techniques themselves, it seems appropriate to mention again the wide variety of methods that have been only partially sampled in the presentation. The previous chapters have attempted to cover the leading published tests and a few of the unpublished ones. Here we will note a few of the many other possibilities to give the reader a sense of the full field. Because many measures of psychological variables are poorly publicized, the new student or worker in assessment is in danger of trying to map territory that someone else may have already explored.

Buros' *Mental Measurements Yearbooks* are, of course, the major resource for finding published tests. In addition to personality and intelligence tests mentioned on these pages, the yearbooks cover many achievement and aptitude tests. Buros includes tests in English, fine arts, foreign languages, mathematics, and social science, and general achievement batteries and aptitude tests in such areas as reading, speech and hearing, sensory-motor skills, mechanical ability and manual dexterity, specific vocational aptitudes, and general multi-aptitude batteries. Buros also lists miscellaneous areas of testing like listening comprehension, socioeconomic status, hypnotic susceptibility, and reasoning ability.

There are also several resources for locating unpublished materials that may also save the student's or test-developer's time. The Educational Testing Service of Princeton, New Jersey, maintains a collection of unpublished tests that is constantly increasing. Chun, Cobb, & French (1975) have published a guide to 3000 sources of assessment measures based on a computerized national repository of social science measures at the Institute of Social Research at the University of Michigan. Comrey, Backer, & Glaser (1973) have published a similar book, *A sourcebook for mental health measures,* which contains over 1000 abstracts describing instruments, and indicating where more information can be obtained. A sample of the topics covered includes alcoholism, crime, drugs, educational adjustment, family interaction, parental behavior, racial attitudes, suicide and death, and teacher attitudes.

As resources for surveys in given fields of assessment, the series of books edited by McReynolds, entitled *Advances in psychological assessment,* provide excellent summaries and evaluations of new developments. McReynolds' volumes cover such areas as the assessment of infants, brain-behavior relations, group clinical tests, community mental health, and the history of assessment itself.

A COMMENT AND CRITIQUE ON ABILITY TESTING

Most of this chapter has dealt with ability testing, in which "intelligence" is the most pervasive and readily confused concept. So-called "IQ tests" have been both the greatest achievement of assessment psychologists and the source of their greatest criticism and consternation. The high value placed on intelligence in the dominant American and Western societies has led to several kinds of over-emphasis on intelligence tests and test results. For one thing, people have tended to make a test result more important than the technical limitations of tests warrant. The reliability of most well-known intelligence tests is high (usually in the .80s or .90s), but even such high figures allow for variation. If tests are repeated over several years' time, some variation is to be expected, and IQ changes are as high as twenty-five to fifty points in certain rare instances, especially if a youngster has gone through periods of maladjustment or parental disturbance (Honzik, 1948; Bayley & Schaefer, 1964). The limitations in the validity of intelligence tests need also to be understood, especially in interpreting results for an individual. Even as high a validity coefficient as .60 on a general scholastic ability test against college grades still does not account for as much as half of the variance among individuals. Many other factors enter into a score. There are only a few studies relating intelligence to success in real life situations over a number of years. Oden (1968), for example, found abundant evidence of achievement in a twenty-five year follow up of children identified by Terman as having high IQs, but the degree of success seemed not to depend on just *how* high the IQ was. Factors like creativity, exploratory interests, economic supports, and environmental opportunities enter into success. Measured intelligence has been found to be both a reflection of past schooling and a predictor of future school success. The close relation of IQ to schooling contaminates evaluation of criteria of occupational success (McClelland, 1973), since diplomas and degrees are hurdles required for many occupations. Occupations requiring school-like activities (such as abstract reasoning, much reading, and manipulation of numbers and words) are likely to require high levels of IQ. But many other real life activities, such as musical, artistic, mechanical, and muscular work are much less related to what is measured by intelligence tests. In any case the IQ must be viewed as *measured* intelligence, not necessarily the *adaptive* intelligence used in everyday living.

Another kind of problem is the overemphasis in most intelligence tests on the kinds of information and values inherent in the white middle class segment of American (or European and perhaps Japanese) society. As we have learned earlier, test content and testing procedures presume opportunities to acquire certain information and certain thinking skills. Test content, test administration, and test norms inevitably reflect such learning, and the attempt to develop tests that are culture-fair to minority groups in this country and to people in other cultures has not been very successful (Brislin et al., 1973). The Jensen controversy in the late 1960s and early 1970s is only one of many disputes over the relative value of intelligence tests and their relationship to racial differences (Cronbach, 1975b). Both psychological scientists and laymen argue about the causes of the persistent findings that ten to twenty IQ points usually separate the averages of groups of American blacks and whites on measures of intelligence (Baughman, 1971; Tyler, 1974)—whether they are due to heredity or environment. It must be remembered that these are *group* differences, and there is much overlap in the distributions of scores. These test findings are only performances, of course, from which we make inferences about a construct called intelligence, and the performances are affected by many factors. Intelligence no doubt is a result of an interaction between inherited potential and a host of environmental factors, and some differences are due to the inadequacy of the measuring instruments (Tyler, 1974; Loehlin, Lindzey, & Spuhler, 1975; Anastasi, 1976). Heredity sets the stage for a wide range in ability development, on which the forces of environment play, especially the early home experiences and peer attitudes about learning. This concept is called the *reaction range* by Gottesman (1968), who shows that people with the same basic inheritance could easily differ ten to twenty points in IQ depending on the way the home and school encourage the development and use of their capabilities. For extensive discussions of the assessment of minority group members, see Sattler, 1974, or Samuda, 1975.

Another idea intelligence testing has overemphasized is the decrement related to age. Early cross-sectional studies of IQ at different ages gave misleading results. Most longitudinal studies have not shown a decrease in total ability until over age sixty. Test scores depend partly on the information in the culture at the time the test was constructed (Schaie, 1974). In a rapidly changing society like that of America, Europe, Japan, and other rapidly modernizing countries, the information and education imparted to one generation is much different from that given another in the course of growing up. Thus we sometimes unfairly test older people in ways more appropriate to the young.

In general, many people have overemphasized the place of intelligence and IQ improvement in the total developmental picture. Earlier we noted that Anderson & Messick (1974) point out in connection with the Headstart program that social competence is a much more important factor in a child's development than IQ improvement. The whole person, with his or her interests, motivations, interpersonal skills, and other characteristics, should be the focus of educational programs—not just the limited kind of tasks found on intelligence tests. For many treatment programs, the IQ is also too abstract or irrelevant. As mentioned in chapter seven, specific behavioral problems must be identified in order to design plans for improvement.

All of these problems of poor usage and overemphasis on intelligence and intelligence tests may make the reader wonder: "Why not throw intelligence testing out altogether?" The answer in most cases is that intelligence, by whatever name we call it, does enter into much human effort, and if we are to make decisions with or about people and understand them, we need to take intelligence into account, estimated in the best way possible. Intelligence and ability tests, if handled with caution and appreciation for their weaknesses, and if used only with decisions for which they are *relevant,* can provide much better assistance than informal procedures like interviews.

Keeping in mind the multitude of abilities and the complexity of mental activities, we see that it is important *not* to base decisions on any single measure of ability and achievement. The wise assessor uses several different kinds of tasks and looks at other information, such as the history of the person and the context of the school or life situation. Any one IQ should also be treated as a *band* or range rather than a single score, keeping in mind the reliability or accuracy of the instrument. The assessor tries to discern the *pattern* of abilities the person shows, not a single score. All but the most severely retarded show a variety of skills and competencies in coping with present and potential environments. Much of what is being said here indicates that intelligence tests, or any tests, will be helpful if they are in the hands of a well trained person who has the client's interests at heart.

Of particular importance in the assessment of ability is an understanding of how and where the person wants to use that ability. Persons of surprisingly modest intellectual capability can master undergraduate college courses if they work hard and persist. Mentally retarded individuals can work well in sheltered work situations. Society needs to make use of motivations and willingness to work wherever those can be found and generate reward systems that help the person learn the necessary skills. On the upper ends of the different kinds of abilities we need to locate or generate situations for challenging and encouraging talent in directions that people want to go. We shall return to some of these questions in the final chapter.

SUMMARY

In this chapter we have discussed the important but often misinterpreted field of cognitive ability testing in its relation to personality. Cognition is a general term for a variety of "thinking" activities. The most common measure of general cognitive ability is the intelligence test, and there is a variety of more specific measures. This broad array of tests can be conceptualized in several ways, such as a factor-analytic hierarchy with general intelligence ("g") or fluid intelligence on top, or a three dimensional cube of 120 abilities in Guilford's Structure of Intellect model.

An example of a widely used intelligence test is the Wechsler Adult Intelligence Scale. We noted, in studying this test, that though research has not associated psychiatric diagnostic types with exact patterns of intellectual functioning, there are many informal ways in which as assessor can make observations and obtain hypotheses about personality while testing for intelligence.

Cognitive styles are ways of thinking and solving problems. They include Witkin's system for studying psychological differentiation (field dependence-independence), Kagan's analytical-global approach to categorizing objects, Kelly's approach to locating the individual constructs along which people think as well as his concept of cognitive complexity, and Rotter's internal and external locus of control. Divergent and convergent thinking is a related area of individual differences. Divergent thinking, which seems to be related to creativity, calls for imagination in giving several answers to a question rather than one correct one.

A competency-based view of personality emphasizes the skills or abilities that people use in their interactions in the environment. Of special interest for the next chapter (on attaining an integrated view of a person) and for research, are the instruments such as the adjective checklists, Q sorts, the semantic differential, and various ratings.

At the end of the chapter we noted some of the pitfalls and over-emphases on the value-laden area of intelligence testing. We particularly noted that one should not make important decisions on the basis of one test, but should look at the total needs and the possibilities for maximum development of the individual. One should distinguish between measured intelligence (the IQ) and adaptive intelligence used in coping with real life situations. Intelligence tests can be of great value for many purposes, if they are used by a well trained person with the client's interests at heart.

SUGGESTED READINGS

GOLDFRIED, M. R. & D'ZURILLA, T. J. A behavioral-analytic model for assessing competence. In C. C. Spielberger (ed.) *Current topics in clinical and community psychology.* Vol. 1. New York: Academic Press, 1969, pp. 151–196. Goldfried and D'Zurilla discuss the concept of competence and point to the importance of relating effectiveness to problematic situations. They illustrate the development of assessment techniques in a study of the adjustment of freshmen at the State University of New York at Stony Brook. McClelland (1973) also emphasizes the need to turn toward the use of life-outcome criteria and the development of repeated achievement profiles in an impassioned plea to focus on competence rather than intelligence with its stultifying labeling dangers.

MASTERSON, The adjective checklist technique: A review and critique. In P. McReynolds (ed.) *Advances in psychological assessment.* Vol. 3. San Francisco: Jossey-Bass, 1975. pp. 275–312. Checking a list of adjectives to describe oneself or someone else is a simple, easily understood, and practical technique for applied and research purposes. This review helpfully takes up the major devices and the evidence for their reliability and validity.

MATARAZZO, D. *Wechsler's measurement and appraisal of adult intelligence* (5th and rev. ed.) Baltimore: Williams & Wilkins, 1972. This book is a major updating and revision of the fourth edition of Wechsler's widely used, basic clinical test on intelligence testing. It covers the nature and history of intelligence, its classification, the concepts of retardation and giftedness, and a thorough description of the Wechsler-Bellevue and Wechsler Adult Intelligence Tests, along with relevant research of reliability, validity, norms, and relations to personality and clinical problems. Sattler's *Assessment of children's intelligence* (1974) is excellent for its discussion of background, issues, and methods.

TYLER, L. E. *Individual differences: Abilities and motivational directions.* Englewood Cliffs, N.J.: Prentice-Hall, 1974. This very readable little book, (230 small pages) is a distillation of research findings and ideas about intelligence, special abilities, creativity, ccognitive styles, interests, biographical information, and general studies of directions of development. Those readers who are particularly interested in research on black-white differences will find *Race differences in intelligence* by Loehlin, Lindzey, & Spuhler (1975) and *Psychological testing of American minorities* by Samuda (1975) comprehensive and helpful. An interesting article pointing to the importance of tradition and culture is Seymour Sarason's "Jewishness, blackishness and the nature-nurture controversy" (1973).

WELSH, S. *Creativity and intelligence: A personality approach.* Chapel Hill: Institute for Research in Social Science, Univ. of North Carolina, 1975. Welsh's book evaluates a number of theories and research approaches, and reports on new research with young people. Welsh sees both what he calls "origence" and "intellectence" as major dimensions of personality. For an overview of the relation of creativity to personality in another culture, see the book by the Indian psychologist, Paramesh (1972).

chapter eleven

Integrating and Communicating Assessment Information

> *Mankind is made up of inconsistencies, and no man acts invariably up to his predominant character. The wisest man sometimes acts weakly, and the weakest sometimes wisely.* —Lord Chesterfield, *Letters to His Son*

In the previous chapters we have been examining isolated procedures for assessing a person. Now we must put together the various pieces of the puzzle to form the whole picture. That the synthesis is not always easy is suggested by the observation from Lord Chesterfield quoted above.

In the sequence of assessment (shown in the first chapter, Figure 1–4), we are at the last stages—the choice of ways to organize information and the choice of manner to present results. The earlier part of the process involved choices about the purposes of the assessment and the strategies and kinds of information to be gathered. These earlier decisions affect the final stages, and this influence is one of the reasons for the importance of arranging for feedback and evaluation of the assessment process so that future assessments will benefit. The entire assessment system exists within a larger network of systems—the agency or office, and the surrounding community in which both the client and the assessor have interests, resources, and interdependencies. The assessor's decisions about reports and other communications must be made with the "consumers" in mind—how best to report findings so that the client or agency can take action and use resources well. In this chapter we will examine psychological reports and ideas, and research concerning assessors' judgmental skills. We will also review the work of some assessment programs in which large amounts of information on many people are combined. Finally we will try to assess the current status of assessment.

ILLUSTRATIONS OF ASSESSMENT PRODUCTS

From the beginning, a most important question for the assessor is "What is the goal?" In answering this question, the assessor must look at both the ultimate purpose (such as the benefit for a client in psychotherapy or the satisfaction of a worker on a new job) and the more immediate goal (such as the report to write for the therapist or the recommendation about selecting a person for a position). Now, at the close of the assessment sequence, the psychologist or other assessor (even those in everyday life) chooses *how to describe the person,* conveying his or her working image to others; *what to decide about the person,* giving probabilities of success to various alternatives for action; and, in some cases, *whether original formulations or questions about the person have given right or wrong answers,* seeing in research situations if hypotheses were logically and statistically confirmed or disproved. A common product of assessment is a report— written, oral, or both. A number of abbreviated examples of reports follow:

A Psychologist's Report to a Social Worker about Perry, an American Indian Boy

Perry, aged four years and two months, was referred from a remote small town by the State Department of Public Assistance, for general developmental evaluation and recommendations about possibilities for adoption and for the counseling of prospective parents. The examination consisted of prolonged free-play interaction and a developmental test. Perry's appearance and physical care were a distinct credit to his present foster mother, as he was neatly dressed and well turned out. Slight initial shyness gave way to doing what he wished and generally ignoring me in the playroom. He obviously enjoyed some interaction, but did not seek it out.

Observations. Perry's acceptance of the examiner and ability to separate easily from the worker who brought him were positive social achievements. His gross motor skills in walking, running, balancing, ball throwing and catching, and general coordination were not notably different from those of most four-year-olds. His performances at hand washing and putting on his coat were below age expectations, however. His fine motor skills showed definite slowness in development. Many young children are able to concentrate on a design to be drawn, but Perry's problem started with the pencil—should he hold it in his fist, between fingers, or finger and thumb? Much of what he accomplished, because he had not learned the basic skill, looked retarded. In language skills, Perry also was out of step. Compared with age-peers, he used language less often and had a smaller vocabulary, less ability to construct coherent sentences, and fewer concepts such as "on" or "inside." As a rough approximation, Perry may be at least eighteen months behind in this area.

Test of learning.   In an effort to elicit Perry's best performance, I gave him a raisin for any good effort at imitating a requested behavior. Even such a crude reinforcement schedule produced immediate and profound results. He did and said things he had seemed unable to do and say earlier in the session. Perry will obviously work hard for something he finds rewarding. However, in the usual situation Perry has a way of acting as if he has not heard the request or doesn't know the answer, which forces the uncertain adult into the position of doing things for him or asking yes/no questions, to which he gestures and doesn't speak.

Recommendations.   Perry can be helped by a variety of programs, among them early schooling such as Headstart, well-selected television programs, and assistance by the present foster parents. Perhaps the most potentially useful idea would be to provide interested adults with a few simple teaching techniques and some ideas about areas to stress. Training sessions here in the clinic would be desirable, but if not possible because of the distance, we can send you a programmed book for parents. (Summarized from Sundberg, Tyler, and Taplin, 1973, pp. 576-77.)

A Counseling Psychologist's Account of Kim's Test Anxiety.

Kim Morrison, an eighteen-year-old first year college student, came to the counseling center after an episode in her biology class. The counselor, Laura Stark, interviewed her for half an hour. Kim told how she had "frozen" while taking her first examination in college. After most of the class had left, her biology instructor noticing she was sitting immobilized with a vacant stare, not having written anything on the examination asked her what was the matter. She burst into tears and told the instructor she could not remember anything she had read. The instructor suggested that she discuss her problem with someone at the college counseling center.

Laura (as the counselor preferred to be called by the students) elicited this story in bits and pieces of the examination, from Kim between sobs. She found out, as Kim calmed down, that Kim came from a small rural town and had never lived away from home before coming to college. Kim had done fairly well in the high school work but had always been afraid of exams and was so upset after some that she vomited afterwards. Laura encouraged her by saying that it was good she was now taking the step to talk about this problem and arranged for an appointment a few days hence. In the meantime, Kim was to fill out the Fear Survey Schedule (FSS) and the MMPI at home. Laura explained that these provided useful and quick ways to get acquainted with her concerns about herself. Laura also asked Kim to jot down a few brief notes on any situations that frightened or worried her in the next few days.

At the time of the second session, Kim was again tearful and reported that she had been very upset when a teacher had announced an exam to be given in two weeks. The counselor reviewed the items on the FSS with Kim and sent the MMPI to be scored. Kim checked many distressing situations on the FSS including speaking in public, entering a room where others were seated, sudden noises, being watched while working, dirt, being criticized, making mistakes, looking foolish, and losing control. Laura reviewed each of these with Kim over the hour. Many of the problems seemed to center around fear of being evaluated or criticized. Taking tests was one clear example of this fear. Laura and Kim discussed the need to look at the general fear of criticism but decided together to work first on the examination anxiety because taking tests was an immediate necessity for surviving in college.

Laura explained what systematic desensitization was and how it worked by having the person gradually face fears or worries while in a state of relaxation. Laura then asked Kim to tell about all kinds of situations in or about classrooms that upset her. Laura wrote thirteen feared situations down on a piece of paper and asked Kim to rank them in order from least to most threatening. Two of the least upsetting were walking into the classroom to listen to a lecture by a friendly instructor and having a friend tell about taking an exam successfully. The most threatening was taking a final exam in a hard course for which she had lost her textbook the day before. Laura also asked Kim to fill out a study habits inventory.

Before the third session, Laura had reviewed the MMPI profile, which showed considerable elevation on Scales 2 (depression) and 7 (psychosthenia) but was otherwise a fairly normal college profile. The MMPI results along with the interviews put her mind at ease about severe disorder and confirmed the decision to concentrate on the test anxiety. Laura also selected certain MMPI items to discuss with Kim at the beginning of the third session. These uncovered a few additional fears and related problems. Laura then explained relaxation procedures to Kim and instructed her to release the tensions in the muscles of each part of her body while reclining in a comfortable chair. While Kim relaxed with closed eyes, Laura asked her to imagine the least threatening situation—just coming to a lecture. Kim was to say when she felt tense. Imagining a few such situations did not disturb Kim's relaxed state, so Laura asked her to imagine the next most anxiety evoking situation, meanwhile continuing her deep relaxation. Moving gradually up the hierarchy and repeating relaxation instructions with images that aroused some tension, Laura and Kim were able to reach the fifth of the thirteen levels that day without much disturbance.

In subsequent sessions, they moved up the anxiety ladder until the most fearful situations could be imagined calmly. In addition, Laura discussed the results of the study skills inventory and suggested some study techniques that Kim might try. Another part of the therapy involved assertiveness training. After working out a ranked list of situations, Laura and Kim agreed on practice assignments outside the counseling session. Beginning with small matters such as refusing to buy something a sales clerk tried to push on her, Kim engaged in progressively more difficult situations for self-assertions. After ten counseling sessions, Kim felt confident enough to discontinue therapy. In the meantime, she had taken three examinations, not completely calmly, since, as Laura pointed out, it is quite normal to have some tension in such situations, but without panic. Doing a routine telephone follow-up three months later, Laura found that Kim had continued her progress and was getting along well in school. (Readers interested in more detail about systematic desensitization and related assessment may refer to Morris, 1975, or Lazarus, 1971).

A Psychologist's Account of a Screening Examination
of a Highway Patrolman Applicant

The following account is a slightly abbreviated quotation from Joseph Matarazzo, 1972, pp. 503–506; it presents his thoughts about the assessment problem, as well as a report on a case. Matarazzo has served as a consultant in the psychological screening of applicants for a police force for many years.

The successful law enforcement applicant in this country during the past few decades typically has had to pass a number of critical hurdles in the hiring process. These usually include a written civil service examination, a test of physical prowess and agility, an extensive medical examination, a psychological examination, and an oral interview before a committee composed of representatives from the law enforcement agency itself, the civil service bureau, and the community at large. This . . . example illustrates an assessment challenge for the psychologist which has become increasingly more frequent in the past few years: namely, an applicant from a disadvantaged segment of our socioeconomic strata whose qualifications appear high in all areas but one—measured intelligence.

The applicant was born in a small rural town outside a large city, the last of four children. . . . His father was a mill worker, who, despite much effort, was unable to find steady work during most of the applicant's formative years. The applicant completed high school . . . and enlisted in the United States Army for four years. He served honorably and was discharged as corporal . . . shortly after his 22nd birthday. He returned home and had a number of construction and manual labor jobs in and around his community before applying for a position with this law enforcement agency a year later. His first try was unsuccessful when he failed the first step in the civil service process, namely a 30-minute, group-administered, written intelligence test. Six months later he tried again, passed this test and also the agility and medical examinations. Following these two steps he was seen by the consulting psychologist.

A summary of the main findings from this psychological examination includes an MMPI entirely within the normal range, the code being '35418-9 '0; Strong Vocational Interest Blank scores high on Farmer, Aviator, Printer, Policeman and Senior CPA; California F scale score of 60. The clinical interview impressions were as follows; "tall, impeccably dressed, somewhat shy, aware of his personal–educational deficits, verbalizes life long ambition to be in a service profession, and no clinical indices of psychopathology.'' The WAIS results reveal a Verbal IQ, Performance IQ and Full Scale IQ of 88, 86, and 86, respectively.

This level of functioning places him at only the 20th percentile for all men and women his age—a level of *measured intelligence* well below average and one not usually believed sufficient for work in law enforcement in today's complex society. Yet, interestingly, this man's socio–educational-military occupational *adaptive behavior* to date, as well as his overall personality integration, his level of motivation, and his complex of personal attitudes and values in regard to public service, in combination, presented a clinical picture of a young man who was functioning in society at a level considerably above that suggested by his measured intelligence alone.

Furthermore, examination of his responses to the individual items on the 11 WAIS subtests, and the subtest scaled scores themselves . . . revealed a fairly *consistent* pattern without evidence of either inter- or intra-subtest scatter, or Verbal-Performance differential, or any other ideas of the clinically suggestive type. . . . Formal personality study by the Rorschach Inkblot Test, MMPI, and other tests . . . revealed no evidence of psychopathology. . . . Rather, the global picture which emerged from both the test and the interview segments of this clinical industrial appraisal was that of a well-integrated young man of average ability, as judged clinically. . . .

The writer has seen this pattern of relatively low measured intelligence relative to actual achievement and its variants at comparatively higher levels of measured intelligence . . . many times among applicants for executive employment, as well as college and professional school, and in each instance, faces the "moment of truth." . . . should his decision be guided by *clinical judgment* which suggests "hire" in this case, or actuarial *prediction* which . . . would suggest "do not hire" inasmuch as a man at this level of measured intelligence would have a much higher probability of job failure in law enforcement than one of higher ability. . . . A lower limit of WAIS Full Scale IQ of about 100 probably is required for the many judgments which a law enforcement agent would have to make in meeting the public and carrying out his other day-to-day responsibilities. To say the writer agonized over this particular decision would be an understatement. Nevertheless, after considerable reflection regarding the validity of such a judgment . . . the recommendation to hire was telephoned in. Along with the recommendation went the additional information that the psychologist, although satisfied with his recommendation, nevertheless felt obliged to communicate the deficit in measured intelligence. The law enforcement administrator decided to hire the applicant.

At the time of this writing the applicant . . . has been on the force a full 11 years. He has received favorable reports from his immediate supervisors, and two official commendations from his department. However, he also has been involved in three minor but costly accidents with his official vehicle and has sustained two injuries in the line of duty, one necessitating hospitalization and home care extending over several months. In this regard, the pattern of scores on clinical scales 1, 2, and 3 of his MMPI (the so-called "Hysteroid V" pattern) will be of interest to practitioners experienced with this clinical tool.

Clinical Psychologist's Report on His Psychotherapy Patient

This abbreviated case description is taken from Blank, (1965, pp. 145–167 and pp. 327–334). The patient is a female, aged 27, married with two children. She has had one-half year of junior college and is not employed outside the home. She was evaluated by her psychotherapist for assistance in planning therapy and to determine the quality and quantity of psychopathology. The tests administered were the MMPI, Interpersonal Checklist, Rorschach, Draw-A-Person, Wechsler Adult Intelligence Scale, and Thematic Apperception Test. In the interview and testing sessions, the patient was friendly though somewhat reserved and emotionally bland.

> The tests reveal an immature, hysterical character structure. The patient characteristically seeks to defend herself from anxiety by repressing sexual and aggressive feelings and by restricting her awareness greatly in such a way as to avoid contact with any thought content that might be related to these feelings. Her cautious, evasive responses to the projective tests reflect this pattern, as do her scores and responses on the WAIS. (Blank, 1965, p. 152)

Her overall IQ was 96, which is in the normal range, but she scored only 89 on the verbal section and 105 on the performance scale. She showed extensive restriction of interests in order to avoid possibly disturbing content. The patient's hysterical defenses have not been successful, however, and she has resorted to obsessive-compulsive mechanisms to allay her anxieties (her MMPI peaks are on Depression and Psychasthenia; Code: 27 '384-0). Sexual material is predominantly threatening as, for example, she rejects Rorschach Card VI, which includes a shape often perceived as a male sex organ. At a preconscious level, strong dependency needs play a major role. Basically, she would like to be taken care of and she resents adult responsibilities. She is hostile toward female figures and looks to men to take care of her, rather than seeking more mature sexual relationships. Consciously, however, she says she would like to be a more responsible, assertive person who can help and care for others.

> At present, the patient seems to be in an extremely vulnerable condition. . . . stress of the sort she would encounter upon resuming family responsibilities would be likely to increase her obsessive-compulsive mechanisms to a disabling degree and to subject her to intense anxiety. Prolonged psychotherapy in a life situation in which she is relatively free from pressures until she is better able to handle them is advisable. Diagnostic Impression: Anxiety and obsessive-compulsive reactions in a hysterical personality. (Blank, 1965.)

Dr. Blank goes on to relate the results of testing to the patient's life situation and to psychotherapy. The patient had been hospitalized shortly before the testing sessions after complaining to her physician about severe depression. Dr. Blank saw her in therapy for over thirty sessions. He points out numerous instances of concurrence between material that came out in therapy and the test results. For instance on the second session, she revealed that she used fainting spells in order to get her husband's attention and though she praised him, she indicated that he expressed little feeling and was hard to get close to. Dr. Blank related this material to TAT themes of people being alone, not really relating to each other, and, at best, arguing. In the course of therapy, the patient began to make visits to her home and talked less about how hopeless and miserable she felt; she was able to have sex relations with her husband again. Blank (1963, p. 167), rating the results of the therapy successful, concludes as follows:

> Despite the depression, agitation and withdrawal aspects presented by the psychological evaluation, there was also conveyed an ego intactness and defensive structure able to tolerate the pressures and probing of intensive psychotherapy. . . . She also indicated on these tests her yearning for and reaching out to people. Another important clue was the need to concentrate on her understanding and working with her tremendous hostile impulses and their relationship to her sexual identity. When this material came up in treatment, frequent referrals back to the test material helped clarify for the therapist what was going on.

Morris Brown, an Extensive Case Study
by a Research Psychologist

The following is a shortened account of an intensive study of one person over a considerable period of time by Robert Holt (1971, pp. 95–199).

> If you were to meet William Morris Brown, you would probably find him likable and eager to please, although not very unusual. He talks with apparent relish, racing along from one thing to another with a naive sort of eagerness at once disarming and refreshing. His face is alert and mobile, and in spite of a smile that seems a little too ready, you would probably put him down as a happy extrovert who would fit into the local service club with ease and satisfaction. At 26, Morris looks like any other energetic young businessman, well satisfied with himself, the world, and all the good "business prospects" in it. . . . Morris is large and compact, without much excess fat, although he is beginning to have trouble keeping his weight down to 194 pounds. . . . He carries his 6-foot frame well and easily, however, with a trace of the athlete in his walk. . . . His well-fed look of stability and maturity is probably a help to Brown in his business. He is a securities salesman and is quite successful for his age. . . . Since graduation, Morris . . . lives alone in an inexpensive rooming house near the college; he makes a considerable proportion of his sales to members of the university community. . . . His present life goes along pretty smoothly to outward appearances. He works hard and takes an afternoon off every few days to play golf, at which he excels. Almost every weekend he gets

away for a while to work on a cabin he is building in the country. On these trips he almost always takes along at least one companion, usually of college age, to help with the work. He has a rather large number of friends. . . . but no intimate ones. Morris rarely goes to a movie because he says movies hurt his eyes, but he likes to read, mostly biographies. He seldom has a date and knows few girls. (Holt, 1971, pp. 95–96)

With this introduction, Holt started a long report on a man whom he and a colleague assessed extensively starting in 1940. At that time and over several months, they interviewed Mr. Brown in detail on his childhood, adolescence, and young adult years. They administered the Study of Values, some other inventories, and an intelligence test; and conducted a constitutional analysis (somatotyping him as above the midpoint on endomorphy and mesomorphy and very low on ectomorphy), and tested him with the TAT, the Rorschach, and free association sessions. They noted that the tests, especially the projective ones, brought out much more psychopathology than was apparent on first impression. He showed great ambivalence about his mother, and his TAT stories portrayed father figures as evil and remote. His father had left the family when he was eight. Synthesizing these diverse sources of information by checking one source against another and using a largely psychoanalytic personality theory, the author formulated the results as:

> The state of confusion and turmoil Morris was in does not approximate any standard diagnostic category, but it brings to mind the kind of condition described by Erikson . . . as a *postadolescent identity crisis.* Morris was chronologically in the time of young adulthood when his peers were rapidly finding life partners with whom to share an intimacy for which he was not yet ready. . . . Morris' conflicts were typical of this condition: dependence on his mother versus rejection of her, need for the approval of others versus fear of involvement, resistance to external constraint and a deficiency in moral restraints versus a seeking for his own form of self-control and morality, and a deep confusion about himself growing out of his basic uncertainty about his sexual identity—am I a man? a woman? some kind of sexually deficient eunuch?. . . . We should remember, too, that the historical era was one of considerable uncertainty and growing uneasiness for young men. In 1942 (the time of the first testing) America was already involved in war and he himself was waiting until some minor medical matters were taken care of so that he could join the Navy as an officer candidate (pp. 162–163).

With an unusual pattern of assets and liabilities on the tests and case history, the psychologists were not sure whether Morris would head toward good adaptation or severe maladjustment.

In 1966 Morris met one of the psychologists again. Morris had seen combat in the Pacific, had returned to the same city to sell securities, and had remained a bachelor. The psychologist proposed a repeat of the investigation and Morris responded with enthusiasm. At this time the following procedures were administered in addition to the projectives and extensive interviews given earlier: the MMPI, Eysenck Personality Inventory, Study of Values, WAIS, Adjective Checklist, California Q Sort, and some tests of cognitive style. In his final report (pp. 191–199) the author indicated that Morris had become an important person in his small town. His prowess at golf led him to travel to many invitational tournaments. He was elected mayor of the town and spent one term in the state legislature. Morris and his mother began to be on increasingly good terms as she accepted him as an adult and made no attempt to interfere in his life; when she died he felt he had been the devoted son she needed. The center of his social life was a rambling house on the coast where he could and often did accommodate many guests. "Uncle Morris" became almost a legendary figure to the boys in his friends' families, swimming, sailing, and playing tennis as well as any teen-ager. Morris at the time of the second testing seemed to have settled down, and seemed to be happy. Now over fifty, he had not changed much in his erotic life. He had had sexual affairs with both women and men, discreetly and rather infrequently, and usually without much tenderness and affection; most of his sexual release was through masturbation. He came close to marrying a college sophomore when he was about thirty-five, a beautiful girl who fell in love with him. Yet

> I was such an emotional wreck that I couldn't see, what is this business of being in love? I mean, it's just a torture—there was nothing good about it. We just badgered each other, killed each other—ecstatically happy for one moment and then made miserable for 24 hours. . . . There was just no peace to it.

The psychologist commented that (pp. 198–99)

> Thanks to Morris' unusual defenses—a blend of isolation, denial, and repression—he has been able to keep the door to sexual activity with males ajar, but not enough to bring against himself the accusation of being a "fairy," which he clearly is not. . . . He has been able to develop an identity in which there are both masculine and feminine elements. And the latter are mainly qualities that were the source of his mother's strength—her moral backbone, her compulsive orderliness and organizing ability, and her kindly nurturance. The role Morris plays with so many of his young friends . . . is a parental one, just as his preferred role in politics is that of a just, impartial parent who emphatically settles the children's squabbles without getting drawn into taking sides. . . . Morris' most recent projective test responses show none of the gory, self-directed destructive imagery that was so blatant in the Rorschach and TAT of 1940. . . . As Morris grew more sure of himself and realized that he was a socially esteemed and estimable person, he was able to get control over the savagely self-punitive superego elements. . . . The importance of Morris' environment should not be overlooked. . . . His being able to get away from the big-city pressure and competition to a small country town where he could live an outdoor life was a weekend safety valve for years, while he began to develop rootedness in the little community. His longtime position

of public trust . . . made mature, moral integrity far more rewarding than any kind of opportunistic attempt at self-serving shortcuts could possibly be. . . . Morris Brown's life history is a good example of an important principle in understanding personality: Early traumas and other unhappy experiences and the growth of such defenses as isolation and denial do not necessarily imply a disturbance in the adult personality.

Before leaving the subject of reports, it is important to note some serious problems in communicating "working images" to others. This is illustrated by a report about a young man written without even seeing a case history or testing data, but knowing only the title of the program and where the case originated. The following abbreviated version of a "completely blind analysis" was presented at a professional meeting for a discussion entitled "A Case Study of Schizophrenia" based on a case from a Veterans Administration hospital (Sundberg, Tyler and Taplin, 1973, p. 577–579):

> The veteran approached the testing situation with some reluctance. He was cooperative with the clinician, but mildly evasive on some of the material. Both the tests and the past history suggest considerable inadequacy in inter-personal relations, particularly with members of the family. . . . It is doubtful whether he has ever had very many close relationships. He has never been able to sink his roots in deeply. He is immature, egocentric, and irritable, and often he misperceives the good intentions of the people around him . . . He tends to be basically passive and dependent, though there are occasional periods of resistance and rebellion against others. Although he shows some seclusiveness and autistic trends, he is in fair contact with reality. Vocationally, his adjustment has been very poor. Mostly he has drifted from one job to another. His interests are shallow . . . At present he is mildly depressed, although a great deal of affect is not shown . . . His intelligence is close to average, but he is functioning below his potential. In summary, this is a long-time inadequate or borderline adjustment pattern. Test results and case history, although they do not give a strong clear-cut diagnostic picture, suggest the diagnosis of schizophrenia, chronic undifferentiated type. Prognosis . . . appears to be poor.

The report rang surprisingly true to those who knew the actual case. Both in this instance and in others involving the description of persons such as the "character reading" from tea leaves or astrological charts, some methods tend to fool people into accepting a report as genuine. For one thing, there are likely to be certain base rates, or frequently seen characteristics, of the people who come for diagnosis or character analysis. In the mental hospital it is unlikely that people would be there if they could not be described as *immature* and *inadequate.* These terms are "universally valid" for patients.

Meehl (1956), using an earlier idea from D.G. Paterson, has called the pseudo-success of such vague and meaningless reports the "Barnum Effect" and warns that it is a very serious problem in communication. People can read projectively into such descriptions whatever they want to read and also tend to accept what is said by a prestigious person. This tendency helps explain the persistent acceptance of standard personality descriptions that are not at all individualized (Forer, 1949; Sundberg, 1955; Hinrichsen and Bradley, 1974; Delprato, 1975; Rosen, 1975). Descriptions supposedly based on projective techniques which seem mysterious to the nonpsychologist, seem to be especially effective (Snyder, 1974), even in other cultures (Diamond and Bond, 1974).

THE MATERIAL TO BE INTEGRATED

The cases illustrate considerable variety in the amount and kind of information the interpreter studies. They range from only an observation and a test for four-year-old Perry to about twenty procedures for Morris. In most clinical situations the number of standard assessment procedures in addition to the interview would be about three or four. Many psychologists would argue that both structured and unstructured tests should be included in a battery since "the structured test represents the more typical of life situations. The unstructured test represents the situation in which the individual has to turn largely to himself to cope. . . . One person may manifest severe and crippling conflicts on the unstructured material, which implies that at the unconscious level he is beset with severe difficulties. Yet at the semi-structured level, he shows good coping capacity." (Jones, Meyer, and Eiduson, 1972). A common battery for adults used in many traditional clinical settings would be an intelligence test (such as the WAIS), the Rorschach, a sentence completion test, and the MMPI. Behaviorally oriented settings tend to use a few checklists, inventories, or record keeping procedures. Special referral questions or problems that come up during the examination might lead the clinician to administer tests of brain damage, special abilities, interests, or fantasy. The variety of assessment procedures is great and assessors will have their own personal preferences.

The crucial matter in the practical setting is defining exactly what one wants to make decisions or develop images about, and how the assessment procedures might best accomplish those particular goals. In everyday life this is also true; we can seldom take the time or have the patience to examine another's life in extreme detail. Yet if we are serious about complete under-standing of the full functioning of a person, we need to develop ways of synthesizing vast amounts of material. A complete psychology would study individuals in all their complexity and bewildering inconsistency. To organize the large amount of information on a person, it may be helpful to think in terms of different views of the same person, just as we may look at a mountain, a piece of sculpture, or an actor in a play from different angles and in different lights and times. To see a person comprehensively we should think of the many systems involved and ask questions relative to different ways to view them. To simplify, we might say that there are five basic areas of *content* about which we should always inquire in understanding the person, each in past and future time:

1. *Physical–physiological questions:* What kind of body does the person have and how does it function? What was the body like in the past and what are the trends for the future?

2. *Social–ecological questions:* What kinds of situations does the person encounter in his/her daily life and what influences come from the larger social structure? How were these in the past and what are the potentials for the future?

3. *Behavioral questions:* What are the person's observable habits, skills, and problematic activities? How have they developed and how are they affected by changes in the situation and reward contingencies?

4. *Self-related questions:* What does the person say about his/her self? What is the history of self-talk or self-evaluation and what is likely to affect it for the future?

5. *Inferred dynamic-symbolic questions:* What would be hypothesized concerning inner conflicts, motives, emotional fixations, and the like based on personality theories? What can be inferred about the person's "symbolic world"? What has been the psychodynamic developmental history and what would be predicted for the future?

As the reader has noticed, no doubt, these five sets of questions cover the gamut of techniques, theories, and system levels. Personality theories and tests tend to pursue highly selected areas of human functioning. By ignoring other areas they gain in simplicity and depth, but lose in complexity and comprehensiveness. In a thorough going study of a person, all of these questions would be asked and the commonalities and discrepancies among the information obtained would be exposed. Practical limitations in time and resources, however, force us to concentrate on only limited aspects of the person. Furthermore, ethical considerations, such as invasion of privacy and respect for the client's preferred limits on a relationship, dictate care in deciding on the extent with which the assessor collects information (Morgenstern, 1976).

THE PERSONALITY ASSESSOR'S INTEGRATING PROCESSES

In collecting information on the person, the assessor has been developing a number of hypotheses about him or her, and the guiding purposes of the assessment have channeled concerns toward possible alternative decisions. After all the data have been collected, the assessor is likely to sit down and read and reread the information, looking at it from different angles. As mentioned in chapter one, the personality assessor can view any observation or finding as a sample of behavior, a correlate of something else, or a sign of some underlying condition that theory would suggest. In analyzing the mass of material, the examiner will particularly notice agreements and disagreements among the findings.

Another important general consideration, mentioned earlier, is the assessor's comparison of the results with his or her own implicit or statistical norms and baserates. What is to be expected in the interview situation or on the tests from different kinds of persons? Any gross deviation from the expectations is informative. The interviewee who never looks the assessor in the eye raises questions about evasiveness, extreme shyness, or perhaps an unusual cultural background. The client who produces a high F score on the MMPI or no popular responses on the Rorschach is deviant and that deviancy calls for an explanation.

Undoubtedly there are many individual differences among clinicians and other assessors as they process the data before them and move to the integration required by reports, recommendations, or other actions. Two research directions have developed in an attempt to clarify how a clinician thinks—thinking aloud, and the statistical representation of clinician choices. Using the *thinking aloud* approach, the investigator simply presents the clinician with a tape recorder and a set of data—test results or other information—and asks for a step by step report of how he or she notices, organizes, and classifies the information, and comes to decisions and recommendations. Variations on this method are called *stimulated recall* and *Interpersonal Process Recall* (Kagan, 1974). In this procedure, a video tape of an interview is played back to the clinician (or the client, for that matter) and a trained facilitator encourages the clinician to remember the thought processes that went on as the interview progressed. Interpersonal Process Recall is used in a variety of ways, particularly in the training of counselors. When training is focused on specific skills such as listening and responding to feelings, this procedure can be an effective training device (Kagan, 1974).

Kleinmuntz (1967, 1970) used thinking aloud to develop a computer *simulation* of a clinician interpreting the MMPI. He selected a clinician whose predictions had been demonstrated to have high accuracy in separating adjusted from maladjusted profiles of college students. Kleinmuntz asked the clinician to describe all details of his subjective processes while making decisions on many profiles. From a compilation of cues and inferences, Kleinmuntz (1967, p. 365) constructed the flow chart shown in Figure 11–1. Such a sequence can then be translated into computer language for a set of decision-rules about classifying profiles or assigning descriptive statements. Procedures like these have been the basis for much of the

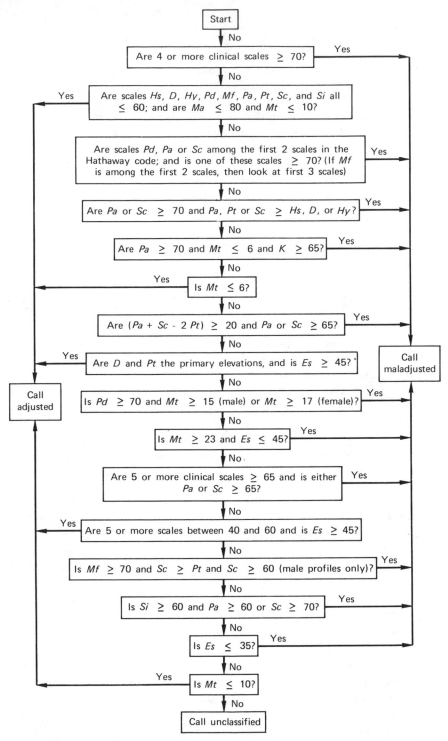

FIGURE 11-1 MMPI decision rules for the identification of maladjustment in college students. (From Kleinmuntz, 1967, p. 365)

computerized interpretation of psychological tests. Such a flow chart may be constructed for any kind of assessment information, including life history data and observations. Nathan (1967) has developed such a system for psychiatric diagnosis, and Kleinmuntz (1968) has constructed a decision-tree of choices in neurological diagnosis through the use of a game like Twenty Questions in which the expert neurologist would have to ask yes/no questions.

The second major investigation of clinical judgment attempts to make a statistical representation of the weights that judges give to the various items of information they have about the person being judged. Hoffman (1960) calls this *paramorphic representation* or a *model* of the clinician's judgments—not a direct representation, but one similar in form that produces the same results. This idea relates to a seminal proposal of Brunswick (1956; elaborated by Hammond et al., 1964), whose *lens model* is represented in Figure 11–2. In the middle of the figure are the facts or information (w–z) that serve as cues for the clinician. These facts might be items like IQ, age, score on the MMPI ego strength scale, and ratings of ability to get along with others. Data on many people would be made available to the clinician–judge who would make predictions about their success in psychotherapy. Through using the correlations that resulted from these predictions for cases that varied widely on the scores, the investigator can derive the weights given each one. Then the investigator can construct a representation of the clinician's judging behavior—a multiple regression equation, which is a formula for predicting one variable from a number of other correlated variables. The regression equation then is the statistical model, or paramorphic representation of the clinician's behavior.

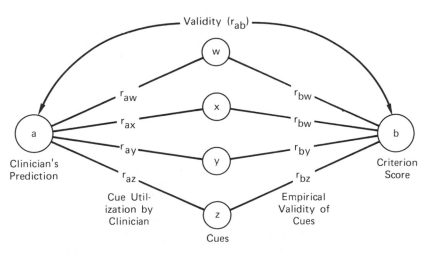

FIGURE 11-2 Clinical prediction paradigm. (From Hammond, Hursch, Todd, 1964, pp. 438-56. Copyright 1964 by the American Psychological Association. Reprinted by permission.)

So far this paramorphic representation says nothing about accuracy, but simply reproduces in a formula what the clinician does in the situation. The right hand side of the lens model can now be used to check the accuracy of the clinician's judgment and the weights attached to each of the cues. An ordinary regression equation could be derived by correlating the several cues with the criterion score, which might be ratings of success in psychotherapy. One study by Goldberg (1970) derived paramorphic models from a group of clinicians and demonstrated their superior accuracy over individual clinical judges.

THE ACCURACY OF CLINICAL JUDGMENT AND PREDICTION

Who is a good judge of others? That question must be very old, and psychologists have produced only a few beginning answers. Taft (1955), reviewing research, concluded that the ability to judge others was related to *age* (until adulthood), *intelligence, esthetic interests* (especially in art and drama), *self-insight, emotional adjustment,* and *social skill.* Taft also noted that the good judge of others possesses *relevant norms* against which to judge a person, is *interested* in the judging task, and is *free* to make accurate judgments about the person (that is, does not have vested interests).

Most of Taft's propositions, and earlier ones by Allport, have not been adequately tested. There are a number of pitfalls and problems in such investigations. Wiggins (1973, p. 180) states that "the ability to judge others is frequently construed as a general trait of the judge that is relatively independent of the persons or qualities judged. However, evidence for the generality of judgmental accuracy is far from conclusive." Reliability of judgments depends on the breadth or narrowness of categories. Judging depends on the situation and on the kind and manner of presentation of the information to be judged. Wiggins (1973, p. 180) also points out that "Available evidence suggests that claims of superior judging ability for clinicians must be viewed with considerable skepticism." When clinicians (including psychologists, psychiatrists, social workers, and others) are lumped together and asked to make predictions from test data, several studies (Goldberg, 1959; Levenberg, 1975) show that they often do no better than secretaries or untrained college students. It is still true, however, that some clinicians are more perceptive and accurate than others. Unfortunately we do not yet know what makes for more accuracy.

One thing we do know, however, is that clinicians cannot out-predict a statistical formula derived for the data that the clinicians are using. This was the conclusion of Paul Meehl's book, *Clinical versus statistical prediction,* which landed like a bombshell among assessment experts in 1954 and generated a flurry of experiments trying to refute Meehl's findings. The basic research design of the series of contests between the clinician, and the statistician or actuary, was (a) to find an outcome that could be predicted (or postdicted) by statistical means, (b) to provide the clinician (or counselor, personnel worker, or others) with the basic data being used in the statistical prediction equation and sometimes additional data on the subjects, and (c) to compare the accuracy of the predictions from the clinicians and from the formula. The first study reported by Meehl is Sarbin's 1943 attempt to predict college grades. For the statistical prediction, a clerk simply put each student's aptitude test score and his or her high school grade rank into an equation developed on an earlier sample. For the clinical predictions, Sarbin gave psychologists the same test scores and grade ranks plus a variety of additional information including other test scores and a biographical form. The judges also interviewed the students before making their predictions of the grades they would receive at the end of the first term in college. The predictions from the statistical formula correlated with actual grades .45 for men and .70 for women; the corresponding predictions of the psychologists correlated .35 and .69, figures that were not significantly different. The formula, involving much less time once it was developed, did fully as well as the experts.

Similar studies have been conducted for the prediction of parole violation, return to prison, recovery from psychosis, personality descriptions, outcome of psychotherapy, medical diagnosis, and job success and satisfaction. In his "box score" of research contrasting clinical and statistical prediction in 1965, Meehl reported fifty-one studies in which thirty-three showed a superiority for the statistician, and seventeen showed no significant difference. Only one study seemed to be in favor of the clinician, and this one was subsequently severely criticized (Goldberg, 1968).

Most of the concern has now shifted to the problem of how to best combine the advantages of the formula with the work of the human assessor. This new concern is supported by Sawyer's reanalysis (1966) of Meehl's data. He found the best prediction method was one in which both judgmental and mechanical input data were available for statistical combination. Thus the clinician is a valuable *source* of input data. Many psychologists, psychiatrists, personnel workers, and others would be content to have as much automation and statistical assistance as possible in their difficult jobs. They recognize the human fallibility in processing complex kinds of data and the extremely subjective quality of many of their judgments.

Assessors in practical situations recognize the impossibility of relying on statistical procedures in most of their work. The tests and other data collection devices often are not available. Even if there are tests, there is seldom sufficient research on their particular, local decision-making situations to justify the direct use of such tools. Such research is needed, and the responsibility falls on professional people to develop and use the best tools possible for their area of expertise. Furthermore, much assessment work requires human judgment because accidental occurrences or special conditions make it necessary to judge whether a test or a formula is applicable in individual cases. The context of assessment also requires human judgment in tailoring assessment to the person. In most professional situations the surrounding administrative system, the availability of job or treatment alternatives, and the many decisions along the way require that there be a skilled person guiding the work. The assessor must relate to the people of the clinic or office, choose assessment procedures, and interpret assessment findings in the light of the "delivery system" with which he works.

LARGE ASSESSMENT PROGRAMS

The investigations that have provided the most important opportunities to study the integration of extensive data about individuals are the large assessment programs. Such "multiple assessment" (Taft, 1959) or "programmatic assessment" projects typically involve extensive interviewing, many tests, and observation procedures carried out by many judges with groups of subjects in a live-in situation, or assessment center. An early step in this direction, as we have noted, was that of Henry Murray and his associates (1938), who studied individuals at the Harvard Psychological Clinic, but the person who is usually given credit for developing "the assessment method" is Simoneit (1940), who organized a large effort to select officers and specialists for the German military establishment. During World War II, Britain and the United States set up similar centers for special selection purposes, and after the war perhaps a dozen civilian programs have been carried out. Wiggins (1973), in an excellent review, lists five American "milestone assessments": The selection of people for espionage work in World War II by the Office of Strategic Services, the study of Air Force officers by the Institute of Personality Assessment and Research at the University of California at Berkeley, the Veterans Administration research on the selection of clinical psychologists at the University of Michigan, the Menninger study of psychiatrists, and the studies of selection for the Peace Corps.

The emphasis in most of these efforts is on the intensive study and evaluation of the "total person," often by the use of observing behavior in ingenious situational tests and by the analysis of expressive behaviors as well as more traditional information from biographical data, and intelligence and personality tests. Usually such large programs try to develop a model of the target personality—a set of qualities presumed to characterize successful persons in their area of study, whether they are spies, officers, or psychiatrists. These models are used to guide the construction of rating scales for the expert judges and to select and develop tests and procedures to bring out crucial characteristics. Final judgments are often made in group meetings of the assessors.

The dramatic and often quoted work of the American Office of Strategic Services during World War II has been alluded to briefly before. Under the charismatic leadership of General William Donovan and a large number of prominent psychologists including Henry Murray, the OSS set up a few secret stations for screening men nominated as candidates for sabotage and espionage work behind enemy lines. All candidates were dressed in the same fatigue uniforms and told to stick to a cover story and not reveal their identity except under specified conditions. Using ideas from their British and German predecessors, the assessors employed leaderless group tasks, stress interviews, and situations such as informal drinking parties in which they tried to get the candidates to break down their cover stories. In addition, many tests and other special procedures were used. Unfortunately, the pressures of war-time emergencies made a good analysis of criterion situations impossible, and follow-up studies were also confused by the fact that people were often assigned to completely different jobs from what had been expected when they were sent to the OSS station. In their report on their activities the OSS staff (1948) gave detailed criticisms of the assessment program.

As illustrations of the subsequent programs that dealt with professional or occupational groups, we shall briefly look at two programs; one on architects and one on the Peace Corps. The architect study was one of a series of studies of creativity and effectiveness conducted over several decades by the Institute of Personality Assessment and Research (IPAR) of the University of California at Berkeley. The founder and long-time head of IPAR was Donald MacKinnon, who had participated in the Harvard assessment work with Henry Murray and also in the OSS studies. The primary group studied consisted of forty architects from sixty-four who had been nominated by experts as being the most creative in the United States. These men spent an intensive weekend at the Berkeley research center. They were contrasted on certain paper and pencil tests with two other less creative groups who were tested by mail—architects who had worked with the first group and architects from the same areas who were not nominated as creative. On many psychological measures, results from the highly creative group were tested for significance against results from the two less creative groups combined. In some instances the highly creative persons were compared with the norms for the tests.

The IPAR study uncovered many differences among the three groups. There were significant differences in self-images. On adjective checklists, the highly creative people checked themselves significantly more often as "inventive, determined, independent, individualistic, enthusiastic, and industrious" than the contrast groups, who more often described themselves as "responsible, sincere, reliable, dependable, clear thinking, tolerant, and understanding" (MacKinnon, 1962, p. 487). As mentioned in the last chapter, the WAIS IQs of members of the highly creative group ranged widely—from 120 to 141 (MacKinnon and Hall, 1972). Though the creative group's average of 132 was a little higher than the two other groups' (130 and 128), there was a large overlap.

Given sufficient intellectual ability, the major factors in creative endeavor seem to lie in a number of personality variables. On the MMPI, for example, the creative architects scored above average on psychopathological scales, not because they were overtly disturbed, but apparently because they were willing to allow themselves to think differently from others and because they had adequate control mechanisms. Another finding characteristic of all male creative groups was a high score on many measures of femininity. There was a correlation of −.49 between rated creativity and scores on the Strong masculinity score, for instance. This finding calls to mind the contention of Bem, (1975), that effectiveness is higher in people with both male and female interests and characteristics. The more creative architects showed high preference on the Barron-Welsh Art Scale for complex, asymmetrical drawings rather than simple symmetrical ones (a correlation of .48 between rated creativity and this scale). The creative ones also tended to use a larger number of colored pieces than the less creative on a mosaic design. "It is clear that creative persons are especially disposed," MacKinnon concluded (p. 489), "to admit complexity and even disorder into their perceptions without being made anxious by the resulting chaos. It is not so much that they like disorder per se, but that they prefer the richness of the disordered to the stark barrenness of the simple." Another significant personality difference was the preference of the creative persons for perceptive and intuitive ways of thinking and knowing, rather than the judgmental and direct-sensing ways (these results arising from the Myers-Briggs Type Indicator, an inventory based on Jungian theory). Creative architects also showed high values for the theoretical and esthetic (on the Allport-Vernon-Lindzey) and gave a large number of unusual responses on the word association test.

As a final example we will look at the assessment work of the Peace Corps, the American overseas volunteer program for less developed countries. President Kennedy inaugurated the program in 1961–62, twenty years after the war-time OSS program. The Peace Corps was handicapped by being an on-going and hurried government project. (In its first year almost 1,000 volunteers were selected, trained, and placed in twelve different countries.) Though they had to make compromises with methodological ideals, the psychologists who worked in the Peace Corps found it possible to profit from the experience gained in previous projects. For one thing, the first director of assessment, Nicholas Hobbs, arranged for decisions about procedures to be related to job descriptions from overseas and saw to it that selection judgments involved people who were knowledgeable about the situations to which the volunteers were going. He set up an elaborate system of screening based on application blanks, well designed letters of recommendation, academic records, language aptitude and placement tests, and medical examinations, to be used before inviting individuals to come for training. Hobbs (1963) resisted pressures for a costly nationwide network of individual interviewers because he knew from research that the increase in validity would be nil. In Figure 11-3 (from Wiggins, 1973, pp. 585 and 587) the top part shows the flow chart of suitability screening before the person was chosen for training. Screening clerks using desribed criteria did much of the pretraining selection. Another early director of selection, Ed Henry (1965), reported that only one of six who initially applied eventually came to the training site. (One half of those invited did not come for various personal reasons.) Most of those who did come were new college graduates, frequently majors in the social sciences or the humanities—the "B.A. generalists."

For its live-in situation, the Peace Corps used the two or three months of training which in the early days was mainly in universities. Centers were set up in Puerto Rico and Hawaii and eventually in the countries of desti- nation, the developing countries in Asia, Africa, and South America. The assessment decisions were made in the two stages shown on the bottom of Figure 11-3, an intermediary selection and a final one, both involving a variety of people associated with the training site and having much informa- tion. At the final selection all members involved had summaries available as each trainee was discussed in turn. Wiggins (1973, p. 588) states "It seems likely that the information on which the final board made its decision was more comprehensive than that available to any other project in the history of personality assessment." The number and kind of tests and other psychological data varied from place to place, but the MMPI, interview information, and peer and staff ratings were always collected. Because a working knowledge of language in remote areas of countries like Nepal, Tanzania, or Colombia was absolutely necessary, much attention was given to language training (about five hours a day) and evaluation of fluency. The data included ratings by field assessment officers and others at the training site, but the final decisive rating was made by the field selection officer, who came from outside. The reason for separating the person making the final choice from the local situation was to provide a more objective and overall perspective, based on a knowledge of other selection programs and usually of the overseas situation too. The field selection officer placed each candi- date in one of three administrative categories: reject, provisional accept, or accept. He or she also rated the accepted volunteers for expected overseas performance. One study (Goldberg, 1966) showed a high correlation between board consensus and the field selection officer's ratings.

What was the outcome of the whole selection process? The major criteria available for evaluation are completion of the full two years of duty and ratings by the Peace Corps field representative in the host country. The early drop-out rate varied from country to country and project to project, averaging around 13 percent. Henry (1965) reported that about half of the drop-outs returned home for family reasons, such as a death or the need to take over a family business. Wiggins (1973, p. 598) notes that an approximately "95 percent valid positive hit rate is an extraordinary statistic for a large-scale selection program of this kind." Summarizing several research reports (Colmen et al., 1964; Wrigley et al., 1966; Jones, 1969), Wiggins (p. 598) states

> The best predictor of overseas performance was the final board rating made by the field selection officer. Peer ratings of overall success ran a strong second. . . . Instructor's ratings and predictions by field assessment officers were also significantly correlated with overseas performance. However, the magnitude of all these correlations was quite modest.

Among measures obtained prior to training, the classification officer's ratings and letters of recommendation appeared the most promising, although the size of their correlations would not justify their being substituted for final board ratings. In his concluding critique, Wiggins (1973, p. 600) states

> Peace Corps selection procedures were not exemplary of every principle of personality assessment . . . but the procedures were surely more sophisticated and more likely to be successful than those of any previous large-scale assessment project. Here it seems appropriate to give credit, not only to those assessment psychologists who served the Peace Corps so well, but to those far-sighted administrators, such as Sargent Shriver, who recognized that effective selection is a scientific problem, as well as an administrative one.

It should be added that the above description of Peace Corps selection applied roughly to the first five years of that organization. In later years there have been many changes, affected by larger events—the Vietnam War, the disenchantment of many American young people with the administrations that supported that war, the resulting decrease in applications, the change of the political party in power in 1968, and the shifting needs of the developing countries toward greater specialization. The Peace Corps was placed under a larger organization for all volunteer programs called ACTION, set up by the Nixon administration. Much of the selection apparatus for screening applicants and trainees was dismantled or changed. Quite specific job descriptions were developed to meet host country needs, such as cattle

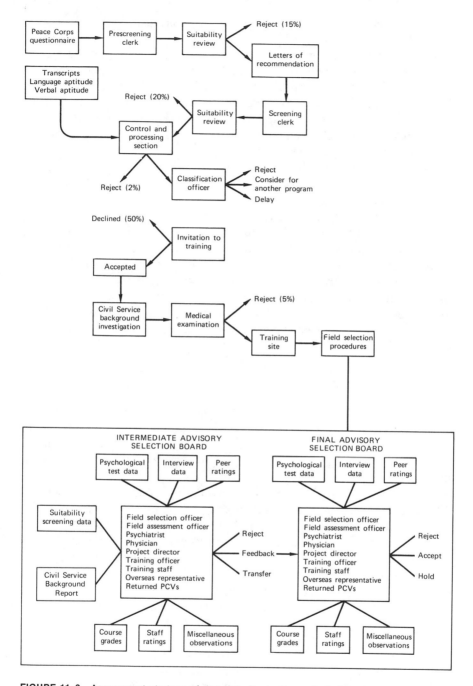

FIGURE 11-3 Assessment strategy of the early Peace Corps, including suitability screening before training (top) and field selection during training (bottom). (From Wiggins, 1973, p. 585 and 587)

breeding or ocean fishing, and selection became more like that for a Civil Service job than for a general, flexible position such as community development. Within the Peace Corps there was considerable debate about the need for extensive psychological work. In the process the numbers of assessment psychologists associated with the Peace Corps dwindled and their function shifted toward counseling and assisting in self-assessment. The results of these changes remain to be evaluated.

At the same time as the Peace Corps assessment was developing, the assessment center idea was starting in large industries. Bray, with American Telephone and Telegraph, has been prominent in developing applications to the selection and study of executives. One book (Bray, Campbell, and Grant, 1974) reports on an eight-year follow-up of over 200 college recruits that shows considerable validity for the assessments employed. Such assessment center work in industry is the major current locus of programmatic assessment. Numbering only about a dozen in all, the large assessment programs have contributed a great deal to theory and techniques in assessment—many tests, procedures for combining information, research findings, and the groundwork for training people in assessment.

CRITIQUE AND COMMENT—THE STATUS OF ASSESSMENT

What overall conclusions can we draw from these small and large efforts at making sense out of information about human beings? Have psychologists arrived at useful and effective ways of synthesizing, communicating, and deciding about persons? If final answers are not in, are we on our way?

Most reviews of the large assessment projects have indicated many disappointments. They mention low predictive validities and few significant results from a great deal of work and expense. One reviewer (Clark, 1960) said the mountain labored and brought forth a mouse. Sometimes it seems as if the large assessment assumption about "safety in numbers" has led to a hodge-podge of confusion rather than clarity of results. If there is any one criticism that stands above all others, it is the failure to solve the *criterion problem*. Some criteria used were too vague and global, like ratings of "general effectiveness"; others were unreliable or of questionable importance. This problem was insufficiently recognized at the beginning of assessment, when (a) knowledge of the criterion could be used in choosing predictors and designing the study, and (b) better criteria could be developed against which to compare the predictors. Wiggins (1973, p. 602) says "Without exception, all these assessment studies fell short of an optimum level of *criterion analysis* that could have guided both the selection of appropriate assessment procedures and the manner in which data were combined."

Cronbach (1970, pp. 677–678), after reviewing a set of large assessment programs, also points to the importance of the criterion, but with a slightly different twist: "The most important requirement for valid assessment is that the assessors understand the psychological requirements of the criterion task." In the Peace Corps research and some of the other successful studies (Vernon, 1950; Holmen et al., 1956) a careful job analysis was made, or the assessment involved ratings by individuals who were familiar with the eventual work situation to which the candidates were going.

Cronbach also concludes that we must not assume that psychological training gives the specialist assessor an advantage. Instead, psychologists need to find people who will make useful judgments no matter what their training. In several studies, peer ratings show up very well against criteria of later success. One study of army officer candidates (Holmen et al., 1956) used recent graduates of the officer candidate school as judges. The validity coefficient of their ratings was .55, about the same as that of peers, which was .58—both very high as such studies go. Gormly and Edelberg (1974) also found peer ratings very useful in locating cross-situational consistency. The probable reason for the frequent success of peer ratings in assessment studies is that peers are similar to the kind of people with whom the person will be working in the future. The true criteria of success in jobs, management, marriage, psychotherapy, or almost any other human activity rest largely on judgments by others. If those particular kinds of "significant others" can be represented in the assessment itself, it is likely that the results will hold up in later performance.

Cronbach also points out that performance tests that are like work samples of the criterion task have considerable validity. Such tasks do not require the assessor to jump to a high level of inference or bring in a lot of intervening personality theory. They can often be judged by nonprofessional assessors. Unfortunately, a number of the large assessment projects did not make much use of work samples based on analysis of the criterion situations. There are dangers in relying on a "model" of an ideally successful person, although the model-building or analytic approach was the one most commonly used in assessment programs.

Many of the same considerations given to "assessment-in-the-large" apply as well to "assessment-in-the-small." On the individual scale the clinician or personnel psychologist is often unfamiliar with the criterion situation, the home life or working conditions of the client. The tests she or he uses are often limited, in no sense work samples. Even occupational aptitude tests show average validity coefficients of only .22 against proficiency criteria and .39 for training criteria (Ghiselli, 1973). The clinician's imperfect memory and combinatory powers are subject to "illusory correlations," (Chapman and Chapman, 1967, 1969), that is, mistaken notions about the significance of observations based on limited or misleading experience. It is also very difficult to process large masses of information. With all these problems in obtaining and combining information into a coherent and useful picture of a person, it may be surprising that there is as much validity to clinical judgment as there is.

Some would recommend that we throw all formal assessment and testing away. But then the question arises, what would be the replacement, since decisions must be made? Whatever might replace current practices should also be subjected to the same tough scrutiny as to reliability, validity, and cost-benefit analysis.

Promising directions for more valid use of assessment procedures are appearing. Particularly exciting are possibilities for research linking human observational resources to computer combinational processes. A "knowledgeable" computer, having a memory for previous problems and similar persons and situations, could call to the attention of the clinician-assessor possibilities to be investigated that the clinician alone might not have considered. Much progress is being made in medical diagnosis of simulated patients, so that professionals can be evaluated and trained (Hoffman, 1974; Kleinmuntz, 1975; Zubin et al., 1975).

These are largely exciting possibilities for the future rather than present resources. What can we conclude would be of value for the "judge of others" right now? Summarizing many of the points made in this book, here are fifteen general suggestions:

1. The primary order of business is clarification of the purposes of the assessment, including ultimate use of the information and kinds of alternatives to be decided. What are the basic questions? What form would make the answers useful? Who will be judging the person in the future?

2. One should remember that all assessment and evaluation activities are parts of an ongoing situation. Assessment is an interpersonal event in a social context; all observations must be interpreted as samples within this context.

3. For all assessors, interviews and observations are the basic tools, but unless they are standardized and the assessor is trained, they must be viewed with considerable skepticism. It is important to be aware of the likelihood of bias and unreliability. To counteract these problems, recheck important information or have several observers.

4. A sequence of scanning and focusing is useful. In most assessments one first needs a quick survey of the person's life situation and problems, and then more detail in areas particularly relevant to the purposes of the assessment.

5. The assessor should be sensitive to the cultural, social, and ethnic background of the person and of himself or herself, and the effects these may have on assessment. In all judgments, this background and the appropriate norms should be kept in mind.

6. Whenever possible the assessor should make use of "hard" procedures, such as standardized tests, statistical prediction methods, and computer information, if relevant. In the absence of tests, one should try to create small work samples, close to the criteria to be used, or use observation in the field.

7. The assessor should develop local base rates, expectancy tables, and norms about behaviors and outcomes when possible. If these cannot be developed by "hard data," he or she should be aware of them through personal impressions and checking with others.

8. In collecting new information, the assessor should direct efforts carefully to a limited amount of data. The important thing is not getting *more*, but getting the *right kind* of information, the kind most relevant to the situation and purposes at hand. Mischel cogently observes (1968, p. 145) "Base rates, direct self-reports, self-predictions, and especially indices of relevant past behavior typically provide the best as well as the cheapest predictions."

9. One should be especially careful about making predictions concerning low probability events—things that seldom happen; the baserates are against them and much evidence will be needed to make such predictions.

10. Jumping to an overly high inference level is risky. One should avoid too much speculation, except for research purposes.

11. In general, one should be aware of several theories, not just one, and should be skeptical of untested theories of personality.

12. The assessor will profit from becoming thoroughly aware of the situation he or she is trying to predict—the criterion situation. The criterion should guide the collection of information and the final prediction or description itself.

13. Whenever possible the assessor should make use of other judges—especially those similar in background to the person being studied and those familiar with the criterion situation.

14. The assessor should keep a record of his or her "batting average," study it, and use it in improving assessment abilities.

15. The utility of the assessment depends finally on effective communication. Checking how well one is transmitting a useful and meaningful image of another person, both in oral and written form, is important to the continually learning assessor.

SUMMARY

The principal problem discussed in this chapter was that of combining the diverse information on individuals into some meaningful whole that meets the purposes of the assessment task. We also noted the problem of reporting called the "Barnum Effect" which is the use of vague or universally valid descriptions that do not individualize the person but are often readily accepted. For comprehensive assessment of a person there are a large number of concepts and methods that might be used, centering around physical–physiological, socio–ecological, behavioral, self-related, and inferred dynamic questions.

The clinician's cognitive processes in integrating a case have been studied by asking the psychologist to think aloud as he or she reviews assessment information and makes decisions. Such reports can be used to develop decision rules and computer programs. Another procedure is to use statistical techniques that correlate elements of a test with the clinician's decisions and build a paramorphic representation of his or her use of those data. We briefly reviewed studies showing the superiority of statistical over clinical prediction and noted the advantage of combining clinical and statistical processes.

The large assessment programs we reviewed—OSS, the IPAR architects, and the Peace Corps—developed interesting procedures and findings, but are costly and provide rather unimpressive validity figures. Most important among the problems of assessment is the criterion. Those projects that seemed to fare best began with a good criterion analysis to guide the assessors in selecting procedures; they often used work samples, and made use of judges who were familiar with the ultimate criterion situation. The final pages noted a number of problems related to clinical judgment and brought together suggestions for improvements made in previous parts of the book.

SUGGESTED READINGS

BRAY, D. W., CAMPBELL, R. J., AND GRANT, D. L. *Formative years in business: A long-term AT&T study of managerial lives.* New York: Wiley, 1974. The assessment center at American Telephone and Telegraph extensively studied 217 persons newly hired for managerial positions, using a number of novel techniques. Eight years later the researchers found that 64 percent who were originally rated high did reach a high level of management compared with only 32 percent who were given a low rating. Huck (1973) finds support for the validity of the assessment center method in a survey. MacKinnon (1975) provides an excellent critical review of the development of assessment centers and some recommendations for the future.

GOLDBERG, L. R. Man versus model of man: a rationale, plus some evidence, for a method of improving on clinical inferences. *Psychological Bulletin,* 1970, 73, 422–432. Goldberg describes and illustrates the development of a paramorphic model of clinicians' decision-making. Using data on clinicians who were differentiating psychotic from neurotic profiles on the MMPI, Goldberg showed that the paramorphic formula was more accurate than the clinicians themselves. He urges clinicians to study their diagnostic behavior and substitute statistical models wherever feasible. This procedure for creating formulas that are more effective than the original human judges is called *bootstrapping.* Another researcher developing models for clinical judgment and information integration is Anderson (1972).

LEVY, L. H. *Psychological interpretation* New York: Holt, Rinehart & Winston. 1963. Levy presents one of the few extensive explorations of theoretical and practical aspects of interpretation. He distinguishes two kinds of diagnostic work—the formal, using "cookbook" rules; and the interpretive, using higher levels of inference. Tallent's *Psychological report writing* (1976) is a thorough and helpfully illustrated discussion of the problems and rationale of good communication about individuals.

KLEINMUNTZ, B. Clinical information processing by computer. In *New directions in psychology,* Vol. 4. New York: Holt, Rinehart & Winston, 1970, pp. 123–210. Kleinmuntz in a clear and readable manner introduces the reader to the many different uses of the computer not only for compiling data but for simulating personality, interacting with a person via a display panel or typewriter, and developing decision-making and diagnostic capabilities. In a shorter article, Kleinmuntz (1975) reviews many of these points and brings them up to date.

MEEHL, P. E. *Psychodiagnosis: Selected papers.* Minneapolis: University of Minnesota Press, 1973. In this collection of papers by an eminent psychologist, the following chapters are particularly relevant: "What can the clinician do well?," "The cognitive activity of the clinician," "When shall we use our heads instead of the formula?," and especially "Why I do not attend case conferences." The rest of the book contains other important and seminal articles in personality assessment. Meehl says "We ought to make our clinical students as acutely aware of the Barnum effect as they are of the dangers of counter transference" (the therapist's overly emotional involvement with the client).

THORNE, F. C. Clinical Judgment. In R. H. Woody and J. D. Woody (eds.), *Clinical assessment in counseling and psychotherapy.* Englewood Cliffs, N.J.: Prentice-Hall, 1972, pp. 30–85. One of the long-time leaders in clinical psychology, Thorne reviews the problems and research on knowing what questions to ask and how to organize the answers in clinical situations. He gives twenty unusual sketches of poor clinical judges such as the pious do-gooder, the textbook parrot, and the long-shot gambler. He concludes (p. 79): "The study of clinical judgment should have first priority in clinical training programs." Several studies suggest the possibility of sex and class biases among clinicians (Abramowitz et al., 1973; Chasen & Weinberg, 1975; DiNardo, 1975).

chapter twelve

Assessment, Society, and the Future

At long last we are beginning to ask, not can it be done, but
should it be done? The challenge is to our ability to anticipate the
second- and third-order consequences of interventions in the
ecosystem before the event, not merely to rue them afterward . . .
we must learn to think through before we act out.
—Leon Eisenberg. The human nature of human nature (1972, p.
123)

This final chapter provides an opportunity to bring together many ideas
that have been mentioned in the previous chapters in order to focus on what
seems to be emerging in assessment and what needs to be considered as we
look at the future. Having discussed assessment techniques one at a time
and in combination, we now need to examine some of the larger questions
about persons and society and explore and speculate about the future
possibilities.

Figure 12–1 illustrates the complex variety in assessment and summarizes
much of what has been presented in previous chapters. The Assessment
Cube shows the different kinds of methods that might be used at different
system levels for different functions. For example the upper left hand
corner in front could be illustrated by a selection interview with an applicant
for a job as a secretary or factory worker. The bottom sub-block in the far

right hand corner would be a projective technique, such as a TAT picture administered to a large sample as part of a national survey of achievement motivation. Some of the sub-blocks are hard to imagine; for instance, a psycho–physiological technique used with a community to evaluate a program. Still, it is not inconceivable that workers doing research on alcoholism and traffic safety might stop drivers in random places in a city to take blood samples before and after an extensive television program against driving "under the influence." The Assessment Cube serves to remind us of at least 125 different combinations in the wide-ranging work of assessment.

CURRENT UNFINISHED BUSINESS—CONCEPTUAL

Without trying to describe the future, we can detect many loose ends, gaps, and unfulfilled promises in assessment. Probably the most important and most difficult is the conceptualization of the field. How should we organize the myriad ideas about assessment into some reasonably coherent entity? On which theories, models, and issues should we concentrate; which

A. Assessment Methods

   1. Projective techniques
   2. Objective techniques
   3. Observations of behavior
   4. Bio-psychological techniques
   5. Interviews

B. System Levels

   1. Individual
   2. Small group
   3. Organization
   4. Community
   5. Region, state or nation

C. Functions

   1. Personnel selection and
     classification
   2. Training and education
   3. Counseling/therapy/system
     change
   4. Program evaluation/planning/data feedback
   5. Instrumentation for research/theory-building

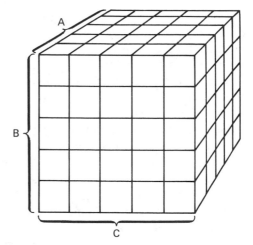

FIGURE 12-1   Assessment cube of methods, systems, and functions

is most promising? If we study Figure 12-1, we must wonder about over-emphases and underemphases. The frequency of efforts in each of the sub-blocks would vary greatly. For instance, almost all psychological assessment concentrates on examining individuals (Level B1). In addition, assessment is usually done in a strange situation for the person—an office or a clinic—seldom in his or her home or at work or play, so that the surrounding context, or environment is seldom noticed or given any importance. How ecologically valid are our assessments then? This book has emphasized certain functions—selection, diagnosis, and image-making for counseling or therapy—much more than others because these are the functions to which assessment psychologists have given most attention. All of these limitations and questions call for conceptual organization, ways of looking at assessment and persons-in-environments, and theories and models that will generate both good practice and good research.

Assessment as a branch of psychology has always had a peculiar relationship to personality theory. While it is undoubtedly true that assessors have at least an implicit theory (Fancher, 1966, 1967), those theories are often not the same as the theories put together by the leading writers on personality. One of the reasons that practical assessment has been limited in its relation to theory is that theories tend to concentrate on one or a few aspects of a person and are not able to bring the whole range of behaviors and experiences into their systems. In recent years interest in large scale personality theory has been waning. The trend in research seems to be toward the development of models and the testing of constructs. Rather than building an all-encompassing theory, a scholar chooses a particular topic such as depression, repression, stress, affiliation, or aggression on which to concentrate investigation. To build a model, the researcher then identifies the important variables, hypothesizes their manner of interaction, and develops measuring devices to test hypotheses derived from the model. Fiske (1971) presents an excellent analysis of the measurement of constructs. A model is less comprehensive but usually more precise than a theory.

Assessment, then, seems to have grown from at least two sources—practical needs with a limited theoretical base and the stimulus provided by general theories and models. Freudians say "aha" when evidences of the Oedipus complex or infantile trauma show up; behaviorists feel satisfied when the antecedents and reinforcers of a problem behavior are identified. Constructs serve the assessor as guidelines of *what to pursue*. A random search over a person's life and current behavior is likely to produce random results; the assessor must know what is important—what to look for in the limited time of his or her practice. It seems unlikely that unaided human processing equipment can do much better than pick out a few salient characteristics of a person (Dawes, 1975; Slovic, 1972). Ultimately the complexity of content must be dealt with by an assessor–machine combination, but for now we need a comprehensive theory that will guide us to what is important.

A tentative attempt to relate a systems-ecological approach to both cognitive and behavioral concepts is illustrated by Figure 12-2 (partly drawing on ideas from Barker, 1968, and from Mischel, 1973). Its purpose is to help keep in mind the continuous feedback loop between the person and the environment as he or she moves through time and space, and at the same time portray the most significant processes within the living organism as stimuli come in and responses occur. At the boundary, immediate stimuli (such as light waves) contact the receiving sense organ (the eye). The optic nerves send stimulation to the brain, which at the same time is receiving stimuli from other sources, including internal bodily stimulation (such as signals from fatigue states or low blood sugar level). The Central Processor is the hypothetical set of activities (or mediating mechanisms) in the brain that deal with the stimulation and ultimately decide on a response. Five assessment related processes are postulated.

A stimulus selection and categorizing process that means the person attends to only some of the massive incoming stimulation and relates it to his or her individual way of organizing and classifying stimuli. Among many plants on the ground, the gardener spies a dandelion and codes or classifies it as a weed to be expunged from this precious place. Relevant assessment devices, mostly of the cognitive style variety, include those for measuring attention among many possibilities in a picture, differentiation of important material from confusing surroundings, and sorting behaviors. Instructions to subjects also serve to alert them to attend to certain aspects of the assessment process.

Self-regulating concepts, such as core personal values, one's sense of identity, and one's plans or programs, provide important background aspects for processing the flow of experience. Related assessment procedures would be instruments studying the hierarchy of values, personal intentions, life goals, methods of organizing one's personal time and space, and ways in which one makes meaning out of events. The self-regulating concepts do not necessarily mean that a person is completely consistent; a desperate situation, the absence of supports for value expression, and momentary confusion from drugs might influence a person to descend to less important values or use different aspects of personality.

Competencies provide the store of personal resources on which the person can call—the ability to think through a problem, knowledge resources, behavioral skills, or the ability to cope with interpersonal difficulties. Assessment procedures would attempt to get at the full range of cognitive and behavioral skills, not only the usual intelligence and ability tests, but also a coordinated battery of interpersonal problem-solving and creative coping skills.

Situational expectations are learned assumptions or conclusions about the relation of behavior to situations and the change in situations over time. They are if-then postulations, "If I smile and agree with her, then she will like me," or "I can only wait to see if he wants to help; if I ask, he will refuse." As yet there are few assessment devices of this kind. The S-R scale of anxiousness by Endler and Hunt (1966), mentioned in chapter six, that asks subjects to specify different responses in different situations, is one of a few

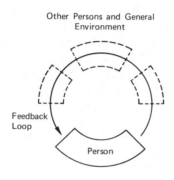

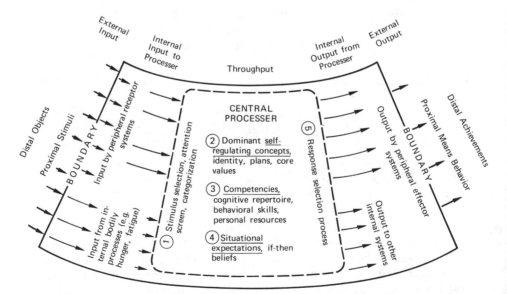

FIGURE 12-2 A cognitive-behavioral view of the personal sector in the continuous flow of interaction with the environment.

illustrations. Psychologists have concentrated more attention on taxonomies of people than on taxonomies of situations, yet common sense tells us that we respond differently at different times and places.

Response selection, the last major activity of the Central Processor, involves the choice of activity in line with the four earlier influences. The response must seem related to the situation, be within the repertoire of the individual, not in violation of what is important, required, or desired by the individual, and included in what was originally noticed. To the person it often seems that the action was the only thing he or she could do at the time; to outsiders other possibilities may be apparent. The individual has been limited by past learnings and present perceptions, and time forces the choice of either action or inaction, which is itself another form of response. Assessment devices are possible here too; the important element is the pattern of action selected under different conditions—not the if–then concepts of the response repertoire, but what the actual behaviors of the person indicate. The person may say many things but do something different. Procedures for the assessment of words versus deeds are needed. From a panoply of potential behaviors, what patterns emerge? These reflect the selection process for different situations. The assessor is likely to need observation or careful reporting of behavior. Stimulated recall, mentioned in the last chapter, may be helpful.

Figure 12–2 does not imply that the assessor stops with the five points of the Central Processor. Assessment must also recognize the context, the feedback mechanisms, and the element of time. Of particular importance is a parallel exploration in the environment with regard to supports for the various cognitive activities, behaviors, and if–then assumptions that are potential in the person. All external behaviors require some kind of support, either financial, physical, social, or emotional. Behavior cannot occur in a vacuum, so the assessor looks at the ecology of the behavior—what it supports and encourages, what it denies importance to or denigrates.

The unfinished conceptual business of psychology is not only to be found in relating techniques to integrating theories and models of personality functioning, but also in the development of a *theory of practice.* We need both inquiries into the ideas that people report to be of value, and analyses of what people actually do, in other words an understanding of "espoused theories" and "theories-in-use" as Argyris and Schön (1974) term them. Assessment should develop a rationale and research support for its activities of decision-making, and be particularly sensitive to image-making in the service of such applied functions as counseling and psychotherapy, and selection and classification. In the first chapter, Figure 1–4 points to system analysis in terms of decision-making. A well-articulated theory of practice would eventually take into account several important sources of socio-psychological concepts: social, organizational, and community psychology. From social psychology, a theory of practice should integrate the understandings about person perception, impression-formation, attributions of causes of behavior, integration of information, decision-making, and problem-solving. Considering larger systems, the complete assessment theory of practice would look at the socio–political–economic factors in organizations and communities, and relate assessment activities to an understanding of the place of decisions and images in social limits and how reports and recommendations influence the development of individuals in society. It would recognize the *Realpolitik* of decision-making in clinics, hospitals, industries, and other large bureaucracies. The task for the future, then, is the development of an understanding of the functioning of assessment in on-going organizational systems and the formulation of relevant policies.

CURRENT UNFINISHED BUSINESS— METHODOLOGICAL

As chapter three and other chapters have indicated, there is almost no limit to the amount of methodological improvement that assessment procedures need. They all could use better validity, reliability, norms, studies of base rates and incremental utility, and aids to interpretation. As emphasized in this book, it is crucially important to develop better *criteria* for judging the validity and effectiveness of individual tests and assessment programs. The APA *Standards for educational and psychological tests* (1974) are seldom fulfilled by current tests, and almost all Buros test reviewers complain about a long list of inadequacies. We know many things that should be done. The question in this complex field of measuring human behavior is how to set priorities with the limited resources at our disposal. Assuming the overriding importance of validity studies for practical assessment, let us look only at a few important directions that seem to be emerging and need more attention:

Situational Assessment and the Interaction of Personal and Situational Characteristics. This major barrier to the assessment of human behavior has been mentioned many times in this book. It is both a conceptual and a methodological block, but one in which there is some progress (Bersoff, 1973; Endler and Hunt, 1966; Mischel, 1973; Price and Bouffard, 1974; Stern, 1970; and others mentioned in chapter five). A large part of the problem is the absence of ways to classify situations and individual difference variables in a congruent manner. Just a short taxonomy of each will lead to an enormous number of interactions. In the personal taxonomy field, Goldberg (1972b, 1975) has pointed out the need to identify key concepts and relations through a systematic analysis of words from the dictionary. Like

Gough (1965), he sees as a valuable resource the "folk concepts," the terms describing personal characteristics strained through the sieve of centuries of usage. Goldberg (1975, 1976) has embarked on an ambitious research program to develop a taxonomy. If a parallel taxonomy of situations perceived by "the folk" could also be developed, the result might prove to be extremely useful. Perceptions are not enough, of course; one must also have evidence from the observation of people in natural situations. Bersoff (1973, p. 897), in proposing the use of "psychosituational" assessment, says "Any assessment procedure that isolates the target person from the significant others who participate in his behavior can be considered, at the very least, incomplete, and, at the most, unethical." The conflict between situationalists and trait theorists is likely to remain strong, replacing the response set controversy of the 1960s. Both sides recognize in some way that the other influence has some importance; behavior is never completely situation-specific, and traits are not completely transitional. Trait theorists have been developing *moderator variables,* such as sex, age, or certain traits, to help account for the differences in the way traits work in different classes of individuals; for instance, a correlation may hold up with a sample of women but not with men. If moderator variables are extended to situations, then the positions of the two antagonists are not far apart (Goldberg, 1972b; Mischel, 1973).

Computer-Assisted Integration of Information and Assistance in Interpretation. Certainly the human brain as an information processer has its limits. The studies on clinical versus statistical prediction reviewed in the last chapter helped define those limits. Furthermore there seem to be absolute limits to the human brain in the number of items it can hold in memory and integrate (Dawes, 1975). As assessment becomes more complex, we shall have to depend more and more on memory aids in order to process information. The full and fair study of a person will require more information than we now receive from tests. It seems likely that there will be psychological check-ups sometime in the future that will give the person essential information about his or her own abilities, interests, and coping skills. Such check-ups may be as commonplace as medical check-ups are now. Programs for differentiating abilities and directions, and integrating them in guidance work and career planning by use of computer technology (Harris, 1974; Katz, 1973) illustrate one kind of possibility. Multidimensional assessment extending over time, recommended by some psychologists (Tyler, 1973) to counteract the simplistic use of single measures in decision-making, will require more attention to integrating processes.

Aptitude-Treatment-Interaction (ATI) Studies. Cronbach (1957, 1975a) has repeatedly pointed to the importance of not only measuring individual differences but also relating these to different programs of learning or treatment. Individuals show differences in learning modes, interests, and cognitive styles. It should not be expected that everyone will benefit equally from the same kind of educational presentation. Some students learn better on their own unstructured time; others achieve well in a highly structured situation. The same applies to therapy and counseling procedures, and to daily coping in natural situations. An ATI technology is beginning to be developed (Cronbach, 1975; Owens, 1968); some (Hunt, 1975) would broaden it to all person—environment interactions.

Criterion Referencing. In chapter two we noted the contrast between norm referencing, which is, judging the significance of a person's obtained score by comparison with a large sample of people, and criterion referencing, which is, determining the significance of a test score by seeing how it relates to an absolute standard or expected success rate based on previous experience. (We also noticed self-referencing, or the comparison of a new score with the individual's previous performance.) The importance of criterion referencing is that it moves away from the use of relative standards, dependent on the particular sample of people on which one has test results, and requires instead that levels of performance be specified. These standards of competency must be relevant to the tasks required. Thus, a demand that tests be criterion referenced would make the test developers devote more attention to clarifying relevant standards and realistic expectations. If the assessor finds that people meet minimal levels of skill or knowledge, then he or she can look for other important characteristics. When criterion referencing is applied to learning situations, it is often called competency-based education. Carver (1975) points out a basic difference in the orientation of test makers toward tests designed simply to measure individual differences (that he calls *psychometric*) and toward tests intended to measure within-individual gain or growth in skills or achievements (which he calls *edumetric*). Criterion referencing calls attention to development of skills.

Study of the Single Individual and Intraindividual Organization. If the psychology of personality and personality assessment is to go very far, it must contend with the uniqueness of each person's life experience and behavior, the situations through which an individual progresses. The time-honored method of studying individual persons is the case study. We need better technology and methodology for such studies. Behavioral assessment has emphasized the individual, but in the process has singled out only problem behaviors to record and organize. We need to study more of the person. A few attempts at developing methods for studies of an N of one are available (Chassan, 1967; Dukes, 1965; Holtzman, 1963; Hoyer, 1974). An important problem was discerned by Carlson (1971) in her extensive review of articles in major personality journals. She found that (p. 209) "not a single published study attempted even minimal inquiry into the organization of personality variables within the individual." As the first chapter stated, a full assessment psychology must cover three aspects of persons: that which is in common with others, that which is shared with some others (which is the major emphasis of personality study to date), and that which is unique.

To these methodological needs, many others could be added such as exploring the relative utility of different strategies of test construction, linear and non-linear production, and different approaches to judgment and decision-making; these and other trends are mentioned by Goldberg (1972b). However, we must stop somewhere and go on to other topics.

CURRENT UNFINISHED BUSINESS—
SOCIAL RESPONSIBILITIES

The growth of testing and psychological assessment during the twentieth century in the United States and many other countries has been an impressive phenomenon. Public and private policy decisions have legitimatized tests as important elements in the selection of draftees in World War I, in admissions procedures to colleges, in employment and classification in industry, and in many individualized situations such as court decisions about insanity or clinical decisions about treatment. The manufacture and sales of tests is a large business, and education and training for testing involves thousands of people and considerable public expense. When an activity reaches such a magnitude and influences in an important way the channeling of people's opportunities, then questions arise and the enterprise must be scrutinized for its worth and its implications for society. It is not surprising that there has been an outcry against ability testing in the 1960s and 70s. In previous chapters we have briefly alluded to some of these societal problems and public policy considerations. Here we will return to them and add further thoughts and evidence. Three dangers stand out—the potential use of assessment for unfair discrimination, the problem of the violation of privacy, and the danger of overvaluing or undervaluing the assessment of persons. persons.

The Danger of Unfair Discrimination.   In one sense of the word, "discrimination" is what assessment is all about—the discrimination between the presence or absence of mental illness, or the discrimination between persons capable of doing a job well and those who would do poorly. However, the word has come to connote another very negative feeling, involving prejudice and bigotry, and it is this pejorative application of the word that is the point of the present discussion. The danger is the exclusion of minority groups, the poor, the handicapped, women, the young, and the old from positions of reward and influence. The administration of standardized tests or other assessment procedures that do not adequately take into account the differences in background, language, model of expression, and test-taking knowledge and attitudes has sometimes had this effect. The simple lack of norms for nonwhites or women on many tests makes the technique already suspect.

In the late 1940s and early 50s, a black sociologist, Allison Davis (1949; Eells et al., 1951), was one of the first people to point out the unfairness of intelligence tests to lower socioeconomic groups. The content of test items are chosen from experiences more likely to be familiar to white middle class than to lower class children, such as taking trips or playing with toys. More recently, Williams (1972) has demonstrated an interesting "turning of the tables" by creating a vocabulary test using black ghetto terms. Few whites can do well on it, but those who do, Williams claims, are likely to have a sensitivity and understanding of black culture. G. K. Bennett (1969), reviewing the uses of tests in personnel work, states "tests yield objective scores which quantify the consequences of disadvantage," and Williams (1971) has decried the "intellectual genocide" of children that results from using tests to label them retarded and place them in special tracks in school. In an extensive survey and study of the relation between intelligence and cultural environment, Philip Vernon (1969) has given ample evidence of the differences in perception and thinking between different cultural and ethnic groups in the United States and other countries. Often cross-cultural differences are due to poor translation, lack of equivalence in content, administrative procedures, inexperience with testing materials, or different attitudes toward achievement and competition (Brislin, Lonner, & Thorndike, 1973). Samuda (1975) has reviewed an extensive compendium of tests developed for use with minority people. In addition to using the most relevant testing methods available, the assessor should never stop the assessment with testing alone. He or she needs to remember that *measured* intelligence or personality in the test situation must be compared with *adaptive* intelligence or personality in the daily life of the client.

To what extent do demonstrated differences in intelligence tests result from genetic differences or from early environment and training? This widely debated question, is largely irrelevant to present decisions about individuals. Individual decisions must be made on the basis of current individual abilities, personality, and potential for learning. The overlap between ethnic and racial groups is so great that decisions must rest on individual study, not group differences. No doubt, both heredity and environment have effects on the development of a person, but at the present time very little can be done about genetic make-up. The usefulness of intelligence or personality tests does not lie in detecting innate differences, but in show-ing the present functioning of the person. It is essential for society to do everything it can to learn how to improve early developmental environ-ments and to find educational and training procedures that will enable persons of all levels of ability and varieties of personality to contribute to their own welfare and that of society. Assessment devices can be used as tools to help diagnose educational, vocational, and social skills and needs and test improvement with regard to them. In understanding how tests are best used with different groups, we must keep in mind that they may be valid *within* a group, even if the meaning of the differences between groups is not clear. Cleary (1968), for example, demonstrated in several colleges that both black and white students showed high correlations (around .50) between academic aptitude tests and grades. The tests worked as well within the black group as within the white. Anastasi (1976, p. 60) writes "To conceal the effects of cultural disadvantages by rejecting tests or by trying to devise tests that are insensitive to such effects can only retard progress toward a genuine solution of social problems. Such reactions toward tests are equivalent to breaking a thermometer because it registers a body temperature of 101 °."

Similar problems arise in regard to adverse discrimination because of sex and age. Items may pigeon-hole boys into traditional masculine roles, such as carpentry and law and girls into so called feminine roles such as nursing, child care, and housework. As mentioned earlier, David Campbell (1972) has revised the widely used Strong test to eliminate sex bias. One study (Abramowitz et al., 1973) identified sex-related ideological biases in clinical judges. Age bias may be as pernicious as sex bias. People in their teens or those over forty, fifty, or sixty are often excluded from participation in jobs simply on the basis of age and not on the basis of ability, energy, interest, or creativity. Assessment procedures may, however, be used to demonstrate the value and potential contributions of persons in nonpreferred age groups. Others who are often unfairly "selected out" include the physically handicapped, the poor, former convicts, and former mental patients. When assessment devices are used as institutional gate-keepers to disqualify and deselect for *irrelevant* reasons, they are preventing the full use of human resources and contributing to society's unrest and alienation. A major concern for assess-ment psychology, then, should be to ensure that tests are relevant to the decisions being made, and to the tasks and treatments being considered. The 1971 U.S. Supreme Court decision (the Griggs vs. Duke Power case) shifted to the employer the resonsibility for proving that selection pro-cedures are relevant and fair. Psychologists are trying to define relevance and determine exact ways to test for it (APA, 1969; Bray & Moses, 1972; Cleary et al., 1975; McNemar, 1975).

The Danger of Violation of Privacy.   Another major concern about assessment procedures is that the information collected may be a threat to individual freedom. The tests may be used to disseminate information that the person does not wish others to know. Knowledge about a person can mean power over that person. This concern is particularly important in connection with personality testing.

The MMPI has frequently been cited as an example. The inventory has a number of items like "I am a religious person" or "I am sometimes attracted to members of the same sex." Some individuals object to answering true or false to such items, but if the applicant is asked to take the test for a job he wants very much, he feels great pressure to answer. Some years ago White, in *The Organization Man* (1956), recommended that people cheat so as to appear normal, though not ideal. If people followed such advice, the utility of the test would be vitiated, even though unusual test-taking attitudes may be detected to some extent. It is also possible to imagine that a person might unintentionally reveal things about himself that could be damaging, perhaps on a projective technique that is unclear about its purposes. In a clinic or hospital there are usually extensive protections for confidential material, and private psychiatrists and psychologists, like lawyers and ministers, are not required to divulge privileged information. But no such care or protection may exist in personnel offices and schoolrooms, and occasionally there are celebrated cases in which confidential material is stolen (such as the case of Daniel Ellsberg's psychiatrist).

In the United States there seem to be trends toward the widespread establishment of personal data banks perhaps keyed to social security numbers. For many practical and research purposes such data banks would be useful. Records kept in computer memories could quickly be scanned for information when a person moves from one place to another. Needless interviews and filling out forms could be avoided. The data bank would make it possible for personologists and other social scientists to study patterns of background events related to personal and social problems, a kind of research impossible without massive numbers of subjects.

But disclosures in the mid-70s of the existence of FBI, CIA, and Defense Department files on many citizens in America and similar records in other countries raised the spectre of Big Brother in Orwell's *1984*, a widely read piece of fiction portraying a society in which there is heavy-handed authoritarian control over everyone. If regional or national data banks for social, scientific, and applied purposes should come into existence, extreme caution must be used to protect privacy so that a person's past history cannot damage his or her future. Some agencies automatically destroy personal files after a certain length of time. A young man who gets arrested with a delinquent gang or who is convicted of a marijuana charge might have the rest of his life greatly affected if this information were readily available. Most persons have some things in their background of which they are not proud. Complete openness of files to hiring agencies or political enemies could lead to exploitation. We cannot predict how personality data and test results might look to others in the future.

The Danger of Overvaluing or Undervaluing Tests.   In the past, tests have been oversold, and still many questionable claims are being put out by commercial test publishers, as many a review in Buros' Mental Measurements Yearbooks can attest. Testing is now big business, and trained professional consultants and testing experts have invested themselves in the use of their favored instruments. Like any organization, testing companies push for their own survival and enrichment. It is easy to overlook the public good in the pursuit of private gain. As with other organizations, the question is a problem of *accountability* and *evaluation.* Publishers and testing services need to be responsible for checking the effectiveness of their products and services. Outside evaluation is also needed to separate false claims and abuse from good results.

But there is also a danger in the wholesale rejection of tests. The protection of privacy and the prevention of unfair discrimination are worthy aims. In order to achieve them, some advocate throwing out all tests as the Soviet Union did in 1936. As has been said previously, however, tests are tools, only as good as the craftspeople who wield them. As Cronbach says (1975, p. 1) "Sound policy is not for tests or against tests; what matters is how tests are used."

Some might respond with the argument—It matters whether you have tools around because they will be used, and often, by fools. Someone has proposed the "law of the hammer"—Give a small boy a hammer, and he will pound all sorts of things with it. People often use this argument in favor of gun control saying that the mere fact that we allow people to have almost unrestricted ownership of guns of all sorts in the United States accounts for our high crime rate in comparison with the other developed countries. Thus it can be argued that having tests, we will often use them inappropriately. Society must decide which tools to make easily accessible, and demonstrate the costs and the benefits for having such implements. Tests, unlike guns, are usually meant to be employed by experts who have had training in their proper interpretation. There are very few casualties and many helpful victories when tests are in the hands of a responsible psychologist who has the client's interest at heart. If we broaden the use of tests in the process of "giving psychology away," as many would advocate (Miller, 1969), we must make distinctions between tests that anyone can safely use and tests that must only be used by experts.

The tester and the opponent of testing face the same hard questions about what the alternatives are. Decision-making must continue about jobs and therapies, and people need and want help in finding work and training most appropriate to their talents and interests. What are the alternative policies for meeting these needs? Which procedures will accomplish the ultimate aims the best way? If objective devices are not used, subjective ones, like interviewing, usually are. We should repeatedly evaluate the effects of interview assessment vs. assessment by means of tests and other techniques. As we have noticed earlier, the most exact procedures have in the past usually produced better results. Another, worse, alternative to assessment may be the use of political pull or cultural bias. Decisions may be made on the basis of ethnic membership or adherence to party doctrine and other considerations clearly irrelevant to the job to be done. Some have argued that this is what should be done with minority groups, to redress past wrongs. But even if one uses a quota system, must one necessarily select randomly from within the groups favored? Dawes (1975) frankly advocates the use of bias in favor of minority groups and women in admitting students to graduate work, he would simply add the difference between the means of the groups to the scores of the minority group member and then proceed in the ordinary manner to select with tests proven predictive of graduate success. Further work on aptitude-treatment interaction may point to special ways of facilitating learning in members of minority groups. The road to equity, while maintaining a realistic concern for talent, is not an easy one. With proper concern and careful study of various policies and their results we may be able to achieve Thomas Jefferson's hope for testing many years ago, that it would help the poor achieve and make use of opportunities they would not otherwise have had (Cronbach, 1975b).

Concerns about possible dangers in the use of tests are part of a widespread questioning of social policies and social directions. The general problem of the contribution of social science to public policy formation is in itself an interesting one. Donald Campbell (1969, p. 409) holds this hope for social scientists:

> The United States and other modern nations should be ready for an experimental approach to social reform, an approach in which we try out new programs designed to cure specific social problems, in which we learn whether or not these programs are effective, and in which we retain, imitate, modify, or discard them on the basis of apparent effectiveness on the multiple imperfect criteria available.

Psychological assessment could make important contributions to the program evaluation side of such experiments (Wortman, 1975). We should not conclude, however, that it will be easy to use assessment techniques in evaluating the effectiveness of programs. Such evaluation must often deal with strong political pressures, with unplanned administrative changes affecting programs, and with emotional resistance to data collection. These and other difficulties showed up in the evaluation of the preschool program for disadvantaged children, Project Headstart (Jensen, 1974; Cronbach,

1975b). Lack of agreement on criteria and the values behind them crippled this project. Policies cannot grow out of facts alone. In planning evaluation projects, we must consider values. As Wortman (1975, p. 566) says, "policy formation originates with the values of the policy maker and society, and . . . these values are most immune to feedback." The major political ideologies differ in the importance they assign to two basic values, freedom and equality (Rokeach, 1973), and these are often difficult if not impossible to balance. Assessment itself can be used in the service of various values. The psychologist and others must ask "Whose interests are being served?"

THE PROBABLE FORCES OF THE FUTURE

In one of my classes, I have asked students to list ten events they saw as likely to happen in their lives in the future, and then to list ten events likely to happen in society or the country. After finishing, I asked them to indicate whether the event would be pleasant or unpleasant. The events of the personal future were rated as overwhelmingly pleasant, and the events of the societal future were rated as overwhelmingly unpleasant. As a research finding, the procedure was so informal that one cannot claim that the results are generalizable, but they suggest the possibility that people see little connection between their personal lives and the happenings in society. If society is turbulent, aren't individuals likely to be affected? For example, Toffler, in *Future Shock* (1970) shows that the rate of social change has become so fast that individuals find it difficult to cope with their environment; individuals are perplexed by an overabundance of choices of ways to live in the post-industrial society. In this section we will look at some major world forces and explore their relevance to the assessment of persons.

Views of the future range from the frightening to the idyllic. For centuries historians and philosophers have examined the past for signs of cyclical or progressive changes. Science fiction since the turn of the century has stimulated the imagination and has sometimes served as society's warning system for impending technological problems. Only since the late 1960s has there been an attempt at more exact procedures for long range future gazing. Three methods for forecasting alternatives have emerged: extrapolation of current trends (for instance the Club of Rome's *Limits to Growth,* Meadows et al., 1972); combining the opinions of experts (the Delphi Method, Helmer, 1966); and games and simulation, often by means of computers ("Futures," the PLATO computer program, and others described by Rojas, 1974). The picture of the world's future portrayed in the *Limits to Growth* is a pessimistic one, showing in various ways that rapid population expansion, pollution and overuse of the world's resources will bring worldwide disaster in the 21st century, early in the century if one uses certain figures, late, using others.

Three problem areas are likely to dominate world thinking during the lives of the readers of this book and to raise fundamental problems of human behavior: *Peace,* Will leaders be able to resolve conflicts other than through proliferation of destruction and resist the ultimate temptation to release a worldwide radioactive holocaust?; *Population,* Will acceptable methods and incentives be found to change human sexual behavior from the production of pregnancies to other forms of expression and pleasure?; and *Pollution,* Will the military-industrial complex and individual citizens agree to sufficient change in life style to prevent the destruction of the life-supporting environment while insuring adequate living standards around the world? The key to many problems is population, since it is closely tied to pollution, food needs, and the use of resources. Projections show the world population reaching ten to sixteen billion about a century after 1970, when the population was 3.6 billion, already an enormous increase from 1.6 billion in 1900 (Brown, 1975; World Population Conference, 1974). In order to make this increase more understandable, one needs to imagine every city four times its 1970 size, with the concomitant increase in demands for food, jobs, and services. Brown foresees other dramatic discontinuities in coming world events, including a shift in political power from industrial countries to those possessing the important raw materials that are steadily growing more scarce.

In each of these giant areas of world concern, assessment psychology can add its small bit by providing measurement methods and concepts. Most use will be made of interviews and questionnaires, but inventories, projective techniques, and observation may supplement the simpler methods. As these problems impinge on individuals in such areas as crowding, social controls, and the need to reduce demand for goods: assessment may be involved in the attempts communities make to improve themselves. Peace, population, and pollution are highly prominent in the current scene, but they are indicators of only a few of the trends, some of which may provide positive opportunities rather than problems. The sociologist, Theodore Caplow (1971) lists fifteen world trends that were in evidence during the last 100 years and are likely to continue. Many of these seem related to assessment: Technological progress, technological diffusion, increase in goods, increase in services, increase in symbols and images, population expansion, occupational specialization, decreasing work effort, equalization of the sexes, urbanization and suburbanization, intensified spatial mobility, erosion of traditional cultures, expansion of government, increasing severity of war, and decreasing autonomy of the natural environment. Caplow also lists eleven trends that are often mentioned but are more difficult to quantify and prove: Increasing anxiety, breakdown of social values, increasing anomie (alienation), increasing deviance, increasing political violence, decline of the family, decline of religion, status equalization, cultural homogenization, global interdependence, and accelerating rates of social change. A number of Caplow's trends point to important problems on which assessment will be working in the future. They also suggest what is likely to happen to the assessment enterprise itself—increasing technology and computerization, increasing mechanization of routine processes of testing, growth in testing organizations and bureaucracies, more specialization of functions, greater variety of techniques, and increasing needs for services.

As population and communication increase, the problems of people become more and more urgent. The economist and social philosopher Kenneth Boulding wrote (1973, p. 20):

> We have been frittering away our resources in weaponry and space and even in organ transplants and sophisticated medicine. We should have been devoting ourselves to studying conflict, identity and human learning. Our massive ignorance about the learning and reality-testing process may well be the ultimate limitation on our ability to solve any of our problems.

So the role of social scientists in society is likely to increase in importance. The psychologist Donald Michael (1973) particularly urges that society engage in long range planning, thinking beyond the immediate years. To plan in a rapidly changing world requires imagination about alternative ways to go and concern for the consequences of actions. Few people at present have such long range perspective. Michael urges the development of a "future-responsive society" that actively fosters examination of images of the future.

In gaining perspective through imagining the future and also through studying history and other cultures, human beings will be moving toward an understanding beyond their own immediate feelings and perceptions. A major challenge is to think of *the common good*. Garett Hardin, a biologist (1968), wrote an often quoted article called "The Tragedy of the Commons" in which he shows that environmental and population problems are not likely to be solved by depending on individual initiative. For example, it was to the personal advantage of each herdsman in the English village to add more cattle to his herd that grazed in the commons, and each kept doing this until eventually all grazing became impossible and the grass was exhausted. Dawes and others (Dawes, 1973; Dawes, Delay, & Chaplin, 1974; Meux, 1973) show *the commons dilemma* to be a form of the often researched "Prisoner's Dilemma" in social psychology where there is a conflict between whether the individual should act for his or her own immediate reward or trust that another person will decide in such a way that both will get an even larger reward. A problem for the future is to develop systems of reward and communications and individual imaginations that will encourage actions maximizing long range values for all. We must learn to assess larger systems rather than the individual alone. The study of human judgment, which is part of the broadly conceived assessment process, is likely to be an increasingly important part of the understanding of policy formation (Hammond, 1974).

PRIORITIES FOR THE ASSESSMENT OF PERSONS

At this end of the book, then, what are some of the most valuable directions for assessment in the future? Assessment is usually seen as a means to accomplish ends or objectives. Now as we contemplate the likely forces of the future, the unfinished business of assessment, and the needs of society, we must ask hard questions about the highest and most important ends toward which assessment should turn. Here are five general areas in which it seems those interested in assessment should concentrate their energies.

Assessment as an Aid to Research on Major World Problems. As mentioned earlier, some problems—population, pollution, and peace—are of such magnitude that everyone should be concerned with them. Many people find them overwhelming, what can an individual do? With imagination, assessment psychology can help in addressing these long range and highly significant matters. For instance, the problems of pollution depend on attitudes toward growth and abilities to think in terms of the ecology and the larger systems. We know how to measure such attitudes and abilities and how to evaluate educational and mass media programs that might change them. Using appropriate techniques, cross cultural and intracultural studies can contribute to understanding the sources of these difficulties (Dawes, 1974).

Social System Indicators for the Prevention of Psychological Disorders and the Enhancement of the Quality of Life. Assessment could be concerned with fire prevention, not just fire fighting. It could help locate the sources of problems and the potentials for assistance to many people, not just by evaluating the patients, clients, and applicants that come to the assessor. In order to give humane and social needs as much attention as technological and economic factors, planners must have ways of measuring social conditions and reporting the findings to decision-makers and the public. In the United States the Council of Economic Advisers has had a powerful influence on national monetary policy, but for social affairs there is no equivalent body. Such a Council of Social Advisers would need regular and extensive sources of information on social problems like crime, mental illness, and educational handicaps (see Bauer, 1966 and Wilcox et al., 1972). Feedback mechanisms would alert society to the dangers of social downturns and areas of social distress just as economic indicators now alert economic planners to unemployment and production problems. Psychological assessment devices and social research techniques should be adapted or invented to reveal both negative and positive indicators of the quality of life. We could look for instances of creative coping with problems, recreational activities, volunteerism in communities, and helpful leadership. Nebulous as many of these ideas may sound, it seems likely that assessment methods could be developed to deal with them. With such feedback, organizations, communities, and national decision-makers would be better able to prevent problems and enhance the quality of life. The mechanism could serve as an early warning system for social distress and give people an image of what their society is like, counteracting the emphasis on the unusual and the deviant that they now receive from the mass media. Television itself would be one of the factors assessed in developing social indicators.

Self-Assessment for Effectiveness.   Somewhat parellel to the first point, assessment might see as its major goal assisting individuals in understanding *themselves.* Most assessment to date has been oriented toward decisions *about* patients, clients, and applicants. With the growing recognition of responsibility to the person ·from whom one collects data, the psychologist is trying to find ways of working *with* persons rather than *on* them. The enhancement of the person, not the diagnosis of deficiency is the aim. Zubin (1972, p. 429) has written ''Psychopathologists in the past have behaved like bookkeepers who had only red ink available. It is high time the assets of patients were counted as well as their liabilities.'' As Toffler (1970) and Milgram (1970) have shown, the problem for many people, especially in urban environments, is the problem of over-choice, the confusing overabundance of possibilities sometimes resulting in shutting out what is really important for the person. People need an understanding of their own values, resources, and priorities to help them choose how they want to live. Tests and other assessment procedures can help. Instead of just using tests as they are at present, we can develop tests that are *exploratory exercises.* They can become instruments not just for decisions and descriptions, but for learning about oneself or a special area of knowledge or skill. The beginnings of the use of assessment for self learning are exemplified by the self directed search in vocational planning by Holland (1974), the course-in-oneself by Dana & Fitzgerald (in press), and the human relations training of Pfeiffer & Heslin (1973) and Pfeiffer and Jones (1971–1974). Meichenbaum (1975) provides a behavioral rationale of self-instruction. Combined with ''field learning'' and environmental simulation, such methods can enable individuals and families to move toward goals they devise.

Accountability and Assessment of Assessment Technology. Part of the development of assessment should include the study of its own implicit and explicit goals and procedures for improving its own systems. It is conceivable that much of present assessment activity is useless. As behaviorists look back on projective testing, they say, "What a waste of time!" The practice of assessment must be looked at from a cost-benefit basis, but not in a narrow-minded, simplistic way. Some sample questions that might be asked are: Do the decisions being made by an agency result in hiring fewer minority group members than would be expected? Why is this happening? Are assessment practices resulting in a "brain drain" from one sector of the community to another? Particular on-going assessment systems must be analyzed, as must the assessment technology as a whole. Where is it going? The aim of any technology assessment is to anticipate consequences before mass production in order to optimize benefits and allocate resources in the development of the most useful methods. Do we need more of certain assessment procedures rather than others? What are criteria for a humane technology? These are some of the important questions that should be asked as the psycho-technology of personal assessment develops (Miller, 1970; Locatis & Gooler, 1975; Wortman, 1975; Gutentag & Struening, 1975).

Widespread Assessment Training and Education for the Understanding of Person-Environment Systems. If assessment is seen as the information gathering and organizing aspect of human systems for their decision and image making functions, then who shall be assessors, and how should they prepare for that role? How should people be educated to make use of systems-oriented assessment resources? Assessment as the art of understanding systems at all levels can be much more widespread than at present. The long range trends are toward more and more human services provided by many kinds of people besides psychologists. Efforts should be directed toward giving them tools and teaching them how to use them. Self-assessment techniques mentioned above are examples at one systems level. Human judgment and some form of assessment are called for in all kinds of work with individuals and communities.

An optimistic view of these five points would see all of these priorities being supported by generous financing and public cooperation in the interest of helping people understand the future of our highly interdependent "Spaceship Earth." A pessimistic view would see the coming decades as a time of either the destruction of humankind through atomic war, population crashes, and industrial poisoning, or the misuse of technology to terrorize and subjugate people. Behavioral scientists and the general public will face many value-laden decisions before the year 2000. These decisions will be posed by such discoveries as how to choose the sex of offspring, provisions for giving intensely gratifying sensations by brain implantations and new mind-altering drugs, instant two-way visual communication, and the ability to control internal organs willfully. These phenomena are already on the horizon and will create a behavioral technology that is the next step up the scale from the current revolution in biology and the earlier revolution in the physical sciences. In our interdependent world, assessment of persons will be involved in these changes.

FINAL COMMENT

Many readers will be in positions in the future to carry out whatever ideas were acquired while reading this book. Kenneth Boulding, surveying the many problems and pessimisms about the current state of the world, wrote (1973, p. 21):

> The dangers and difficulties of the present time are very great. Nevertheless, the only unforgivable sin is despair, for that will justify itself. Man is very far from having exhausted the potential of his extraordinary nervous system. The troubles of the 20th century are not unlike those of adolescence—rapid growth beyond the ability of organizations to manage, uncontrollable emotion, and a desperate search for identity. Out of adolescence, however, comes maturity in which physical growth with all its attendant difficulties comes to an end, but in which growth continues in knowledge, in spirit, in community, and in love; it is to this that we look forward as a human race. This goal, once seen with our eyes, will draw our faltering feet towards it.

SUMMARY

In this last chapter, we have returned to a consideration of major issues and the interaction of assessment with the larger social system. The further development of assessment needs to relate to personality theory and a theory of action. A cognitive-behavioral-ecological view of personality was proposed, with a postulated Central Processer that involves stimulus selection and categorizing, self-regulating concepts, a competency repertoire, situational expectations, and response selection. Methodological unfinished business includes the need for situational and person-situation interaction assessment, computer assisted integration of information and interpretation, aptitude-treatment interaction studies, criterion-referencing, and studies of single individuals and intraindividual organization. The unfinished business of assessment's social responsibilities include dealing with the dangers of bias against minorities and other groups, the undermining of privacy and the over- and under-valuation of tests. Assessment needs to develop better ways of showing accountability for its actions and evaluating its cost-effectiveness.

Looking at the likely world events in the future, we noted the predominance of problems from population expansion, pollution, and peace-breaking. It is evident that individual lives will be touched by these giant problems, and one can speculate on the possibilities for the contribution of assessment to research on these problems and on the remediation of their disturbing effects. Long-range planning will require considerable imagination, flexibility, and a perspective on "the common good."

Developmental priorities for the assessment of persons include aids to research on major world problems, social system indicators, self-assessment of competencies, evaluation of assessment technology, and education for understanding person-environment systems. One may take a pessimistic or an optimistic view of the future, but in any case at the center of one's thoughts are questions about the ways of living an individual life, and the ways to better understand persons and enhance the quality of life.

SUGGESTED READINGS

CLEARY, T. A., HUMPHREYS, L. G., KENDRICK, S. A., & WESMAN, A. Educational uses of tests with disadvantaged students. *American Psychologist,* 1975, 30, 15–40. This APA report provides excellent background information and discussion of issues concerning ability testing especially as it relates to fairness to minority students. The authors state that (p. 24) "By and large, *when properly applied and interpreted,* they [general mental ability tests] have predicted future learning for all segments of our society with modest but significant validity and generalizability." An article by Arvey & Mussio (1974) presents a model for demonstrating whether employment tests discriminate against minorities by testing a large sample of applicants. Padilla & Ruiz (1975) give a critique of personality assessment and test interpretation of Mexican Americans.

CRONBACH, L. J. Five decades of public controversy over mental testing. *American Psychologist,* 1975, 30, 1–14. Cronbach reviews the history of public attacks on testing, especially intelligence testing, with particular attention to the furor over Arthur Jensen's 1969 article and racism. Cronbach's review and discussion of aptitude-treatment interaction (1975) is another important article.

FAWCETT, J. T. Psychological research on family size and family planning in the United States. *Professional Psychology,* 1974, 5, 334–344. This brief summary by a leading expert in population psychology can introduce the reader to one world problem area in which assessment devices have made some contribution.

MICHAEL, D. N. *On learning to plan—and planning to learn.* San Francisco: Jossey-Bass, 1973. Michael urges the development of future responsive, societal learning. Such an approach to long-range planning would require radical changes of organizations and social norms. He incorporates other futurist thinking in discussing new ideas of competence, and states (p. 6) "the future is our present responsibility."

SCHWITZGEBEL, R. L. Behavior instrumentation and social technology. *American Psychologist,* 1970, 25, 491–499. Schwitzgebel imaginatively discusses the emerging and foreseeable possibilities of such innovations as automated public opinion polling and behavioral prosthetics, and presents some of the professional and public problems of their use. The special issue of the *American Psychologist* on instrumentation (March, 1975) outlines advanced technology and its uses such as biofeedback, measurement of genital response, tactile communication, and radio telemetry in clinical work. As a sharp contrast, the reader might like to see the humanist and existential approach to assessment by Dana & Leech (1974). In Kline's edited book (1973) largely by British authors discussing new testing approaches, Bannister and Bott write movingly of the political assumptions in testing and the implicit contract between the two human beings in the assessment dyad.

TYLER, L. E. Design for a hopeful psychology. *American Psychologist,* 1973, 28, 1021–1029. In a presidential address to the APA, Leona Tyler analyzes promising signs of change, including the reorientation of assessment from selection to classification and improvement of self-knowledge, the shift from unidimensional to multidimensional thinking, and a general decline in elitism. In considering policy formation she places great emphasis on the perception of and choice among different alternatives for the future.

WORTMAN, P. M. Evaluation research: A psychological perspective. *American Psychologist,* 1975, 30, 562–575. Wortman provides an excellent overview of program evaluation and how it relates to values and policy making. The definitive comprehensive reference is the handbook by Gutentag & Struening (1975). Readers may also be interested in Donald Campbell's proposals (1969) for ways in which social change may be studied by psychologists in "the experimenting society." Zuniga (1975) discusses Campbell's ideas and the problems posed for social scientists during the turmoil of Chile's Unidad Popular period. Argyris (1975) presents some of the dangers in applying results from experimental social psychology. Bronfenbrenner (1974) outlines needs and problems in relating developmental research to public policy and the lack of usable knowledge about behavior in the natural environment.

Bibliography

ABELSON, R. P. Simulation of social behavior. In G. Lindzey and E. Aronson (eds.) *The handbook of social psychology.* (2nd ed.), Vol. 2. Reading, Mass.: Addison-Wesley, 1968, pp. 274-356.

ABRAMOWITZ, S. I., ABRAMOWITZ, C. V., JACKSON, C., & GOMES, B. The politics of clinical judgment: What nonliberal examiners infer about women who do not stifle themselves. *Journal of Consulting and Clinical Psychology,* 1973, 41, 385-391.

ADINOLFI, A. A. Relevance of person perception research to clinical psychology. *Journal of Consulting and Clinical Psychology,* 1971, 37, 167-176.

ADORNO, T. W., et al. *The authoritarian personality.* New York: Harper and Row, 1950.

ALLEN, K. E., HART, B. M., BUELL, J. S., HARRIS, F. R., & WOLF, M. M. Effects of social reinforcement on isolate behavior of a nursery school child. *Child Development,* 1964, 35, 511-518.

ALLEN, R. M. *Personality assessment procedures.* New York: Harper, 1958.

ALLEN, T. W. Review of J. Annett, *Feedback and human behavior.* Baltimore: Penguin, 1969. *Journal of Personality Assessment,* 1972, 36, 78-79.

ALLPORT, G. W. *Personality, a psychological interpretation.* New York: Holt, 1937.

ALLPORT, G. W. *The use of personal documents in psychological science.* New York: Social Science Research Council Bulletin No. 49, 1942.

ALLPORT, G. W. The open system in personality theory. *Journal of Abnormal Psychology,* 1960, 61, 301–311.

ALLPORT, G. W. *Pattern and growth in personality.* New York: Holt, Rinehart & Winston, 1961.

ALLPORT, G. W. *Letters from Jenny.* New York: Harcourt Brace, 1965.

ALLPORT, G. W. & ODBERT, H. S. Trait-names; A psycho-lexical study. *Psychological Monographs,* 1936, 47 (1, Whole No. 211).

American Psychological Association, *Ethical standards of psychologists.* Washington, D.C.: American Psychological Association, 1953.

American Psychological Association. Ethical standards of psychologists. *American Psychologist,* 1968, 23, 357–361.

American Psychological Association. *Standards for educational and psychological tests.* Washington, D.C.: American Psychological Association, 1974.

American Psychological Association. Instrumentation in psychology. *American Psychologist,* 1975, 30, No. 3 (Special issue).

American Psychological Association Committee on Scientific and Professional Ethics and Conduct. Draft: Ethical standards of psychologists. *APA Monitor,* 1975, 6, No. 11, 18–19.

American Psychological Association Task Force on Employment Testing of Minority Groups. Job testing and the disadvantaged. *American Psychologist,* 1969, 24, 637–650.

American Psychological Association Task Force on Issues of Sexual Bias in Graduate Education, Guidelines for nonsexist use of language. *American Psychologist,* 1975, 30, 682–685.

ANASTASI, A. *Psychological testing* (4th ed.) New York: Macmillan, 1976.

ANDERSON, N. H. Looking for configurality in clinical judgment. *Psychological Bulletin,* 1972, 78, 93–102.

ANDERSON, S. & MESSICK, S. Social competency in young children. *Developmental Psychology,* 1974, 10, 282–293.

ARGYLE, M. & LITTLE, B. R. Do personality traits apply to social behavior? *Journal for the Theory of Social Behaviour,* 1972, 2, 1–35.

ARGYRIS, C. Dangers in applying results from experimental social psychology. *American Psychologist,* 1975, 30, 469–485.

ARGYRIS, C. & SCHÖN, D. A. *Theory in practice: Increasing professional effectiveness.* San Francisco: Jossey-Bass, 1974.

ARKOWITZ, H., LICHTENSTEIN, E., McGOVERN, K., & HINES, P. The behavioral assessment of social competence in males. *Behavior Therapy,* 1975, 6, 3–13.

ARMSTRONG, J. S. & SOELBERG, P. On the interpretation of factor analysis. *Psychological Bulletin,* 1968, 70, 361–364.

ARTHUR, A. Z. Diagnostic testing and the new alternatives. *Psychological Bulletin,* 1969, 72, 183–192.

ARVEY, R. D. & MUSSIO, S. J. A validation strategy for the "nonsample." *Professional Psychology,* 1974, 5, 264–266.

ASH, P. The reliability of psychiatric diagnoses. *Journal of Abnormal and Social Psychology,* 1949, 44, 272–276.

Associated Press. Russian high schoolers face crucial exams. *Christian Science Monitor,* 1974, September 3, p. 5C.

AVERILL, J. R. & OPTON, E. M., Jr. Psychophysiological assessment: Rationale and problems. In P. McReynolds (ed.) *Advances in psychological assessment.* Vol. 1, Palo Alto: Science and Behavior Books, 1968, pp. 265–288.

AXELROD, S., HALL, R. V., WEIS, L., & ROHER, S. Use of self-imposed contingencies to reduce the frequency of smoking behavior. In M. J. Mahoney & C. E. Thoresen, *Self-control: Power to the person.* Monterey, California: Brooks-Cole, 1974.

BAIER, D. E. & DUGAN, R. E. Factors in sales success. *Journal of Applied Psychology,* 1957, 41, 37–40.

BAKER, B. C. XYY chromosome syndrome and the law. *Criminologica,* 1970, 7, 2–35.

BALES, R. F. *Interaction process analysis.* Cambridge, Mass.: Addison-Wesley, 1950.

BALES, R. F. Interaction process analysis. In D. L. Sills (ed.) *International encyclopedia of the social sciences.* Vol. 7. New York: Macmillan and Free Press, 1968, pp. 465–471.

BALES, R. F. *Personality and interpersonal behavior.* New York: Holt, Rinehart & Winston, 1970.

BALTES, P. B. & SCHAIE, K. W. (eds.) *Life-span developmental psychology: Personality and socialization.* New York: Academic Press, 1973.

BANAKA, W. H. *Training in depth interviewing.* New York: Harper & Row, 1971.

BANCROFT, J. H. J. The application of psychophysiological measures to the assessment and modification of sexual behaviour. *Behaviour Research and Therapy,* 1971, 9, 119–130.

BANDURA, A. A social learning interpretation of psychological dysfunctions. In P. London and D. Rosenhan (eds.) *Foundations of abnormal psychology.* New York: Holt, Rinehart & Winston, 1968.

BANDURA, A. *Principles of behavior modification.* New York: Holt, Rinehart & Winston, 1969.

BANNISTER, D. (ed.) *Perspectives in personal construct theory.* London: Academic Press, 1970.

BARCHAS, J. D., STOLK, J. M., CIARANELLO, R. D., & HAMBURG, D. A. Neuroregulatory agents and psychological assessment. In P. McReynolds (ed.) *Advances in psychological assessment,* Vol. 2. Palo Alto: Science and Behavior Books, 1971, pp. 260–92.

BARKER, R. G. (ed.) *The stream of behavior.* New York: Appleton-Century-Crofts, 1963.

BARKER, R. G. & WRIGHT, H. F. *One boy's day.* New York: Harper, 1951.

BARKER, R. G. *Ecological psychology.* Stanford: Stanford University Press, 1968.

BARLOW, D. H., AGRAS, W. S., & LEITENBERG, H. Experimental investigations in the use of covert sensitization in the modification of sexual behavior. In R. W. Rubin and C. M. Franks (eds.) *Advances in behavior therapy.* Vol. 3. New York: Academic Press, 1970.

BARNES, M. & BERKE, J. *Mary Barnes, two accounts of a journey through madness.* New York: Harcourt Brace, 1971.

BARRON, F. *Personal soundness in university graduate students, an experimental study of young men in the sciences and professions.* Berkeley: University of California Press, 1954.

BARTHELL, C. N. & HOLMES, D. S. High school yearbooks: A nonreactive measure of social isolation in graduates who later became schizophrenic. *Journal of Abnormal Psychology,* 1968, 73, 313–316.

BARTLETT, C. J. & GREEN, C. G. Clinical prediction: Does one sometimes know too much? *Journal of Counseling Psychology,* 1966, 13, 267–270.

BASS, B. M. The leaderless group discussion. *Psychological Bulletin,* 1954, 51, 465–492.

BATESON, G., JACKSON, D. D., HALEY, J., & WEAKLAND, J. H. Toward a theory of schizophrenia. *Behavioral Science,* 1956, 1, 251–264.

BAUER, R. A. (ed.) *Social Indicators.* Cambridge, Mass.: MIT Press, 1966.

BAUGHMAN, E. E. *Black Americans.* New York: Academic Press, 1971.

BAYLEY, N. & SCHAEFER, E. S. Correlations of maternal and child behaviors and the development of mental abilities: Data from the Berkeley Growth Study. *Monographs, Society for Research in Child Development,* 1964, 29, No. 6.

BECK, A. T., WARD, C. H., MENDELSON, M., MOCK, J. E., & ERBAUGH, J. K. Reliability of psychiatric diagnosis 2: A study of consistency of clinical judgments and ratings. *American Journal of Psychiatry,* 1962, 119, 351–357.

BECK, S. J. How the Rorschach came to America. *Journal of Personality Assessment,* 1972, 36, 105–108.

BEM, S. L. Sex role adaptability: One consequence of psychological androgeny. *Journal of Personality and Social Psychology,* 1975, 31, 634–643.

BENJAMIN, A. *The helping interview.* Boston: Houghton Mifflin, 1969.

BENNETT, G. K. Factors affecting the value of validation studies. *Personnel Psychology,* 1969, 22, 265–268.

BERGIN, A. E. The evaluation of therapeutic outcomes. In A. E. Bergin & S. L. Garfield (eds.) *Handbook of psychotherapy and behavior change: An empirical analysis.* New York: Wiley, 1971, pp. 217–270.

BERGIN, A. E. & GARFIELD, S. L. *Handbook of psychotherapy and behavior change: An empirical analysis.* New York: Wiley, 1971.

BERGMANN, M. S. Limitations of method in psychoanalytic biography: A historical inquiry. *Journal of the American Psychoanalytic Association,* 1973, 21, 833–850.

BERNE, E. *Games people play.* New York: Grove, 1964.

BERRIEN, F. K. *General and social systems.* New Brunswick, N.J.: Rutgers University Press, 1968.

BERRY, J. W. Temne and Eskimo perceptual skills. *International Journal of Psychology,* 1966, 1, 207–229.

BERSOFF, D. N. Silk purses into sows' ears: The decline of psychological testing and a suggestion for its redemption. *American Psychologist,* 1973, 28, 892–899.

BIJOU, S. W. & PETERSON, R. F. Functional analysis in the assessment of children. In P. McReynolds (ed.), *Advances in psychological assessment,* Vol. 2. Palo Alto: Science & Behavior Books, 1971, pp. 63–78.

BINGHAM, W. V. D. & MOORE, B. V. *How to interview.* New York: Harper and Row, 1924.

BIRDWHISTELL, R. L. *Kinesics and context: Essays on body motion communication.* Philadelphia: University of Pennsylvania Press, 1970.

BIRREN, J. E. (ed) *Handbook of aging and the individual.* Chicago: University of Chicago Press, 1959.

BLANK, L. *Psychological evaluation in psychotherapy: Ten case histories.* Chicago: Aldine, 1965. Materials quoted reprinted by permission of the author and Aldine Publishing Co.

BLOCK, J. *The Q-sort method in personality assessment and psychiatric research.* Springfield, Ill.: Thomas, 1961.

BLOCK, J. *The challenge of response sets.* New York: Appleton-Century-Crofts, 1965.

BLOCK, J. *Lives through time.* Berkeley: Bancroft, 1971.

BLUM, G. S. *The Blacky pictures and manual.* New York: Psychological Corp., 1950.

BLUM, G. S. A guide for research use of the Blacky pictures. *Journal of Projective Techniques,* 1962, 26, 3–29.

BLUM, G. S. Assessment of psychodynamic variables by the Blacky Pictures. In P. McReynolds (ed.), *Advances in psychological assessment,* Vol. 1. Palo Alto: Science & Behavior Books, 1968, pp. 150–168.

BODIN, A. M. Conjoint family assessment: An evolving field. In P. McReynolds (ed.) *Advances in psychological assessment,* Vol. 1. Palo Alto: Science & Behavior Books, 1968, pp. 223–243.

BOLZ, C. R. Personality types. In R. M. Dreger (ed.) *Multivariate personality research: Contributions to the understanding of personality in honor of Raymond B. Cattell.* Baton Rouge, La.: Claitor's Publishing Division, 1972.

BORKOVEC, T. D. & Craighead, W. E. The comparison of two methods of assessing fear and avoidance behaviour. *Behaviour Research and Therapy,* 1971, 9, 285–291.

BOULDING, K. E. Towards a 21st century politics. *Span,* 1973, 14 (Jan.), 16–21.

BOWERS, K. S. Situationalism in psychology: On making reality disappear. Department of Psychology Research Report No. 37. Waterloo, Ont.: University of Waterloo, September 1972.

BRAGINSKY, B. M. & BRAGINSKY, D. D. *Mainstream psychology: A critique.* New York: Holt, Rinehart & Winston, 1974.

BRAY, D. W., CAMPBELL, R. J., & GRANT, D. L. *Formative years in business: A long-term A T & T study of managerial lives.* New York: Wiley, 1974.

BRAY, D. W. & GRANT, D. L. The assessment center in the measurement of potential for business management. *Psychological Monographs,* 1966, 80, No. 17 (Whole No. 625).

BRAY, D. W. & MOSES, J. L. Personnel selection. In P. H. Mussen & M. R. Rosenzweig (eds.) *Annual Review of Psychology,* Vol. 23. Palo Alto: Annual Reviews, 1972, pp. 545–576.

BREGER, L. *From instinct to identity: The development of personality.* Englewood Cliffs, N.J.: Prentice-Hall, 1974.

BRIGGS, P. F., ROUZER, D. L., HAMBERG, R. L., & HOLMAN, T. R. Seven scales for the Minnesota-Briggs History Record with reference group data. *Journal of Clinical Psychology, Monograph Supplement,* 1972, No. 36.

BRISLIN, R. W., LONNER, W. J., & THORNDIKE, R. M. *Cross-cultural research methods.* New York: Wiley, 1973.

BRONFENBRENNER, U. Developmental research, public policy, and the ecology of childhood. *Child Development,* 1974, 45, 1–5.

BROWN, L. R. The discontinuities before us. *The Futurist,* 1975, 9, 122–131.

BROWN, R. *Social psychology.* New York: Free Press, 1965.

BROZEK, J. To test or not to test: Trends in the Soviet views. *Journal of the History of the Behavioral Sciences,* 1972, 8, 243–248.

BRUHN, A. R. & REED, M. R. Simulation of brain damage on the Bender-Gestalt Test by college subjects, *Journal of Personality Assessment,* 1975, 39, 244–255.

BRUNSWIK, E. *Perception and the representative design of psychological experiments.* Berkeley: University of California Press, 1956.

BUBER, M. *I and thou.* (2nd ed.) Trans. by R. G. Smith. New York: Scribner, 1958.

BUCHWALD, A. M. Verbal utterances as data. In H. Feigl & G. Maxwell (eds.) *Current issues in the philosophy of science.* New York: Holt, 1961, pp. 461–468.

BUCKLEY, W. (ed.) *Modern systems research for the behavioral scientist: a sourcebook.* Chicago: Aldine-Atherton, 1968.

BUHLER, C. & MASSARIK, F. (eds.) *The course of human life.* New York: Springer, 1968.

BURDOCK, E. I. & HARDESTY, A. S. Psychological test for psychopathology. *Journal of Abnormal Psychology,* 1968, 73, 62–69.

BUROS, O. K. (ed.) *The fifth mental measurements yearbook.* Highland Park, N.J.: Gryphon Press, 1959.

BUROS, O. K. (ed.) *The sixth mental measurements yearbook.* Highland Park, N.J.: Gryphon Press, 1965.

BUROS, O. K. *Personality tests and reviews.* Highland Park, N.J.: Gryphon Press, 1970.

BUROS, O. K. (ed.) *The seventh mental measurements yearbook,* Vols. 1, 2. Highland Park, N.J.: Gryphon Press, 1972.

BUTCHER, J. N. (ed.) *MMPI: Research developments and clinical applications.* New York: McGraw Hill, 1969.

BUTCHER, J. N. (ed.) *Objective personality assessment: Changing perspectives.* New York: Academic Press, 1972.

BYRD, E. A study of validity and constancy of choice in a sociometric test. *Sociometry,* 1951, 14, 175–181.

CAMPBELL, D. P. The Strong Vocational Interest Blank: 1927–1967. In P. McReynolds (ed.) *Advances in Psychological Assessment,* Vol. 1. Palo Alto: Science and Behavior Books, 1968, pp. 105–130.

CAMPBELL, D. P. *Handbook for the Strong Vocational Interest Blank.* Stanford, Ca.: Stanford University Press, 1971.

CAMPBELL, D. P. The practical problems of revising an established psychological test. In J. N. Butcher (ed.) *Objective personality assessment.* New York: Academic Press, 1972, pp. 117–130.

CAMPBELL, D. T. Reforms as experiments. *American Psychologist,* 1969, 24, 409–427.

CAMPBELL, D. T. & FISKE, D. W. Convergent and discriminant validation by the multitrait-multimethod matrix. *Psychological Bulletin,* 1959, 56, 81–105.

CANADY, H. G. The effect of "rapport" on the IQ: A new approach to the problem of racial psychology. *Journal of Negro Education,* 1936, 5, 209–219.

CANNELL, C. F. & KAHN, R. L. Interviewing. In G. Lindzey and E. Aronson (eds.) *Handbook of social psychology* (2nd ed.) Vol. 2, Reading, Mass.: Addison-Wesley, 1968, pp. 526–595.

CAPLOW, T. *Elementary sociology.* Englewood Cliffs, N.J.: Prentice-Hall, 1971.

CARKHUFF, R. R. *Helping and human relations.* New York: Holt, Rinehart & Winston, 1969.

CARLSON, J. S. & FULLMER, D. W. *College norms.* Eugene: Counseling Center, University of Oregon, 1959.

CARLSON, R. Where is the person in personality research? *Psychological Bulletin,* 1971, 75, 203–219.

CARLSON, R. Studies of Jungian typology: I. Memory, social perception, and social action. *Journal of Personality,* 1973, 41, 559–576.

CARSON, R. C. *Interaction concepts of personality.* Chicago: Aldine, 1969.

CARTWRIGHT, D. S. *Introduction to personality.* Chicago: Rand McNally, 1974.

CARTWRIGHT, D. S. Trait and other sources of variance in the S-R Inventory of Anxiousness. *Journal of Personality and Social Psychology,* 1975, 32, 405–414.

CARVER, R. P. Two dimensions of tests: Psychometric and edumetric. *American Psychologist,* 1975, 29, 512–518.

CASH, T. F., BEGLEY, P. J., McCOWN, D. A. & WEISE, B. C. When counselors are heard but not seen: Initial impact of physical attractiveness. *Journal of Counseling Psychology,* 1975, 22, 273–279.

CASON, H. Common annoyances. *Psychological Monographs,* 1930, 40, No. 182.

CATTELL, R. B. *Description and measurement of personality.* Yonkers-on-Hudson, N.Y.: World, 1946.

CATTELL, R. B. *Personality: A systematic, theoretical and factual study.* New York: McGraw-Hill, 1950.

CATTELL, R. B. Principles of design in projective or misperception tests of personality. In H. H. Anderson & G. L. Anderson (eds.) *An introduction to projective techniques.* New Jersey: Prentice-Hall, 1951.

CATTELL, R. B. Theory of fluid and crystallized intelligence: A critical experiment. *Journal of Educational Psychology,* 1963, 54, 1–22.

CATTELL, R. B. *The scientific analysis of personality.* Baltimore: Penguin Books, 1965.

CATTELL, R. B. *Personality and mood by questionnaire.* San Francisco: Jossey-Bass, 1973.

CATTELL, R. B. How good is the modern questionnaire? General principles for evaluation. *Journal of Personality Assessment,* 1974, 38, 115–129.

CATTELL, R. B. & WARBURTON, F. *Principles of objective personality measurement, and a compendium of objective tests.* Urbana, IL: University of Illinois Press, 1967.

CAUTELA, J. R. & KASTENBAUM, R. A reinforcement survey schedule for use in therapy, training and research. *Psychological Reports,* 1967, 20, 1115–1130.

CHAPMAN, L. J. & CHAPMAN, J. P. Genesis of popular but erroneous psycho-diagnostic observations. *Journal of Abnormal Psychology,* 1967, 72, 193–204.

CHAPMAN, L. J. & CHAPMAN, J. P. Illusory correlation as an obstacle to the use of valid psychodiagnostic signs. *Journal of Abnormal Psychology,* 1969, 74, 271–280.

CHASEN, B. & WEINBERG, S. L. Diagnostic sex-role bias: How can we measure it? *Journal of Personality Assessment,* 1975, 39, 620–629.

CHASSAN, J. B. *Research design in clinical psychology and psychiatry.* New York: Appleton-Century-Crofts, 1967.

CHILD, D. *The essentials of factor analysis.* New York: Holt, Rinehart & Winston, 1970.

CHRISTIE, R. & GEIS, F. L. *Studies in Machiavellianism.* New York: Academic Press, 1970.

CHRISTIE, R. & JAHODA, M. (eds.) *Studies in the scope and method of the authoritarian personality.* Glencoe, Ill.: Free Press, 1954.

CHUN, KI-TAEK, COBB, S. & FRENCH, J. R. P., JR. *Measures for psychological assessment: A guide to 3000 original sources and their applications.* Ann Arbor, MI: Institute of Social Research, 1975.

CIMINERO, A. R., CALHOUN, K. S., & ADAMS, H. E. (eds.) *Handbook for behavioral assessment.* New York: Wiley, 1976 (in press).

CLARK, K. E. The mountain's mouse. *Contemporary Psychology,* 1960, 5, 72–73.

CLARK, R. A. Projective measurement of experimentally induced levels of sexual motivation. *Journal of Experimental Psychology,* 1952, 44, 391–399.

CLEARY, T. A. Test bias: Prediction of grades of Negro and white students in integrated colleges. *Journal of Educational Measurement,* 1968, 5, 115–124.

CLEARY, T. A., HUMPHREYS, L. G., KENDRICK, S. A., & WESMAN, A. Educational uses of tests with disadvantaged students. *American Psychologist,* 1975, 30, 15–40.

COAN, R. W. *The optimal personality: An empirical and theoretical analysis.* New York: Columbia University Press, 1974.

COHEN, H. D. & SHAPIRO, A. A method for measuring sexual arousal in the female. *Psychophysiology,* 1971, 8, 251–252 (Abstract).

COHEN, J. & LEFKOWITZ, J. Development of a biographical inventory blank to predict faking on personality tests. *Journal of Applied Psychology,* 1974, 59, 404–405.

COHEN, J. & STRUENING, E. L. Opinions about mental illness in the personnel of two large mental hospitals. *Journal of Abnormal and Social Psychology,* 1962, 64, 349–360.

COLBY, K. M. *Ten criticisms of PARRY.* Stanford: Stanford Artificial Intelligence Laboratory, 1974.

COLBY, K. M., HILF, F. D., WEBER, S., & KRAEMER, H.C. Turing-like indistinguishability tests for the validation of a computer simulation of paranoid processes. *Artificial Intelligence,* 1972, 3, 199–221.

COLBY, K. M., WATT, J., & GILBERT, J. P. A computer method of psychotherapy. *Journal of Nervous and Mental Diseases,* 1966, 142, 148–152.

COLMEN, J. G., KAPLAN, S. J., & BOULGER, J. R. Selection and selection research in the Peace Corps. Research Note No. 7, Washington, D.C.: Research Division, Peace Corps, August, 1964.

COMREY, A. L., BACKER, T. E., & GLASER, E. M. *A sourcebook for mental health measures.* Los Angeles: Human Interaction Research Institute, 1973.

CONSTANTINOPLE, A. An Eriksonian measure of personality development in college students. *Developmental Psychology,* 1969, 1, 357–372.

CORTES, J. B. & GATTI, F. M. *Delinquency and crime: A biopsychosocial approach.* New York: Seminar, 1972.

CRADDICK, R. A. Sharing oneself in the assessment procedure. *Professional Psychology,* 1975, 6, 279–282.

CRAIK, K. H. The assessment of places. In P. McReynolds (ed.), *Advances in psychological assessment,* Vol. 2. Palo Alto.: Science and Behavior Books, 1971 pp. 40–62.

CRAIK, K. H. Environmental psychology. In M. Rosenzweig & L. Porter (eds.) *Annual Review of Psychology,* 1973, 24, 403–421.

CRESSEN, R. Artistic quality of drawings and judges' evaluation of the DAP. *Journal of Personality Assessment,* 1975, 39, 132–137.

CRONBACH, L. J. The two disciplines of scientific psychology. *American Psychologist,* 1957, 12, 671–684.

CRONBACH, L. J. *Essentials of psychological testing,* 3rd ed. New York: Harper & Row, 1970.

CRONBACH, L. J. Beyond the two disciplines of scientific psychology. *American Psychologist,* 1975, 30, 116–127 . (a)

CRONBACH, L. J. Five decades of public controversy over mental testing. *American Psychologist,* 1975, 30, 1–14. (b)

CRONBACH, L. J. & GLESER, G. C. *Psychological tests and personnel decisions,* 2nd ed. Urbana, Ill.: University of Illinois Press, 1965.

CRONBACH, L. J., GLESER, G. C., NANDA, H., & RAJARATNAM, N. *The dependability of behavioral measurements: Theory of generalizability for scores and profiles.* New York: Wiley, 1972.

CRONBACH, L. J. & MEEHL, P. E. Construct validity in psychological tests. *Psychological Bulletin,* 1955, 52, 281–302.

CROWNE, D. P. & MARLOWE, D. *The approval motive.* New York: Wiley, 1964.

DAHLSTROM, W. G., WELSH, G. S., & DAHLSTROM, L. E. *An MMPI handbook, Vol. 1, Clinical interpretation* (rev. ed.) Minneapolis: University of Minnesota, 1972.

DAHLSTROM, W. G., WELSH, G. S., & DAHLSTROM, L. E. *An MMPI handbook, Vol. 2, Research developments and applications* (rev. ed.). Minneapolis: Univ. of Minnesota Press, 1975.

DAILEY, C. A. *Assessment of lives.* San Francisco: Jossey-Bass, 1971.

DAMARIN, F. L. Cattell's mill (a review of R. B. Cattell, *Personality and mood by questionnaire*). *Contemporary Psychology,* 1975, 20, 452–453.

DANA, R. H. & FITZGERALD, J. Educational self-assessment: A course-in-oneself. *College Student Journal* (in press).

DANA, R. H. & LEECH, S. Existential assessment. *Journal of Personality Assessment,* 1974, 38, 428–435.

DARLEY, J. G. & HAGANAH, T. *Vocational interest measurement: Theory and practice.* Minneapolis: University of Minnesota Press, 1955.

DARLEY, S. A. & KATZ, I. Heart rate changes in children as a function of test versus game instructions and test anxiety. *Child Development,* 1973, 44, 784–789.

DAVIDSON, P. O., & COSTELLO, C. G. (eds.) *N = 1: Experimental studies of single cases.* New York: Van Nostrand Reinhold, 1969.

DAVIS, A. Poor people have brains, too. *Phi Delta Kappan,* 1949, 30, 294–295.

DAVIS, W. E. Race and the differential power of the MMPI. *Journal of Personality Assessment,* 1975, 39, 138–140.

DAWES, R. M. *Fundamentals of attitude measurement.* New York : Wiley, 1972.

DAWES, R. M. The common dilemma game: An N-person mixed-motive game with a dominating strategy for defection. *Oregon Research Institute Research Bulletin,* 1973, 13, No. 2.

DAWES, R. M. Shallow psychology. *Oregon Research Institute Research Bulletin,* 1975, 15, No. 2.

DAWES, R. M. Multivariate selection of students in a racist society: A systematically unfair approach. In M. Zeleny (ed.) *Multiple Criteria Decision Making: Kyoto, 1975.* New York: Springer Verlag, 1976 (in press).

DAWES, R. M., DELAY, J., & CHAPLIN, W. The decision to pollute. *Environment and Planning,* 1974, 6, 3–10.

DELLAS, M. & GAIER, E. L. Identification of creativity: The individual. *Psychological Bulletin,* 1970, 73, 55–73.

DELPRATO, D. J. Face validity of test and acceptance of generalized personality descriptions. *Journal of Personality Assessment,* 1975, 39, 345–348.

DERMER, M. & THIEL, D. L. When beauty may fail. *Journal of Personality and Social Psychology,* 1975, 31, 1168–1176.

DIAMOND, M. J. & BOND, M. H. The acceptance of "Barnum" personality interpretations by Japanese, Japanese-American, and Caucasian American college students. *Journal of Cross-Cultural Psychology,* 1974, 5, 228–235.

DICKSON, C. R. Role of assessment in behavior therapy. In P. McReynolds (ed.) *Advances in psychological assessment.* Vol. 3. San Francisco: Jossey-Bass, 1975, pp. 341–388.

DiMASCIO, A., BOYD, R. W., & GREENBLATT, M. Physiological correlates of tension and antagonism during psychotherapy: A study of "interpersonal physiology." *Psychosomatic Medicine,* 1957, 19, 99–104.

DiNARDO, P. A. Social class and diagnostic suggestion as variables in clinical judgment. *Journal of Consulting and Clinical Psychology,* 1975, 43, 363–368.

DOHRENWEND, B. S. Life events as stressors: A methodological inquiry. *Journal of Health and Social Behavior,* 1973, 14, 167–175. (a)

DOHRENWEND, B. S. Social status and stressful life events. *Journal of Personality and Social Psychology,* 1973, 28, 225–235. (b)

DOHRENWEND, B. P. & DOHRENWEND, B. S. Social and cultural influences on psychopathology. In M. R. Rosenzweig & L. W. Porter (eds.) *Annual review of psychology.* Vol. 25. Palo Alto: Annual Reviews, 1974, pp. 417–452.

DOHRENWEND, B. S. & DOHRENWEND, B. P. (eds.) *Stressful life events: Their nature and effects.* New York: Wiley, 1974.

DOLL, E. A. *The measurement of social competence.* Minneapolis: Educational Test Bureau, 1953.

DOOB, L. W. Behavior and grammatical style. *Journal of Abnormal and Social Psychology,* 1958, 56, 398–401.

DOOB, L. W. *Patterning of time.* New Haven: Yale University Press, 1971.

DuBois, P. H. *A history of psychological testing.* Boston: Allyn & Bacon, 1970.

DUKES, W. F. N = 1. *Psychological Bulletin,* 1965, 64, 74–79.

DUNNETTE, M. D. *Personnel selection and placement.* Belmont, Cal.: Wadsworth, 1966.

DWYER, J. & MAYER, J. Psychological effects of variations in physical appearance during adolescence. *Adolescence,* 1969, 3, 353–380.

EDGINGTON, E. S. A new tabulation of statistical procedures used in APA journals, *American Psychologist,* 1974, 29, 25–26.

EDWARDS, A. L. *The social desirability variable in personality assessment and research.* New York: Dryden, 1957.

EELLS, K., DAVIS, A., HAVIGHURST, R. J., HERRICK, V. E., & TYLER, R. W. *Intelligence and cultural differences.* Chicago: University of Chicago Press, 1951.

EISENBERG, L. The *human* nature of human nature. *Science,* 1972, 176, 123–128.

EISLER, R. M., HERSEN, M., MILLER, P. M., & BLANCHARD, E. B. Situational determinants of assertive behaviors. *Journal of Consulting and Clinical Psychology,* 1975, 43, 330–340.

EKMAN, P. & FRIESEN, W. V. Nonverbal behavior in psychotherapy research. In J. M. Shlien (ed.) *Research in psychotherapy.* Vol. III. Washington, D.C.: American Psychological Association, 1968, pp. 179–216.

ELLISON, R. L., JAMES, L. R., FOX, D. G., & TAYLOR, C. W. The identification of talent among Negro and White students from biographical data. Washington, D.C.: Office of Education, Bureau of Research. Final Report Project 9-H-033, 1970.

ELLSWORTH, R. B., FOSTER, L., CHILDERS, B., ARTHUR, G., & KROEKER, D. Hospital and community adjustment as perceived by psychiatric patients, their families, and staff. *Journal of Consulting and Clinical Psychology Monographs,* 1968, 32, No. 5, Part 2, 1–41.

EMERY, F. E. (ed.) *Systems thinking.* Harmondsworth, Middlesex: Penguin, 1969.

ENDICOTT, J. & SPITZER, R. L. The value of the standardized interview for the evaluation of psychopathology. *Journal of Personality Assessment,* 1972, 36, 410–417.

ENDLER, N. S. The person versus the situation—a pseudo issue? A response to Alker. *Journal of Personality,* 1973, 41, 287–303.

ENDLER, N. S. & HUNT, J. McV. Sources of behavioral variance as measured by the S-R inventories of anxiousness. *Psychological Bulletin,* 1966, 65, 336–346.

ENDLER, N. S. & HUNT, J. McV. Generalizability of contributions from sources of variance in the S-R Inventories of Anxiousness. *Journal of Personality,* 1969, 37, 1–24.

ENDLER, N.S., HUNT, J. McV., & ROSENSTEIN, A. J. An S-R Inventory of Anxiousness. *Psychological Monographs,* 1962, 76 (Whole No. 536).

ENGLISH, H. B., & ENGLISH, A. C. *A comprehensive dictionary of psychological and psychoanalytical terms.* Essex, England: Longman Group, 1958.

ERIKSON, E. H. *Childhood and society.* New York: Norton, 1950.

ERIKSON, E. H. *Young man Luther: A study of psychoanalysis and history.* New York: Norton, 1958.

ERIKSON. E. H. *Identity: Youth and crisis.* New York: Norton, 1968.

ERIKSON, E. H. *Gandhi's truth: On the origins of militant nonviolence.* New York: Norton, 1969.

ERIKSON, E. H. *Life history and the historical moment.* New York: Norton, 1975.

ERON, L. D. A normative study of the Thematic Apperception Test. *Psychological Monographs,* 1950, 64, No. 9.

EVANS, B. *Dictionary of quotations.* New York: Delacorte Press, 1968.

EVANS, I. M. & NELSON, R. O. A curriculum for the teaching of behavior assessment. *American Psychologist,* 1974, 29, 598–606.

EXNER, J. E. & EXNER, D. E. How clinicians use the Rorschach. *Journal of Personality Assessment,* 1972, 36, 403–408.

EYSENCK, H. J. The effects of psychotherapy: an evaluation. *Journal of Consulting Psychology,* 1952, 16, 319–324.

EYSENCK, H. J. *The structure of human personality.* New York: Wiley, 1953.

EYSENCK, H. J. *The effects of psychotherapy.* New York: International Science Press, 1966.

EYSENCK, H. J. *The biological basis of personality.* Springfield, Ill.: Charles Thomas, 1967.

FANCHER, R. E. Explicit personality theories and accuracy in person perception. *Journal of Personality,* 1966, 34, 252–261.

FANCHER, R. E. Accuracy versus validity in person perception. *Journal of Consulting Psychology,* 1967, 31, 264–269.

FAWCETT, J. T. Psychological research on family size and family planning in the United States. *Professional Psychology,* 1974, 5, 334–344.

FELNER, R. D., STOLBERG, A., & COWEN, E. L. Crisis events and school mental health referral patterns of young children. *Journal of Consulting and Clinical Psychology,* 1975, 43, 305–310.

FESTINGER, L. *A theory of cognitive dissonance.* Stanford: Stanford University Press, 1957.

FILSKOV, S. B. & GOLDSTEIN, S. G. Diagnostic validity of the Halstead-Reitan neuropsychological battery. *Journal of Consulting and Clinical Psychology,* 1974, 42, 382–388.

FINE, S. A. & WILEY, W. W. *An introduction to functional job analysis: A scaling of selected tasks from the social welfare field.* Kalamazoo, Mich.: W. E. Upjohn Institute for Employment Research, 1971.

FISCHER, C. T. Intelligence defined as effectiveness of approaches. *Journal of Consulting and Clinical Psychology,* 1969, 33, 668–674.

FISKE, D. W. *Measuring the concepts of personality.* Chicago: Aldine, 1971.

FLANAGAN, J. C. The critical incident technique. *Psychological Bulletin,* 1954, 51, 327–358.

FOA, U. G. Convergences in the analysis of the structure of interpersonal behavior. *Psychological Review,* 1961, 68, 341–353.

FORER, B. R. The fallacy of personal validations: A classroom demonstration of gullibility. *Journal of Abnormal and Social Psychology,* 1949, 44, 118–123.

FORSYTH, R. P., & FAIRWEATHER, G. W. Psychotherapeutic and other hospital treatment criteria: The dilemma. *Journal of Abnormal and Social Psychology,* 1961, 62, 598–604.

FRANK, L. K. Projective methods for the study of personality. *Journal of Psychology,* 1939, 8, 389–413.

FREDERIKSEN, N. Toward a taxonomy of situations. *American Psychologist,* 1972, 27, 114–123.

FREEMAN, H. E. & GIOVANNONI, J. M. Social psychology of mental health. In G. Lindzey & E. Aronson (eds.) *The handbook of social psychology.* Reading, Ma.: Addison-Wesley, 1969, pp. 660–719.

FRENCH, J. W. Effect of anxiety on verbal and mathematical examination scores. *Educational and Psychological Measurement,* 1962, 22, 553–564.

FREUD, A. *The ego and the mechanisms of defense.* New York: International Universities Press, 1946.

FREUD, S. Fragment of an analysis of a case of hysteria. In *The standard edition of the complete psychological works of Sigmund Freud.* Vol. 7. London: Hogarth, 1953, pp. 3–122. (Originally published in 1905.)

FREUND, K. A laboratory method for diagnosing predominance of homo- or hetero-erotic interest in the male. *Behavioural Research and Therapy,* 1963, 1, 85–93.

FREUND, K., SEDLACEK, F., & KNOB, K. A simple transducer for mechanical plethsymography of the male genital. *Journal of the Experimental Analysis of Behavior,* 1965, 8, 169–170.

FRIEDLANDER, F. & GREENBERG, S. Effects of job attitudes, training and organization climate on performance of the hard-core unemployed. *Journal of Applied Psychology,* 1971, 55, 287–295.

FRYREAR, J. L., NUELL, L. R., & RIDLEY, S. D. Photographic self-concept enhancement of male juvenile delinquents. *Journal of Consulting and Clinical Psychology,* 1974, 42, 915.

FULKERSON, S. C. Some implications of the new cognitive theory for projective tests. *Journal of Consulting Psychology,* 1965, 29, 191–197.

GAMBLE, K. R. The Holtzman Inkblot Technique: A review. *Psychological Bulletin,* 1972, 77, 172–194.

GARRETT, H. E. *Statistics in psychology and education.* (5th ed.) New York: Longmans, 1958.

GAUQUELIN, M. *The scientific basis of astrology.* New York: Stein & Day, 1969.

GEER, J. H. The development of a scale to measure fear. *Behaviour Research and Therapy,* 1965, 3, 45–53.

GEER, J. H. Direct measurement of genital responding. *American Psychologist,* 1975, 30, 415–418.

GERARD, R. W. Comments. In J. Cole & R. Gerard (eds.) *Psychopharmacology: Problems in evaluation.* Washington, D.C.: National Academy of Sciences National Research Council, 1956.

GERGEN, K. J. AND BACK, K. W. Aging, time perspective, and the preferred solutions in international conflicts. *Journal of Conflict Resolution,* 1965, 9, 177–186.

GETTER, H. & WEISS, S. D. The Rotter Incomplete Sentences Blank Adjustment Score as an indicator of somatic complaint frequency. *Journal of Projective Techniques and Personality Assessment,* 1968, 32, 266.

GETZELS, J. W. & JACKSON, P. W. *Creativity and intelligence.* New York: Wiley, 1962.

GHISELLI, E. E. The validity of occupational aptitude tests. *Personnel Psychology,* 1973, 26, 461–477.

GIBB, C. A. Leadership. In G. Lindzey & E. Aronson (eds.) *The handbook of social psychology.* (2nd ed.) Vol. 4, Reading, Ma.: Addison-Wesley, 1969, pp. 205–282.

GILBERSTADT, H. & DUKER, J. *A handbook for clinical and actuarial MMPI interpretation.* Philadelphia: Saunders, 1965.

GILMORE, S. K. *The counselor-in-training.* Englewood Cliffs, N.J.: Prentice-Hall, 1973.

GILMORE, S. K. Personal communication, 1976.

GLASER, R. Instructional technology and the measurement of learning outcomes. *American Psychologist,* 1963, 18, 510–522.

GLASGOW, R. E. & ARKOWITZ, H. Behavioral assessment of male and female social competence and heterosexual dyadic interactions. *Behavior Therapy,* 1975, 6, 488–498.

GLENNON, J. R., ALBRIGHT, L. E., & OWENS, W. A. Jr., *A catalog of life history items.* Washington, D.C.: American Psychological Association, Division 14, 1966.

GLUECK, S. & GLUECK, E. *Unravelling juvenile delinquency.* New York: Commonwealth Fund, 1950.

GOETHALS, G. W., & KLOS, D. S. (eds.) *Experiencing youth: First person accounts.* Boston: Little, Brown, 1970.

GOFFMAN, E. *The presentation of self in everyday life.* Garden City, N.Y.: Doubleday, 1959.

GOLDBERG, L. R. The effectiveness of clinicians' judgments: The diagnosis of organic brain damage from the Bender Gestalt Test. *Journal of Consulting Psychology,* 1959, 23, 25–33.

GOLDBERG, L. R. Diagnosticians versus diagnostic signs: The diagnosis of psychosis versus neurosis from the MMPI. *Psychological Monographs,* 1965, 79, No. 9 (Whole No. 602).

GOLDBERG, L. R. Reliability of Peace Corps Selection Boards: A study of interjudge agreement before and after board discussions. *Journal of Applied Psychology,* 1966, 50, 400–408.

GOLDBERG, L. R. Seer over sign: The first "good" example? *Journal of Experimental Research in Personality,* 1968, 3, 168–171.

GOLDBERG, L. R. Man versus model of man: A rationale, plus some evidence, for a method of improving on clinical inferences. *Psychological Bulletin,* 1970, 73, 422–432.

GOLDBERG, L. R. A historical survey of personality scales and inventories. In P. McReynolds (ed.) *Advances in psychological assessment,* Vol. 2. Palo Alto: Science and Behavior Books, 1971, pp. 293–336.

GOLDBERG, L. R. Parameters of personality inventory construction and utilization: A comparison of prediction strategies and tactics. *Multivariate Behavioral Research Monographs,* 7, No. 2, 1972. (a)

GOLDBERG, L. R. Some recent trends in personality assessment. *Journal of Personality Assessment,* 1972, 36, 547–560. (b)

GOLDBERG, L. R. The exploitation of the English language for the development of a descriptive personality taxonomy. Paper presented at the American Psychological Association meetings, Montreal, August, 1973.

GOLDBERG, L. R. Objective diagnostic tests and measures. *Annual review of psychology,* Vol. 25. Palo Alto: Annual Reviews, 1974, pp. 343–366.

GOLDBERG, L. R. Toward a taxonomy of personality descriptive terms: a description of the ORI taxonomy project. *Oregon Research Institute Technical Report,* 1975. Vol. 15, No. 2.

GOLDBERG, L. R. Language and personality: Toward a taxonomy of trait descriptive terms. *Istanbul Studies in Experimental Psychology,* 1976, Vol. 12 (in press).

GOLDBERG, P. A review of sentence completion methods in personality assessment. *Journal of Projective Techniques and Personality Assessment,* 1965, 29, 12–45.

GOLDBERGER, L. & HOLT, R. R. Experimental interference with reality contact: Individual differences. In P. Solomon, P. E. Kubzansky, P. H. Leiderman, J. H. Mendelson, R. Trumbull, & D. Wexler (eds.) *Sensory deprivation.* Cambridge, Ma.: Harvard University Press, 1961, pp. 130–142.

GOLDEN, M. Some effects of combining psychological tests on clinical inferences. *Journal of Consulting Psychology,* 1964, 28, 440–446.

GOLDFRIED, M. R. & D'ZURILLA, T. J. A behavioral-analytic model for assessing competence. In C. D. Spielberger (ed.) *Current topics in clinical and community psychology,* Vol. 1. New York: Academic Press, 1969, pp. 151–196.

GOLDFRIED, M. R. & D'ZURILLA, T. J. *Assessment and facilitation of effective behavior in college freshmen.* Final report submitted to the National Institute of Mental Health for research grant No. MH15044, 1972.

GOLDFRIED, M. R. & D'ZURILLA, T. J. Prediction of academic competence by means of the Survey of Study Habits and Attitudes. *Journal of Educational Psychology,* 1973, 64, 116–122.

GOLDFRIED, M. R. & KENT, R. N. Traditional versus behavioral personality assessment: A comparison of methodological and theoretical assumptions. *Psychological Bulletin,* 1972, 77, 409–420.

GOLDFRIED, M. R. & SPRAFKIN, J. N. *Behavioral personality assessment.* Morristown, N.J.: General Learning Corporation, 1974.

GOLDFRIED, M. R., STRICKER, G., & WEINER, I. B. *Rorschach handbook of clinical and research applications.* Englewood Cliffs, N.J.: Prentice-Hall, 1971.

GOLDMAN, L. *Using tests in counseling* (2nd ed.). New York: Appleton-Century-Crofts, 1971.

GOLDMAN, L. Test information in counseling: A critical view. In Educational Testing Service, *Measurement for self-understanding and personal development.* Princeton, N.J.: ETS, 1973.

GOODSTEIN, L. D. & LANYON, R. I. (eds.) *Readings in personality assessment.* New York: Wiley, 1971.

GORMLY, J. & EDELBERG, W. Validity in personality trait attribution. *American Psychologist,* 1974, 29, 189–193.

GOTTESMAN, I. J. Biogenetics of race and class. In M. Deutsch, I. Katz, & A. R. Jensen (eds.) *Social class, race and psychological development.* New York: Holt, Rinehart & Winston, 1968, pp. 11–51.

GOUGH, H. G. On making a good impression. *Journal of Educational Research,* 1952, 46, 33–42.

GOUGH, H. G. *California Psychological Inventory Manual.* Palo Alto: Consulting Psychologists Press, 1957.

GOUGH, H. G. Cross-cultural studies of the socialization continuum. *American Psychologist,* 1960, 15, 410 (abstract).

GOUGH, H. G. Conceptual analysis of psychological test scores and other diagnostic variables. *Journal of Abnormal Psychology,* 1965, 70, 294–302.

GOUGH, H. G. An interpreter's syllabus for the California Psychological Inventory. In P. McReynolds (ed.) *Advances in psychological assessment,* Vol. 1. Palo Alto: Science and Behavior Books, 1968, pp. 55–79.

GOUGH, H. G. A cluster analysis of home index status items. *Psychological Reports,* 1971, 23, 923–929.

GOUGH, H. G. & HEILBRUN, A. B. *The Adjective Check List Manual.* Palo Alto: Consulting Psychologists Press, 1965.

GOUGH, H. G. & LAZZARI, R. A 15-item form of the F scale and a cross-cultural application. *Journal of Psychology,* 1974, 88, 39–46.

GOUGH, H. G. & QUINTARD, G. A French application of the CPI Social Maturity Index. *Journal of Cross-Cultural Psychology,* 1974, 5, 247–252.

GOUGH, H. G. & SANDHU, H. S. Validation of the CPI socialization scale in India. *Journal of Abnormal and Social Psychology,* 1964, 68, 544–547.

GRAHAM, F. K. & CLIFTON, R. I. Heart-rate change as a component of the orienting response. *Psychological Bulletin,* 1966, 65, 305–320.

GRANTHAM, R. J. Effects of counselor sex, race and language style on black students in initial interviews. *Journal of Counseling Psychology,* 1973, 20, 553–559.

GREEN, E. E., FERGUSON, D. W., GREEN, A. M., & WALTERS, E. D. *Preliminary report on Voluntary Controls Project: Swami Rama.* Topeka: Menninger Foundation, 1970.

GREEN, H. B. & KNAPP, R. H. A much-needed and timely analysis (A review of L. W. Doob, *Patterning of Time*). *Contemporary Psychology,* 1973, 18, 456–457.

GRIER, W. H. & COBBS, P. M. *Black rage.* New York: Basic Books, 1968.

GRONLUND, N. E. *Sociometry in the classroom.* New York: Harper, 1959.

GROSS, E. & STONE, G. P. Embarrassment and the analysis of role requirements. *American Journal of Sociology,* 1964, 70, 1–15.

GUILFORD, J. P. (ed.) *Printed classification tests.* Washington, D.C.: Government Printing Office, 1947.

GUILFORD, J. P. *Personality.* New York: McGraw-Hill, 1959. (a)

GUILFORD, J. P. Three faces of intellect. *American Psychologist,* 1959, 14, 469–479. (b)

GUILFORD, J. P. *The nature of human intelligence.* New York: McGraw-Hill, 1967.

GUION, R. M. *Personnel testing.* New York: McGraw-Hill, 1965.

GUMP, P., SCHOGGEN, P., & REDL, F. The camp milieu and its immediate effects. *Journal of Social Issues,* 1957, 13, 40–46.

GURIN, G., VEROFF, J., & FELD, S. *Americans view their mental health.* New York: Basic Books, 1960.

GUTENTAG, M. & STRUENING, E. L. (eds.) *Handbook of evaluation research.* Vols. 1 and 2. Beverly Hills, Ca.: Sage, 1975.

GYNTHER, M. D., FOWLER, R. D., & ERDBERG, P. False positives galore: The application of standard MMPI criteria to a rural, isolated, Negro sample, *Journal of Clinical Psychology,* 1971, 27, 234–237.

HALL, C. S., & LINDZEY, G. *Theories of personality,* 2nd ed. New York: Wiley, 1970.

HAMMER, E. F. *The clinical application of projective drawings.* Springfield, Ill: Thomas, 1958.

HAMMOND, K. R. Human judgment and social policy. Report No. 170. Institute of Behavioral Science, University of Colorado, Boulder, April, 1974.

HAMMOND, K. R., HURSCH, C., & TODD, F. J. Analyzing the components of clinical inference. *Psychological Review,* 1964, 71, 438–456.

HANNA, J. V. Estimating intelligence by interview. *Educational and Psychological Measurement,* 1950, 10, 420–430.

HARDIN, G. The tragedy of the commons. *Science,* 1968, 162, 1243–1248.

HARRIS, D. B. *Children's drawings as measures of intellectual maturity: A revision and extension of the Goodenough Draw-A-Man Test.* New York: Harcourt, Brace & World, 1963.

HARRIS, J. The computer: Guidance tool of the future. *Journal of Counseling Psychology,* 1974, 21, 331–339.

HARSHBERGER, D. & MALEY, R. F. (eds.) *Behavior analysis and systems analysis: An integrative approach to mental health programs.* Kalamazoo, MI: Behaviordelis, 1974.

HARTMANN, H. *Ego psychology and the problem of adaptation.* New York: International Universities Press, 1958.

HARTSHORNE, H. & MAY, M. A. *Studies in deceit.* New York: Macmillan, 1928.

HARTSHORNE, H., MAY, M. A., & MALLER, J. B. *Studies in service and self-control. New York: Macmillan, 1929.*

HARTSHORNE, H., MAY, M. A., & SHUTTLEWORTH, F. K. *Studies in the organization of character.* New York: Macmillan, 1930.

HASE, H. D. & GOLDBERG, L. R. The comparative validity of different strategies of deriving personality inventory scales. *Psychological Bulletin,* 1967, 67, 231–248.

HATHAWAY, S. R. & MCKINLEY, J. C. *The Minnesota Multiphasic Personality Inventory* (rev.) New York: Psychological Corp., 1951.

HATHAWAY, S. R. & MEEHL, P. E. *An atlas for the clinical use of the MMPI.* Minneapolis: University of Minnesota Press, 1951.

HAYWOOD, H. C., FILLER, J. W., SHIFMAN, M. A., & CHATELANAT, G. Behavioral assessment in mental retardation. In P. McReynolds (ed.) *Advances in psychological assessment.* Vol. 3. San Francisco: Jossey-Bass, 1975, pp. 96–136.

HEILBRONER, R. L. *An inquiry into the human prospect.* New York: Norton, 1974.

HEINRICH, P. & TRIEBE, J. K. Sex differences in children's human figure drawings. *Journal of Personality Assessment,* 1972, 36, 263–267.

HELMER, O. *Social technology.* New York: Basic Books, 1966.

HENNING, J. J. & LEVY, R. H. Verbal-performance IQ differences of white and Negro delinquents on the WISC and WAIS. *Journal of Clinical Psychology,* 1967, 23, 164–168.

HENRY, E. R. What business can learn from Peace Corps selection and training. *Personnel,* 1965, 42, 17–25.

HENRY, W. E. *The analysis of fantasy: The thematic apperception technique in the study of personality.* New York: Wiley, 1956. ©1956 John Wiley & Sons, Inc. Reprinted by permission of John.Wiley & Sons, Inc.

HERSEN, M. & BELLACK, A. S. (eds.) *Behavioral assessment: A practical handbook.* New York: Pergamon, 1976 (in press).

HESS, E. H. Pupillometric assessment. In J. M. Shlien (ed.) *Research in psychotherapy,* Vol. 3. Washington, D.C.: American Psychological Association, 1968, pp. 573–583.

HILL, E. F. *The Holtzman inkblot technique.* San Francisco: Jossey-Bass, 1972.

HINRICHSEN, J. J. & BRADLEY, L. A. Situational determinants of personal validation of general personality interpretations. *Journal of Personality Assessment,* 1974, 38, 530–534.

HOBBS, N. A psychologist in the Peace Corps. *American Psychologist,* 1963, 18, 47–55.

HOFFMAN, M. L. An interview method for obtaining descriptions of parent-child interaction. *Merrill-Palmer Quarterly,* 1957, 56, 1–12.

HOFFMAN, P. J. The paramorphic representation of clinical judgment. *Psychological Bulletin,* 1960, 57, 116–131.

HOFFMAN, P. J. Physicians appraise other physicians: Improving the decisions of a medical specialty board. *Oregon Research Institute Research Bulletin,* Vol. 14, No. 4. Eugene, Oregon: Oregon Research Institute, 1974.

HOGAN, R. *Personality theory: the personological tradition.* Englewood Cliffs, N.J.: Prentice-Hall, 1976.

HOLLAND, J. L. *Making vocational choices: A theory of careers.* Englewood Cliffs, N.J.: Prentice-Hall, 1973.

HOLLAND, J. L. *The self directed search: A guide to educational and vocational planning.* Palo Alto: Consulting Psychologists Press, 1974.

HOLMEN, M. G. et al. An assessment program for OCS applicants. *HumRRO Technical Report,* No. 26, 1956.

HOLMES, D. S. The conscious control of thematic projection. *Journal of Consulting and Clinical Psychology,* 1974, 42, 323–329.

HOLMES, T. H. & MASUDA, M. Life change and illness susceptibility. *Separation and depression.* AAAS, 1973, pp. 161–186.

HOLMES, T. H. & RAHE, R. H. The social readjustment rating scale. *Journal of Psychosomatic Research,* 1967, 11, 213.

HOLSTI, O. R. *Content analysis for the social sciences and humanities.* Reading, Ma.: Addison-Wesley, 1969.

HOLT, R. R. Gauging primary and secondary processes in Rorschach responses. *Journal of Projective Techniques,* 1956, 20, 14–25.

HOLT, R. R. *Assessing personality.* New York: Harcourt, Brace Jovanovich, 1971.

HOLTZMAN, W. H. Statistical models for the study of change in the single case. In C. W. Harris (ed.) *Problems in measuring change.* Madison: University of Wisconsin Press, 1963.

HOLTZMAN, W. H. New developments in Holtzman Inkblot Technique. In P. McReynolds (ed.) *Advances in psychological assessment.* Vol. 3. San Francisco: Jossey-Bass, 1975, pp. 243–274.

HOLTZMAN, W. H. THORPE, J. W., SWARTZ, J. D., & HERRON, E. W. *Inkblot perception and personality: Holtzman Inkblot Technique.* Austin: University of Texas Press, 1961.

HONZIK, M. P., MACFARLANE, J. W., & ALLEN, L. The stability of mental test performance between two and eighteen years. *Journal of Experimental Education,* 1948, 17, 309–324.

HORNER, A. J. The evolution of goals in the life of Clarence Darrow. In C. Buehler & F. Massarik (eds.) *The course of human life.* New York: Springer, 1968, pp. 64–75.

HOROWITZ, M. J. A study of clinicians' judgments from projective test protocols. *Journal of Consulting Psychology,* 1962, 26, 251–256.

HOVEY, H. B. The questionable validity of some assumed antecedents of mental illness. *Journal of Clinical Psychology,* 1959, 15, 270–272.

HOYER, W. J. Aging as intraindividual change. *Developmental Psychology,* 1974, 10, 821–826.

HUCK, J. R. Assessment centers: A review of external and internal validities. *Personal Psychology,* 1973, 26, 191-212.

HUFF, E. M. & NAGEL, D. C. Psychological aspects of aeronautical flight simulation. *American Psychologist,* 1975, 30, 426-439.

HUMMEL, T. J., LICHTENBERG, J. W., & SHAFFER, W. F. CLIENT 1: A computer program which simulates client behavior in an initial interview. *Journal of Counseling Psychology,* 1975, 22, 164-169.

HUNT, D. E. Person-environment interaction: A challenge found wanting before it was tried. *Review of Educational Research,* 1975, 45, 209-230.

HUTT, M. L. *The Hutt adaptation of the Bender-Gestalt Test* (2nd Ed.) New York: Grune & Stratton, 1969.

HUTT, M. L. & BRISKIN, G. J. *The clinical use of the revised Bender-Gestalt Test.* New York: Grune & Stratton, 1960.

HUTT, M. L. & GIBBY, R. G. *An atlas for the Hutt adaptation of the Bender-Gestalt Test.* New York: Grune & Stratton, 1970.

INSEL, P. M. & MOOS, R. H. Psychological environments: Expanding the scope of human ecology. *American Psychologist,* 1974, 29, 179-188.

JACKSON, D. N. Personality Research Form manual. Goshen, N.Y.: Research Psychologists Press, 1967.

JACKSON, D. N. A sequential system for personality scale development. In C. D. Spielberger (ed.) *Current topics in clinical and community psychology,* Vol. 2. New York: Academic Press, 1970, pp. 61-96.

JAMES, W. *Principles of psychology,* Vol, 1. New York: Holt, 1890.

JANIS, I. L., MAHL, G. F., KAGAN, J., & HOLT, R. R. *Personality: Dynamics, development and assessment.* New York: Harcourt, Brace Jovanovich, Inc. 1969. Copyright © 1969, 1971 by Harcourt, and reprinted by permission.

JENSEN, A. R. How much can we boost IQ and educational achievement. *Harvard Educational Review,* 1969, 39, 1-123.

JENSEN, A. R. *Educational differences.* New York: Barnes & Noble, 1974.

JOHNSON, O. G., & BOMMARITO, J. W. *Tests and measurements in child development: A handbook.* San Francisco: Jossey-Bass, 1971.

JOHNSON, R. K. & MEYER, R. G. The locus of control construct in EEG Alpha rhythm feedback. *Journal of Consulting and Clinical Psychology,* 1974, 42, 741-756.

JONES, E. E., KANOUSE, D. E., KELLEY, H. H., NISBETT, R. E., VALINS, S., & WEINER, B. *Attribution: Perceiving the causes of behavior.* Morristown, N.J.: General Learning Press, 1972.

JONES, M. C., ALBERT, PETER, & WATSON, JOHN B. *American Psychologist,* 1974, 29, 581-583.

JONES, M. C., BAYLEY, N., MACFARLANE, J. W., & HONZIK, M. P. (eds.) *The course of human development: Selected papers from the longitudinal studies, Institute of Human Development, the University of California, Berkeley.* Waltham, Mass.: Xerox College Pub., 1971.

JONES, N. F., MEYER, M., & EIDUSON, B. An introductory lecture on personality assessment. *Journal of Personality Assessment,* 1972, 36, 479-492.

JONES, R. R. Selection and overseas experiences of Peace Corps Volunteers. Final Report, Peace Corps Contract No. 80-1539. Eugene, Or: Oregon Research Institute. August, 1969.

JONES, R. R., REID, J. B., & PATTERSON, G. R. Naturalistic observation in clinical assessment. In P. McReynolds (ed.) *Advances in psychological assessment,* Vol. 3. San Francisco: Jossey-Bass, 1975, pp. 42–95.

JUNG, C. G. The association method. *American Journal of Psychology,* 1910, 21, 219–269.

KADUSHIN, A. *The social work interview.* New York: Columbia University Press, 1972.

KAGAN, J., MOSS, H. A., & SIGEL, I. E. Psychological significance of styles of conceptualization. In J. C. Wright and J. Kagan (eds.) *Basic cognitive processes in children. Monograph of the Society for Research in Child Development,* 1963, Serial No. 86, 73–124.

KAGAN, N. Influencing human interaction—eleven years with IPR. In B. A. Jacobs, R. K. Buschman, R. F. Dency, D. T. Schaeffer, & J. Stieber (eds.) *Counselor training: Short-term client systems: Manual for trainers.* Arlington, Va: National·Drug Abuse Training Center, 1974, pp. 329–346.

KANFER, F. H. & GRIMM, L. G. Promising trends toward the future development of behavior modification: Ten related areas in need of exploration. In W. E. Craighead, A. E. Kazdin, & M. J. Mahoney (eds.) *Behavior modification: Principles, issues, and applications.* Boston: Houghton Mifflin, 1975.

KANFER, F. H. & SASLOW, G. Behavioral analysis: an alternative to diagnostic classification. *Archives of General Psychiatry,* 1965, 12, 529–538.

KANFER, F. H. & SASLOW, G. Behavioral diagnosis. In C. M. Franks (ed.) *Behavior therapy: Appraisal and status.* New York: McGraw-Hill, 1969, pp. 417–444.

KAPLAN, B. (ed.) *Studying personality cross-culturally.* Evanston, Il.: Row, Peterson, 1961.

KATZ, D. The functional approach to the study of attitudes. *Public Opinion Quarterly,* 1960, 24, 163–204.

KATZ, M. R. Career decision-making: A computer-based system of interactive guidance and information (SIGI). In *Measurement for self-understanding and personal development.* Princeton, N.J.: Educational Testing Service, 1973, pp. 43–69.

KELLY, E. L. Consistency of the adult personality. *American Psychologist,* 1955, 10, 659–681.

KELLY, G. A. *The psychology of personal constructs,* Vol. 1. *A theory of personality;* Vol. 2. *Clinical diagnosis and therapy.* New York: Norton, 1955.

KELLY, G. A. The theory and technique of assessment. In P. R. Farnsworth & Q. McNemar (eds.) *Annual review of psychology.* Vol. 9. Palo Alto: Annual Reviews, 1958, pp. 323–352.

KELLY, J. G. The ecological analogy and community work. Paper presented at the symposium, ''Public Policy and Ecological Change,'' International Society for the Study of Behavioral Development Biennial Conference, University of Surrey, Guildford, England, July, 1975.

KELMAN,H. C. *A time to speak: On human values and social research.* San Francisco: Jossey-Bass, 1968.

KELMAN, H. C. Attitudes are alive and well and gainfully employed in the sphere of action. *American Psychologist,* 1974, 29, 310–324.

KENISTON, K. Inburn: An American Ishmael. In R. W. White (ed.) *The study of lives.* New York: Atherton, 1963, pp. 40–70.

KILPATRICK, D. L. & SPREEN, O. A revision of the Halstead category test for children aged 9 to 15. *Psychology in the Schools,* 1973, 10, 101–106.

KILPATRICK, F. P. & CANTRIL, H. Self-anchoring scaling: A measure of individuals' unique reality worlds. *Journal of Individual Psychology,* 1960, 16, 158–170.

KIMMEL, H. D. Instrumental conditioning of anatomically mediated responses in human beings. *American Psychologist,* 1974, 29, 287–296.

KING, S. H. *Five lives at Harvard: Personality change through college.* Cambridge, Ma.: Harvard University Press, 1973.

KIRKPATRICK, J. J., EWEN, R. B., BARRETT, R. S., & KATZELL, R. A. *Testing and fair employment.* New York: New York University Press, 1968.

KLASSEN, D., ROTH, A., & HORNSTRA, R. K. Perception of life events as gains or losses in a community survey. *Journal of Community Psychology,* 1974, 2, 330–336.

KLEIN, R. H. & IKER, H. P. The lack of differentiation between male and female in Schreber's autobiography. *Journal of Abnormal Psychology,* 1974, 83, 234–239.

KLEINMUNTZ, B. *Personality measurement.* Homewood, Il.: Dorsey Press (now Krieger), 1967.

KLEINMUNTZ, B. *Formal representation of human judgment.* New York: Wiley, 1968.

KLEINMUNTZ, B. Clinical information processing by computer. In *New directions in psychology,* Vol. 4. New York: Holt, Rinehart &Winston, 1970, pp. 123–210.

KLEINMUNTZ, B. The computer as clinician. *American Psychologist,* 1975, 30, 379–387.

KLETT, C. J. & PUMROY, D. K. Automated procedures for psychological assessment. In P. McReynolds (ed.) *Advances in psychological assessment,* Vol. 2. Palo Alto: Science & Behavior Books, 1971, pp. 14–39.

KLINE, P. (ed.) *New approaches in psychological measurement.* New York: Wiley, 1973.

KLOPFER, W. G. & TAULBEE, E. S. Projective tests. In M. R. Rosenzweig & L. W. Porter (eds.) *Annual review of psychology,* Vol. 27. Palo Alto: Annual Reviews, 1976, pp. 543–567.

KLUCKHOHN, C., MURRAY, H. A. & SCHNEIDER, D. M. (eds.) *Personality in nature, society, and culture.* New York: Knopf, 1953.

KOSTKA, M. P. & GALASSI, J. P. Group systematic desensitization versus covert positive reinforcement in the reduction of test anxiety. *Journal of Counseling Psychology,* 1974, 21, 464–468.

KOSTLAN, A. A method for the empirical study of psychodiagnosis. *Journal of Consulting Psychology,* 1954, 18, 83–88.

KRAPFL, J. E. Accountability through cost-benefit analysis. In D. Harshbarger & R. F. Maley (eds.) *Behavior analysis and systems analysis: An integrative approach to mental health programs.* Kalamazoo, Mi.: Behaviordelia, 1974, pp. 238–257.

KUNCE, J. T., RAYAN, J. J., & ECKELMAN, C. C. Violent behavior and differential WAIS characteristics. *Journal of Consulting and Clinical Psychology,* 1976, 44, 42–45.

LACEY, J. I. Somatic response patterning and stress: Some revisions of activation theory. In M. H. Appley & R. Trumbull (eds.) *Psychological stress.* New York: Appleton-Century-Crofts, 1967, pp. 14–42.

LaForge, R. Research use of the ICL. *Oregon Research Institute Technical Report* 3, No. 4, Eugene, Or.: Oregon Research Institute, 1963.

LaForge, R. & Suczek, R. F. The interpersonal dimension of personality. III. An interpersonal check list. *Journal of Personality,* 1955, 25, 94–112.

Lambley, P. The dangers of therapy without assessment. *Journal of Personality Assessment,* 1974, 263–265.

Lang, P. J. Automatic control or learning to play the internal organs. In T. Barner, L. V. DiCara, J. Kamiya, N. E. Miller, D. Shapiro, & J. Stoyva (eds.) *Biofeedback and self-control.* Chicago: Aldine-Atherton, 1971. (a)

Lang, P. J. The application of psychophysiological methods to the study of psychotherapy and behavior modification. In A. E. Bergin & S. L. Garfield (eds.) *Handbook of psychotherapy and behavior change: An empirical analysis.* New York: Wiley, 1971, pp. 75–125. (b)

Lang, P. J. & Lazovik, A. D. Experimental desensitization of a phobia. *Journal of Abnormal and Social Psychology,* 1963, 66, 519–525.

Langer, W. C. *The mind of Adolf Hitler: The secret wartime report.* New York: Basic Books, 1972.

Lanyon, R. I. Technological approach to the improvement of decision making in mental health services. *Journal of Consulting and Clinical Psychology,* 1972, 39, 43–98.

Lanyon, R. I. & Goodstein, L. D. *Personality assessment.* New York: Wiley, 1971.

Lay, C. H., Burron, B. F., & Jackson, D. N. Base rates and informational value in impression formation. *Journal of Personality and Social Psychology,* 1973, 28, 390–395.

Lazarus, A. A. Group therapy of phobic disorders by systematic desensitization. *Journal of Abnormal and Social Psychology,* 1961, 63, 504–510.

Lazarus, A. A. *Behavior therapy and beyond.* New York: McGraw-Hill, 1971.

Lazarus, R. S. *Psychological stress and the coping process.* New York: McGraw-Hill, 1966.

Lazarus, R. S. Stress. In D. L. Sills (ed.) *International encyclopedia of the social sciences.* New York: Macmillan and Free Press, 1968, pp. 337–348.

Lazarus, R. S. A cognitively oriented psychologist looks at biofeedback. *American Psychologist,* 1975, 30, 553–561.

Lazarus, R. S., Opton, E. M., Nomikos, M. S., & Rankin, N. O. The principle of short-circuiting of threat: Further evidence. *Journal of Personality,* 1965, 33, 622–635.

Lazarus, R. S., Speisman, J. C., Mordkoff, A. M., & Davison, L. A. A laboratory study of psychological stress produced by a motion picture film. *Psychological Monographs,* 1962, 76, Whole No. 553.

Leary, T. *The interpersonal diagnosis of personality.* New York: Ronald Press, 1957.

Ledvinka, J. Race of interviewer and the language elaboration of black interviewees. *Journal of Social Issues,* 1971, 27, 185–197.

Lehman, H. C. The age decrement in outstanding scientific creativity. *American Psychologist,* 1960, 15, 128–134.

Leitenberg, H. The use of single-case methodology in psychotherapy research. *Journal of Abnormal Psychology,* 1973, 82, 87–101.

LERNER, E. A. *The projective use of the Bender Gestalt.* Springfield, Ill.: Thomas, 1972.

LeSHAN, L. L. Time perspective and social class. *Journal of Abnormal and Social Psychology,* 1952, 47, 589–592.

LESSING, E. E. Demographic, developmental, and personality correlates of length of future time perspective (FTP). *Journal of Personality,* 1968, 36, 183–201.

LESSINGER, L. M. Robbing Dr. Peter to pay Paul: Accounting for our stewardship of public education. *Educational Technology,* 1971, 11, 11–14.

LEVENBERG, S. B. Professional training, psychodiagnostic skill, and Kinetic Family Drawings. *Journal of Personality Assessment,* 1975, 39, 389–393.

LEVINE, D. Why and when to test: The social context of psychological testing. In A. I. Rabin (ed.), *Projective techniques in personality assessment: A modern introduction.* New York: Springer, 1968, pp. 553–580.

LEVINE, D. A cross-national study of attitudes toward mental illness. *Journal of Abnormal Psychology,* 1972, 80, 111–114.

LEVY, L. H. *Psychological interpretation.* New York: Holt, Rinehart & Winston, 1963.

LEVY, L. H. & DUGAN, R. D. A factorial study of personal constructs. *Journal of Consulting Psychology,* 1956, 20, 53–57.

LEWINSOHN, P. M. Assessment of clinical (diagnostic) skill: Illustration of a quantitative approach. *Professional Psychology,* 1971, 2, 303–304.

LEWINSOHN, P. M. Psychological assessment of patients with brain injury. Project report, Research Grant No. RD–15–P–55299/9–04, Social and Rehabilitation Service, Department of Health, Education and Welfare, Washington, D.C., 1973.

LEWINSOHN, P. M. & GRAF, M. A follow-up study of persons referred for vocational rehabilitation who have suffered brain injury. *Journal of Community Psychology,* 1973, 1, 57–62.

LEWINSOHN, P. M. & LIBET, J. Pleasant events, activity schedules, and depressions. *Journal of Abnormal and Social Psychology,* 1972, 79, 291–295.

LIFTON, R. J. & OLSON, E. *Explorations in psycho-history.* New York: Simon & Schuster, 1974.

LINDZEY, G. On the classification of projective techniques. *Psychological Bulletin,* 1959, 56, 158–168.

LINDZEY, G. *Projective techniques and cross-cultural research.* New York: Appleton-Century-Crofts, 1961.

LINDZEY, G. & BYRNE, D. Measurement of social choice and interpersonal attractiveness. In G. Lindzey & E. Aronson (eds.) *The handbook of social psychology* (2nd ed.) Vol. II. Reading, Mass.: Addison-Wesley, 1968, pp. 452–525.

LINDZEY, G. & KALNINS, D. Thematic Apperception Test: Some evidence bearing on the "hero assumption." *Journal of Abnormal and Social Psychology,* 1958, 57, 76–83.

LITTLE, K. B. & SHNEIDMAN, E. S. Congruencies among interpretations of psychological test and anamnestic data. *Psychological Monographs,* 1959, 73, No. 6 (Whole No. 476).

LOCATIS, C. N. & GOOLER, D. D. Evaluating second-order consequences: Technology assessment and education. *Review of Educational Research,* 1975, 45, 329–353.

LOEHLIN, J. C., LINDZEY, G., & SPUHLER, J. N. *Race differences in intelligence.* San Francisco: Freeman, 1975.

LOEVINGER, J. Objective tests as instruments of psychological theory. *Psychological Reports,* 1957, 3, 635–694 (Monograph No. 9).

LOEVINGER, J. The meaning and measurement of ego development. *American Psychologist,* 1966, 21, 195–206.

LOEVINGER, J. Theories of ego development. In L. Breger (ed.) *Clinical-cognitive psychology.* Englewood Cliffs, N.J.: Prentice-Hall, 1969, pp. 83–135.

LOEVINGER, J. *Ego development: Conceptions and theories.* San Francisco: Jossey-Bass, 1976.

LOEVINGER, J. & WESSLER, R. *Measuring ego development,* Vol. 1, *Construction and use of a sentence-completion test.* San Francisco: Jossey-Bass, 1970.

LOEVINGER, J., WESSLER, R., & REDMORE, C. *Measuring ego development,* Vol. 2, *Scoring manual for women and girls.* San Francisco: Jossey-Bass, 1970.

LOMBARDI, D. N. Eight avenues of life style consistency. *Individual Psychologist,* 1973, 10, 5–9.

LOPEZ, F. M., Jr. *Evaluating executive decision making.* New York: American Management Association, 1966.

LORD, F. M. & NOVICK, M. R. *Statistical theories and mental test scores.* Reading, Ma.: Addison-Wesley, 1968.

LORR, M., McNAIR, D. M., KLETT, C. J., & LASKY, J. J. Evidence of ten psychotic syndromes. *Journal of Consulting Psychology,* 1962, 26, 185–189.

LORR, M. & SUZIEDELIS, A. Modes of interpersonal behavior. *British Journal of Social and Clinical Psychology,* 1969, 8, 124–132.

LUBIN, B., WALLIS, R. R., & PAINE, C. Patterns of psychological test usage in the United States: 1935–1969. *Professional Psychology,* 1971, 2, 70–74.

LUMSDEN, J. Test theory. In M. R. Rosenzweig & L. W. Porter (eds.) *Annual review of psychology,* Vol. 27. Palo Alto: Annual Reviews, 1976, pp. 251–280.

LUSHENE, R. E., O'NEIL, H. F., & DUNN, T. Equivalent validity of a completely computerized MMPI. *Journal of Personality Assessment,* 1974, 38, 353–361.

LYKKEN, D. T. Psychology and the lie detector industry. *American Psychologist,* 1974, 29, 725–739.

MAAS, H. S. & KUYPERS, J. A. *From thirty to seventy.* San Francisco: Jossey-Bass, 1974.

MACCORQUODALE. K. & MEEHL, P. E. On a distinction between hypothetical constructs and intervening variables. *Psychological Review,* 1948, 55, 95–107.

MACHOVER, K. *Personality projection in the drawing of the human figure.* Springfield, Ill.: Thomas, 1949.

MACKINNON, D. W. The nature and nurture of creative talent. *American Psychologist,* 1962, 17, 484–495.

MACKINNON, D. W. Personality and the realization of creative potential. *American Psychologist,* 1965, 20, 273–281.

MACKINNON, D. W. Human assessment: Perspective and context for current practice. Paper presented at the American Psychological Association meetings, Chicago, 1975.

MACKINNON, D. W. & HALL, W. B. Intelligence and creativity. *Proceedings XVIIth International Congress of Applied Psychology,* Vol. II. Brussels: Editest, 1972, pp. 1883–1888.

MacPhillamy, D. J. & Lewinsohn, P. M. Depression as a function of levels of desired and obtained pleasure. *Journal of Abnormal Psychology,* 1974, 83, 651–657.

Maddi, S. *Personality theories: A comparative analysis.* Homewood, Il.: Dorsey, 1972.

Madison, P. *Personality development in college.* Reading, Ma.: Addison-Wesley, 1969.

Mahrer, A. R. (ed.) *New approaches to personality classification.* New York: Columbia University Press, 1970.

Mandelbaum, D. G. The study of life history: Gandhi. *Current Anthropology,* 1973, 14, 177–206.

Manning, H. M. Programmed interpretation of the MMPI. *Journal of Personality Assessment,* 1971, 35, 162–176.

Marjoribanks, K. Environment, social class, and mental abilities. *Journal of Educational Psychology,* 1972, 62, 103–109.

Marjoribanks, K. Another view of the relation of environment to mental abilities. *Journal of Educational Psychology,* 1974, 66, 460–463.

Marks, P. A., Seeman, W., & Haller, D. L. *The actuarial use of the MMPI with adolescents and adults.* Baltimore: Williams and Wilkins, 1974.

Masling, J. The influence of situational and interpersonal variables in projective testing. *Psychological Bulletin,* 1960, 57, 65–85.

Masling, J. Role-related behavior of the subject and psychologist and its effect upon psychological data. In D. Levine (ed.), *Nebraska symposium on motivation,* 1966. Lincoln, Ne.: University of Nebraska Press, 1966, pp. 67–103.

Masterson, S. The adjective checklist technique: A review and critique. In P. McReynolds (ed.) *Advances in psychological assessment.* Vol. 3. San Francisco: Jossey-Bass, 1975, pp. 275–312.

Matarazzo, J. D. *Wechsler's measurement and appraisal of adult intelligence.* (5th ed.) Baltimore: Williams and Wilkins, 1972.

Matarazzo, J. D. & Wiens, A. N. *The interview: Research on its anatomy and structure.* Chicago: Aldine-Atherton, 1972.

Matarazzo, J. D., Wiens, A. N., Saslow, G., Dunham, R. M., & Voas, R. B. Speech durations of astronaut and ground communicator. *Science,* 1964, 143, 148–150.

Matthews, C. G., Shaw, D. J., & Kløve, H. Psychological test performances in neurologic and "psuedo-neurologic" subjects. *Cortex,* 1966, 2, 244–253.

Mayman, M., Schafer, R., & Rapaport, D. Interpretation of the Wechsler-Bellevue Intelligence Scale in personality appraisal. In H. H. Anderson & G. L. Anderson (eds.) *An introduction to projective techniques.* Englewood Cliffs, N.J.: Prentice-Hall, 1951, pp. 541–580.

Mazlish, B. *In search of Nixon—A psychohistorical inquiry.* New York: Basic Books, 1972.

McClelland, D. C. *The achieving society.* Princeton, N.J.: Van Nostrand, 1961.

McClelland, D. C. Testing for competence rather than for "intelligence." *American Psychologist,* 1973, 28, 1–14.

McClelland, D. C. Love and power: The psychological signals of war. *Psychology Today,* 1975, 8, No. 8, 44–48.

McFALL, R. M. The effects of self-monitoring on normal smoking behavior. *Journal of Consulting and Clinical Psychology,* 1970, 35, 135–142.

McGUIRE, W. J. The nature of attitudes and attitude change. In G. Lindzey & E. Aronson (eds.) *The handbook of social psychology* (2nd ed.) Vol. 3, Reading, Ma.: Addison-Wesley, 1969, pp. 136–314.

McNEMAR, Q. On so-called test bias. *American Psychologist,* 1975, 30, 848–851.

McQUEEN, L., FEHNEL, R., MOURSUND, J., MUÑOZ, R., & SUNDBERG, N. *Assessing interpersonal skills in the human services: Special project final report to the Cooperative Assessment of Experiential Learning.* Eugene, Or.: Wallace School of Community Service & Public Affairs, University of Oregon, 1975.

McREYNOLDS, P. (ed.) *Advances in psychological assessment.* Vol. 1. Palo Alto: Science & Behavior Books, 1968.

McREYNOLDS, P. (ed.) *Advances in psychological assessment.* Vol. 2. Palo Alto: Science & Behavior Books, 1971.

McREYNOLDS, P. (ed.) *Advances in psychological assessment.* Vol. 3. San Francisco: Jossey-Bass, 1975. (a)

McREYNOLDS, P. Historical antecedents of personality assessment. In P. McReynolds (ed.) *Advances in psychological assessment.* Vol. 3. San Francisco: Jossey-Bass, 1975, pp. 477–532. (b)

MEADOWS, D. H., MEADOWS, D. L., RANDERS, J., & BEHRENS, W. W. *The limits to growth: A report for the Club of Rome's project on the predicament of mankind.* New York: Signet, 1972.

MEEHL, P. E. *Clinical versus statistical prediction.* Minneapolis: University of Minnesota Press, 1954.

MEEHL, P. E. Wanted—a good cookbook. *American Psychologist,* 1956, 11, 263–272.

MEEHL, P. E. Some ruminations on the validation of clinical procedures. *Canadian Journal of Psychology,* 1959, 13, 102–128.

MEEHL, P. E. The cognitive activity of the clinician. *American Psychologist,* 1960, 15, 19–27.

MEEHL, P. E. Seer over sign: the first good example. *Journal of Experimental Research in Personality,* 1965, 1, 27–32.

MEEHL, P. E. Reactions, reflections, projections. In J. N. Butcher (ed.) *Objective personality assessment.* New York: Academic Press, 1972, pp. 131–184. (a)

MEEHL, P. E. Specific genetic etiology, psychodynamics, and therapeutic nihilism. *International Journal of Mental Health,* 1972, 1, 10–27. (b)

MEEHL, P. E. *Psychodiagnosis: Selected papers.* Minneapolis: University of Minnesota Press, 1973.

MEEHL, P. E., LYKKEN, D. T., SCHOFIELD, W., & TELLEGEN, A. Recaptured-item technique (RIT): A method for reducing somewhat the subjective element in factor naming. *Journal of Experimental Research in Personality,* 1971, 5, 171–190.

MEEHL, P. E. & ROSEN, A. Antecedent probability and the efficiency of psychometric signs, patterns, or cutting scores. *Psychological Bulletin,* 1955, 52, 194–216.

MEGARGEE, E. I. *The California Psychological Inventory handbook.* San Francisco: Jossey-Bass, 1972.

MEHTA, P. H., ROHILA, P.K., SUNDBERG, N. D., & TYLER, L. E. Future time perspectives of adolescents in India and the United States. *Journal of Cross-Cultural Psychology,* 1972, 3, 293–302.

MEICHENBAUM, D. Self-instructional methods. In F. H. Kanfer and A. P. Goldstein (eds.) *Helping people change.* New York: Pergamon, 1975, pp. 357–392.

MENNE, J. M. A comprehensive set of counselor competencies. *Journal of Counseling Psychology,* 1975, 22, 547–553.

MESSICK, S. The standard problem: Meaning and values in measurement and evaluation. *American Psychologist,* 1975, 30, 955–966.

MEUX, E. P. Concern for the common good in an N-person game. *Journal of Personality and Social Psychology,* 1973, 28, 414–418.

MICHAEL, D. N. *On learning to plan—and planning to learn.* San Francisco: Jossey-Bass, 1973.

MIKLICH, D. R. Radio telemetry in clinical psychology. *American Psychologist,* 1975, 30, 419–425.

MILGRAM, S. The experience of living in cities. *Science,* 1970, 167, 1461–1468.

MILLER, G. A. Psychology as a means of promoting human welfare. *American Psychologist,* 1969, 24, 1063–1075.

MILLER, G. A. Assessment of psychotechnology. *American Psychologist,* 1970, 25, 991–1001.

MILLER, G. A., GALANTER, E., & PRIBRAM, K. H. *Plans and the structure of behavior.* New York: Holt, Rinehart & Winston, 1960.

MILLER, J. G. The nature of living systems. *Behavioral Science,* 1971, 16, 277–301.

MILLON, T. & DIESENHAUS, H. I. *Research methods in psychopathology.* New York: Wiley, 1972.

MILLS, R. B., McDEVITT, R. J., & TONKIN, S. Situational tests in metropolitan police recruit selection. *Journal of Criminal Law, Criminology and Police Science,* 1966, 57, 99–106.

MISCHEL, W. Preference for delayed reinforcement and social responsibility. *Journal of Abnormal and Social Psychology,* 1961, 62, 1–7.

MISCHEL, W. *Personality and assessment.* New York: Wiley, 1968.

MISCHEL, W. Continuity and change in personality. *American Psychologist,* 1969, 24, 1012–1018.

MISCHEL, W. Toward a cognitive social learning reconceptualization of personality. *Psychological Review,* 1973, 80, 252–283.

MOLISH, H. B. Projective methodologies. In P. H. Mussen & M. R. Rosenzweig (eds.) *Annual review of psychology,* Vol. 23, Palo Alto: Annual Reviews, 1972, pp. 577–614.

MOOS, R. H. Behavioral effects of being observed: Reactions to a wireless radio transmitter. *Journal of Consulting and Clinical Psychology,* 1968, 32, 383–388.

MOOS, R. H. Conceptualizations of human environments. *American Psychologist,* 1973, 28, 652–665.

MOOS, R. H. Assessment and impact of social climate. In P. McReynolds (ed.) *Advances in psychological assessment.* Vol. 3. San Francisco: Jossey-Bass, 1975, pp. 8–41.

MOOS, R. H. & INSEL, P. M. (eds.) *Issues in social ecology: Human milieus.* Palo Alto: National Press, 1974.

MORGAN, C. D. & MURRAY, H. A. A method for investigating fantasies: The Thematic Apperception Test. *Archives of Neurology and Psychiatry,* 1935, 34, 289–306.

MORGANSTERN, K. P. Behavioral interviewing: The initial stages of assessment. In M. Hersen & A. S. Bellack (eds.) *Behavioral assessment: A practical handbook.* New York: Pergamon, 1976 (in press).

MORRIS, R. J. Fear reduction methods. In F. H. Kanfer & A. P. Goldstein (eds.) *Helping people change.* New York: Pergamon Press, 1975, pp. 229–272.

MOURSUND, J. P. *Evaluation: An introduction to research design.* Monterey, Ca.: Brooks/Cole, 1973.

MUNTER, P. O. Psychobiographical assessment. *Journal of Personality Assessment,* 1975, 39, 424–428.

MURPHY, G. *Human potentialities.* New York: Basic Books, 1958.

MURRAY, H. A. *Explorations in personality.* New York: Oxford, 1938.

MURRAY, H. A. *Thematic Apperception Test manual.* Cambridge, Ma.: Harvard University Press, 1943.

MURRAY, H. A. Some basic psychological assumptions and conceptions. *Dialectica,* 1951, 5, 266–292.

MURRAY, H. A. Preparations for the scaffold of a comprehensive system. In S. Koch (ed.) *Psychology: A study of a science,* Vol. 3, *Formulations of the person and the social context.* New York: McGraw-Hill, 1959, pp. 7–54.

MURSTEIN, B. I. *Theory and research in projective techniques (emphasizing the TAT).* New York: Wiley, 1963.

MURSTEIN, B. I. (ed.) *Handbook of projective techniques.* New York: Basic Books, 1965.

MURSTEIN, B. I. Discussion for current status of some projective techniques. *Journal of Projective techniques and Personality Assessment,* 1968, 23, 229–239. (a)

MURSTEIN, B. I. Effect of stimulus, background, personality, and scoring system on the manifestation of hostility on the TAT. *Journal of Consulting and Clinical Psychology,* 1968, 32, 355–365. (b)

MURSTEIN, B. I. & WOLF, S. R. Empirical test of the "levels" hypothesis with five projective techniques. *Journal of Abnormal Psychology,* 1970, 75, 38–44.

MUSSEN, P. H. (ed.) *Carmichael's manual of child psychology.* (3rd ed.) Vols. 1 & 2. New York: Wiley, 1970.

NATHAN, P. E. *Cues, decisions and diagnoses.* New York: Academic Press, 1967.

NESSELROADE, J. R. & BALTES, P. B. Adolescent personality development and historical change: 1970–72. *Monographs of the Society for Research on Child Development,* 1974, 39 (1, Serial No. 154).

NEWCOMB, T. M. An approach to the study of communicative acts. *Psychological Review,* 1953, 60, 393–404.

NEWMAN, S. H., BOBBITT, J. M., & CAMERON, D. C. The reliability of the interview method in an officer candidate evaluation program. *American Psychologist,* 1946, 1, 103–109.

NORMAN, W. T. *2800 personality trait descriptors: Normative operating characteristics for a university population.* Department of Psychology, University of Michigan: April, 1967.

NORMAN, W. T. Psychometric considerations for a revision of the MMPI. In J. N. Butcher (ed.) *Objective personality assessment.* New York: Academic Press, 1972, pp. 59–83.

ODEN, M. H. The fulfillment of promise: 40 year follow-up of the Terman gifted group. *Genetic Psychology Monographs,* 1968, 77, 3–93.

ODUM, C. L. A study of time required to do a Rorschach examination. *Journal of Projective Techniques,* 1950, 14, 464–468.

Office of Strategic Services Staff. *Assessment of men.* New York: Holt, Rinehart & Winston, 1948.

OSGOOD, C. E. & LURIA, Z. A blind analysis of a case of multiple personality using the Semantic Differential. *Journal of Abnormal and Social Psychology,* 1954, 49, 579–591.

OSGOOD, C. E., SUCI, G. J., & TANNENBAUM, P. H. *The measurement of meaning.* Urbana, Il.: University of Illinois Press, 1957.

OWENS, W. A. Toward one discipline of scientific psychology. *American Psychologist,* 1968, 23, 782–785.

OWENS, W. A. Cognitive, non-cognitive, and environmental correlates of mechanical ingenuity. *Journal of Applied Psychology,* 1969, 53, 199–208.

OWENS, W. A. A quasi-actuarial basis for individual assessment. *American Psychologist,* 1971, 26, 992–999.

OWENS, W. A. Background data. In M. D. Dunnette (ed.) *Handbook of industrial psychology.* New York: Rand-McNally, 1975.

OWENS, W. A. & HENRY, E. R. *Biographical data in industrial psychology, a review and evaluation.* Greensboro, N.C.: The Creativity Research Institute, The Richardson Foundation, 1966.

PACKARD, V. *A nation of strangers.* New York: McKay, 1972.

PADILLA, A. M. & RUIZ, R. A. Personality assessment and test interpretation of Mexican Americans: A critique. *Journal of Personality Assessment,* 1975, 39, 103–109.

PALMER, J. O. *The psychological assessment of children.* New York: Wiley, 1970.

PAPAJOHN, J. & SPIEGEL, J. *Transactions in families.* San Francisco: Jossey-Bass, 1975.

PARAMESH, C. R. *Creativity and personality.* Madras, India: Janatha, 1972.

PASAMANICK, B. & KNOBLOCH, H. Early language behavior in Negro children and the testing of intelligence. *Journal of Abnormal and Social Psychology,* 1955, 50, 401–402.

PASCAL, G. R. & SUTTELL, B. J. *The Bender-Gestalt Test: Quantification and validity for adults.* New York: Grune & Stratton, 1951.

PASKEWITZ, D. A. Biofeedback instrumentation: Soldering closed the loop. *American Psychologist,* 1975, 30, 371–379.

PASSINI, F. T. & NORMAN, W. T. A universal conception of personality structure? *Journal of Personality and Social Psychology,* 1966, 4, 44–49.

PATTERSON, G. R. Behavioral intervention procedures in the classroom and in the home. In A. E. Bergin & S. L. Garfield (eds.) *Handbook of psychotherapy and behavior change: An empirical analysis.* New York: Wiley, 1971, pp. 751–775.

PATTERSON, G. R. A basis for identifying stimuli which control behaviors in natural settings. *Child Development,* 1974, 45, 900 911.

PATTERSON, G. R., RAY, R. S., & SHAW, D. A. Direct intervention in families of deviant children. *Oregon Research Institute Research Bulletin,* 1968, 8, 9.

PAUL, G. L. *Insight vs. desensitization in psychotherapy.* Stanford: Stanford University Press, 1966.

PAULSON, M. J., GROSSMAN, S. & SHAPIRO, G. Child-rearing attitudes of foster home mothers. *Journal of Community Psychology,* 1974, 2, 11–14.

PAYNE, A. F. *Sentence completions.* New York: N. Y. Guidance Clinic, 1928.

PELLIGRINI, R. J. The astrological "theory" of personality: An unbiased test by a biased observer. *Journal of Psychology,* 1973, 85, 21–28.

PERRY, D. K. Validities of three interest keys for U.S. navy yeomen. *Journal of Applied Psychology,* 1955, 39, 134–138.

PETERSON, D. R. Behavior problems of middle childhood. *Journal of Consulting Psychology,* 1961, 25, 205–209.

PETERSON, D. R. *The clinical study of social behavior.* New York: Appleton-Century-Crofts, 1968.

PETRULLO, L. & BASS, B. M. (eds.) *Leadership and interpersonal behavior.* New York: Holt, Rinehart & Winston, 1961.

PFEIFFER, J. W. & HESLIN, R. *Instrumentation in human relations training: A guide to 75 instruments with wide application to the behavioral sciences.* Iowa City: University Associates, 1973.

PFEIFFER, J. W. and JONES, J. E. (eds.) *A handbook of structured experiences for human relations training.* Vols. 1, 2, 3, 4. La Jolla, Cal.: Universities Associates, 1971–74.

PHILLIPS, L. *Human adaptation and its failures.* New York: Academic Press, 1968.

PHILLIPS, L. & DRAGUNS, J. G. Classification of the behavior disorders. In P. H. Mussen & M. R. Rosenzweig (eds.) *Annual review of psychology,* Vol. 22. Palo Alto: Annual Reviews, 1971, pp. 447–482.

POLAK, F. *The image of the future,* Vol. II. (Translated by E. Boulding.) The Netherlands: A. W. Sijhoff, 1961.

PORTEUS, S. P. *Porteus Maze Test: Fifty year's application.* Palo Alto: Pacific Books, 1965.

POTKAY, C. R. The role of personal history data in clinical judgment: A selective focus. *Journal of Personality Assessment,* 1973, 37, 203–213.

PRICE, R. H. & BOUFFARD, D. L. Behavioral appropriateness and situation constraint as dimensions of social behavior. *Journal of Personality and Social Psychology,* 1974, 30, 579–586.

PROLA, M. A review of the Transcendence Index. *Journal of Personality Assessment,* 1972, 36, 8–12.

PURCELL, K. The Thematic Apperception Test and antisocial behavior. *Journal of Consulting Psychology,* 1956, 20, 449–456.

QUAY, H. C. Personality patterns in pre-adolescent delinquent boys. *Educational and Psychological Measurement,* 1966, 26, 99–110.

RABIN, A. I. Time estimation of schizophrenics and non-psychotics. *Journal of Clinical Psychology,* 1957, 13, 88–90.

RABIN, A. I. (ed.) *Projective techniques in personality assessment: A modern introduction.* New York: Springer, 1968.

RABKIN, J. G. Opinions about mental illness: A review of the literature. *Psychological Bulletin,* 1972, 153–171.

RABKIN, L. Y. (ed.) *Psychopathology and literature.* San Francisco: Chandler, 1966.

RAHE, R. H., MAHAN, J. L., & ARTHUR, R. J. Prediction of near-future health change from subjects' preceding life changes. *Journal of Psychosomatic Research,* 1970, 14, 401.

RAPOPORT, A. & WALSTEN, T. S. Individual decision behavior. In P. H. Mussen & M. R. Rosenzweig (eds.) *Annual Review of Psychology,* Vol. 23, Palo Alto: Annual Review, 1972, pp. 131–176.

RAUSH, H. L., DITTMAN, A. T., & TAYLOR, T. J. Person, setting, and change in social interaction. *Human Relations,* 1959, 12, 361–378.

REICHENBACH, H. *Experience and prediction, an analysis of the foundations and the structure of knowledge.* Chicago: University of Chicago Press, 1938.

REIK, T. *Listening with the third ear.* New York: Farrar, Straus and Giroux, 1948.

REIMANIS, G. Psychological development, anomie, and mood. *Journal of Personality and Social Psychology,* 1974, 29, 355–357.

REITAN, R. M. Certain differential effects of left and right cerebral lesions in human adults. *Journal of Comparative and Physiological Psychology,* 1955, 48, 474–477.

REITAN, R. M. Assessment of brain-behavior relationships. In P. McReynolds (ed.) *Advances in psychological assessment.* Vol. 3. San Francisco: Jossey-Bass, 1975, pp. 186–242.

REITAN, R. M. & FITZHUGH, K. B. Behavioral deficits in groups with cerebral vascular lesions. *Journal of Consulting and Clinical Psychology,* 1971, 37, 215–223.

REYNOLDS, W. M. and SUNDBERG, N. D. Recent research trends in testing. *Journal of Personality Assessment,* 1976, 40, 228–233.

RICE, S. A. Contagious bias in the interview. *American Journal of Sociology,* 1929, 35, 420–423.

RICH, J. *Interviewing children and adolescents.* New York: St. Martin's Press, 1968.

RIMM, D. C. & MASTERS, J. C. *Behavior therapy: Techniques and empirical findings.* New York: Academic Press, 1974.

RINN, J. L. Structure of phenomenal domains. *Psychological Review,* 1965, 72, 445–466.

ROBACK, H. B. Human figure drawings: Their utility in the clinical psychologist's armamentarium for personality assessment. *Psychological Bulletin,* 1968, 70, 1–19.

ROBACK, H. B., LANGEVIN, R., & ZAJAC, Y. Sex of free choice figure drawings by homosexual and heterosexual subjects. *Journal of Personality Assessment,* 1974, 38, 154–155.

ROETHLISBERGER, F. J. & DICKSON, W. J. *Management and the worker.* Cambridge, Ma.: Harvard University Press, 1939.

ROFF, M. & RICKS, D. F. (eds.) *Life history research in psychopathology.* Minneapolis: University of Minnesota Press, 1970.

ROFF, M., ROBINS, L. N., & POLLACK, M. (eds.) *Life history research in psychopathology.* Vol. 2. Minneapolis: University of Minnesota Press, 1972.

ROGERS, C. R. *Client-centered therapy.* Boston: Houghton, 1951.

ROGERS, C. R. The necessary and sufficient conditions of therapeutic personality change. *Journal of Consulting Psychology,* 1957, 21, 95–103.

ROGERS, C. R. & DYMOND, R. F. *Psychotherapy and personality change.* Chicago: University of Chicago Press, 1954.

ROJAS, B. Futuristics, games and educational change. In A. Toffler (ed.) *Learning for tomorrow.* New York: Vintage Books, 1974.

ROKEACH, M. *Open and closed mind.* New York: Basic Books, 1960.

ROKEACH, M. *Beliefs, attitudes and values.* San Francisco: Jossey-Bass, 1968.

ROKEACH, M. *The nature of human values.* New York: Free Press, 1973.

RORSCHACH, H. *Psychodiagnostics: A diagnostic test based on perception.* (4th ed.) New York: Grune & Stratton, 1942. (Originally published in 1921.)

ROSEN, G. M. Effects of source prestige on subjects' acceptance of the Barnum Effect: Psychologist versus astrologer. *Journal of Consulting and Clinical Psychology,* 1975, 43, 95.

ROSENHAN, D. L. On being sane in insane places. *Science,* 1973, 250–258.

ROTTER, J. B. Word association and sentence completion methods. In H. H. Anderson and G. L. Anderson (eds.) *An introduction to projective techniques.* Englewood Cliffs, N.J.: Prentice-Hall, 1951, pp. 279–311.

ROTTER, J. B. *Social learning and clinical psychology.* New Jersey: Prentice-Hall, 1954.

ROTTER, J. B. Generalized expectancies for internal vs. external control of reinforcement. *Psychological Monographs,* 1966, 80 (Whole No. 609).

ROTTER, J. B., CHANCE, J. E., & PHARES, E. J. (eds.) *Applications of a social learning theory of personality.* New York: Holt, Rinehart & Winston, 1972.

ROTTER, J. B. & RAFFERTY, J. E. *The Rotter Incomplete Sentences Test.* New York: Psychological Corporation, 1950.

ROWE, F. B. Assessment in the Peace Corps. In A. W. Asten (Chm.), The revolt against assessment—Where do we go from here? Symposium presented at the meeting of the Eastern Psychological Association, Washington, D. C., May, 1973.

ROYCE, J. E. Does person or self imply dualism? *American Psychologist,* 1973, 28, 883–886.

RUNKEL, P. J. & McGRATH, J. E. *Research on human behavior.* New York: Holt, Rinehart & Winston, 1972.

RUSSELL, E. W., NEURINGER, C., & GOLDSTEIN, G. *Assessment of brain damage.* New York: Wiley, 1970.

RYCHLAK, J. F. *A philosophy of science for personality theory.* Boston: Houghton Mifflin, 1968.

SALES, S. M., GUYDOSH, R. M., & IACONO, W. Relationship between "strength of the nervous system" and the need for stimulation. *Journal of Personality and Social Psychology,* 1974, 29, 16–22.

SAMUDA, R. J. *Psychological testing of American minorities: Issues and consequences.* New York: Dodd, Mead & Co., 1975.

SANDIFER, M. G., PETTUS, C., & QUADE, D. A study of psychiatric diagnosis. *Journal of Nervous and Mental Disease,* 1964, 139, 350–356.

SANDLER, B. E. Eclecticism at work: Approaches to job design. *American Psychologist,* 1974, 29, 767–773.

SANDLER, H., McCUTCHEON, E. P., FRYER, T. B., ROSITANO, S., & WESTBROOK, R., & HARO, P. Recent NASA contributions to biomedical telemetry. *American Psychologist,* 1975, 30, 257–264.

SARASON, S. B. Jewishness, blackishness, and the nature-nurture controversy. *American Psychologist,* 1973, 28, 962–971.

SARASON, S. B., DAVIDSON, K. S., LIGHTHALL, F. F., WAITE, R. R., & RUEBUSH, B. K. *Anxiety in elementary school children.* New York: Wiley, 1960.

SARASON, S. B., MANDLER, G., & CRAIGHILL, P. G. The effect of differential instructions on anxiety and learning. *Journal of Abnormal and Social Psychology.* 1953, 47, 561–565.

SARBIN, T. R. A contribution to the study of actuarial and individual methods of prediction. *American Journal of Sociology,* 1943, 593–602.

SARBIN, T. R. & ALLEN, V. L. Role theory. In G. Lindzey & E. Aronson (eds.) *Handbook of social psychology,* Vol. 1 (2nd ed.) Reading, Ma.: Addison-Wesley, 1968, pp. 488–567.

SARBIN, T. R. & JONES, D. S. An experimental analysis of role behavior. *Journal of Abnormal and Social Psychology,* 1956, 51, 236–241.

SARBIN, T. R., TAFT, R., & BAILEY, D. E. *Clinical inference and cognitive theory.* New York: Holt, Rinehart & Winston, 1960.

SARMA, D. V. N. Letter to the editor. *Journal of Personality Assessment,* 1974, 38, 66.

SATTLER, J. M. *Assessment of children's intelligence.* Philadelphia: Saunders, 1974.

SAUNDERS, T. R. Toward a distinctive role for the psychologist in neurodiagnostic decision-making. *Professional Psychology,* 1975, 6, 161–166.

SAWYER, J. Measurement and prediction, clinical and statistical. *Psychological Bulletin,* 1966, 66, 178–200.

SCHAEFER, C. E. & ANASTASI, A. A biographical inventory for identifying creativity in adolescent boys. *Journal of Applied Psychology,* 1968, 52, 42–48.

SCHAEFER, E. & BELL, R. Development of a parental attitude research instrument. *Child Development,* 1958, 29, 339–261.

SCHAFER, R. *The clinical application of psychological tests.* New York: International Universities Press, 1948.

SCHAIE, K. W. Translations in gerontology—from lab to life: Intellectual functioning. *American Psychologist,* 1974, 29, 802–807.

SCHAIE, K. W. & LABOUVIE-VIEF, G. Generational versus ontogenetic components of change in adult cognitive behavior: A fourteen-year cross-sequential study. *Developmental Psychology,* 1974, 10, 305–320.

SCHMIDT, H. O. & FONDA, C. P. Reliability of psychiatric diagnosis: A new look. *Journal of Abnormal and Social Psychology,* 1956, 52, 262–267.

SCHOFIELD, W. & BALIAN, L. A comparative study of the personal histories of schizophrenic and nonpsychiatric patients. *Journal of Abnormal and Social Psychology,* 1959, 59, 216–225.

SCHOGGEN, P. Environmental forces in the everyday lives of children. In R. G. Barker (ed.) *The stream of behavior.* New York: Appleton-Century-Crofts, 1963, pp. 42–69.

SCHULZ, D. A. *Coming up black: Patterns of ghetto socialization.* Englewood Cliffs, N.J.: Prentice-Hall, 1969.

SCHUTZ, W. C. *FIRO: A three-dimensional theory of interpersonal behavior.* New York: Rinehart, 1958.

SCHUTZ, W. C. *FIRO-B.* Palo Alto: Consulting Psychologists Press, 1967.

SCHWITZGEBEL, R. L. Behavior instrumentation and social technology. *American Psychologist,* 1970, 25, 491–499.

SCHWITZGEBEL, R. L. & SCHWITZGEBEL, R. K. (eds.) *Psychotechnology: Electronic control of mind and behavior.* New York: Holt, Rinehart & Winston, 1973.

SCOTT, R. D. & JOHNSON, R. W. Use of the Weighted Application Blank in selecting unskilled employees. *Journal of Applied Psychology,* 1967, 51, 393–395.

SCOTT, W. A. Attitude measurement. In G. Lindzey & E. Aronson (eds.) *The handbook of social psychology.* (2nd ed.) Vol. 2. Reading, Ma.: Addison-Wesley, 1968, pp. 204–273.

SECHREST, L. B. Incremental validity: A recommendation. *Educational and Psychological Measurement,* 1963, 23, 153–158.

SECHREST, L. & BRYAN, J. H. Astrologers as useful marriage counselors. *Trans-Action,* 1968, 6, 34–36.

SECORD, P. F. & BACKMAN, C. W. *Social psychology.* New York: McGraw-Hill, 1964.

SELLS, S. B. A multivariate model of personality. In J. R. Royce (ed.) *Contributions of multivariate analysis and psychological theory.* London: Academic Press, 1973.

SHAH, S. A. & BORGAONKAR, D. S. The XYY chromosomal abnormality: Some "facts" and some "fantasies?" *American Psychologist,* 1974, 29, 357–359.

SHAPIRO, D. & CRIDER, A. Psychophysiological approaches to social psychology. In G. Lindzey & E. Aronson (eds.) *Handbook of social psychology* (2nd ed.) Reading, Ma.: Addison-Wesley, 1969, pp. 1–49.

SHELDON, W. H. *The varieties of temperament: A psychology of constitutional differences.* New York: Harper, 1942.

SHELDON, W. H. *Atlas of men.* New York: Harper, 1954.

SHNEIDMAN, E. S. Plan 11. The logic of politics. In L. Arons and M. A. May (eds.) *Television and human behavior.* New York: Appleton-Century-Crofts, 1963, pp. 177–199.

SHONTZ, F. C. *Research methods in personality.* New York: Appleton-Century-Crofts, 1965.

SIESS, T. F. & JACKSON, D. N. The Personality Research Form and vocational interest research. In P. McReynolds (ed.) *Advances in psychological assessment.* Vol. 2. Palo Alto: Science and Behavior Books, 1971, pp. 109–132.

SILVERMAN, B. I. Studies of astrology. *Journal of Psychology,* 1971, 77, 141–149.

SIMONEIT, M. *Deutsches Soldatentum, 1914–1939.* Berlin: Junker und Buennhaupt, 1940.

SINES, L. K. The relative contribution of four kinds of data to accuracy in personality assessment. *Journal of Consulting Psychology,* 1959, 23, 483–492.

SINGER, J. L. Imagination and waiting ability in young children. *Journal of Personality,* 1961, 29, 296–313.

SKINNER, B. F. *The behavior of organisms.* New York: Appleton-Century-Crofts, 1938.

SKINNER, B. F. *Science and human behavior.* New York: Macmillan, 1953.

SKINNER, B. F. *Beyond freedom and dignity.* New York: Knopf, 1971.

SLOVIC, P. From Shakespeare to Simon: Speculations—and some evidence about man's ability to process information. *Oregon Research Institute Monograph,* 1972, 12, No. 2.

SMITH, A. G. (ed.) *Communication and culture.* New York: Holt, Rinehart & Winston, 1966.

SMITH, M. B. Personal values in the study of lives. In R. W. White (ed.) *The study of lives.* Englewood Cliffs, N.J.: Prentice-Hall, 1963, pp. 324–347.

SNEDDEN, D. Measuring general intelligence by interview. *Psychological Clinic,* 1930, 19, 131–134.

SNIDER, J. G. & OSGOOD, C. E. *Semantic differential technique: A sourcebook.* Chicago: Aldine, 1969.

SNYDER, C. R. Acceptance of personality interpretations as a function of assessment procedures. *Journal of Consulting and Clinical Psychology,* 1974, 42, 150. (a)

SNYDER, C. R. Why horoscopes are true: The effects of specificity on acceptance of astrological interpretations. *Journal of Clinical Psychology,* 1974, 30, 557–580. (b)

SONSTEGARD, M. Life style identification and assessment. *Individual Psychologist,* 1973, 10, 1–4.

SOSKIN, W. F. Influence of four types of data on diagnostic conceptualization in psychological testing. *Journal of Abnormal and Social Psychology,* 1959, 58, 69–78.

SOSKIN, W. F. & JOHN, V. P. The study of spontaneous talk. In R. B. Barker (ed.) *The stream of behavior.* New York: Appleton-Century-Crofts, 1963, pp. 328–381.

SPIELBERGER, C. D. (ed.) *Anxiety and behavior.* New York: Academic Press, 1966.

STEPHENSON, W. *The study of behavior: Q-technique and its methodology.* Chicago: University of Chicago Press, 1953.

STERN, G. G. *People in context: Measuring person-environment congruence in education and industry.* New York: Wiley, 1970.

STERN, G. G., STEIN, M. I., & BLOOM, B. S. *Methods in personality assessment.* Glencoe, Ill.: Free Press, 1956.

STONE, H. K. & DELLIS, N. P. An exploratory investigation into the levels hypothesis. *Journal of Projective Techniques,* 1960, 24, 333–340.

STORMS, M. D. Videotape and the attribution process: Reversing actors' and observers' points of views. *Journal of Personality and Social Psychology,* 1973, 27, 165–175.

STRAUSS, M. E., GYNTHER, M. D., & WALLHERMFECHTEL, J. Differential misdiagnosis of blacks and whites by the MMPI. *Journal of Personality Assessment,* 1974, 38, 55–60.

STRONG, E. K., Jr. *Vocational interests 18 years after college.* Minneapolis: University of Minnesota Press, 1955.

STROUDENMIRE, J. Effects of muscle relaxation training on state and trait anxiety in introverts and extroverts. *Journal of Personality and Social Psychology, 1972,* 24, 272–275.

SUINN, R. M. & OSKAMP, S. *The predictive validity of projective measures.* Springfield, Il.: Thomas, 1969.

SULLIVAN, H. S. *The interpersonal theory of psychiatry.* New York: W. W. Norton, 1953.

SUNDBERG, N. D. The acceptability of "fake" versus "bona fide" personality test interpretations. *Journal of Abnormal and Social Psychology,* 1955, 50, 145–147.

SUNDBERG, N. D. The practice of psychological testing in clinical services in the United States. *American Psychologist,* 1961, 16, 79–83.

SUNDBERG, N. D. A method for studying sensitivity to implied meanings. *Gawein* (Journal of Psychology, University of Nijmegen, Netherlands), 1966, 15, 1–8.

SUNDBERG, N. D. & BACHELIS, W. The fakability of two measures of prejudice: The California F Scale and Gough's Pr Scale. *Journal of Abnormal and Social Psychology,* 1956, 52, 140–142.

SUNDBERG, N. & BALLINGER, T. Nepalese children's cognitive development as revealed by drawings of man, woman and self. *Child Development,* 1968, 39, 969–985.

SUNDBERG, N. D., ROHILA, P. K., & TYLER, L. E. Values of Indian and American adolescents. *Journal of Personality and Social Psychology,* 1970, 16, 374–397.

SUNDBERG, N. D., TYLER, L. E., & TAPLIN, J. R. *Clinical psychology: Expanding horizons* (2nd ed.) Englewood Cliffs, N.J.: Prentice-Hall, 1973.

SUPER, D. E., et al. *Computer-assisted counseling.* New York: Teachers College Press, 1970.

SWENSON, C. H. Empirical evaluations of human figure drawings. *Psychological Bulletin,* 1957, 54, 431–466.

SWENSON, C. H. Empirical evaluations of human figure drawings. *Psychological Bulletin,* 1968, 70, 20–44.

SZALAI, A. et al. *The use of time.* The Hague: Mouton, 1973.

TAFT, R. The ability to judge people. *Psychological Bulletin,* 1955, 52, 1–23.

TAFT, R. Multiple methods of personality assessment. *Psychological Bulletin,* 1959, 56, 333–352.

TAGIURI, R. Person perception. In G. Lindzey & E. Aronson (eds.) *Handbook of social psychology* Vol. 3. (2nd ed.) Reading, Ma.: Addison-Wesley, 1969. pp. 395–449.

TANNER, J. M. Physical growth. In P. H. Mussen (ed.) *Carmichael's manual of child psychology* (3rd ed.), Vol. 1. New York: Wiley, 1970, pp. 77–156.

THARP, R. G. & WETZEL, R. J. *Behavior modification in the natural environment.* New York: Academic Press, 1969.

THORESEN, C. E. & MAHONEY, M. J. *Behavioral self-control.* New York: Holt, Rinehart & Winston, 1974.

THORNDIKE, E. L. The nature, purposes and general methods of measurements of educational products. In *Seventeenth Yearbook of the National Society for the Study of Education. Part II: Measurement of Educational Products.* Bloomington, Ill.: Public School Publishing Company, 1918.

THORNDIKE, R. M. & KLEINKNECHT, R. A. Reliability of homogeneous scales of reinforcers: A cluster analysis of the Reinforcement Survey Schedule. *Behavior Therapy,* 1974, 5, 58–63.

THORNE, F. C. Clinical judgment. In R. H. Woody & J. D. Woody (eds.) *Clinical assessment in counseling and psychotherapy.* Englewood Cliffs, N.J.: Prentice-Hall, 1972, pp. 30–85.

THURSTONE, L. L. Attitudes can be measured. *American Journal of Sociology,* 1928, 33, 1, 529–554.

THURSTONE, L. L. The dimensions of temperament. *Psychometrika,* 1951, 16, 11–20.

TIFFIN, J., PARKER, B. J., & HABERSTAT, R. W. The analysis of personnel data in relation to turnover on a factory job. *Journal of Applied Psychology,* 1947, 31, 615–616.

TOFFLER, A. *Future shock.* New York: Random House, 1970.

TOMKINS, S. S. & MINER, J. B. *The Picture Arrangement Test.* New York: Springer, 1957.

TORRANCE, E. P. *Guiding creative talent.* Englewood Cliffs, N.J.: Prentice-Hall, 1962.

TRUAX, C. B. & CARKHUFF, R. R. *Toward effective counseling and psychotherapy.* Chicago: Aldine-Atherton, 1967.

TWENTYMAN, C. T. & McFALL, R. M. Behavioral training of social skills in shy males. *Journal of Consulting and Clinical Psychology,* 1975, 43, 384–395.

TYLER, L. E. Towards a workable psychology of individuality. *American Psychologist,* 1959, 14, 75–81.

TYLER, L. E. Research explorations in the realm of choice. *Journal of Counseling Psychology,* 1961, 8, 195–201.

TYLER, L. E. *The psychology of human differences* (3rd ed.) New York: Appleton-Century-Crofts, 1965.

TYLER, L. E. *Tests and measurements,* (2nd ed.) Englewood Cliffs, N.J.: Prentice-Hall, 1971.

TYLER, L. E. Human abilities. In P. H. Mussen & M. R. Rosenzweig (eds.) *Annual review of psychology.* Palo Alto: Annual Reviews, 1972, pp. 177–206.

TYLER, L. E. Design for a hopeful psychology. *American Psychologist,* 1973, 28, 1021–1029.

TYLER, L. E. *Individual differences.* Englewood Cliffs, N.J.: Prentice-Hall, 1974.

TYLER, L. E., SUNDBERG, N. D., ROHILA, P. K., & GREENE, M. M. Patterns of choices in Dutch, American, and Indian adolescents. *Journal of Counseling Psychology,* 1968, 15, 522–529.

ULLMAN, L. P. & KRASNER, L. *A psychological approach to abnormal behavior* (2nd ed.) Englewood Cliffs, N.J.: Prentice-Hall, 1975.

VANDENBURG, S. G. Human behavior genetics: Present status and suggestions for future research. *Merrill-Palmer Quarterly of Behavior and Development,* 1969, 15, 121–154.

VANDENBERG, S. G. What do we know today about the inheritance of intelligence and how do we know it? In R. Cancro (ed.) *Intelligence: Genetic and environmental influences.* New York: Grune & Stratton, 1971, pp. 182–218.

VARBLE, D. L. Current status of the Thematic Apperception Test. In P. McReynolds (ed.) *Advances in psychological assessment.* Vol. 2. Palo Alto: Science & Behavior Books, 1971, pp. 216–235.

VERNON, P. E. The validation of civil service selection board procedures. *Occupational Psychology,* 1950, 24, 75–95.

VERNON, P. E. *Personality assessment: A critical survey.* New York: Wiley, 1964.

VERNON, P. E. *Intelligence and cultural environment.* London: Methuen, 1969.

VERNON, P. E. & PARRY, J. B. *Personnel selection in the British forces.* London: University of London Press, 1949.

VINITSKY, M. A forty-year follow-up on the vocational interests of psychologists and their relationship to career development. *American Psychologist,* 1973, 28, 1000–1009.

WAGNER, E. E., DARBES, A., & LECHOWICK, T. P. A validation study of the Hand Test Pathology score. *Journal of Personality Assessment,* 1972, 36, 62–64.

WALLACE, J. An abilities conception of personality: Some implications for personality measurement. *American Psychologist,* 1966, 21, 132–138.

WALLACE, J. What units shall we employ? Allport's question revisited. *Journal of Consulting Psychology,* 1967, 31, 56–64.

WALLACE, M. W. & RABIN, A. I. Temporal experience. *Psychological Bulletin,* 1960, 57, 213–236.

WATERMAN, A. S., GEARY, P. S., & WATERMAN, C. K. Longitudinal study of changes in ego identity status from the freshman to the senior year at college. *Developmental Psychology,* 1974, 10, 387–392.

WATSON, R. I. Historical review of objective personality testing: The search for objectivity. In B. M. Bass and I. A. Berg (eds.) *Objective approaches to personality assessment.* Princeton, N.J.: Van Nostrand, 1959, pp. 1–23.

WEBB, E. Character and intelligence. *British Journal of Psychology Monograph Supplement,* 1915, III.

WEBB, E. J., CAMPBELL, D. T., SCHWARTZ, R. D., & SECHREST, L. *Unobtrusive measures: Nonreactive research in the social sciences.* Chicago: Rand McNally, 1966.

WECHSLER, D. Intelligence defined and undefined: A relativistic appraisal. *American Psychologist,* 1975, 30, 135–139.

WEICK, D. E. Systematic observational methods. In G. Lindzey & E. Aronson (eds.) *The handbook of social psychology,* Vol. 2 (2nd ed.), Reading, Ma.: Addison-Wesley, 1968, pp. 357–451.

WEISS, R. L. Operant conditioning techniques in psychological assessment. In P. McReynolds (ed.) *Advances in psychological assessment.* Vol. 1, Palo Alto: Science and Behavior Books, 1968, pp. 169–190.

WEISS, R. L. Contracts, cognition and change: A behavioral approach to marriage therapy. *Counseling Psychologist,* 1975, 5, 15–26.

WEISS, R. L. & MARGOLIN, G. Assessment of marital conflict and accord. In A. R. Ciminero, K. S. Calhoun, & H. E. Adams (eds.) *Handbook of behavioral assessment.* New York: Wiley, 1977, pp. 555–602.

WELSH, G. S. Adjective check list descriptions of Freud and Jung. *Journal of Personality Assessment,* 1975, 39, 160–168. (a)

WELSH, G. S. *Creativity and intelligence: A personality approach.* Chapel Hill: Institute for Research in Social Science, University of North Carolina, 1975. (b)

WERRIMONT, P. F. Re-evaluation of a weighted application blank for office personnel. *Journal of Applied Psychology,* 1962, 47, 417–419.

WHITE, R. W. Motivation reconsidered: The concept of competence. *Psychological Review,* 1959, 66, 297–333.

WHITE, R. W. *Lives in progress* (3rd ed.) New York: Dryden Press, 1975.

WHYTE, W. H., Jr. *The organization man.* New York: Simon & Schuster, 1956.

WICKRAMASEKERA, I. Heart rate feedback and the management of cardiac neurosis. *Journal of Abnormal Psychology,* 1974, 83, 578–580.

WIENER, D. N. Subtle and obvious keys for the Minnesota Multiphasic Personality Inventory. *Journal of Consulting Psychology,* 1948, 12, 164–170.

WIENS, A. N. The assessment interview. In I. B. Weiner (ed.) *Clinical methods in psychology.* New York: Wiley, 1976, pp. 3–60.

WIGGINS, J. S. *Personality and prediction: Principles of personality assessment.* Reading, Ma.: Addison-Wesley, 1973.

WIGGINS, J. S., RENNER, K. E., CLORE, G. L., & ROSE, R. J. *The psychology of personality*. Reading, Mass.: Addison-Wesley, 1971.

WIGGINS, J. S. & VOLLMAR, J. The content of the MMPI. *Journal of Clinical Psychology,* 1959, 15, 45–47.

WILCOX, L. D., BROOKS, R., BEAL, G. M., & KLONGLAN, G. E. *Social indicators and societal monitoring: An international annotated bibliography*. San Francisco: Jossey-Bass, 1972.

WILKINSON, R. *The broken rebel: A study in culture, politics, and authoritarian character*. New York: Harper and Row, 1972.

WILLIAMS, R. J. *Biochemical individuality*. New York: Wiley, 1956.

WILLIAMS, R. L. Abuses and misuses in testing black children. *The Counseling Psychologist,* 1971, 2, 62–73.

WILLIAMS, R. L. The Black Intelligence Test of Cultural Homogeneity (BITCH) —100: A culture-specific test. Paper presented at the American Psychological Association meetings. Honolulu, September, 1972.

WINCH, R. F. & MORE, D. M. Does TAT add information to interviews? Statistical analysis of the increment. *Journal of Clinical Psychology,* 1956, 12, 316–321.

WINETT, R. A. & WINKLER, R. C. Current behavior modification in the classroom: Be still, be quiet, be docile. *Journal of Applied Behavior Analysis,* 1972, 5, 499–504.

WITKIN, H. A. & BERRY, J. W. Psychological differentiation in cross-cultural perspective. *Journal of Cross-Cultural Psychology,* 1975, 6, 4–87.

WITKIN, H. A., DYK, R. B., FATERSON, H. F., GOODENOUGH, D. R., & KARP, S. *Psychological differentiation*. New York: Wiley, 1962.

WITKIN, H. A., GOODENOUGH, D. R., & KARP, S. A. Stability of cognitive style from childhood to young adulthood. *Journal of Personality and Social Psychology,* 1967, 7, 291–300.

WITKIN, H. A., LEWIS, H. B., HERTMAN, M., MACHOVER, K., MEISSNER, P. B., & WAPNER, S. *Personality through perception: An experimental and clinical study*. New York: Harper & Row, 1954.

WITTSON, C. L. & HUNT, W. A. The predictive value of the brief psychiatric interview. *American Journal of Psychiatry,* 1951, 107, 582–585.

WOLFF, W. T. & MERRENS, M. R. Behavioral assessment: A review of clinical methods. *Journal of Personality Assessment,* 1974, 38, 3–16.

WOLMAN, B. B. (ed.) *The psychoanalytic interpretation of history*. New York: Basic Books, 1971.

WOLPE, J. *Psychotherapy by reciprocal inhibition*. Stanford, Ca.: Stanford University Press, 1958.

WOLPE, J. & LAZARUS, A. A. *Behavior therapy techniques: A guide to the treatment of neuroses*. Oxford: Pergamon Press, 1966.

World Population Conference, *World Population Year, August, 1974*. Washington, D.C.: U.S. Department of State, 1974.

WORTMAN, P. M. Evaluation research: A psychological perspective. *American Psychologist,* 1975, 30, 562–576.

WRIGLEY, C., COBB, J., & KLINE, D. Validities of the Peace Corps training measures. *Computer Institute for Social Science Research, Research Report No. 5,* East Lansing: Michigan State University, March, 1966.

ZIFFERBLATT, S. M. Behavioral systems. In C. E. Thoresen (ed.) *Behavior modification in education.* Chicago: University of Chicago Press, 1973, pp. 317–350.

ZIGLER, E. & PHILLIPS, L. Social effectiveness and symptomatic behaviors. *Journal of Abnormal and Social Psychology,* 1960, 61, 231–238.

ZILLER, R. C. *The social self.* New York: Pergamon, 1973.

ZUBIN, J. Discussion of symposium on newer approaches to personality assessment. *Journal of Personality Assessment,* 1972, 36, 427–434.

ZUBIN, J., ERON, L. D., & SCHUMER, F. *An experimental approach to projective techniques.* New York: Wiley, 1965.

ZUBIN, J., SALZINGER, K., FLEISS, J. L., GURLAND, B., SPITZER, R. L., ENDICOTT, J., & SUTTON, S. Biometric approach to psychopathology. In M. R. Rosenzweig & L. W. Porter (eds.) *Annual Review of Psychology,* Vol. 26. Palo Alto: Annual Reviews, 1975, pp. 621–671.

ZUÑIGA, R. B. The experimenting society and radical social reform: The role of the social scientist in Chile's Unidad Popular experience. *American Psychologist,* 1975, 30, 99–115.

Index